Finding Faith in Foreign Policy

Finding Faith in Foreign Policy

Religion and American Diplomacy in a Postsecular World

GREGORIO BETTIZA

OXFORD
UNIVERSITY PRESS

OXFORD
UNIVERSITY PRESS

Oxford University Press is a department of the University of Oxford. It furthers
the University's objective of excellence in research, scholarship, and education
by publishing worldwide. Oxford is a registered trade mark of Oxford University
Press in the UK and certain other countries.

Published in the United States of America by Oxford University Press
198 Madison Avenue, New York, NY 10016, United States of America.

© Oxford University Press 2019

Library of Congress Cataloging-in-Publication Data
Names: Bettiza, Gregorio, 1979– author.
Title: Finding faith in foreign policy : religion and American diplomacy in a
postsecular world / Gregorio Bettiza.
Description: 1st [edition]. | New York : Oxford University Press, 2019. |
Includes bibliographical references and index.
Identifiers: LCCN 2018053854| ISBN 9780190949464 (hardcover : alk. paper) |
ISBN 9780190949488 (electronic publication) |
ISBN 9780190949495 (oxford scholarship online)
Subjects: LCSH: United States—Religion. | Religion and politics—United States. |
Religion and international relations—United States. | United States—Foreign relations.
Classification: LCC BL2525.B495 2019 | DDC 201/.727—dc23
LC record available at https://lccn.loc.gov/2018053854

9 8 7 6 5 4 3 2 1

Printed by Sheridan Books, Inc., United States of America

to Katie

CONTENTS

TABLES

ACKNOWLEDGMENTS

This book began in earnest with my own conversion. Not a religious conversion, but rather an intellectual one to a postsecular sensibility. Although I grew up in Rome where the presence of the sacred is acutely felt, mine was a family of *laici*. We were a rare breed in post-World War II Italy with its stark social and political divide between Communists and Christian Democrats. Unlike many on the left, we were not vehemently atheists or anti-clerical. But neither were we practicing Catholics or enthusiastic supporters of an active church in the public sphere. Religion was valued, but exclusively in the private sphere. Importantly, being surrounded by the artistic feats from a bygone era of Papal power and statues like those of the sixteenth-century "heretic" Giordano Bruno—burned at the stake in Campo de' Fiori, a square where I passed countless hours hanging out with friends during high school—I implicitly believed that religion would have an ever-diminishing role in the future of humankind.

Fast forward to the mid-2000s. I was now living in Washington, DC, working for the World Bank. My belief in progress had led me to pursue a career in development. Yet the world around me defied many of my assumptions and expectations. The president of the United States—a country that represented to my eyes the very embodiment of modernity—was George W. Bush, a born-again Christian. The events of 9/11 had brought Islam center stage in world politics and by 2003, Western armies to the heart of Mesopotamia in the name of the "war on terror." Samuel Huntington's fantasy of clashing civilizations seemed ominously prophetic. The development programs I was working on at the time regularly took me to Jerusalem, where the giant of religion was anything but a sleeping force. All of a sudden a thought struck me: rather than having become a relic of the past, at the dawn of the twenty-first century, religion mattered in incredibly powerful ways, not least in world politics. Many of the assumptions about faith I held were being upended. I needed to understand more.

So began the journey that led me to embark on this project. Along the way I was fortunate to benefit from the support of a great many people and institutions, to whom I am profoundly indebted. First, I have benefited from the exceptionally supportive and inspiring scholars who supervised, mentored, and examined my PhD dissertation from which this book arose. Katerina Dalacoura, my supervisor, has taught me how to think like a scholar. Her analytical rigor, open-mindedness, and ability to challenge assumptions have been an enduring source of inspiration. From Michael Cox I learned a great deal about American foreign policy and about not shying away from asking the big and important questions of our times. Daniel Philpott, whose writings introduced me to the field of religion and international relations (IR), kindly took time out of a busy trip to London to examine my dissertation. For that I am forever grateful as well as for his continuous advice throughout the years. Research for my dissertation would not have been possible without the generous funding I received from the LSE IDEAS Stonex Scholarship. I also benefited greatly from Visiting Fellowships with the Center for Transatlantic Relations and with the Global History and Theory Program at SAIS Johns Hopkins University, who hosted me in Washington DC respectively in the summers of 2011 and 2017.

My thinking about IR and religion has been shaped by the many people who have generously taken the time to read and comment my research, or simply discuss ideas with me. At the LSE, the International Theory Research Workshop, LSE IDEAS, and *Millennium* have provided an incredibly fertile intellectual environment. During my time there I benefitted enormously from the insights and wisdom of Kirsten Ainley, Amnon Aran, Barry Buzan, Kim Hutchings, Nick Kitchen, George Lawson, and Arne Westad, and from lively debates with my fellow doctorates Manuel Almeida, Adel Altoraifi, Filippo Dionigi, Alex Edwards, Rebekka Friedman, Jasmine Gani, Andrew Jillions, Jorge Lasmar, Roberto Orsi, Kevork Oskanian, Ramon Pacheco Pardo, Vassilios Paipais, Chris Phillips, and Meera Sabaratnam.

A Max Weber Postdoctoral Fellowship from the European University Institute (EUI) allowed me to begin writing this book. For support, comments, and advice while in Florence, I would like to thank Pasquale Annicchino, Maria Birnbaum, Adam Bower, Pasquale Ferrara, Anna Grzymala-Busse, Ulrich Krotz, Nadia Marzouki, Olivier Roy, and Kristina Stoeckel. A special mention should go to my friends and co-organizers of the Max Weber Historical Sociology Reading Group, in particular Philip Balsiger, Simon Jackson, and David Pretel. My current colleagues in the politics department at the University of Exeter have been instrumental in helping me refine and sharpen the book's arguments. Particular thanks go to Stephane Baele, John Heathershaw, Bice Maiguashca, Irene Fernandez-Molina, David Lewis, Beverley Loke, Alex Prichard, Claudio Radaelli, and Doug Stokes. Charles Doran, Dan Hamilton, Erik Jones, and Matthias Matthijs at SAIS Johns Hopkins University have likewise provided invaluable support.

Earlier ideas and book chapters have been presented at countless conferences, seminars, and panels on religion around the world. I am grateful to Mariano

Barbato, Clifford Bob, David Bukley, Grace Davie, Jim Guth, Jeffrey Haynes, Peter Henne, Lee Marsden, Fabio Petito, Nukhet Sandal, Elizabeth Shakman Hurd, Peter Mandaville, David Montgomery, Michael Rectenwald, and Scott Thomas for their insightful suggestions, constructive criticism, and thought-provoking conversations at different stages of the project. I am also particularly indebted to the many civil society and faith-based activists, religious leaders, policy analysts, scholars, and US government officials who took time to speak with me during my fieldwork and discuss the issues raised by my research.

Special thanks go to David McBride and his staff at Oxford University Press for their support and help throughout multiple stages of the project. This book owes much also to the extremely generous feedback and constructive comments provided by two anonymous reviewers. I am also especially grateful to Gabi Recknagel for meticulously editing the manuscript and making it far more readable. Needless to say, I am entirely responsible for the content and conclusions of this book.

A number of people encountered throughout my life have in different ways inspired this project. Filippo Mazzarelli, whose love of life I have always admired and faith I have always envied. Emiliano Alessandri, the right person at the right time, showed me "the way of the PhD." And Mervyn Frost, who first sparked my interest in IR while attending his lectures during my Masters at King's College many years ago. The scholarly seed that became this book was planted then.

Finally, I thank my family. My parents, Ludina Barzini and Enzo Bettiza, have instilled in me the passion for politics and curiosity for the world without which this book would never exist in the first place. My mother's relentless confidence in me has provided an endless source of support throughout my life. I also owe a huge debt of gratitude to my American in-laws, Janie and Bernie McCabe. They have always made me feel at home away from home, welcoming debates about religion and politics—subjects notoriously unfit for polite conversation—around the dinner table. Bernardo and Giorgia were born while I was working on this book. They have brought immense joy and often reminded me—whether I liked it or not—that there is more to life than my intellectual musings.

It is difficult to describe the depth of gratitude that I feel toward my wife and best friend, Katie. Her love, patience, and encouragements have kept me going through the ups and downs of a project that has taken roughly a decade and our entire married life thus far to complete. It is to her that this book is dedicated.

Exeter
November 2018

Portions of Chapter 5 appeared as "Constructing Civilisations: Embedding and Reproducing the 'Muslim World' in American Foreign Policy Practices and Institutions since 9/11," *Review of International Studies* 41, no. 3 (July 2015): 575–600. Permission to reprint the material here is granted by Cambridge University Press.

ABBREVIATIONS

ACLU	American Civil Liberty Union
AEI	American Enterprise Institute
BMENA	Broader Middle East and North Africa
CFBCI	Center for Faith-Based and Community Initiatives
CFR	Council on Foreign Relations
CIRIS	Cambridge Institute on Religion and International Studies
CSID	Center for the Study of Islam and Democracy
CSIS	Center for Strategic and International Studies
CVE	Countering Violent Extremism
EPPC	Ethics and Public Policy Center
EU	European Union
DoD	Department of Defense
FBO	faith-based organization
FCO	UK Foreign and Commonwealth Office
FoRB	freedom of religion and belief
FSI	Foreign Service Institute
GAO	Government Accountability Office
ICRD	International Center for Religion and Diplomacy
IGE	Institute for Global Engagement
IRCU	Inter-Religious Council of Uganda
IRF	International Religious Freedom
IRFA	International Religious Freedom Act
ISIS	Islamic State of Iraq and the Levant
LGBTQ	lesbian, gay, bisexual, transgender, and queer/questioning
MEPI	Middle East Partnership Initiative
NAE	National Association of Evangelicals
NGO	non-governmental organization

NSC	National Security Council
NSS	National Security Strategy
OIC	Organization of Islamic Conference/Cooperation
OIG	Office of Inspector General
OIRF	Office of International Religious Freedom
PEPFAR	President's Emergency Plan for AIDS Relief
PCC	Policy Coordination Committee
RGA	Office of Religion and Global Affairs
UN	United Nations
USAID	United States Agency for International Aid
USCIRF	United States Commission on International Religious Freedom
USG	United States Government
USIP	United States Institute of Peace
WFDD	World Faith Development Dialogue
WHOFBI	White House Office of Faith-Based Initiatives, a general term I use for the Bush-era White House Office of Faith-Based and Community Initiatives, the Obama-era White House Office of Faith-Based and Neighborhood Partnerships, and the Trump administration's White House Office of Faith and Opportunity Initiative
WINEP	Washington Institute for Near East Policy

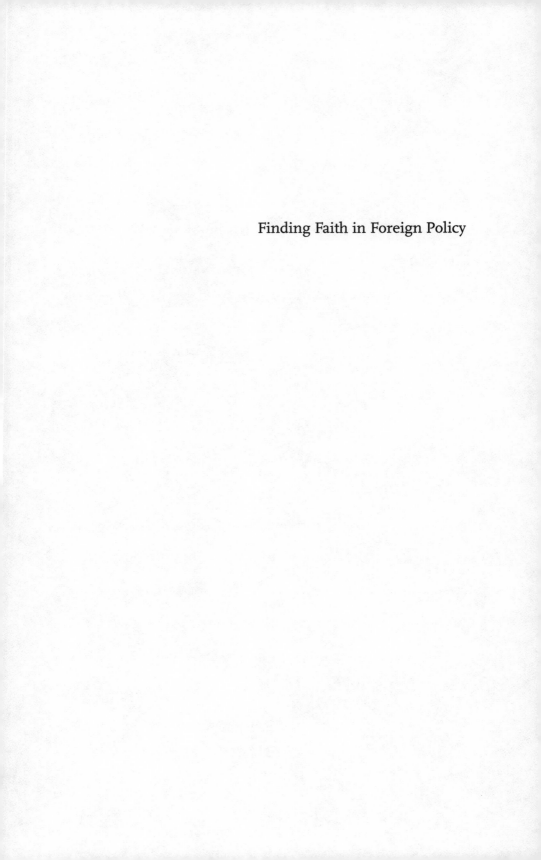

Finding Faith in Foreign Policy

CHAPTER 1 | Introduction

Religion as Subject and Object
of US Foreign Policy

[We] need to recognize that in a world where people of all faiths are
migrating and mingling like never before, where we are this global
community . . . we ignore the global impact of religion, in my judgment,
at our peril. . . . So I say to my fellow State Department employees, all of
them, wherever you are, I want to reinforce a simple message: I want you
to go out and engage religious leaders and faith-based communities in our
day-to-day work. Build strong relationships with them and listen to their
insights and understand the important contributions that they can make
individually and that we can make together.
                                    —Secretary of State John Kerry, August 2013

WITH THESE WORDS, AMERICA'S Secretary of State John Kerry announced the
creation of an Office of Faith-Based Community Initiatives in the Department
of State on August 7, 2013. Like a faithful flock, American diplomats were now
given a new and important mission: to let the world know that from now on
the United States embraces religions and religious communities as important partners for the common good. That same month, President Obama's US
Strategy on Religious Leader and Faith Community Engagement set out the
office's vision and direction. This new strategy and State Department office—
renamed in 2015 the Office of Religion and Global Affairs—marked a turning
point in the two-decade long effort to institutionalize what in policy circles is
generally referred to as "religious engagement," namely, the idea that greater
capacity should be built in American diplomacy to understand and mobilize
religious actors and dynamics to advance the nation's security interests, humanitarian concerns, and liberal values abroad.

The emergence of a policy of religious engagement represented another
milestone, however. This event was not unique, but marked the culmination

of a broader, historically novel turn toward systematically making religion both a subject and object of American foreign policy across a range of domains. Indeed, religious engagement was one among four different, but also interconnected, foreign policy frameworks with an explicit focus on religion that came into being between the late 1990s, in the aftermath of the Cold War, and the end of the Obama presidency—which is the temporal focus of this book.

The very first explicitly religious framework materialized when in 1998 Congress unanimously passed the International Religious Freedom Act (IRFA) during the second Clinton presidency. The IRFA directed American diplomats and presidents to act "on behalf of individuals persecuted in foreign countries on account of religion," and to monitor and respond to "violations of religious freedom" around the world.[1] From then on a range of soft and hard power tools—economic sanctions, diplomatic engagements or arm-twisting, naming and shaming, and programming—would be increasingly used to intervene in foreign lands to secure the rights of religious groups and individuals and to promote environments favorable to the flourishing of what American foreign policymakers identified as religion and religious liberty. Such activities would be coordinated by a novel office and an Ambassador-at-Large for International Religious Freedom in the State Department, and an independent United States Commission on International Religious Freedom (USCIRF). In 2015, a further Special Advisor for Religious Minorities in the Near East and South/Central Asia was added to the mix and by 2016 Congress passed a new bill—the Frank R. Wolf International Religious Freedom Act—deepening and expanding the provisions of the original 1998 act.

The second religiously oriented foreign policy framework came into being as soon as President George W. Bush stepped into the White House in January 2001. "In every instance where my Administration sees a responsibility to help people," Bush explained during his presidential campaign, "we will look first to faith-based organizations."[2] And so he did. By launching the Faith-Based and Community Initiatives and other programs like the President's Emergency Plan for AIDS Relief (PEPFAR), President Bush considerably expanded the capacity of the American state to partner with faith-based organizations in the making of foreign aid policy and the delivery of humanitarian and development assistance abroad. These initiatives allowed new ideas and networks to be harnessed to reach those in need worldwide. They also introduced new norms that made it possible for the most religiously infused of organizations—like for instance Franklin Graham's Samaritan's Purse—to receive funding even if these blurred the boundaries between missionary and humanitarian work, or designed HIV/AIDS prevention programs on theologically informed views mandating abstinence rather than condom use. An Office of Faith-Based and Community Initiatives was created in the White House and an affiliate center

---

[1] IRFA (1998).
[2] Bush quoted in White House (2008, 1).

was established in the United States Agency for International Development (USAID) to promote and oversee these initiatives. With the arrival of the Obama administration, and much to the dismay of many of the Democratic president's liberal supporters,[3] most of the policies, norms, and institutions that had been put in place by President Bush were continued or even expanded.

Soon after planes were tragically flown into the symbols of American economic and military power at the shout of *Allahu Akbar* (God is the greatest) on September 11, 2001 (9/11), a further religiously oriented foreign policy framework came into being. In the context of America's war on terror, the United States would increasingly seek to pacify and reform the societies, politics, and theologies of the people and countries that became associated and identified with the religion invoked by the terrorists. Before 9/11, neither Muslims nor Islam hardly, if ever, featured as an organized category in and object of US foreign policy. Now they would become the main targets, first of the Bush administration's "freedom agenda," and then of President Obama's attempts to defuse notions of civilizational clashes between the West and Islam (epitomized by his famous 2009 speech in Cairo calling for a "new beginning between the United States and Muslims around the world").[4] Simultaneously both administrations, with President Bush's "war of ideas" and President Obama's Countering Violent Extremism (CVE) policies, sought to steer Islamic debates, practices, and education in order to delegitimize the interpretations and narratives articulated by *jihadist* groups such as Al Qaeda or the Islamic State of Iraq and the Levant (ISIS). The intent was to promote, instead, what came to be variously identified as moderate, liberal, true, peaceful, or good Muslims and Islam. Once more, a novel institutional infrastructure emerged to devise and implement all of these policies. This included the appointment of America's first-ever "ambassadors" to Muslims, notably symbolized by the Special Envoy to the Organization of Islamic Cooperation (OIC) and the Special Representative to Muslim Communities.

These multiple explicitly religious foreign policy frameworks constitute what this book calls *religious foreign policy regimes*. Individually I label these, in the order in which they were introduced here, the Religious Engagement, the International Religious Freedom, the Faith-Based Foreign Aid, and the Muslim and Islamic Interventions regimes. Taken together these regimes would come to form a broader, constantly evolving, whole. A *foreign policy regime complex* on religion whose purpose has been to advance the United States' interests and values globally by managing and marshaling in an increasingly structured way the power of faith in the post-Cold War world. I use the concepts of regime and regime complex to capture something more multifaceted than simply a change in policy. Adopting a regime perspective means starting by exploring the emergence of religion as an issue area in American foreign policy, along with the

---

[3] Berlinerblau and Salmon in Berkley Center (2009, 4:44–5:33); Kopsa (2013).
[4] Obama (2009b).

TABLE 1.1 Religious Foreign Policy Regimes and Regime Complex Timeline, 1992–2016

CLINTON (1993–1996)	CLINTON (1997–2000)	BUSH (2001–2004)	BUSH (2005–2008)	OBAMA (2009–2012)	OBAMA (2013–2016)
	International Religious Freedom				
		Faith-Based Foreign Aid			
		Muslim and Islamic Interventions			
					Religious Engagement

practices, norms, and institutions that have then been put in place to address and govern it.[5] Table 1.1 provides an overview and timeline that stretches from the first Clinton to the second Obama presidency of the four religious foreign policy regimes.

The emergence of religion as a specific issue area in American foreign policy since the end of the Cold War is in itself a remarkable phenomenon. First, the breadth and depth with which religion has become a subject and object of US foreign policy is qualitatively and quantitatively unprecedented in the country's modern history. More puzzling still, these developments fly in the face of the general social scientific consensus of the twentieth century, championed by thinkers such as Max Weber, Karl Marx, Friedrich Nietzsche, and Sigmund Freud, which saw the disenchantment of the world and God's demise as inescapable byproducts of modernization. If faith was supposed to be relegated to the dustbin of history, why has religion been operationalized to the extent that it has in US foreign policy within the past couple of decades? Put differently, what do these developments tell us about the role and place of religion in world politics in the twenty-first century?

The book aims to give an answer to these puzzles while also addressing several more specific questions raised by this new, systematic turn toward religion in the formulation and implementation of US foreign policy. First, what explains the emergence and evolution of the regime complex with its four disparate regimes and under the watch of three very different presidencies (Clinton, Bush, and Obama)? Second, in what ways have the boundaries between state and religion, faith and foreign policy been redefined by the regimes? Third, what are the global effects of the growing entanglements between the sacred and the foreign policy of, arguably, the most powerful state in the international system today?

The next section begins to answer some of these questions as it introduces the book's core concepts and arguments. These are grounded in a theoretical

---

[5] The book applies to foreign policy insights drawn from literatures on domestic policy regimes (May and Jochim 2013; Wison 2000), international regimes (Hasenclever, Mayer, and Rittberger 2000; Krasner 1983; Kratochwil and Ruggie 1986), and international regime complexes (Keohane and Victor 2011; Raustiala and Victor 2004).

framework which combines scholarship in the sociology of religion, with sociological theories of international relations (IR),[6] namely Constructivism, International Historical Sociology, and English School. Theory will be largely kept implicit throughout the introduction, as chapter 2 will delve into it in greater detail. The section that follows, then, situates this book's arguments within the wider literature and highlights its contributions. Lastly, I move on to definitional and methodological issues, and conclude with the plan of the book.

The Arguments

In this section I put forward the book's three main arguments about the causes and consequences of the progressive and systematic operationalization of religion in American foreign policy since the end of the Cold War.

First Argument: The Macro and Micro Causes of the Operationalization of Religion

Why has religion become an organized subject and object of American foreign policy in the past three decades? One of the most obvious explanations that may immediately come to mind when attempting to answer this question would be to point at the role played by internationally driven events such as the 9/11 attacks and the growing influence of Islam more generally in world politics. As important as these phenomena are, they can hardly help us make sense of foreign policy regimes that predated 9/11 such as the regimes on International Religious Freedom and on Faith-Based Foreign Aid. Another not entirely erroneous assumption would be to turn to the role played by President George W. Bush, whose Christian faith and born-again experience featured large in his public persona.[7] Once more, though, a causal account that chiefly relied on the figure of President Bush would be unsatisfactory, since both the International Religious Freedom and the Religious Engagement regimes appeared, respectively, before and after his presidency.

Central to my argument is that events like 9/11 and personalities like those of President Bush can only be fully understood when placed in a wider macro social and historical context defined by the emergence of a *postsecular world society*.[8] This postsecular world society has come about as a result of two simultaneously occurring religio-secular processes: a growth in the political salience

---

[6] When international relations is referred to as a discipline, the acronym IR will be used hereafter; the term will be spelled out in full when used in a wider or general context.

[7] Aikman (2004); Mansfield (2003).

[8] The concept of "postsecularism" draws inspiration from Jürgen Habermas (Habermas 2008a, 2008b; 2006; Habermas and Mendieta 2010; Habermas et al. 2010), while that of "world society" is indebted to English School thinking (Buzan 2018; 2004). See chapter 2 for a more in-depth discussion about this book's use of these concepts and terminology.

of religion globally, and the development of a postsecular consciousness. The former process, also known as the "global resurgence of religion,"[9] refers to the rising political influence and clout that religious actors, identities, beliefs, practices, and symbols have gained worldwide since the 1970s—not just within Islam, but across most other major religious traditions such as Christianity, Judaism, Buddhism, and Hinduism. These changes are accompanied by the rise of what, borrowing from Jürgen Habermas, I label "postsecular consciousness": a mode of thinking rooted in mounting critiques of secularization theories and secular knowledge paradigms seen as misrepresenting and marginalizing the role of religion in modern times.[10]

The growing political salience of religion and the emergence of a postsecular consciousness explain why religion has come to matter more in world politics today—and with it indirectly in American foreign policy—than had been expected throughout much of the twentieth century. Embedded in and reacting to these wider developments are a multiplicity of agents who, at the micro-level, have come forward intent on making religion a structured subject and object of American foreign policy. I call these agents, drawing also on the work of Vyacheslav Karpov and Sadia Saeed, *desecularizing actors*.[11] It is these actors, I contend, who translate macro postsecular developments into foreign policy changes. They do so especially through the articulation and deployment of a number of *desecularizing discourses*. In their most general form, these discourses present a particular religious regime as the principled or strategically necessary solution to the perceived secular shortcomings of American foreign policy in the context of a world marked by religions' continued and growing power.

Desecularizing actors are a disparate lot, with different—and at times conflicting—backgrounds, ideas, interests, and priorities, which explains why a plurality of religious foreign policy regimes, and understandings thereof, exist. Some actors, which I label *desecularizing activists*, operate at the civil society and grass-roots level, and are connected to particular religious denominations, institutions, and movements. These activists are an expression of the rising tide of religious lobbying and advocacy in America on foreign policy matters which, although cutting across multiple religious traditions,[12] is represented most strikingly by the politicization of Protestant Evangelicals and the Christian Right.[13] Another set of actors are what I call *desecularizing experts*. These cultural elites—intellectuals, scholars, or policy analysts—are often tied to a burgeoning range of initiatives across religious and secular universities,

---

[9] I generally prefer, borrowing from Bellin (2008), the notion of "growing political salience" of religion rather than the more widely adopted terminology of "return" or "resurgence" of religion (e.g. Hatzopoulos and Petito (2003); Thomas (2005); Toft, Philpott, and Shah (2011)). The conceptual reasons for this linguistic choice are discussed in chapter 2, especially note 20.
[10] For seminal critiques of secularization theory see Berger (1999b); Casanova (1994). For critiques of secularism as a form of ideology see Asad (2003a); Connolly (1999).
[11] Karpov (2010); Saeed (2016).
[12] See especially Pew Research Center (2012).
[13] Marsden (2008); Mead (2006).

well-established think tanks, and novel faith-based "think-and-do tanks." They act as an epistemic community producing policy-relevant knowledge about religion in world affairs. A third range of actors fall into a category that I label *desecularizing policymakers*. These are individuals who hold positions of power or authority within state institutions including the President of the United States, Secretaries of State, or Members of Congress.

In short, I argue that being attentive to the macro-historical religious and intellectual changes encapsulated by the concept of the postsecular world society enables us to understand why religion is becoming an increasingly salient issue in American foreign policy, despite predictions that modernity was supposed to be secular. Attention to these macro developments also allows us to identify the complex range of global and domestic forces that lie at the origin of the different regimes—including those represented by 9/11 or by President Bush. It is in this larger context that a disparate range of desecularizing actors have simultaneously come forward since the end of the Cold War, and in ever greater numbers in the aftermath of 9/11, seeking to operationalize religion in US foreign policy across a multiplicity of domains.[14]

Second Argument: Shifting Secular–Religious Boundaries and the Desecularization of US Foreign Policy

The second key argument of the book is that the emergence of the four individual regimes and the overarching regime complex are produced by—and are themselves producing—multiple processes of foreign policy desecularization (hence the labeling of actors and discourses here as "desecularizing"). Desecularization occurs as secular and secularist settlements are contested, weakened, and rolled back.[15] Such processes redefine the boundaries and sustain new entanglements between state and church, faith and knowledge that manifest themselves in a greater capacity, acceptance, and willingness to include religion more systematically as a subject and object of US foreign policy.

I identify four parallel processes of desecularization, which vary in degree according to regime. I label these *institutional, epistemic, ideological,* and *state-normative* desecularization.[16] Institutional desecularization involves "material" changes, whereby new institutions and practices emerge that include in a more structured manner religious actors and voices in the making and implementation of foreign policy. Epistemic, ideological, and state-normative

---

[14] For accounts similarly inspired by sociological approaches to IR—including Historical Sociology, the English School, and Constructivism—that seek to explain changes in foreign policy practices and institutions by combing macro-structural developments and micro-agentic dynamics, see Alden and Aran (2012, ch. 6); Carlsnaes (1992); Hill (2003, chs. 7–8); Mabee (2007).

[15] Peter Berger (1999a) first introduced the term desecularization, mostly to mean the persistence and revival of religion in the modern world. I draw here on the work of Vyacheslav Karpov (2010) and Sadia Saeed (2016), who reconceptualize desecularization as a process of contestation of existing secular settlements.

[16] This categorization is inspired by José Casanova's (2011) multiple definitions of secularization and secularism.

desecularization, instead, constitute "ideational" changes in the knowledge, mentalities, culture, and norms that dominate within foreign policy milieus. Epistemic desecularization leads to an understanding of religion as something that matters, rather than being irrelevant, in world politics. Ideological desecularization leads to a view of religion as a positive, rather than negative and dangerous, force in international relations. Through the lens of state-normative desecularization, informal and formal norms regulating state–religion relations, which in the United States are identified with the Establishment Clause of the Constitution's First Amendment, are reinterpreted toward a more accommodationist rather than a separationist stance.

Third Argument: The Effects on Global Religious-Secular Landscapes

The regimes are leading the most powerful state in the international system to intervene ever more systematically in, and potentially influencing and transforming, religious and secular landscapes worldwide. I am not the first to make this observation. Indeed, the effects and consequences of making religion an increasingly structured subject and object of US foreign policy have elicited a flurry of policy and normative debates. On the one side of the argument are regime advocates who suggest that the operationalization of religion is valuable since it empowers marginalized religious voices and is necessary for creating a more peaceful, prosperous, and democratic world in an era of resurging religions. On the other side of the debate are the critics who claim that the religious turn in international policy only empowers orthodox/official rather than heterodox/unofficial religion, and can contribute to exacerbating divisions, conflict, terrorism, poverty, and neocolonial practices globally.[17]

Where this book differs from current discussions is in its attempt to neither celebrate nor indict change, but to understand and explain it. Hence I am less concerned with asking whether the advent of America's foreign policy regime complex on religion represents a positive or negative development, or whether it is making the world a better or worse place. My aim, instead, is to unpack how the desecularization of US foreign policy is making the world a *different* place, especially a religiously different one. Herein lies the crux of my third argument, which is that the foreign policy regimes are affecting global religious and secular landscapes in three particular ways: (i) they potentially reshape global religious realities along American norms and interests; (ii) they contribute to religionizing world politics; and (iii) they promote and diffuse similar religious regimes in international policy.

---

[17] An excellent place to start for an overview of the heated debates pitting proponents and critiques of these regimes—especially in the context of the International Religious Freedom and Religious Engagement ones—are a number of online forums hosted by *The Immanent Frame* (2013; 2012/2013; 2010/2011). See also Philpott and Shah (2016).

Shaping Global Religious Realities along American Norms and Interests

With religion becoming an ever more institutionalized subject and object of American foreign policy, the world's superpower has become increasingly entangled in global religious realities and dynamics. In the case of some regimes—like the International Religious Freedom and the Muslim and Islamic Interventions ones—their intent is explicitly to generate particular religious outcomes (for instance, promote religious tolerance or encourage moderate Islam). In the case of other regimes—notably those concerning Faith-Based Foreign Aid and Religious Engagement—religion is less the direct target of the foreign policy intervention. Instead, faith-based actors and perspectives are treated mostly as a means in the pursuit of ostensibly nonreligious ends (for instance, reducing poverty or resolving the Israeli-Palestinian conflict). Nonetheless, these regimes ultimately end up indirectly affecting the fortunes of the religious institutions, communities, and traditions that the US government does—or does not—partner with and thus empowers—or disempowers—through its foreign policy efforts. As I argue and show in the book, when the United States meddles in global religious landscapes, it will try to shape them—whether explicitly or implicitly—in ways that may reflect (a) American national interests; (b) its party political and ideological cleavages; (c) the country's religious identity, demographics, and norms; or (d) the priorities of specific domestically based desecularizing actors who dominate a particular policy space at any given moment.[18]

Religionizing World Politics

By making religion a subject and object of American foreign policy, the regimes simultaneously contribute to making faith *matter* more in world political discourses and practices. This is what I mean by religionization. Religionization may occur through mechanisms of "elevation." Elevation may take place as the regimes facilitate the presence of faith-based actors and voices both in the formulation and implementation of American foreign policy, as well as in the public sphere of societies around the world as religious actors and perspectives are mobilized to promote religious liberty, reform Islam, or fight poverty, for instance. Religionization may occur also through mechanisms of "categorization." Categorization occurs as official foreign policy discourses, institutions, and practices produce from the top-down, or reproduce from the

---

[18] The notion that the US may be transforming religious landscapes according to its norms and values is rooted in a constructivist (Menchik 2017) and historical sociological (Agensky 2017) understanding of religion as a category and social entity that does not have an essential and timeless character, but one that is profoundly shaped by and contingent on politics, history and context. Similar conclusions for individual religious foreign policies have been reached for instance by Hurd (2014a) on international religious freedom, Marsden (2012) on faith-based initiatives, or McAlister (2013) for religious engagement. This book seeks to present the most systematic—as of yet—explanation of these dynamics across policy areas.

ground up, a world where religious markers of identity and explanations of world politics are privileged over others.[19]

Promoting and Diffusing Religious Regimes in International Policy

As Elizabeth Shakman Hurd highlights, the operationalization of religion is a global phenomenon.[20] Indeed, over the past two decades we have seen a plurality of countries, such as the United Kingdom or Italy, and multilateral institutions, such as the European Union (EU) or the United Nations (UN), build their capacity to understand, draw upon, and govern global religious dynamics to promote development, reduce violence and terrorism, or advance liberal norms. This book shows how the globalization of policies with a religious focus is connected in important ways to changes in American foreign policy itself. Developments in the American context can lead to the diffusion and promotion of religious policies internationally through two types of dynamics. One sees the United States at the forefront of the operationalization of a particular religious foreign policy regime globally. In such circumstances we are likely to observe a linear process of regime diffusion from the United States to other states and institutions. The second dynamic involves processes of knowledge circulation and mutual learning between the United States and other parties that have already developed similar policies in their own contexts. In such circumstances, we will nonetheless tend to find American-based experts and policymakers seeking to coordinate and lead existing global efforts.

Situating the Arguments

The book's purpose is to provide one of the most theoretically and empirically comprehensive explorations to date of the complex causes, evolving structure, and global effects of the operationalization of religion in American foreign policy. It focuses mainly on changes taking place between the end of the Cold War and the second Obama presidency—with attention given, especially in the concluding chapter, to ongoing developments under President Trump. Along the way, this study draws from and makes a number of contributions to current scholarship and debates on religion in American foreign policy, the discipline of IR, and the social sciences more broadly.

First, this book makes a direct contribution to scholarly debates about the character and shifting boundaries between the secular and the religious in contemporary world politics. As others have argued before, this monograph also highlights the ideological (rather than neutral) nature of secularism,[21] and emphasizes the historically contingent nature of secular–religious

---

[19] On the productive power of discourse and practices in generating identities and meanings, see Barnett and Finnemore (1999); Milliken (1999). Religionization through categorization is noted, among others, by Hurd (2014b) in the context of the International Religious Freedom regime and by Bettiza (2015), and Mandaville (2010b) when it comes to policies targeting Muslims and Islam.
[20] Hurd (2015).
[21] Asad (2003a); Connolly (1999); Hurd (2008); Philpott (2002).

arrangements and settlements.[22] It furthermore stresses in novel and original ways the importance of taking into account the relations and interactions between both large-scale impersonal macro social forces and changes (in our case, the emergence of a postsecular world society) and the role of agency and contestation at the micro-level (in our case, desecularizing actors and their discourses) to explain variations in processes of secularization and desecularization across time and space.[23]

Ultimately, this project advances forms of postsecular knowledge and consciousness as it examines and unpacks ongoing American foreign policy changes. Yet it also shows how such forms of postsecular knowledge and consciousness—especially those produced in the context of the American academy and other expert intellectual and policy milieus—do not just reflect but also influence events in world politics. They can, in fact, produce that same religiously fervent reality that American experts are busy analyzing, as these experts deliberately or unwittingly contribute—alongside other desecularization actors—to the operationalization of religion in American foreign policy. In other words, while the present book adds to a growing literature on the impact of religion's resurgence in the discipline of IR and the practices of world politics, it also reveals in original ways how this very scholarship and the scholars engaged in producing this knowledge about religion in international affairs are themselves reshaping the world we live in.

Second, this book understands and frames the religious turn in American foreign policy primarily as a qualitatively and quantitatively historically novel phenomenon. Such a claim to novelty can invite a number of well-meaning criticisms, especially by scholars who would argue that continuity rather than change characterizes the role played by religion in American foreign policy. In anticipation of such criticism I will respond to two potential lines of critique, while simultaneously emphasizing what is unique about this study and the arguments it makes.

One line of critique could point to the fact that religion has always mattered in American society, politics, and thus foreign policy.[24] Such voices would have an illustrious intellectual forefather, namely Alexis de Tocqueville. Tocqueville magisterially reported the deep entanglement between religion and American politics since the country's very origin.[25] Not surprisingly, he was also among

---

[22] Gorski (2003); Kuru (2009).

[23] For a similar argument suggesting the need to reconcile large scale structures and processes with agents and actions to explain secularization/desecularization, see Mayrl (2016). For accounts that privilege large-scale structural forces to explain processes of secular–religious change, see Bruce (2011); Norris and Inglehart (2004); Shah and Toft (2006). For literature emphasizing instead contingency and political conflicts among agents, see Berger, Davie, and Fokas (2008); Gorski (2003); Lisovskaya and Karpov (2010); Smith (2003).

[24] For extensive overviews on religion in American history, society and politics see Guth, Smidt, and Kellstedt (2009); Wald and Calhoun-Brown (2018).

[25] Tocqueville (2000, 358) famously noted in his seminal book *Democracy in America* how upon his arrival "the religious aspect of the country was the first thing that struck my attention."

the earliest critics of the idea that progress and modernization went hand in hand with secularization.[26] Indeed, a growing body of literature shows how religious belonging and beliefs have shaped American foreign policy across decades if not centuries by influencing public opinion, the worldview of presidents, or through the advocacy and lobbying activities of domestic religious organizations and movements.[27] Likewise, there is an extensive literature on the grand strategic consequences of the religiously infused, mostly Protestant, lenses through which Americans see themselves and their country's place in the world as "exceptional."[28]

While this literature extensively discusses the numerous *religious influences* on American foreign policy, it does not however comprehensively chart the recent emergence of *religious regimes*. Put differently, this book's attention is not exclusively on so-called value driven policies, which may include for example foreign policies like US support for Israel or attempts to curb global human trafficking. Rather, its emphasis is on policies that make religion an explicit subject and object of their focus.[29] The distinction between a religiously infused American identity and a nonreligiously attuned foreign policy practice is fittingly captured by Madeleine Albright as follows:

> During my adult years, western leaders gained political advantage by deriding "godless communism"; otherwise, I cannot remember any leading American diplomat (even the born-again Christian Jimmy Carter) speaking in depth about the role of religion in shaping the world. Religion was not a respecter of national borders; it was above and beyond reason; it evoked the deepest passions; and historically, it was the cause of much bloodshed. Diplomats in my era were taught not to invite trouble, and no subject seemed more inherently treacherous than religion.[30]

Secretary Albright's assessment, delivered in the mid-2000s, no longer accurately reflects the present-day condition of American foreign policy. Diplomats are increasingly, and systematically, being invited to understand, govern, and partner with religion around the world. This is what I mean when arguing that a qualitative and quantitative change has occurred in the operationalization of religion in the making and implementation of American foreign policy.

---

[26] He argued: "There are certain populations in Europe whose unbelief is only equalled by their ignorance and their debasement, whilst in America one of the freest and most enlightened nations in the world fulfils all the outward duties of religious fervor" (Tocqueville 2000, 357–358).
[27] For the role of religion in influencing presidential foreign policy worldviews and practices see Bacevich and Prodromou (2004); Marsden (2011). On the role of multiple Christian denominations see Rock (2011). On Protestant Evangelicals in general see Amstutz (2014); Mead (2006); on the Christian Right in particular see Croft (2007); Marsden (2008). On Catholic orders see Byrnes (2011). On Jewish groups and more broadly the Israeli Lobby, which is not just a "Jewish" or "religious" lobby, since it includes also Christian Zionists and secular Neoconservatives, see Mearsheimer and Walt (2007). For a look at religion, public opinion, and foreign policy, see Froese and Mencken (2009); Guth (2009; 2011). For more historical perspectives which take into account all the various levels at which religion can play a role, see Inboden (2010); Preston (2012).
[28] Literature is vast here: see, for example, Hoover (2014); Lieven (2005); McDougall (1997). For seminal work on American exceptionalism, but not specifically related to foreign policy, see Lipset (1996).
[29] I thank Anna Gryzmala-Busse for helping me clarify this point.
[30] Albright (2006, 8).

Another line of critique emphasizing continuity over change may object that America's religious foreign policy regimes are not a post-Cold War phenomenon. A corollary to this argument would be to question exactly how secular the institutional, cultural, and normative structures of US foreign policy actually were before the 1990s. Indeed, there have been countless instances during and before the Cold War when policymakers did address religious issues and engage religious actors in the pursuit of particular foreign policy objectives. American presidents sought Christian and Islamic allies globally, for example, in their fight against the Soviet Union and Communism.[31] Concerns for the state of religious freedom internationally and attempts to export such norms abroad have punctuated American history.[32] This was notable, for instance, in President Roosevelt's famous "Four Freedoms" speech—which included the freedom of worship—delivered in the context of America's imminent entrance into World War II.[33] Similarly, faith-based organizations—particularly Catholic and Mainline Protestant—were never completely excluded from US humanitarian practices and development programs abroad.

However, except in a few isolated instances—such as the appointment in 1984 of a US ambassador to the Holy See—the institutional architecture of American foreign policy had hardly any bureaucratic position or any specific office explicitly oriented toward religion. Likewise, as the voices of countless desecularizing actors I quote throughout the book attest, a generalized perception exists that the intellectual, cultural, and normative milieus within which foreign policymakers operated before the 1990s left little or no space for taking seriously and consistently approaching religion in world affairs.

In short, there is little doubt that historically US presidents and policymakers have often been concerned with the ebbs and flows of religions and have attempted to marshal and direct faith-based actors in the service of America's national interest. Yet I would also argue that for most of the twentieth century all of this took place—when and if it did at all—in sporadic, ad hoc, circumscribed, and often concealed ways. Since the 1990s, instead, such efforts have been carried out in an ever more structured, institutionalized, widespread, and explicit manner. Put differently, the impulse to draw on and intervene in religious dynamics around the world is undoubtedly not new. What is novel is the breadth and depth through which such processes are being carried out and their bureaucratization has been achieved. This has taken place not by chance or coincidence, but through persistent efforts by some to contest established secular settlements and modes of thinking, and open up foreign policy institutions and foreign policymakers minds to religion. Even Hurd, who is keen to stress the historical continuity of policy interventions in global religious affairs, acknowledges how contemporary developments are nonetheless "unprecedented in size, scope, and reach."[34]

---

[31] Inboden (2010); Kirby (2003); Preston (2012, part VII).
[32] For scholarship placing America's contemporary international religious freedom policy in historical perspective, see Mahmood (2012); Su (2016).
[33] Roosevelt (1941).
[34] Hurd (2015, 16).

The third important contribution this monograph makes to current debates can be found in its effort to comprehensively explain the parallel rise of four distinct post-Cold War religious foreign policies, while simultaneously showing how these constitute the parts of a larger whole: an uncoordinated and loosely integrated regime complex. In fact, the current literature on the operationalization of religion in American foreign policy tends to explore the different policies—the promotion of religious freedom abroad, faith-based initiatives, counterterrorism practices targeting Muslims and Islam, or emerging efforts to engage religious actors around the world—separately and in isolation.[35]

There are some exceptions, most notably represented by Hurd's recent projects and 2015 book *Beyond Religious Freedom*, which do seek to draw parallels and connections between the array of different policies with a religious focus that have emerged in past decades.[36] Yet there are considerable differences between this monograph and Hurd's writings. First, while Hurd touches upon the multiple ways in which faith is being operationalized across policy domains, her work tends to privilege one policy area over others, namely religious freedom. This study, instead, gives equal conceptual and empirical weight to different regimes alongside the International Religious Freedom one—such as the Faith-Based Foreign Aid, Muslim and Islamic Interventions, and Religious Engagement regimes—and seeks to highlight not just their common characteristics but also the differences between them. Second, Hurd examines policy changes from a global perspective and across a range of countries and international institutions. This book focuses on changes in the foreign policies of one particular state, the United States. This is warranted, I would argue, given the pre-eminent role that America plays in world politics in general and in diffusing its models for operationalizing religion in foreign policy across different contexts in particular. Finally, Hurd's critical-theoretical perspective leads her to underplay causal analysis.[37] A theoretically informed explanation of why and how religion has increasingly become a subject and object of foreign and international policy is thus still generally missing—a gap in knowledge this book seeks to fill.

Finally, I also want to be explicit about what this book does *not* do. Two caveats are in order here. The first caveat is that this study concentrates chiefly on the operationalization of religion in American *foreign policy* understood mostly as diplomatic practice and statecraft, rather than in *national security* understood as military operations and intelligence. This means that I focus primarily on changes in institutions, policies, and norms taking place at the level of the presidency/White House, the State Department, and USAID. I only marginally address developments taking place in more security-oriented

---

[35] See for instance Hertzke (2004) on religious freedom, Marsden (2012) on faith-based initiatives, and Bettiza (2015) on interventions focused on Muslims and Islam.

[36] Hurd (2015); also Hurd and Sullivan (2014); Hurd (2012b).

[37] On the lack of causal analysis in Hurd's work, see the debate between Thomas (2016) and Hurd (2016).

branches of the government such as the Department of Defense, CIA, and Homeland Security.[38]

The second caveat is that this book is not designed to explicitly gauge the strength and influence of the religious foreign policy regimes and the overarching complex vis-à-vis other foreign policy efforts. It certainly acknowledges that the regimes exist in constant dynamic tension with other competing policy interests and priorities. Generally, though, the approach taken here tends to strike a balance between two positions. At one end are critics of the regimes that fear a complete break down in the separation of religion and state. And at the other end are regime advocates who regularly lament that despite the emergence of the regimes, US foreign policy continues to overwhelmingly neglect religious considerations and dynamics in global politics.

Definitions and Methodology

Defining Religion

Religion, a central concept of the book, still remains to be defined. This is no simple task since religion is an essentially contested concept, with multiple—often mutually exclusive—existing definitions. No pretense is made here to resolve these longstanding and often thorny debates. What I wish to do, though, is to highlight the perspective I have adopted for this study, explain why I have done so, and what consequences flow from this particular understanding of religion for my analysis.

This book takes a constructivist-inspired *participant approach* to religion. This perspective represents, I would argue, a *via media* between two poles that dominate the current debate about the nature of religion in IR. On one side of the debate can be found substantivist approaches. These adopt a definition of religion that purports to capture its independent, universal, and transhistorical essence (or substance). The definition provided generally frames religion as a set of beliefs, practices, and communities referring to the supernatural and the transcendental,[39] which are presented in stark contraposition to secular ideologies, practices, and actors. On the other side of the debate are critical approaches which deconstruct the concept of religion and the religious-secular divide, understood to be the products of a specifically Western historical experience and a discourse designed to impose certain categories of thought and power relations onto the world.[40] Critical scholarship reveals in important ways the limits of substantivist approaches by persuasively highlighting the contested and contingent nature of what gets to be defined as religion across time and space. Yet this literature also paradoxically risks dissolving its

---

[38] For scholarship in this area, see *Religion State and Society* (2011) and the *Review of Faith & International Affairs* (2009).

[39] For an explicitly substantivist perspective on religion in IR, see Toft, Philpott, and Shah (2011).

[40] See Asad (2003b; 1993); Dressler and Mandair (2011); Van der Veer (2001). In IR see Hallward (2008); Hurd (2008).

own religious subject and object of inquiry as it relentlessly deconstructs the religious-secular binary.

The starting point of a participant approach to religion is to move away from scholarly discourses, and with it from the attempt to specify or critique exactly what religion is or is not.[41] The focus of a participant perspective is, citing Vincent Pouliot, "on what it is that *social agents*, as opposed to analysts, take to be real" (emphasis in original).[42] A participant perspective does not necessarily entail that the scholar should accept the religious-secular dichotomy as natural or clear-cut, but only that it matters for actors in the social world and in international politics. Put differently, a participant perspective allows scholars to treat religion as a distinctive social fact (as substantivists do),[43] without being insensitive to the possibility of contestation and change across time and place (as critical approaches do).

Mona Kanwal Sheikh eloquently makes this point as follows:

> People do . . . use the distinctions between secular and religious, fill these categories with distinctive content, and engage in disputes over them. It is to take the constructivist [i.e., critical] point too far to conclude that the distinction is not valid in any sense, for at a minimum religion and secularism are important and meaningful categories in the everyday language of people and sometimes they appear in direct ideological confrontations. . . . In practice, it matters what individuals and communities have come to understand by religion.[44]

Markus Dressler, who actively contributed to the critical perspective on religion, has come to acknowledge "the limits of this pursuit."[45] As Dressler argues, in a nod toward the value of a participant perspective, "no matter how disputed religio-secularism is as an academic project, its basic promises [*sic*] still function as a powerful device of world-ordering and political engagement." Indeed, Dressler quite fittingly suggests that without understanding the logic of religious-secular world-ordering and the politics that flow from it, it would be difficult, for example, to make sense of the institutionalization of the religious engagement agenda. This book contends that this same logic accounts not just for the creation of the Office of Religion and Global Affairs in the State Department, but also for the emergence of the other regimes and, by extension, of the wider American foreign policy regime complex on religion.

---

[41] A range of emerging approaches to religion are seeking to include the concerns of the critical perspective, while also attempting to move "beyond critique" (*The Immanent Frame* 2014) and salvage the category of religion. These postcritical perspectives, so to speak, follow a range of paths. One includes the participant perspective adopted here. Another path being taken concentrates on "practices" (Riesebrodt 2012), while others are seeking to "broaden" or "disaggregate" the definition of religion beyond the Euro- and Christian-centric understandings that underpin the substantivist approach (e.g., Laborde 2014; Wilson 2012).

[42] Pouliot (2007, 364).

[43] Social facts are "those facts that are produced by virtue of all the relevant actors agreeing that they exist." Ruggie quoted in Pouliot (2007, 364). Pouliot (2007, 364) notes that "to know whether a social fact is 'really real' makes no analytical difference; the whole point is to observe whether agents take it to be real and to draw the social and political implications that follow".

[44] Sheikh (2012, 373).

[45] Dressler (2014); compare with Dressler and Mandair (2011).

Methodology

Empirical research was conducted following a qualitative methodology. Information and data for the case studies on the four religious foreign policy regimes—International Religious Freedom, Faith-Based Foreign Aid, Muslim and Islamic Interventions, and Religious Engagement—was gathered, analyzed, and triangulated from three main sources.

First, fifty-eight semistructured interviews were undertaken with a broad range of actors. Interviewees were approached primarily on account of their involvement with one or more of the religious foreign policy regimes, whether in their role as advocates, implementers, or critics of the regimes. Others, who may have been less familiar with the policy changes under investigation, were nonetheless approached because of their knowledge and expertise of religion in American society and politics more broadly. In selecting interviewees, particular attention was given not to privilege the perspectives of one set of actors, but to be as wide-ranging and inclusive as possible. Thus interviewees included advocates and activists from faith-based or secular non-governmental organizations supportive or critical of the different religious foreign policy regimes; analysts and experts belonging to secular and religious think tanks across the conservative-liberal ideological and theological spectrum; scholars tied to religious and secular universities; and policymakers from the Clinton, Bush, and Obama administrations. Interviews took place either in person or by phone or Skype, during the months of June 2010, June–July 2011, and April–July 2015. These were carried out largely during fieldwork in the United States, mostly around the Washington, DC area, but included also a visit to Liberty University in Virginia, notorious for being founded by Jerry Falwell, a pastor and pivotal figure in the creation of the modern Christian Right movement. A full list of interviewees is provided in Annex 2.

A second method of data collection was through direct observation at conferences, workshops, and interfaith roundtables while conducting fieldwork in the United States. Where possible, nonpublicly available documents were also collected during interviews and observations.

Third, data was retrieved from primary sources produced by Congress, government bureaucracies, law- and policymakers, as well as faith-based and secular non-governmental organizations, think tanks, and universities. These sources include, among others, policy strategies and reports, legal bills, newspaper articles, speeches, sermons, memoirs, blog posts, website content, mailing lists, and newsletters.

Data was analyzed combining the methods of discourse analysis and process tracing.[46] In terms of discourse analysis, I adopted what Benjamin Banta labels "critical discourse analysis" (CDA), rather than the more widely used "poststructural discourse theory" (PDT) approach. In contrast to PDT, which

---

[46] On combining discourse analysis with process tracing to make causal inferences, see Klotz and Lynch (2006); Lupovici (2009); Pouliot (2007).

views discourse as the main source for understanding social reality in isolation from the outside world, CDA views discourse as "differentiated from the realm of extra-discursive practice, placed in dialectical relation to this wider realm of social relations, and analyzed as a possible causal mechanism in the generation of social phenomena, alongside these other mechanisms."[47]

Through such a lens, I sought to retrieve actors' meanings, understandings, and policy preferences expressed in what I have called as principled and strategic desecularizing discourses. Then, using what Derek Beach and Rasmus Brun Pedersen label "explaining-outcome" process tracing,[48] I situated these discourses in the context of a more complex causal chain of events. In particular, desecularizing discourses were placed in relation to two further contributing causal factors—critical junctures and exogenous trends— to explain the circumstances leading to the successful contestation by desecularizing actors of existing secular settlements and the emergence and evolution of the various religious foreign policy regimes over time. Along the way I engaged in theory-guided empirical analysis whereby my explanation of American foreign policy change was informed also by more general understandings of how institutions, practices, ideas, and norms change in world politics. The analysis thus involved a constant dialogue, as George Lawson puts it, "between empirical data, conceptual abstractions, and causal explanations."[49]

Reconstructing the historical chain of events and processes leading to the observed outcomes from participants' accounts and interpretations of their reality as collected through interviews, participant observation, and other primary sources was not always simple. All the more so, as this study simultaneously sought to take seriously participants' subjective perspectives constitutive of desecularizing discourses, while also attempting to contextualize these discourses and explore their causal impact on the world around them. As a result, I sought to the best of my ability to triangulate information collected across different milieus—secular or religious, conservative or liberal, grassroots or governmental—in order to identify common patterns and cross-check data to gain a fuller picture of the events taking place. Hence, when an individual or report is quoted in the main text of the book, the footnote generally accompanying the statement will likely include a range of what may appear at first as redundant references. These are employed with two specific purposes in mind: either to demonstrate that a particular perspective voiced by an actor

---

[47] Banta (2013, 379); also Kurki (2007); Wight (2004).

[48] Process tracing is a methodological tool used to "trace the links between possible causes and observed outcomes" (George and Bennett 2005, 6). As Beach and Pedersen (2013, 18) argue, "explaining-outcome" process tracing focuses on "craft[ing] a minimally sufficient explanation of a puzzling outcome in a specific historical case." They contrast this approach to "theory-testing" and "theory-building" variants of process tracing, which are mostly concerned with making generalizable inferences about the presence/absence of a theorized causal mechanism.

[49] Lawson (2007, 409).

or report I quote in the main text is more widely shared and thus constitutive of a specific desecularizing discourse, or to suggest that a similar account of events and facts offered by one source has been given elsewhere, ideally originating from a different standpoint.

Plan of the Book

The chapter that follows this introduction, chapter 2, lays the conceptual and theoretical groundwork for the book's empirical cases, based on a sociologically informed approach to IR theory. It defines more explicitly what I mean by postsecular world society. It then fleshes out how macro-level postsecular developments can lead to foreign policy changes through the intervening role of desecularizing actors at the micro-level as these seek to contest the secularity of American foreign policy through the deployment of multiple types of desecularizing discourses in order to operationalize religion. It goes into greater conceptual depth in defining the institutional, epistemic, ideological, and state-normative desecularizing processes taking place as religion progressively becomes a subject and object of US foreign policy. Finally, consistent with the theoretical premises of the study, the chapter identifies a threefold typology of global religious-secular effects which the foreign policy regimes and the overall complex are expected to produce.

The theory chapter is followed by four empirical cases exploring the causes, shape, and effects of the different religious foreign policy regimes. These cases are chronologically and thematically ordered. They start from the first regime to emerge in the late 1990s, the International Religious Freedom regime (chapter 3), followed by the Faith-Based Foreign Aid regime (chapter 4), the Muslim and Islamic Interventions regime (chapter 5), and finally the Religious Engagement regime (chapter 6). While the analysis in each case stops at the end of the Obama administration, the concluding sections highlight ongoing developments under the Trump administration. Each chapter follows a similar structure, but with important allowances for the unique conditions of each case.

The final and concluding chapter, chapter 7, provides more than a mere summary of the book's arguments. It serves two main purposes. First, it aims to bring together and emphasize the connections between the four different regimes. Having explored these independently across the empirical chapters, the conclusion shows how, taken together, the separate regimes form the contours of a broader overarching American foreign policy regime complex on religion. The second purpose of the conclusion is to tease out the wider implications of this study and highlight a number of areas for further research and thinking. These areas include assessing the strength of the book's theoretical framework in light of ongoing developments under the Trump administration; understanding in greater depth the changes occurring to the religious realities and traditions that America draws from and intervenes in around the world; investigating further how the American experience with operationalizing religion in its foreign policy relates and compares to similar policy changes taking place elsewhere; and reflecting on what the growing attempts by the United States to manage and mobilize religion globally means for world politics and international order in the twenty-first century more broadly.

| Theorizing US Foreign Policy
in a Postsecular World Society

The assumption that we live in a secularized world is false. The world
today, with some exceptions . . . is as furiously religious as it ever was,
and in some places more so than ever. This means that a whole body of
literature by historians and social scientists loosely labeled "secularization
theory" is essentially mistaken.

—Peter Berger, 1999[1]

Whether governments around the world like it or not, this resurgence of
religion has meant that they would now have to reckon with religion in a
way that they did not forty, fifty, or sixty years ago.

—Monica Duffy Toft, Daniel Philpott, and Timothy Samuel Shah, 2011[2]

This approach to religion, as something that can be operationalised, has
gathered extraordinary academic and international public policy traction.
It is influential in ways that have yet to be fully accounted for in the
discipline and beyond.

—Elizabeth Shakman Hurd, 2012[3]

THIS CHAPTER LAYS OUT the theoretical framework which guides this book's explanation of the causes, evolving structures, and global effects of the post-Cold War turn toward operationalizing religion in US foreign policy. Such turn is exemplified by the rise from the late 1990s onward of four explicitly religious foreign policies, what I define as *religious foreign policy regimes*. They are the International Religious Freedom regime (since 1998), the Faith-Based Foreign Aid regime (since 2001 and predating 9/11), the Muslim and Islamic Interventions regime (since 2001 and following 9/11), and the Religious Engagement regime (since 2013).

---

[1] Berger (1999a, 2).
[2] Toft, Philpott, and Shah (2011, 15).
[3] Hurd (2012b, 945).

While these regimes are distinct and at times even in competition with one another, they also share a number of features. Most notably they share a similar focus on religion, and with that they often share a set of overlapping and interconnected policy agendas and institutional architectures. Taken together these four religious foreign policy regimes constitute the main pillars of a broader whole, namely an evolving US *foreign policy regime complex* on religion. The regime complex is underpinned by an overarching purpose, which is to manage and marshal the power of faith globally in the pursuit of America's interests and values abroad.

I apply the concepts of regime and regime complex, generally used in literatures on domestic and international regimes, to the field of foreign policy.[4] I do so in order to capture something more multifaceted than simply a change in policy. The notion of regime is used here as a way to make sense of a "constellation of ideas, institutional arrangements, and interests" as well as the resulting combination of policies, rules, and actions that "make up the governing arrangements for addressing particular problems."[5] Thus, a regime perspective focuses the analysis on a particular problem or issue and then works backward to unpack and explain the ideas, interests, actors, institutional configurations, policy assemblages, and norms—which together constitute the contours of a regime—that are put in place to address and manage that particular problem or issue.

The literature on international regimes has shown how individual regimes can combine in either tightly or loosely knit ways to form larger configurations of either "nested regimes" or "regime complexes" designed to address a broader set of issues.[6] Nested regimes refer to a semihierarchical set of regimes with a recognizable structure and an identifiable chain of responsibilities and command. Regime complexes comprise a loosely coupled and overlapping set of specific regimes, "linked more or less closely to one another, sometimes conflicting, usually mutually reinforcing" with no "overall architecture or hierarchy that structures the whole set."[7] In our case, as we shall see further in chapter 6, attempts have been made during the Obama administration to bring together the four religious foreign policy regimes into a more coherent nested regime under the umbrella of the religious engagement agenda. Conversely, with the Trump presidency, efforts are seemingly under way to eliminate or fold the Religious Engagement regime under the International Religious Freedom one. As of late-2018 things appear still in flux and thus we remain with a plurality of regimes structured around the contours of a complex.

---

[4] For the literature on domestic policy regimes, see, for example, May and Jochim (2013); Wison (2000). For that on international regimes, see Hasenclever, Mayer, and Rittberger (2000); Krasner (1983); Kratochwil and Ruggie (1986).

[5] May and Jochim (2013, 446).

[6] Keohane and Victor (2011); Raustiala and Victor (2004); see also May and Jochim (2013, 429, 438–440).

[7] Keohane and Victor (2011, 7–8).

The sustained turn toward making religion an organized subject and object of US foreign policy, represented by the rise of the regime complex, is quite a remarkable and in many respects novel development. Religion, to be sure, has never been completely absent from American foreign policy calculations, rhetoric, and practices.[8] Presidents and policymakers alike have regularly called upon the power of faith and religious actors to advance American interests and values abroad throughout the centuries. Yet as the introduction and the four case study chapters show in greater detail, historically there were practically no institutional structures (special appointees, commissions, offices) in the foreign policy bureaucracy explicitly focused on religion, and the general cultural, intellectual, and normative milieu from which US foreign policymakers tended to operate was rather inhospitable to systematically taking religious actors and factors seriously in world politics. The breadth and depth with which religion has been systematically included and operationalized, since the end of the Cold War, in American foreign policy thinking, institutions, and practices—I would hence argue—is qualitatively and quantitatively unprecedented in the country's modern history.

This development is rather puzzling for a number of reasons. First, the emergence of religion as an issue in American foreign policy is surprising, since it challenges often-unquestioned assumptions of an ever more secularizing and disenchanted world. This view was originally articulated in the nineteenth and early twentieth centuries by many of the founding fathers of the modern social sciences such as Max Weber and Karl Marx, and more fully codified by secularization theorists in the second half of the twentieth century.[9] If we live in a world marked by the death of God, to paraphrase Friedrich Nietzsche, why are we seeing a growing focus on and institutionalized attention toward religion in American foreign policy in the past three decades, straddling the end of the twentieth and the beginning of the twenty-first century?

A second puzzle arises when seeking to make sense not just of why religion has been operationalized in US foreign policy in the past decades, but also why it has been operationalized along different regimes and at different moments since the end of the Cold War. The shape, form, and timing in which religion has been brought into American foreign policymaking and implementation across different yet related regimes, and within the space of three very different presidencies—the Clinton, Bush, and Obama ones, which are the main focus of this book—needs a compelling explanation that remains elusive to this day.

Third, much has been made of the eminently secular character of the modern institution of the State, in general, and of the American state, in particular, with its important tradition of church–state separation.[10] This profound institutional separation in the United States exists in parallel to, if not even

---

[8] See, for instance, Preston (2012).
[9] For an excellent overview of the development of secularization theory see Gorski (2003).
[10] See, for example, Fox (2006), whose large N comparative study identifies the United States as having the highest levels of separation of religion and state in the world.

actively facilitating the, maintenance of a highly religious society and public sphere.[11] While the boundary between faith and politics in the United States is often extremely blurred and entanglements in this sphere are generally valued,[12] attempts to separate sharply state institutions and practices from religious ones are instead a social and constitutional norm. The operationalization of explicitly religious foreign policies challenges such an understanding of the state and seems to suggest that the institutional and normative boundaries between the religious and the secular are currently being redefined. If so, how and with what consequences?

A fourth and final puzzle revolves around the possible international effects of the growing entanglement and enmeshment between faith and the foreign policy of arguably the most powerful state in the international system today. Importantly, as the United States has increasingly come to intervene through its regimes in global religious landscapes and dynamics, are these being reshaped and transformed by the superpower? If so, how and in what ways?

This chapter develops a specific conceptual framework that will guide the rest of the book and, importantly, allows us to provide answers to these four puzzles. This framework will be based on a middle-range theoretical approach, grounded in a critical realist philosophy, which combines in an analytically eclectic manner insights from the sociology of religion with sociologically informed IR theories, namely Constructivism, International Historical Sociology, and the English School.[13] Overall such philosophical and theoretical stance leads this book to embrace a number of distinctive perspectives on the relationship between theory and empirical reality; the nature of and relationship between the international system, the state, and its foreign policy; the nature of causality and change in the social world; and the concepts of religion and the secular. These implications are developed more clearly throughout the rest of the chapter.

Explaining the Complex Causes

In order to address the first two puzzles—why religion has been operationalized in US foreign policy at all in a supposedly secularizing world, and why different regimes have been institutionalized at different times—it is vital to adopt a

---

[11] Finke and Stark (2005).

[12] For example, a recent Pew Research Center (2014a) poll surveying Americans' views of desirable/undesirable presidential traits—including experience in the military, being gay or lesbian, or having smoked marijuana—identified atheism as the most negative of all.

[13] On middle-range theorizing and analytical eclecticism see Sil and Katzenstein (2010); also Bennett (2013). For examples of links and overlaps between Historical Sociology, Constructivism, and the English School in IR see Buzan (2004); Buzan and Lawson (2013); Hobson and Hobden (2002); Lawson (2007); Reus-Smit (2008); Reus-Smit (2002). For the critical realist philosophical underpinnings of Historical Sociological theorizing in IR see Curtis and Koivisto (2010); Lawson (2007, 357–358). For a critical realist understanding of Constructivism see Wendt (1999). For sociologists of religion grounding their thinking in a critical realist philosophy see Gorski (2013); Smith (2008).

view of causality as *complex*, as it is understood by critical realist-informed middle-range theory. Middle-range theory positions itself between abstract grand theories and largely descriptive accounts of specific historical contexts or events. Compared to more neopositivist approaches, middle-range theorizing is neither concerned with uncovering law-like regularities nor with isolating a single, independent factor or variable that explains all outcomes. Yet unlike some interpretivist and poststructural accounts of science, middle-range theorizing does not entirely abandon the goal of providing causal explanations, while nonetheless viewing causality often as "complex."[14]

According to this perspective the aim is not to displace, but rather to draw on and combine the insights of different theoretical traditions in order to build conceptual frameworks that, as Milja Kurki suggests, can take into account the "complex interaction of a variety of different kinds of causal factors," whether structures, actors, material objects, ideas, events, and processes that lead to particular outcomes.[15] Middle-range theorizing focuses the attention on identifying the multiple causal conditions and mechanisms which combine into sequences and processes, explaining particular states of affairs or change, within a specific spatio-temporal context or across cases. In our case, I suggest that we need to take into consideration (a) macro-structural processes which provide the context for (b) the emergence of specific agents and discourses at the micro-level, and explore how these relate to (c) a set of further contributing factors, in order to explain the post-Cold War operationalization of religion along a multiplicity of regimes in US foreign policy.

First, to explain why religion has increasingly become a subject and object of American foreign policy, we need to place the United States in (a) a specific macro-level global and historical context experiencing the emergence of a *postsecular world society* over the past decades. Then, in order to explain variation in regime types, we need to identify (b) those *actors* who at the micro-level are producing and reacting to these wider social and historical changes, and who make the case through the articulation of specific discourses that American foreign policy needs to adapt and respond to ongoing macro-level developments. Finally, in order to explain the when and how the regimes have emerged and evolved over time, we need to pay further attention to (c) specific *critical junctures* and a complex range of *exogenous trends*. I now turn to exploring in greater detail these multiple causal factors and how they combine to bring about the observed outcomes.

---

[14] On middle-range theoretical notions of complex causality, see Bennett (2013); Kurki (2007; 2006); Sil and Katzenstein (2010).
[15] Kurki (2006, 202).

Macro-Level Changes: The Emergence of a Postsecular World Society

To explain why religion has become an increasingly organized subject and object of US foreign policy in the aftermath of the Cold War, despite long held assumptions of an ever more secularizing world, I argue that the American state needs to be placed within a wider macro historical and global context undergoing a particular set of transformations. I define such context as one that has been witnessing the emergence, especially from the 1970s onward, of a *postsecular world society* which is affecting simultaneously America's domestic and external environment. I attach particular meanings both to the concept of the "postsecular" and to that of "world society," which I will now unpack.

The "postsecular" is a concept most notoriously popularized in recent years by the German philosopher and social theorist Jürgen Habermas.[16] This concept, like most concepts in the social sciences, escapes a clear-cut definition. "The very notion of postsecularism has proven to be no less ambiguous or elusive than secularism itself," Joseph Camilleri notes. "Its proponents are far from agreed on its meaning, its explanatory potential, or its normative implications."[17] I take here an analytical approach to the postsecular. That is, I am interested in exploring, to use Camilleri's terminology, the "explanatory potential" of the postsecular in international relations in general and to American foreign policy changes in particular. This approach is substantially different from most of the current literature in IR, which has largely tackled the "normative implications" of the postsecular, in line with Habermas' political philosophical concerns.[18]

Building on Habermas and others, I argue that the notion of the postsecular points to two parallel, and often mutually reinforcing, processes that have taken place in the past decades. One is more sociological-political and the other centers instead around a change in ideas and knowledge. These processes are: (i) the growing political salience of religion globally, and (ii) a reflexive turn in secular thought leading to the emergence of a postsecular consciousness.[19] The first process refers to the growing influence and clout that religious actors, identities, beliefs, practices, and symbols have gained in local and international politics—including in the United States—in multiple and

---

[16] Habermas (2008a, 2008b; 2006); Habermas et al. (2010); Habermas and Mendieta (2010). For wider discussions and debates in the social sciences on the postsecular, inspired by the work of Habermas, see Calhoun, Juergensmeyer, and VanAntwerpen (2011); Calhoun, Mendieta, and VanAntwerpen (2013); Gorski et al. (2012b).

[17] Camilleri (2012, 1020); see also Beckford (2012).

[18] For more normatively oriented postsecular scholarship in the discipline of IR, see Barbato and Kratochwil (2009); Mavelli and Petito (2014); *Review of International Studies* (2012). For a more analytical approach, see Bettiza and Dionigi (2015).

[19] The distinction between the two postsecular processes identified here is not arbitrary, but builds upon similar distinctions made by Habermas (2008b, 21) and others. As Gorski et al. (2012a, 2) argue: "The question of the post-secular poses two lines of inquiry: first, determinations about the state of religiosity in the world; second, understanding the new ways that social scientists, philosophers, historians, and scholars from across disciplines are and are not paying attention to religion."

context-specific ways since the 1970s. These trends are also often referred to as constituting a global "resurgence" or "return" of religion.[20]

The modern rise of the state and of multiple secular ideologies—such as nationalism, socialism, communism, fascism, and liberalism—during the seventeenth and twentieth centuries, profoundly marginalized and undermined the authority of religion, in the international sphere first and the domestic one thereafter.[21] Politics throughout the twentieth century was characterized by wars pitting states against each other on the basis of conflicting political and economic projects, which were also eminently secular. During World War II, for instance, warring camps were divided along the lines of Fascist, Communist, and Democratic states. The Cold War saw regions and countries worldwide parceled according to secular idioms such as First, Second, and Third Worlds; the Capitalist West and the Communist East; the free and un-free world; or imperialists and anti-imperialists.

Similarly, the struggle for colonial independence in the Global South was often framed in secular nationalist terms. In the postcolonial world secularist modernizing projects were the norm, as in Nehru's India. The Zionist movement that led to the founding of Israel in 1948 was largely secular nationalist in character. Across Muslim-majority countries, too, secular forces were on the march throughout the twentieth century, whether in the form of Kemalism in Turkey or Arab nationalism across the Middle East. Stalin's quip in the 1930s— "The Pope? How many divisions has he got?"—symbolically captured the idea of the fading relevance and power of religions. Unsurprisingly, contemporary secularization theories would be most explicitly codified at the height of the Cold War itself.[22]

Yet toward the end of the twentieth century, cracks started to appear in modern secular political and ideological edifices. Although subsumed, religions had not completely died out. In fact, they would start to reassert themselves with a "vengeance"—as Gilles Kepel put it—from the 1970s onward.[23] This resurgence of religion has taken many shapes and forms. It has

---

[20] When using the terminology of "growing political salience" of religion I draw from Bellin (2008). I prefer this language to the more commonly used notion of religion's "return" or "resurgence" (e.g., Hatzopoulos and Petito 2003; Thomas 2005; Toft, Philpott, and Shah 2011). Pointing to the growing political salience of religion does not imply some kind of comeback of religion from a previous bygone era. This is a highly contentious issue, with a range of scholars—like Haynes (2006), Hurd (2008), and Wilson (2012), for example—suggesting that religion never really completely went away from politics to begin with. Moreover the notion of growing political salience more clearly highlights processes connected to the politicization of religion, thus discarding a wide range of other sociologically relevant, but only indirectly politically significant, religious phenomena. These include, for example, the continued vitality of religious beliefs and traditions or the proliferation of new religious movements in the modern world (e.g., Pentecostalism in the developing world), which some authors (e.g., Berger 1999a, and Thomas 2010)—but not all (e.g., Toft, Philpott, and Shah 2011)—include in their definition of religious resurgence. Having said this, for practical and stylistic reasons, I will employ from time to time the terminology of "religious resurgence" throughout the book.
[21] On the secularization of the international system, see Philpott (2000). On nationalism as an alternative source of belonging and norms to religions, see Anderson (2006).
[22] Berger (1969); Martin (1978).
[23] Kepel (1994); see also Berger (1999b); Casanova (1994).

become notable, for instance, in the contemporary growth of fundamentalist movements spanning most religious traditions, including Christianity, Islam, Judaism, or Buddhism; in the politicization of religious beliefs in the form of political Islam, the American Christian Right, Jewish nationalism, engaged Buddhism, or Hindu nationalism; or in the emergence of novel forms of identity politics based on religious and civilizational invocations of Confucian, Islamic, Christian, Orthodox, or Judeo-Christian values.[24]

Such dynamics have increasingly and relentlessly intersected with world political events, whether in the case of the Islamic revolution of 1979 in Iran or the fall of the "Godless" Soviet Union in 1989 undermined in part by a Catholic Pope in Europe (John Paul II), a Catholic Union in Poland (*Solidarność*), and Muslim religious fighters in Afghanistan (the *Mujahidin*). The post-Cold War era has witnessed the rise of conflicts pitting warring parties against each other seemly along religious-sectarian lines, most notably captured by the disintegration of Yugoslavia. The terrorist attacks of September 11, 2001, committed at the dawn of the twenty-first century by a group claiming to act in the name of Islam, brought religion to the center of contemporary international relations. Even in ostensibly secular Western Europe, religion has forcefully entered public debates, including how to best integrate and accommodate its growing Muslim population, whether references should be made to Europe's "Christian roots" in the context of the drafting of the EU's constitution, or whether the European project should be enlarged to include Muslim-majority countries such as Turkey.

The second postsecular process involves instead a parallel change in mentalities. This ideational development is exemplified by a self-reflexive turn in secular thought, leading to the emergence of what Habermas labels a "postsecular consciousness."[25] A postsecular consciousness is most evident in the mounting intellectual and political critiques of secular knowledge paradigms variably faulted for misunderstanding, misrepresenting, or marginalizing religion in social life and world politics. Such critique takes prevalently three forms.

Postsecular consciousness appears as a theoretical and historical revision of the secularization thesis and its paradigmatic influence over the social sciences. In the past decades, scholars have poked holes in the theory's teleological prediction that modernity, and parallel observable trends toward the functional differentiation of religion from other spheres of social and political life, implied the demise of belief or religion's irremediable privatization and loss of public relevance.[26] Others have challenged secularization theory's

---

[24] The literature on the contemporary rise of fundamentalism, politically engaged theologies, and forms of religiously infused identity politics is vast. For seminal contributions in these fields, see Barber (1992); Huntington (1996); Juergensmeyer (2008); Marty and Appleby (1991–1995). For seminal contributions in the discipline of IR, see Hatzopoulos and Petito (2003); Thomas (2005); Toft, Philpott, and Shah (2011).

[25] Habermas and Mendieta (2010); also Habermas (2006).

[26] For seminal critiques of secularization theory see Berger (1999b); Casanova (1994).

universalist and homogenizing assumption, arguing that there are "multiple" ways of being modern that do not exclude religion,[27] as well as a variety of historically and politically contingent secular arrangements and secularizing paths.[28] We can call this the "sociological postsecular perspective."

Postsecular consciousness takes also the form of novel normative reflections and projects. These projects find in religious traditions possibilities for overcoming the pathologies of liberal, capitalist, secular modernity. Thus, they seek to contest the restrictions that certain secularist, especially laicist, arrangements impose on the participation of religious individuals and organizations in the public sphere and politics, while highlighting the important contributions that religious insights and voices can make to the common good. We find here thinkers who—either from more secular or religious sensibilities—seek to formulate updated normative frameworks open to mutually advantageous accommodations and learning processes between the secular and the religious.[29] We may call this the "normative postsecular perspective."

Finally, postsecular consciousness expresses itself also within certain critical-theoretical, whether poststructural or postcolonial, strands of thought. This line of reasoning is concerned with revealing and deconstructing what it considers to be the ideological, oppressive, and exclusionary—rather than supposedly neutral, impartial, and inclusive—nature of the secular, and its doctrinal companion, secularism. The secular is thought of as a site of domination and control, a site that seeks to identify and categorize something like "religion" as its opposite, in order to marginalize it from politics and sustain particular forms of power, often those of the modern state.[30] We may call this the "critical postsecular perspective."

Although the sociological, normative, or critical postsecular perspectives originate—to borrow from Luca Mavelli and Fabio Petito—"from different sensibilities and concerns," they nonetheless all "articulate sketches of postsecular visions that encourage us to think beyond current secular frameworks."[31] This change in consciousness has opened the scholarly and intellectual doors toward a budding interest in the production of knowledge about religion as well as greater appreciation and legitimation of religion as a way of thinking about and being in the world.

Going back to our two dimensions constitutive of a postsecular world society—(i) religions' growing political salience and (ii) rise in postsecular consciousness—there has been a tendency in the IR literature to view these

---

[27] Eisenstadt (2000).
[28] See Berger, Davie, and Fokas (2008); Cady and Hurd (2010); Fox (2006); Kuru (2009); Smith (2003).
[29] Habermas and especially his dialogues with Cardinal Ratzinger (Habermas and Ratzinger 2006) is exemplary of this postsecular strand of thought. See also Taylor (2007); Dallmayr and Manoochehri (2007). For similar perspectives in the discipline of IR see Barbato and Kratochwil (2009); Mavelli and Petito (2014).
[30] Exemplary voices here are those of Asad (2003a; 1993); Cavanaugh (2009); Connolly (1999). For perspectives closer to IR see Hurd (2008); Wilson (2012).
[31] Mavelli and Petito (2012, 932).

processes as distinct and mutually exclusive, rather than as deeply entangled. On the one hand, we find accounts that suggest that greater secular reflexivity is a result or needs to come about as we experience the growing political salience of religion in the world.[32] On the other hand are those who instead see this change in consciousness and the abandonment of previously held secularist lenses as generating a greater appreciation for (the continued relevance of) religion and thus with it a misplaced narrative of religious "resurgence."[33] Gorski et al. pithily summarize this tension with the following question: "Which world has changed—the 'real' one or the scholarly one?"[34]

Similarly to Gorski et al., who also adopt critical realist philosophical foundations, I argue that both worlds are changing at the same time.[35] These changes are partly occurring independently from one another while also partly mutually reinforcing each other as changes in practices inform ideas, and changes in ideas inform practices. Put differently, as Tarak Barkawi and George Lawson argue about the co-constitutive relationship between history and theory: "theory is made in history, and it helps to make history."[36]

As we shall see, this means that both processes constitutive of a postsecular world society carry independent explanatory power in accounting for the operationalization of religion in US foreign policy. In other words, both the growing political vibrancy of religion and postsecular consciousness are the conditions of possibility for the emergence of America's foreign policy regime complex on religion. This point is, for instance, implicitly acknowledged by Michael Desch as follows:

> The combination of a grudging intellectual realization that social science needs to deal with religion, in combination with dramatic examples of religion reasserting

---

[32] Philpott (2002).

[33] Haynes (2006); Hurd (2008); Wilson (2012).

[34] Gorski et al. (2012a, 2).

[35] Broadly speaking, critical realism stakes a position between positivist empiricist and hermeneutical interpretivist philosophies of science. Compared to more radical interpretivist approaches, critical realism is ontologically realist in the sense that it recognizes a reality that is mind-independent from those who wish to know it. Compared to positivist philosophies, it is epistemologically critical in the sense that is sees science as a human activity that is inevitably mediated by cultural and historical context, human language and social power (Joseph and Wight 2010; Kurki 2007; Patomäki and Wight 2000; Jackson 2011, ch. 4).

[36] Barkawi and Lawson (2017, 1). Postsecular thought should not be simply seen as a reflection of empirical and historical changes connected with the growing political salience of religion. A series of intellectual developments—the crisis of secular ideologies and projects (whether socialist or liberal), poststructural and postcolonial critiques of universalizing Enlightenment assumptions, the cultural and linguistic turns in the social sciences and humanities—have without doubt contributed to opening the door for the growing interest in religion in the academy partly independently from real-world religious dynamics. Yet the assumption that postsecular consciousness is mostly an intellectual construct divorced from wider developments and events connected with religion's growing political salience is problematic too. Ontologically it is problematic—from this author's philosophical perspective—because it suggests that there is little reality beyond our own interpretations and discourses. Empirically it is problematic because it assigns too much power to scholars in shaping the world most people live in, one where religious beliefs, communities, rituals, and symbols are experienced "in practice" (Riesebrodt 2012) beyond what we as scholars say or do.

itself into international politics, is starting to put religion back on the intellectual and policy agendas.[37]

Having defined how I employ the concept of the postsecular in this book, I now turn to defining what I understand by "world society." I base this concept in English School thinking about the international system. English School scholars divide the international system along two different types of societies, the "international society" of states and interstate relations, and the "world society" of non-state actors and transnational cultural, economic, and social forces. The concept of "international society" captures the distinctiveness of the state in modern times or more generally of any sort of independent political community throughout history. "World society" instead captures the complexity of nonstate transnational and interhuman relations that exist simultaneously as aspects of international reality.[38] Neither society supersedes the other; rather, they exist alongside each other with a degree of autonomy but also in constant interaction with one another.[39] From this perspective, events and developments at the world society level can exercise both domestic and international pressures on a state's foreign policy and thus bring about change. Likewise, foreign policies can themselves influence wider global transnational social forces and processes.[40]

Conceptually grounding the two postsecular processes—the growing political salience of religion and the emergence of postsecular consciousness—at the level of world society allows us to account for the multiple simultaneous domestic and international pressures that are contributing to the emergence of the four distinct, yet interconnected, religious foreign policy regimes. This conceptual move brings together different levels of analysis in one framework and overcomes more standard ways of explaining foreign policy change that generally rely on only one level or "image"—whether focusing on individuals (first image), the nature of the state and domestic politics (second image), or international factors (third image).[41] In fact, the operationalization of religion

---

[37] Desch (2013, 15).

[38] Buzan (2004, 87–89). See also Bull (2002, 266–271); Buzan (2018); Hobson, Lawson, and Rosenberg (2010, 2–4).

[39] This understanding of the international system is distinct from those that either posit the state—as Realists do for instance—as the primary unit of analysis and overlook non-state actors, and those—like Marxist theorists instead—which concentrate on non-state economic actors and forces and view state behavior predominantly as a mere reflection of capitalist agents and structures.

[40] For historical sociological and English School views of how world society interacts and influences the foreign policy of states, and vice versa, see Alden and Aran (2012, ch. 6), and Hill (2003, chs. 7–8). This book is mostly concerned with the study of what Carlsnaes and Guzzini (2011) define as Foreign Policy (FP), which is a broader domain of research compared to a particular body of scholarship recognized as principally concerned with studying foreign policy known as Foreign Policy Analysis (FPA). FPA is generally focused on investigating the multiple influences that impact the *decision-making process* leading to a *specific foreign policy output*. It largely takes a snapshot view of the decision-making process, where the state and its foreign policy structures are seen essentially as given. A FP approach taken here instead, rather than being singularly concerned with decision-making and outputs, investigates the origin, development, and evolution of institutions, practices, ideas, and norms that structure and constitute a state's foreign policy.

[41] Waltz (1959).

in US foreign policy challenges standard ways of explaining change to a state's foreign policy that generally focus on only one level of analysis.

The shortcomings of approaches that make a clear-cut distinction between different levels of analysis are several in our case. If we were to focus only on first-image causes, for example, we could explain some but not all of the regimes. Let us take here the role played by President George W. Bush, whose Christian faith and born-again experience was a central feature of his public persona and thus may be viewed as a driving force in the operationalization of religion in American foreign policy.[42] As we shall see in the case study chapters, President Bush undoubtedly played a pivotal role in bringing about the Faith-Based Foreign Aid regime through executive orders. Yet the Bush explanation can hardly account for the extensive domestic religious lobbying in support of the Faith-Based Foreign Aid regime itself. These domestic forces would likewise influence Barack Obama's decision to extend and expand the regime, despite that among the liberal and progressive milieus supporting the Democratic president many saw the Bush-era faith-based agenda as controversial and hoped it would be rolled back. President Bush, and American presidents more generally, also had little to do with the emergence of the International Religious Freedom regime, for instance, which was institutionalized before the Bush presidency and not through executive action, but by Congress.

Focusing solely on second-image causes related to domestic factors and politics would equally leave us with only a partial picture. Much of the attention here could revolve around the influence of domestic religious groups in general and the Christian or Religious Right in particular.[43] Domestic religious movements and advocacy groups did certainly play an important role in the adoption of the International Religious Freedom and Faith-Based Foreign Aid regimes. Yet focusing only on these forces would discount the key role played by presidents in authorizing the creation and shaping the implementation of such regimes. Moreover, focusing solely on domestic religious lobbying and advocacy cannot take into account neither the rise of the Muslim and Islamic Interventions regime, nor of the Religious Engagement one. These regimes, as we shall see, came into being mostly thanks to pressures exercised by more circumscribed international affairs and policy experts in Washington, DC reacting to events and developments originating outside of the United States, rather than being championed by broader domestic religious constituencies.

Explanations relying exclusively on third-image international factors would likewise be incomplete. Accounts here, for instance, could point to international trends and events with a notable religious dimension, such as the rise

---

[42] The relationship between religion and the American presidency is a complex one, and there is a long history of either personally devout presidents or political leaders adept at mobilizing the religious sentiments of their compatriots (Smith 2006). In this context, however, the George W. Bush presidency has been often singled out as one of the most explicitly religious presidency of the post-World War II era (Aikman 2004; Mansfield 2003).

[43] See, for example, Marsden (2008); Mead (2006).

of political Islam and the attacks of 9/11, as drivers of the religious turn in US foreign policy. As we shall see, these developments are indeed closely linked to the emergence of the Muslim and Islamic Interventions regime and, to some extent, help explain the institutionalization of the religious engagement agenda. The 9/11 explanation, however, cannot account for the development of the International Religious Freedom and Faith-Based Foreign Aid regimes, which in fact emerged before the 2001 terrorist attacks.

In sum, explanations that rely on only one specific image or factor—whether individual leaders, domestic politics, or international forces—remain incomplete and partial on their own. What is needed is a framework that helps to connect these different images. This is what the concept of world society enables us to do, as it captures macro developments taking place transnationally both within and outside the United States. In short, it allows us to analyze the multiple simultaneous domestic and international forces that have come about in the past three decades putting pressure on American foreign policy to adapt and respond both to the growing political salience of religion and to the rise of postsecular consciousness.

Micro-Level Dynamics: Desecularizing Actors and Discourses

In order to address the second puzzle—explaining why there is a variety of religious foreign policy regimes and how these came about at different times since the end of the Cold War—we need to connect macro-level historical and global developments to micro-level analysis. More specifically, we need to look at the creative actions of agents that are producing and responding to the emergence of a postsecular world society and who are responsible for directly causing changes in American foreign policy. Put differently, the emergence of a postsecular world society is a contextual necessary condition that enables the operationalization of religion in American foreign policy at this particular historical juncture, but it does not cause it on its own.[44] To explain how religion has become an increasingly structured subject and object of US foreign policy, we need to pay attention to a wide variety of actors at the micro-level whose identities and interests are co-constitutive of, but whose behaviors are not determined by, macro postsecular processes.[45]

I call these actors *desecularizing actors*. These actors are the causal link between postsecular developments within world society—religious resurgence and postsecular consciousness—and the rise of multiple religious foreign policy regimes since the late 1990s. Peter Berger first introduced the term "desecularization," by which he mostly meant the persistence and revival of religion in the modern world.[46] Vyacheslav Karpov has further qualified this

---

[44] See Mahoney, Kimball, and Koivu (2009) for a discussion on the logics of historical explanation, sequence analysis, and necessary and sufficient conditions.
[45] On the mutual constitution of social structures and agents, see Carlsnaes (1992); Wendt (1987); Wight (1999).
[46] Berger (1999a).

concept to indicate a process of contestation of, and reversal from, a previously secularized and secular state of affairs.[47] Similarly, Sadia Saeed notes that processes of desecularization emerge "when social actors seek to efface the perceived distance between "religious" and "secular" domains."[48] As I will argue in greater detail in this chapter's next section, the renegotiation of previously settled boundaries between the secular and the religious, faith and politics, church and state in American foreign policy is precisely what desecularizing actors work toward in order to successfully institutionalize a specific religious foreign policy regime.[49] Overall, the framework I develop here, seeks to reconcile more traditional sociological accounts that explain processes of secularization/desecularization by stressing the role of large-scale macro developments, with newer perspectives that approach secular-religious changes as the result of contingent political conflicts rooted in the ideologies, interests, and actions of particular agents at the micro-level.[50]

I identify three broad categories of desecularizing actors: activists, experts, and policymakers.[51] *Desecularizing activists* are generally faith-based leaders and organizations embedded in and constitutive of the wider process of religious resurgence in American society. These actors, which can be thought of also as religious "norm entrepreneurs" operating at the civil society and grassroots level,[52] mobilize domestically in the United States to lobby and advocate "from below" for their preferred religious foreign policy regimes.

Desecularizing activists come in different shapes and forms. One particularly vocal and politically important constituency is composed by politicized Evangelicals and by individuals and organizations tied to the Christian Right movement.[53] Increasingly their ranks are flanked by representatives of a reorganized Christian Left movement.[54] More broadly, desecularizing activists are represented by the exponential growth, since the 1970s, of religious advocacy and lobbying organizations in Washington, DC concerned with international

---

[47] Karpov (2010); also Lisovskaya and Karpov (2010).
[48] Saeed (2016, 24).
[49] I extend the analysis of desecularization beyond the domestic sphere, where it is often confined (Lisovskaya and Karpov 2010; Saeed 2016), and apply it to explain changes in foreign policy.
[50] For a similar attempt to reconcile large scale structural processes with agents' actions to explain variations in secularization/desecularization, see Mayrl (2016). Compared to Mayrl, who focuses on domestic education policy rather than foreign policy, the broader context I focus on within which actors pursue their religious-secular political struggles is represented by the macro transnational world society level rather than the meso-level of the state. For scholarship that emphasizes either large-scale structural forces and processes or contingency and political conflicts among agents—but not necessarily both—to explain secular–religious change, see note 23 in chapter 1.
[51] I draw from, but also revisit, Karpov's (2010, 251–255) notion of "counter-secularization activists and actors."
[52] In much constructivist literature, norm entrepreneurs are secular and generally advocate for the adoption of a range of human rights norms (Finnemore and Sikkink 1998). Recently scholarship has emerged conceptualizing religiously based actors as norm entrepreneurs, for instance Adamson (2005); Bettiza and Dionigi (2015); Bob (2015).
[53] On the history and politics of the American Christian Right, see Wald and Calhoun-Brown (2018, ch. 8); Wilcox and Larson (2006).
[54] See Hall (1997); Olson (2007).

issues.[55] Such activism generally cuts across religious communities and denominations—from Christian, to Muslim, Jewish, Buddhist, Mormon, or Baha'i—as well as across conservative and liberal theological orientations. The most pressing issue for desecularizing activists is often the physical and spiritual well-being of their specific religious community worldwide, as well as that of other religions and possibly humanity more broadly at times. These actors view American foreign policy as having long unjustly ignored their voices and faith-based concerns.

Desecularizing experts are cultural elites such as intellectuals, scholars, pundits, and policy analysts. These often, although not exclusively, exhibit some kind of personal religious commitment, but most importantly they are the carriers and producers of postsecular ideas and consciousness (whether analytical, normative, or critical). Being generally tied to universities, think tanks, and policy research institutes, these actors constitute an amorphous "epistemic community" whose claim to expertise is based on particular forms of knowledge—practical, theological, or social scientific—about religion.[56] Desecularizing experts thus tend to have a triple orientation as committed religious individuals, as scholarly analysts of religion, and as policy-engaged actors on matters of religion. Although these experts are outside government, they often have extensive contacts and interactions with policymakers. As such, in their efforts to champion any one particular religious foreign policy regime, they can be seen as doing so through high-level "lateral" forms of engagement—they advocate "from the side," so to speak, rather than from below, as is the case with activists.

Desecularizing experts are commonly connected to a proliferating number of new centers, initiatives, research projects, or task forces housed in academic institutions, well-known think tanks, or novel faith-based "think-and-do tanks,"[57] which explore issues at the nexus of religion and international affairs and actively seek to disseminate this knowledge to foreign policy practitioners. Religiously based universities have established themselves as important leaders in this sector. These include Georgetown University, with its Berkley Center for Religion, Peace, and World Affairs created in 2006 and the Center for Muslim-Christian Understanding founded in 1993; the University of Notre Dame, with an important research program on Religion, Conflict, and Peacebuilding housed in the Kroc Institute since 2000; Baylor University and its Institute for Studies of Religion launched in 2004; and the International

---

55 Pew Research Center (2012).
56 An epistemic community is "a network of professionals with recognized expertise and competence in a particular domain and an authoritative claim to policy-relevant knowledge within that domain or issue area" (Haas 1992, 3; see also Adler and Haas 1992). Sandal (2011) broadens the definition of epistemic community beyond scientific experts to include also religious leaders and organizations.
57 These are institutes that do not just seek to conduct policy-relevant research and influence the public debate (the "think" part), but also take a more proactive role in lobbying governments and carrying out their own programs (the "do" part).

Center for Law and Religion Studies founded in 2000 at Brigham Young University.

Initiatives and centers focused on issues of religion in world affairs have been created in recent decades also across a wide range of more secular universities with important connections to policy milieus in Washington, DC. Harvard University's Belfer Center hosted between 2007 and 2012 the Initiative on Religion in International Affairs and since 2018 its Divinity School and Kennedy School have joined efforts in a new Religion, Conflict, and Peace Initiative; Yale University's MacMillan Center has, since the mid-2000s, a number of ongoing projects focused on religion in international affairs; Johns Hopkins' School for Advanced International Studies (SAIS) labeled its 2009–2010 academic year the "Year of Religion," and launched a Global Politics and Religion Initiative between 2012 and 2014; and George Mason University hosts the Center for World Religions, Diplomacy, and Conflict Resolution since 2003 and the Ali Vural Ak Center for Global Islamic Studies since 2009.

Major think tanks and policy research institutes have joined this booming intellectual enterprise. These include the Council on Foreign Relations (CFR), which in 2006 established a Religion and Foreign Policy Initiative; the Brookings Institution, which has demonstrated a growing interest on the nexus between religion and foreign policy since 2001,[58] and established in 2003 the Project on US Relations with the Islamic World; the United States Institute of Peace (USIP), which launched in 2001 a Religion and Peacemaking Program which has evolved taking multiple forms over the years; the Hudson Institute's Center on Islam, Democracy, and the Future of the Muslim World since 2006 and a Center for Religious Freedom since 2007; and the Pew Research Center's Forum on Religion and Public Life, launched in 2001 (recently renamed Pew Research Center on Religion and Public Life). Adding to this are the countless reports on religion in general and Islam in particular drafted since the early 2000s by think tanks such as the Center for Strategic and International Studies (CSIS),[59] the Rand Corporation,[60] or the Chicago Council on Global Affairs.[61]

A further novel development is the emergence of faith-based think-and-do tanks with an explicit interest in religion in world politics. Some of the most visible ones include the International Center for Religion and Diplomacy (ICRD) founded in 1999, the Center for the Study of Islam and Democracy (CSID) founded in 1999, the Institute for Global Engagement (IGE) founded in 2000, and the Religious Freedom Institute founded in 2016. Other, more established and long-standing think tanks with a religious bent, such as the Ethics and Public Policy Center (EPPC), founded in 1976, have also started paying greater attention to religious dynamics and trends outside of the United States from

---

[58] See the volume by Brian Hehir (2004), which came out from a Brookings event in the early 2000s.
[59] Danan and Hunt (2007).
[60] Benard (2003); Rabasa et al. (2007); Rabasa et al. (2004).
[61] Appleby and Cizik (2010).

the 1990s onward.[62] Many of the voices and activities emerging from this heterogeneous epistemic community are generally concerned with what they see as America's inability to understand, approach, and mobilize religion globally in the pursuit of its national interest, however this may be defined.

Desecularizing policymakers are political or bureaucratic actors sitting in Congress, the White House, or across the foreign policy bureaucracy. Compared to activists and experts, desecularizing policymakers are less central in articulating and setting the intellectual agenda on religion in foreign policy. Desecularizing policymakers sitting in the halls of power have a key role nonetheless. When influenced by activists and experts they push "from within" and authorize "from above" the operationalization of religion across the different regimes. As we shall see, members of Congress and President Bush were instrumental in institutionalizing, respectively, the International Religious Freedom and the Faith-Based Foreign Aid regimes. Neoconservatives in the Bush administration were central in defining the early stages of the Muslim and Islamic Interventions regime. Particular members of the Obama administration made the religious engagement agenda, first articulated by experts outside government, their own and actively championed it across the foreign policy bureaucracy.

Desecularizing actors bring about their preferred religious foreign policy regimes through a number of causal pathways and mechanisms. First and foremost, they do so by articulating and deploying what I label *desecularizing discourses*. Understanding the role of discourses in general and desecularizing discourses in particular is pivotal to the analysis for three main reasons. I argue that desecularizing discourses fulfill three key functions: (a) they articulate novel policy paradigms and contest established foreign policy arrangements; (b) they provide shared meanings and create a conceptual space around which different formations of desecularizing actors can come together; and (c) they act as a causal mechanism that brings about change. I now further unpack and explain these different functions.

First, desecularizing discourses act as (a) conveyors and carriers of the ideas or, to use Peter Hall's expression, the "policy paradigms" that underpin each of the four religious foreign policy regimes. Policy paradigms do not just specify "the goals of policy and the kind of instruments that can be used to attain them," but they also contribute to defining "the very nature of the problems they are meant to be addressing."[63] In other words, policy paradigms embody specific ways of seeing, talking, and defining problems, which in turn shape the kinds of solutions offered, and the types of policies proposed. "A paradigm is like a lens that filters information and focuses attention," Carter Wison explains. "It embodies particular assumptions about the policy problem—its

---

[62] Cromartie (2005). Peter Berger's seminal 1999 edited volume *The Desecularization of the World* was published under the auspices of the EPPC.
[63] Hall (1993, 279).

cause, its seriousness, its pervasiveness, those responsible for creating it, or ameliorating it, and the appropriate governmental response."[64]

At their most basic, desecularizing discourses argue that the secularity of American foreign policymaking and implementation is highly problematic, especially in the context of a postsecular world society. It is this contestation of the secular character of US foreign policy, along with their call for the in-stitutionalization of a particular religious regime, that earns such discourses and the actors who articulate and deploy them, the label "desecularizing." In other words, just by seeking to influence foreign policy on the basis of one's religious persuasion and values—say, for instance, in support of a particular country such as Israel, a particular issue such as combating human trafficking, or a military intervention such as that in Iraq in 2003—does not necessarily qualify an actor as desecularizing. Rather, actors only become desecularizing if they dispute the settled boundaries between the secular and the religious in order to open up greater space for including religion as a distinct subject and object of American foreign policy thinking and practices.

In their broadest and more abstract form, desecularizing discourses come in two varieties: principled and strategic. *Principled desecularizing discourses* generally articulate "beliefs about right and wrong" and about what is "just and unjust"—to borrow from Nina Tannenwald's definition of "principled ideas"—and thus prescribe the appropriate norms of principled conduct.[65] Principled desecularizing discourses are most often, although not exclu-sively, articulated by desecularizing activists and take the following general form: "American foreign policy is too secular and has long unjustly neglected and excluded the concerns of faith-based actors and communities. Such ex-clusion has become even more problematic and discriminatory at a time when religions are seeking a greater role in the public sphere and are major contributors to the common good. As such, in order to rectify this unjustified and unfair neglect, American foreign policy should operationalize religious foreign policy regime X."

Strategic desecularizing discourses are articulated most explicitly, although not exclusively, by desecularizing experts. These discourses are strategic because—to borrow from Nina Tannenwald's definition of "causal ideas"— they lay out "beliefs about cause-effect, or means-end, relationships" and "de-rive authority from the fact that they are espoused by epistemic communities or by other relevant elites."[66] This type of discourse is commonly articulated along the following general lines: "Over the past decades, faith has come to matter more in international politics and hence to America's national interest. American foreign policy needs to overcome its secular biases, which prevent it from understanding and addressing the important role of religion around the world. American interests would be better served if it considered religious

---

[64] Wison (2000, 257).
[65] Tannenwald (2005, 16).
[66] Ibid.

perspectives and solutions to global problems, which can be achieved by operationalizing religious foreign policy regime Y."

The second function of desecularizing discourses is (b) providing shared meanings and creating a conceptual space around which different formations of desecularizing actors debate and discuss, agree and disagree, form broad and at times opposing coalitions, in the overall common pursuit of operationalizing religion in American foreign policy.[67] Sharing discourses, like sharing a language, does not mean that all actors will agree on everything all the time, but it does mean that they will be able to communicate and understand each other. As we shall see in the case studies, there are often important policy disagreements and conflicting priorities among desecularizing actors. These include diverging understandings of how a specific regime should be institutionalized and implemented, and competition between actors championing different regimes altogether.

Indeed, advocacy for the operationalization of religion is riven with conflicts and friction among desecularizing actors themselves. These tensions are rooted in the diversity of their identities (secular or religious), ideological orientations (whether political or theological, conservative, or progressive), interests (whether partisan/sectarian, nationalist, or internationalist), and views of national security and foreign affairs. Yet despite these important differences, desecularizing actors all share a similar conceptual space—which desecularizing discourses reflect and represent—based on a concern with the greater role that religion ought to play for principled or strategic reasons as a subject and object of US foreign policy.

In other words, desecularizing actors—whether activists, experts, or policymakers—share an overarching concern with operationalizing religion in US foreign policy, but nonetheless have often very different understandings of how this should be done. A conceptually fruitful way to capture these similarities and differences, is to think of desecularizing actors as coming together in different formations, as *constellations, networks, coalitions,* and *constituencies.* A *constellation* is constituted by a broad, heterogeneous, loosely knit, and uncoordinated set of desecularizing actors. These generally share an interest in operationalizing one particular regime, say International Religious Freedom; however, they mobilize around very different and at times opposite understandings of how such regime should be implemented and what its purpose should be. Within constellations we can find more homogeneous, but still somewhat loosely knit, *networks* of desecularizing actors. In networks, actors share a similar theological or ideological orientation, as well as a particular view of how a specific religious regime should be operationalized, but on the whole their efforts to mainstream religion in foreign policy are largely uncoordinated. *Coalitions* and *constituencies* are more tightly knit and coherent groupings of desecularizing actors, within a wider network or constellation,

---

[67] See also the notion of "discourse coalition" by Hajer (1993).

that mobilize and lobby together around a shared view of a religious foreign policy regime. Coalitions bring different types of actors—activists, experts, and policymakers—together, while constituencies are prevalently represented by one typology of desecularizing actor – say, experts. Stressing different formations is key, also, to grasp how regimes are often the result of a compromise between competing perspectives within a constellation of desecularizing actors, and on how they evolve over time depending on which networks, coalitions, and constituencies of desecularizing actors hold sway over the policymaking process under different administrations.

Desecularizing discourses, lastly, act (c) as a causal mechanism to bring about policy change.[68] Such change occurs as desecularizing discourses are articulated and deployed to *persuade* policymakers to adopt a particular religious foreign policy regime. Persuasion is "a social process of communication that involves changing beliefs, attitudes, or behavior in the absence of overt coercion," as Jeffrey Checkel explains. "It entails convincing someone through argument and principled debate."[69] Persuasion may either be more superficial if changes are made for political expedience and lead to a more temporary and instrumental adoption of new ideas, or it may go deeper and lead to more sustained change through processes of socialization and the internalization of new ideas and possibly new identities.

Contributing Factors: Critical Junctures and Exogenous Trends

Desecularizing actors and discourses play a key role in what is often a more complex causal story leading to regime emergence and evolution. The ability of actors to institutionalize their regime of choice and shape the same regime along their preferred outcomes depends not solely on what they say and do, but also on the presence of two further contributing factors—or what could also be referred to as INUS conditions.[70] These factors are critical junctures and exogenous (i.e., non-postsecular) trends.

Critical junctures are significant, relatively short-lived, intense moments of social, political, or economic change or crises, which may open up space for reconsidering old or proposing new institutional and policy arrangements.[71] Critical junctures do not directly and on their own cause change. They can provide unsettled times when policymakers may be particularly receptive to new ideas and which desecularizing actors can exploit to persuade them into

---

[68] My understanding of discourse as a causal mechanism here is anchored to what Benjamin Banta (2013) calls "critical discourse analysis" (CDA), compared to the more commonly adopted "poststructural discourse theory" (PDT). See the methodology section in chapter 1 for a fuller discussion of CDA.
[69] Checkel (2006, 364).
[70] INUS stands for "an *insufficient* but *necessary* part of a condition which is itself *unnecessary* but *sufficient* for the result" (Mackie cited in Mahoney, Kimball, and Koivu 2009, 129). INUS causes are neither necessary nor sufficient for an explanation rather they constitute a cause in a larger combination of causes that is sufficient for explaining a particular outcome.
[71] For seminal scholarship on "critical junctures," see Capoccia and Kelemen (2007); Mahoney (2000); Pierson (2004, ch. 5).

adopting a particular religious foreign policy regime. Two types of events are important to our causal story.

One set of events are domestic political changes, most notably presidential elections and the installment of new administrations. As new presidents and administrations bring with them different and novel ideas and personnel, an opening is generated for desecularizing actors to influence foreign policy. Another type of event is constituted by international shocks and crises that desecularizing actors present as revealing, on the one hand, the growing political salience of religion in international relations and, on the other hand, the secular limits of American foreign policy in adequately predicting, understanding, or responding to them.[72] Events which thus appear critical to desecularizing actors include, for instance, the end of the Cold War and the demise of Communism, the post-Cold War rise in civil conflicts often pitting warring parties along sectarian divides, the attacks of 9/11 organized by Al Qaeda, the US failures to pacify Iraq in the aftermath of the 2003 invasion, the continued growth in Islamist terrorism represented most starkly by the emergence of ISIS (the Islamic State of Iraq and the Levant) following the 2011 Arab Spring, and mounting violence directed toward religious groups and minorities around the world. All these instances would lend themselves to be framed by desecularizing actors as moments of radical change and crisis intimately connected to the growing role and significance of religion in world politics.

Exogenous trends are not single events or moments of acute crisis, but longer-term ideational, economic, social, or political developments that occur over years and decades. These trends are conceptualized as "exogenous" because they are unrelated to postsecular processes taking place in parallel and with no apparent connection to the resurgence of religion or the rise of postsecular consciousness. Similarly to critical junctures, exogenous trends create favorable conditions that desecularizing actors can indirectly benefit from or directly exploit to advance their principled or strategic concerns for the operationalization of religion. For instance, as chapter 3 shows, the successful institutionalization of the International Religious Freedom regime cannot be explained without appreciating the post-Cold War expansion in human rights advocacy that was simultaneously taking place at the time.

Upon regime operationalization, we can expect a level of *path dependency* to set in, ensuring that regimes persist over time.[73] While path dependency suggests that regime change will not be the default condition, it does not mean that incremental or abrupt institutional and policy developments cannot occur, whether through decay, the broadening of institutional arrangements and functions, or conversion to an entirely new role. Hence I expect that regime

---

[72] I draw here also from more interpretative approaches to critical junctures (Widmaier, Blyth, and Seabrooke 2007; also Guzzini 2012). These suggest that particular shocks and crises, do not speak for themselves, but acquire salience when they become constructed as critical by certain actors pushing for specific outcomes and changes.

[73] The discussion here draws on Historical Institutionalist theorizing, which is increasingly being applied in the study of IR (Fioretos 2011) and foreign policy (Mabee 2011; 2007).

change and evolution will occur in some cases, which will depend on the complex set of causes that explain regime rise in the first place, including: shifts in the forces and agents that sustain and generate a postsecular world society; the rise of new or the decline of old desecularizing actors and their agendas; the presence of critical junctures (new administrations and international crisis); and the evolution of long-term exogenous trends.

To summarize my arguments so far, in order to understand and explain the rise of America's religious foreign policy regimes and the overall complex, I have proposed to situate the American state within a wider macro global and historical context defined by the emergence of a postsecular world society. This context gives rise to and is being reproduced by a multiplicity of desecularizing actors which pressure American foreign policy institutions and policymakers to respond and adapt to a domestic and international environment marked by the growing political salience of religion and ever more powerful postsecular intellectual currents. The success of these actors in operationalizing their preferred foreign policy regime is dependent upon their articulation and deployment of principled and strategic desecularizing discourses, and on the presence of two further contributing causal conditions, namely critical junctures and exogenous trends.

Shifting Secular-Religious Boundaries and Foreign Policy Desecularization

As pointed out in the previous section, desecularizing actors consider the secularity of American foreign policy as intrinsically problematic, and on this premise, they contest, challenge and seek to renegotiate existing arrangements. The aim of their challenge is to shift and loosen state–religious boundaries in order to open up space for religious actors and perspectives to be systematically brought into the foreign policy decision-making and implementation process. Borrowing from Sadia Saeed's conceptualization of desecularization, I expect the religion–state entanglements emerging in foreign policy from these processes of contestation to occur "while leaving the basic structural differentiation that characterizes modern societies intact."[74] Understanding desecularization as a "historically contingent and instituted" process, as Saeed does,[75] allows to appreciate how religious norms, practices, and actors can become increasingly entwined with some features of US foreign policy while nonetheless the latter continues to retain its autonomous logic on the whole.

Put differently, as religion becomes entangled with particular aspects of foreign policy, this sphere of social and political activity largely maintains its primary function as a vehicle through which a country defends and advances its interests internationally, and manages its relations with other states and

---

[74] Saeed (2016, 23).
[75] Ibid.

foreign publics. Desecularization through Saeed's lens, hence, "does not entail an erosion of the secular disciplinary and symbolic powers of the nation-state, which may in fact be further strengthened through it."[76] We should thus not expect the operationalization of religion in US foreign policy to undermine the American state as such, but rather to provide novel resources for asserting its influence—whether positive, according to supporters of the regimes, or negative, according to critics—in world politics.

But what exactly do desecularizing actors mean when they suggest that American foreign policy is too secular, and what kind of state–religious renegotiations do they seek to bring about? Desecularizing activists, experts, and policymakers' contestation of American foreign policy secularity develops—I contend—along four main lines. They contest it—and here I draw inspiration from José Casanova's multiple definitions of secularization and secularism—for being too secular *institutionally, epistemically, ideologically*, and *state-normatively*.[77] Hence, through the deployment of desecularizing discourses these actors wish to generate processes of institutional, epistemic, ideological, and state-normative desecularization. These processes are essential for the successful operationalization of the various religious foreign policy regimes. As we shall see in a moment, institutional desecularization requires "material" changes to be made to American foreign policy bureaucracies and practices, while epistemic, ideological, and state-normative desecularization require instead "ideational" changes in knowledge, mentalities, culture, and norms. Although it is important to keep these processes conceptually distinct, they are often intertwined and mutually reinforcing (e.g., changes in practices can lead to changes in norms and vice versa).

The problem of *institutional secularization*, in the eyes of desecularizing actors, is the excessive separation and distance that exists between America's foreign policy bureaucracy on the one hand, and religious actors and perspectives on the other. This becomes apparent in the sheer absence, according to desecularizing actors, of dedicated government offices and positions capable of understanding and addressing the role of religion in world politics, a deficiency further underlined by the lack of relevant policies which purposely focus on and target religious forces and dynamics internationally.

Successful contestation of this state of affairs leads to a process of *institutional desecularization* characterized by the progressive structured entanglement between foreign policy institutions and religious actors and perspectives. The aim is to reduce the distance between state and religion by putting in

---

[76] Ibid., 24.
[77] Casanova (2011). My understanding of institutional secularization, for instance, draws on secularization understood as the functional differentiation between religion and other spheres of life including the state. My distinction between epistemic, ideological, and state-normative secularism applied to the realm of foreign policy is inspired by Casanova's distinction between the categories of phenomenological secularism, secularism as ideology, and secularism as statecraft doctrine. For other approaches unpacking how different kinds of secular assumptions inform and structure the foreign policy of the US and European states, see Gutkowski (2013); Hurd (2008).

place new arrangements whereby religious leaders, experts, organizations, and communities can be formally and informally included in ever more structured ways in the formulation and delivery of American foreign policy. Institutional desecularization involves, first, building the bureaucratic architecture of any one particular religious foreign policy regime. This is done by creating new religion-oriented roles, positions, or offices mostly—although not exclusively— within the White House, State Department, or USAID, and populating these mostly—although not exclusively—with religious leaders, activists, and experts brought in through the "revolving door" practice.[78] Second, institutional desecularization occurs with the emergence of new foreign policy practices (whether policies, initiatives, programs, etc.) designed explicitly either to mobilize religious actors and perspectives in the pursuit of certain goals, or to target certain states, communities, organizations, or individuals identified primarily by their religious identity and beliefs.

A particular regime may generate either lower or higher levels of institutional desecularization depending on the extent of the state–religion entanglements it produces and sustains. There is no neat figure or concept that can measure or capture in a clear-cut way how much institutional desecularization has occurred. This may vary, for instance, according to the size of the regime's institutional architecture and the numbers of religious voices that populate it, the proximity of a regime's institutional architecture to the key centers of foreign policy decision-making and thus its ability to influence US conduct abroad, and the extent to which American foreign policy implementation partners with and harnesses the energy of religious actors worldwide (especially by funding them).

The problem of *epistemic secularism*, according to desecularizing actors' perception, is that the American foreign policy establishment is trapped in a mindset that views religion as marginal or irrelevant in the world. This mentality is seen as rooted in an un-reflexive acceptance of secularization theory and paradigms that present religion as declining or as an epiphenomenal force to more concrete economic and security interests. What follows, then, is not only the belief that religion is unimportant, but also that it has little or no relevance to American foreign policy.

Successful contestation of this mentality leads to different degrees of *epistemic desecularization* that generate a view that is either "attentive" of religion or even one that "reifies" religion as the most important factor in social life and international relations. A religiously attentive perspective is one that recognizes the importance of religion in world affairs, compared to treating it as irrelevant, but also stresses the complex ways in which faith interacts

---

[78] This is a highly institutionalized practice in the US whereby individuals from across different civil society sectors—business, academia, policy research, advocacy, and, increasingly, religious sectors— are often called upon to take up assignments within government for a particular period of time, following which they go back to positions outside of government. Thanks to the revolving door practice, nongovernmental actors have direct, rather than mediated, access to policymaking.

with a wide variety of economic, social, political, and historical factors to produce certain outcomes or manifestations. In perspectives that reify religion, complexity is often sidelined and religion is generally presented as the dominant and single most important factor in determining identities, meanings, conducts, events, and outcomes.

The problem of *ideological secularism*, from a desecularizing actor's perspective, is that it sustains in the minds of American foreign policymakers a view of religion as an overwhelmingly negative and problematic force in the world. Seen through an ideologically secularist lens, religion thus mostly appears as a regressive, premodern, irrational, and intolerant force, which should be kept out of international politics (and foreign policy) in order for there to be progress and peace in the world. Compared to an epistemic secularist perspective, which does not take an a priori normative stance for or against religion but simply treats it as an irrelevant factor, an ideological secularist perspective, instead, can view religion as an important force but mostly for the worst, while considering the secular to be inherently progressive, modern, and rational.

It needs to be noted that not all forms of secularism that embed within them a theory and value judgment about what religion is and does are purely hostile to religion.[79] Hence, following also Casanova, *ideological secularism* (which this book is concerned with) should be distinguished from *political secularism* (which is not a focus of this book). As the Georgetown University-based scholar observes, the latter "does not need to share the same negative assumptions about religion" as the former does.[80] Political secularism, for Casanova, is "actually compatible with a positive view of religion as a moral good or as an ethical communitarian reservoir of human solidarity and republican virtue," but what it would like to do is "to contain religion within its own differentiated 'religious' sphere and . . . maintain a secular public democratic sphere free from religion."[81]

Successful contestation leads to different degrees of *ideological desecularization* that manifest themselves in two overarching views of religion. One is a view of religion as complex and often "ambivalent" force, which can be both good and bad.[82] In this understanding, religion's impact in the world is seen as producing both desirable and undesirable, positive and negative outcomes depending upon context and circumstances. Another view, associated with a process of greater ideological desecularization, can lead to the "positive essentialization" of religion. Here religion—especially that which is labeled as true, authentic, and real religion—is represented as inherently good (e.g., peaceful, charitable, compassionate, and socially, economically, and politically useful). Positively essentialized religion is then juxtaposed against either

---

[79] I would like to thank one of the reviewers for pushing me to clarify this important point.
[80] Casanova (2011, 69).
[81] Ibid.
[82] For a classical statement on the "ambivalence of the sacred," see Appleby (2000). For a critique of the good/bad religion dichotomy see Hurd (2015, ch. 2); Mamdani (2002).

the supposedly corrupted, highjacked, or inauthentic religion mobilized in the service of violence by terrorists for instance, or to the limits of secular modes of living, thinking, and acting.

The problem of *state-normative secularism*, from a desecularizing actor's point of view, is that norms—formal rules or informal shared understandings—regulating state–religion relations are all too often interpreted as mandating little or no interaction with religion in the context of foreign policy. In the case of the United States, norms regulating state–religious relations are captured by the first two "religious" clauses of the Constitution's First Amendment the Establishment and the Free Exercise Clause. These read: "Congress shall make no law respecting an establishment of religion, or prohibiting the free exercise thereof." My use of the concept of state-normative secularism refers mostly to "strict separationist" interpretations of the Establishment Clause, which seeks to keep the state and faith-based actors and concerns as separate as possible, even if this may mean favoring nonreligion over religion.[83]

Successful contestation of a strict separationist interpretation of the Establishment Clause leads to processes of *state-normative desecularization* that vary in degree. At the far end of the spectrum, a strict separationist take on state–religion relations can be replaced by some kind of religious "establishment," whereby one or multiple religions are formally declared to be the state's official religion/s and explicitly embedded in or supported by the state. In between these two arrangements—strict separation and establishment—exists a vast gray area often occupied by what are identified as "accommodationist" perspectives on the Establishment Clause. An accommodationist position generally means treating religious voices and actors equally to secular ones, while not favoring religion over the secular, or one religion over another. However, in practice, accommodation is hardly if ever completely neutral. Accommodation often leads to some kind of state preference—however implicit—of certain religions and ways of being religious over others or even of religion over nonreligion.

To sum up my arguments so far: when desecularizing actors discursively contest the secularity of American foreign policy in order to operationalize their preferred religious foreign policy regime—whether International Religious Freedom, Faith-Based Foreign Aid, Muslim and Islamic Interventions, or Religious Engagement—they contest multiple and different aspects of this secularity. The emergence of each regime thus requires, but also further generates, four parallel processes of foreign policy desecularization: institutional, epistemic, ideological, and state-normative. The degree of desecularization

---

[83] Pew Research Center (2009c) and Davis (2010) offer, respectively, a briefer or more comprehensive overview of the complex debates around the meaning of these two clauses and the state–religion interactions these regulate in the US. It is important to note that strict separationist interpretations of the Establishment Clause have, historically, often not been exclusively advocated by humanist, secularist or civil rights groups have, but rather by religious minorities, including minority Christian Protestant denominations and sects seeking to curb the influence of more establishmentarian religious traditions such as the Anglican/Episcopal and Catholic churches.

across these four areas is likely to vary according to regime, with differences mostly rooted in the worldviews and preferences of the desecularizing actors championing and influencing a particular religious foreign policy regime over time.

Global Effects

The progressive and structured opening up of American foreign policymaking and implementation to faith over the past two decades means that the world's superpower has come to enmesh itself with and intervene in global religious dynamics and landscapes in ever more systematic ways. Intended to manage and marshal religion for a plurality of ends, the regime complex thus can have the power to transform—whether intentionally or not—religious and secular realities in the world. This issue has elicited a spirited debate on whether such foreign interventions in global religious affairs are a positive or a negative development.[84]

The historical sociological lens underpinning this study leads it primarily to focus on understanding the secular and religious changes that American foreign policy is generating in the international system, rather than celebrating or critiquing them. As Andrew Linklater aptly puts it: "the plain desire to understand social and political change is often the primary motivation for pursuing historical-sociological inquiry."[85] Thus this study's main concern is with identifying and unpacking the key ways in which the desecularization of American foreign policy is contributing to making the world a religiously *different* place, rather than a *better* or *worse* one. In particular, I suggest that the four regimes and the overall regime complex are intervening and potentially changing global religious and secular landscapes in three key ways:

(i)   shaping global religious realities along American norms and interests;
(ii) contributing to processes of religionization of world politics; and
(iii) diffusing and promoting similar religious regimes in international policy.

The first two effects follow the theoretical consideration that not only (postsecular) developments at the world society level can lead to shifts in states' foreign policies (via specific agents), but also that these shifts in turn can themselves produce particular (religious) changes and outcomes within world society. The third effect, instead, focuses on how changes in US foreign policy may be affecting through dynamics of norm and policy diffusion also what other states in international society may be doing.

---

[84] See note 17 in chapter 1 for references to these debates.
[85] Linklater (2009, 137). Jonathan Agensky (2017), for instance, has recently explored from a historical sociological perspective the entangled history between religion and the global political transformations of the nineteenth century, and how the latter shaped and were themselves reshaped by the former.

Shaping Global Religious Realities Along American Norms and Interests

America's religious foreign policy regimes adopt a wide range of policy tools and diplomatic practices to achieve their desired outcomes. These include normative persuasion, bargaining, sanctioning, and naming and shaming to alter identities and behaviors; transferring (or withholding) economic resources, social recognition, legitimacy, and knowledge to selected faith-based partners through specific programs and initiatives; coopting religious individuals and organizations into the foreign policymaking and implementation process; and "governing at a distance,"[86] through the production of reports and ranking mechanisms with the intent to incentivize particular identities, norms, interests, and practices and disincentive others. In the case of some regimes, for example the International Religious Freedom and the Muslim and Islamic Interventions regimes, states and societies are targeted through a mix of the policy tools and diplomatic practices identified here in order to explicitly and directly produce certain desired religious outcomes. In the case of other regimes, such as the Faith-Based Foreign Aid and Religious Engagement ones, policy instruments are used instead mostly to produce nonreligious objectives such as reducing poverty or resolving conflicts.

As the United States intervenes through multiple means and in more or lesser purposeful ways in the midst of global religious realities at the world society level, I expect these to be potentially transformed along American understandings and practices of faith. Such an assumption is based on the theoretical premise underpinning this book according to which what is understood as constituting "religion" and, especially, what is considered to be "appropriate religion" is historically contingent and context-specific.[87] In particular, I contend that the types of religious understandings and practices that the regimes will—explicitly or implicitly, directly or indirectly—seek out, support, and encourage will inevitably reflect certain logics. These are logics that influence the making and implementation of American foreign policy in general and of the religious regimes more specifically. I identify four particularly salient logics likely to be in play.

One logic will be driven by the desire to manage and promote religious dynamics and actors that can contribute to advance America's national interest. What is in America's national interest may of course be defined in multiple ways. To simplify, we can distinguish between more narrow and immediate security concerns or longer-term international order building objectives. Security interests may involve, for instance, fighting and winning the war on terror against groups claiming to act in the name of a particular religion. Longer-term order building objectives may involve promoting democracy, international human rights norms, development and market economies, and ultimately

---

[86] Broome and Quirk (2015).
[87] See section "Definitions and Methodology" in chapter 1.

what scholars like John Ikenberry have defined as the liberal international order.[88] Thus one can expect that religiosities that can contribute to enhance US security or advance a liberal international order will be empowered through American foreign policy regimes; those that cannot will be ignored or opposed.

A second logic will be driven by the desire to govern and mobilize religious dynamics and actors in ways that reflect the political-ideological proclivities of different administrations, especially along conservative/progressive and Republican/Democratic cleavages. I assume that political-ideological differences among administrations will manifest themselves in distinct foreign policy priorities and objectives, and in different approaches toward religion and religious actors.[89] This implies that Republican and Democratic administrations would tend to seek alliances with and support those religious actors, interpretations, and agendas that match their foreign policy interests and party ideological commitments.

A third logic potentially at play will reflect the United States' own distinctive religious demographics, history, and normative arrangements. The United States is a country marked by a dominant Christian, especially Protestant, identity and population, which is both open to but also at times in tension with a decidedly pluralist religious culture and society.[90] This background and identity can mold the ways in which Americans define religion, mostly centered on individually held beliefs and a denominational view of faith communities as voluntary associations that can be easily entered or abandoned, which generalizes a particular Protestant understanding of religion and religious pluralism.[91] Moreover, the way that Americans view the role of faith in the public sphere generally derives from a vantage point powerfully shaped by a set of important constitutional norms that define the relationship between the American state and religion. These norms, as already mentioned earlier, are encoded in the Establishment and Free Exercise Clauses of the Constitution's First Amendment, which mandate the institutional separation of church and state and prevent the federal government from restricting citizens' exercise of religion. The conjecture here is that the complex factors that define the religious experience and identity of Americans at the domestic level are likely to be projected onto and exported in the world through the regimes.

The fourth and final logic around which global religious landscapes could be reshaped by American foreign policy interventions may reflect the narrower interests and normative concerns of the faith-based activists, experts, and

---

[88] Ikenberry (2001; 2011).

[89] On the role of party and ideological affiliation on US foreign policy, see Dueck (2010). On different party attitudes to religion in contemporary American politics, see Claassen (2015); Putnam and Campbell (2010).

[90] For an excellent overview of these issues see Wald and Calhoun-Brown (2018). For a classic statement on the constant tensions and accommodations which take place between a demographically and culturally dominant Protestant country and other Christian denominations and religious traditions, see Herberg (1955).

[91] See Asad (2011) in general, but also Casanova (2010) and Wilson (2012) for a closer look at the American case in particular.

policymakers that support a particular religious foreign policy regime. "What is important to understand about religious actors is that religious politics, even when it converges with that of the state," Daniel Philpott notes, "emanates from beliefs, practices, and communities that themselves are prior to politics."[92] Translated to our case, this means that religious actors will seek to bend US foreign policy as much as they can to serve the interests and values of their (often transnational) religious communities in particular or of religion more broadly, rather than exclusively those of the American state as such.[93]

In short, I hypothesize that as the United States increasingly intervenes in global religious landscapes and communities, these may be reshaped to reflect American national interests, party politics and ideology, religious identity and norms, as well as the priorities of specific domestically based desecularizing actors. These four logics are not mutually exclusive. They may be present individually or more often in combination, to a lesser or greater extent, across the four religious foreign policy regimes.

Religionizing World Politics

As American foreign policy changes and adapts to a world of resurging religions and perceptions thereof, its foreign policy is likely to multiply and further such processes of resurgence. I expect that the four regimes individually, and the overall complex more broadly, contribute to making religion matter more in the ways that world politics is discussed and practiced. This is what I mean by "religionization," which I conceptualize as potentially occurring through two types of mechanisms: objective elevation and subjective categorization.

All regimes are intended to generate dynamics of religious elevation as they seek to open up space for and empower faith-based actors and traditions in world politics, especially those deemed in line with American foreign policy and societal interests, norms, and identities (as discussed earlier). Such dynamics can take place, for example, as religious actors and perspectives are increasingly called upon to participate in the making of the world's most powerful state's foreign policy, or mobilized on the ground globally to combat terrorism, climate change, poverty, and so on. All these developments increase, rather than decrease, the role of religion in international relations.

Religionization also occurs through more subjective mechanisms of categorization.[94] Religious categorization takes place as American foreign policy institutions, rhetoric and practices assign and uphold, by producing from the top-down or reproducing from the ground up, religious identities in and explanations of world politics. Elizabeth Shakman Hurd points to similar

---

[92] Philpott (2009, 193).
[93] See Byrnes (2011), and Mearsheimer and Walt (2007) for examples of how the interests of particular religious and ethnic advocates/lobbies can be in tension with the foreign policy priorities of the US.
[94] Barnett and Finnemore (1999); Milliken (1999).

dynamics, when she argues that international religious freedom policies lead to the "confessionalization" of world politics. In her words:

> Under a regime of religious freedom, individuals and groups are described, and often legally defined, in religious or sectarian terms rather than on the basis of other social bonds and affiliations—for example, as groups based on social class, historical ties, neighborhood bonds, kinship networks, or professional associations. . . . Religious identity and difference are taken as the natural foundation of social order, as just the way things are. This engenders a "confessionalization" of public life.[95]

The mechanism of religionization through categorization differs from elevation in that it highlights instead how the regimes contribute to socially construct the very same religious categories, subjectivities, and factors that they often seek to objectively govern, manage, and mobilize. Indeed, as scholars working from a poststructural and postcolonial perspective remind us, religious realities are not simply to be found out there in the social world, but are often "made."[96] Despite the intersubjective nature of this process, categorization does also have real material manifestations and consequences. Individuals, communities, and sites are either included or excluded, targeted or ignored, through different means (military, economic, or diplomatic), according to the labels and identities they subscribe to themselves or are given by others—notably, in our case, US foreign policymakers.

Religionization through categorization takes place at two levels. One level involves the breadth and depth at which religious idioms and frames inform and structure American foreign policy discourses, institutions, and practices. The other depends on changes happening in world politics. In particular, this depends on the extent to which processes of socialization into the religious categories (re)produced by US foreign policy occur on the ground. Socialization may be more superficial, whereby local actors instrumentally adopt religious idioms for the purposes of "marketing"[97] themselves to gather international attention and resources from American foreign policymakers. Or it may go even deeper as actors internalize the religious roles, identities, and interests ascribed to them by the foreign policy regimes.[98] While both dynamics could be theoretically plausible, it will be harder for this book—which focuses on changes in American foreign policy rather than developments on the ground—to empirically demonstrate whether and the extent to which socialization processes around the world are taking place at all.

---

[95] Hurd (2013b).
[96] Dressler and Mandair (2011); Van der Veer (2001).
[97] Bob (2005).
[98] The literature on global-local dynamics of socialization is vast, for a good place to start see Checkel (2005).

Regime Diffusion in International Policy

The operationalization of religion is not just an American phenomenon, but an increasingly global one.[99] Networks of international religious freedom advocates and novel institutional arrangements designed to promote such norms internationally, for instance, have sprung up in Canada, the United Kingdom, Italy, and within EU institutions since the 2000s. Initiatives designed to increase partnerships with faith-based organizations for the delivery of humanitarian and development assistance have taken place from the late 1990s onward in the context of multilateral donors such as the World Bank and the UN, as well as across bilateral ones such as the United Kingdom's Department for International Development (DFID) and the Australian Agency for International Development (AusAID). Strategies and policies aimed at winning the hearts, minds, and souls—so to speak—of Muslims in the context of the war on terror are being implemented in the United Kingdom and across many other Western countries since 2001. Foreign ministries in places like France and Italy are also building their capacity to better understand and engage with religions.

This flurry of activity can certainly be explained by referring to the same macro changes and micro-level forces—the emergence of a postsecular world society and the activities of desecularizing actors situated in and reproducing such macro processes—that account for the changes in US foreign policy. In other words, countries and institutions around the world may be subject to the same international and domestic, macro and micro pressures to operationalize religion as America is. This may not be the whole story, however.

In fact, at close scrutiny, the turn toward faith-based policies internationally often emerged in the aftermath, or if already present elsewhere it frequently expanded following, the operationalization of religion in the American context. This may not be a coincidence. It is plausible to assume that some kind of connection between American policy changes and similar developments elsewhere in the world may be at work too. I hypothesize that such connections may be of two broad kinds: a more linear process of norm and policy diffusion from the United States to other contexts, and another less linear process of knowledge circulation and mutual learning between the United States and other countries and international institutions.[100]

In those instances where the operationalization of religion emerged or considerably took off in different international settings in the aftermath of the American experience, I would expect to find linear processes of regime diffusion taking place from the United States to other contexts. Diffusion in these instances may occur directly or indirectly. In the former case, much of the

---

[99] Hurd (2015).

[100] Conceptually I draw here on constructivist-inspired literature on norm/policy diffusion and circulation. See, for example, Acharya (2013); Finnemore and Sikkink (1998); Simmons, Dobbin, and Garrett (2006).

agency resides with American actors—activist, experts, or policymakers tied to a particular regime—who take on the role of international policy entrepreneurs, and advocate change and share experiences across boundaries with the explicit objective of promoting similar arrangements elsewhere. In the latter case, most of the agency would reside with non-American civil society actors and policymakers who carefully observe and learn from the superpower's experience with the intent of reproducing or expanding similar arrangements in their own context.

In those circumstances where certain religious policy regimes developed internationally in important ways before or in parallel to the religious turn in American foreign policy, I hypothesize that we are still likely to see some connections emerging between these disparate developments. I would expect that in such instances American foreign policy changes may be affecting the global policy landscape in a less linear and unidirectional way, and we may instead be witnessing dynamics more akin to processes of knowledge circulation and mutual learning. In such circumstances American activists, experts, and policymakers tied to any one particular regime would both draw from the experience of others, as well as actively share their own knowledge with the hope of influencing the global international religious policy environment. Given the size and power of the United States, we may also expect to find American agents at the center and forefront of emerging networks seeking to share knowledge and coordinate activities across contexts.

Conclusion

This chapter laid out the theoretical and conceptual framework, grounded in a sociological approach to IR theory and a critical realist philosophy, used in this monograph to explain the causes, forms, and effects of the operationalization of religion—since the early 1990s to the end of the Obama presidency in 2016— in US foreign policy. This operationalization is most apparent in the institutionalization of four religious foreign policy regimes: International Religious Freedom, Faith-Based Foreign Aid, Muslim and Islamic Interventions, and Religious Engagement. These four distinct regimes share a number of features which constitute them into a larger whole, namely a foreign policy regime complex dedicated to marshaling and managing the power of faith globally to advance American values and interests abroad.

To enable us to understand why religion has progressively and systematically become a subject and object of American foreign policy since the end of the Cold War, this chapter argued that the United States should be placed within a particular macro historical and global context. This is a context defined by the emergence of a postsecular world society exercising a range of international and domestic pressures on American foreign policy. Yet to causally explain in more detail how religion became operationalized in US foreign policy across different issue areas and during distinct presidencies, we need to pay attention to how macro-level postsecular transformations are translated into policy developments via the actions of particular desecularizing actors at the micro-level.

Through the articulation and deployment of desecularizing discourses, desecularizing actors come forward to contest what they view as the problematic secularity of American foreign policy in the context of a novel postsecular age. As they contest established worldviews, norms, and practices on either principled or strategic grounds, they also seek to persuade policymakers to adopt new explicitly religious foreign policies. The success of these actors in institutionalizing their preferred religious foreign policy regime very much depends on the presence of two further contributing factors: critical junctures and exogenous trends. Both of these factors are crucial. They generate a favorable environment for the operationalization at first and evolution at later stages of each regime.

Secular contestation, and the adoption of the regimes, also leads to more underlying processes of foreign policy desecularization. These include processes of institutional desecularization, whereby new institutions and practices emerge to include religious actors and voices in the making and execution of foreign policy; epistemic desecularization, whereby religion is no longer viewed as irrelevant to social life and world politics; ideological desecularization, whereby religion is no longer viewed exclusively as a problem; and state-normative desecularization, whereby norms demanding a strict separation between state and church are relaxed. The shifting boundaries that such processes entail do not radically undermine foreign policy as an independent sphere of social and political activity. Rather, they open up spaces for particular, novel and deeper forms of religion–state entanglements that extend American influence in world politics both over and through religion.

Processes of desecularization also mean that American foreign policy increasingly intervenes, and thus becomes ever more enmeshed, in global religious and secular realities. It is my contention—and the aim of the analysis of the four cases that follow—that the religious foreign policy regimes are likely to produce three broad international effects: (i) transform global religious landscapes in ways that are informed by and resemble particular American norms and interests; (ii) inject more religion in discourses and practices of world politics through processes of elevation and categorization; and (iii) contribute to the proliferation and expansion of similar religious regimes internationally across countries and institutions through linear (direct and indirect) or circular processes of norm and policy diffusion.

CHAPTER 3 | International Religious Freedom

The right to freedom of religion is under renewed and, in some cases,
increasing assault in many countries around the world.
—International Religious Freedom Act, 1998[1]

IN 1998 CONGRESS PASSED the International Religious Freedom Act (IRFA),
making the monitoring and promotion of religious freedom internationally
an organized and sustained foreign policy of the United States. Formulated
in response to the perceived increase in religious violence and persecution
worldwide since the end of the Cold War, as the quote at the beginning of the
chapter suggests, the IRFA constituted a watershed moment in the American
foreign policy landscape. It heralded the birth of America's first contemporary,
explicitly religious, foreign policy regime: the *International Religious Freedom
regime*.[2] From now on, US foreign policymakers were mandated to systematically foster an international environment conducive to the liberty and flourishing of religions in general, and—as this chapter will argue—some ways of
being religious in particular.

A multifaceted institutional architecture was established to implement
America's international religious freedom policy. At first this included an
Office of International Religious Freedom (OIRF) in the State Department,
headed by an Ambassador-at-Large for International Religious Freedom (IRF
ambassador),[3] and an independent United States Commission on International
Religious Freedom (USCIRF). Nearly two decades later, the Near East and
South Central Asia Religious Freedom Act of 2014 added to this architecture a

---

[1] International Religious Freedom Act (1998).
[2] A caveat is in order here. Religious freedom is of course not solely—or not strictly—a *religious* norm
and issue, but one closely tied to secular liberal and democratic values designed to guarantee the
peaceful coexistence of religiously diverse societies. It is also however a norm that, today, mostly religious actors and communities seek to advance and benefit from (e.g., Hertzke and Philpott 2000).
[3] Ambassadors-at-large are ambassadors that are not appointed to a particular country or diplomatic
post, but are instead assigned a special duty or mission.

new post, that of Special Advisor for Religious Minorities in the Near East and South and Central Asia.

It must be said that concerns about religious freedom do have a long pedigree in American history. The idea that the United States stands as a beacon of religious liberty in a world marked by religious persecutions and discriminations is intimately ingrained in the country's conscience, tied to particular narratives of America's founding moments by persecuted Puritans, and codified in the Free Exercise Clause of the Constitution's First Amendment. Attention to religious freedom in foreign policy is not entirely novel either. Franklin Delano Roosevelt's 1941 Four Freedoms speech, delivered as the United States was preparing to enter World War II, included the "freedom of worship" and is considered one of the earliest expressions of a foreign policy interest in this norm. Some see the US postwar reconstruction of Germany and Japan along liberal democratic lines as having been motivated by the aim to promote religious liberty. Likewise, Americans were instrumental in ensuring that norms about freedom of religion and belief would be included in the Universal Declaration of Human Rights.[4]

During the Cold War, presidents and members of Congress repeatedly positioned the United States on the side of religious liberty against the totalitarian forces of "Godless" Communism.[5] In the late 1970s under the Carter administration the State Department started compiling annual reports on human rights, which included a modest section on infringements of religious freedom. In a highly symbolic gesture, President Reagan granted asylum in the early 1980s to a group of Pentecostals who, arguing they were being persecuted for their religious beliefs by Soviet authorities, breached US embassy doors in Moscow asking for refuge in the United States. A major foreign policy development in support of religious communities abroad was the adoption by Congress of the Jackson-Vanik Amendment in 1974. The amendment sought to deny normal trade relations status to the Soviet Union because of Moscow's efforts to restrict Soviet Jewish emigration to Israel.

This brief historical sketch serves to illustrate that America's contemporary concern for international religious freedom did not spring from a vacuum. Yet what is also apparent is that prior to 1998, actions for religious liberty abroad whether in the form of speeches or diplomatic initiatives were carried out in an ad hoc manner rather than in a structured approach. Up until the end of the Cold War, the freedom of religious individuals and communities was not something that American foreign policymakers had been required to systematically think about, let alone monitor or advance. As Thomas Farr, a staunch advocate of this policy, notes: "You could say twenty years or so ago, there were

---

[4] For a comprehensive historical overview of America's efforts to promote religious liberty abroad, see Su (2016). On Franklin Delano Roosevelt, see also Preston (2012, 319–326). On postwar Japan see Thomas (2014).

[5] Su (2016, ch. 5); also Inboden (2010) and Preston (2012, Parts VII and VIII).

no [international religious freedom] practices, that wouldn't be entirely correct, there were practices that were not institutionalized."[6]

Things have changed remarkably since the rise of the International Religious Freedom regime in the late 1990s. The question is, what has prompted these normative, institutional and policy developments to take place at that particular moment in time? The next section outlines the constellation of desecularizing actors and their discourses championing the cause of international religious freedom in American foreign policy. I further consider the wider social and historical postsecular forces in which these constituencies and their advocacy efforts are embedded, and highlight important critical junctures and exogenous trends that help to explain the emergence of the regime in the late 1990s and its subsequent evolution over the decades. In the two sections that follow I explore and explain the structure, institutions, and practices of the regime from the Clinton to the Obama administrations. The chapter then unpacks the types and degrees of foreign policy desecularization—institutional, epistemic, ideological, and state-normative—that have taken place and are reproduced by the International Religious Freedom regime. The section that follows outlines the global effects of the regime and how this is potentially shaping religious and secular realities worldwide. The chapter concludes by summarizing its main findings and reflecting on ongoing developments under the Trump administration.

Desecularizing Actors and Discourses in Context

With the fall of the Berlin Wall in 1989, a range of diverse religious organizations, faith-based advocates, policy analysts, and scholars came forward to contest the perceived secularity of American foreign policy and advocate with growing vigor that the United States take a more active role in stemming what they viewed as religious persecution worldwide and advancing religious liberty abroad. What would be a rather heterogeneous constellation of actors can be grouped into two broad coalitions both approaching religious freedom from a principled angle, and a third more coherent constituency of actors emerging after the attacks on 9/11 mostly putting forward a strategic understanding of international religious freedom in foreign policy.

Particularist Principled Desecularizing Discourse: Stemming the Persecution of Christians

The first and most vocal constituency mobilizing for a more systematic US foreign policy approach toward matters of religious liberty came together in a coalition of desecularizing activists, experts and policymakers in the early and mid-1990s around a *particularist principled desecularizing discourse*. This

---

[6] Farr in Berkley Center (2017, 1:13–1:25).

discourse presented the global persecution of Christians as a persistent and dangerously growing international scourge in the post-Cold War era. According to these actors, Christian persecution was not only endemic in the world's remaining Communist countries—such as China, North Korea, or Vietnam—but was also dangerously increasing in Muslim-majority ones as well. The coalition championing this cause would argue that the United States had a moral obligation to halt the oppression of Christians. Not only that, but that this duty was all too often ignored because, as Richard Land—then-president of the Ethics and Religious Liberty Commission of the Southern Baptist Convention—argued:

> An increasingly secularized West and its leadership beliefs tend to be indifferent and often uncomprehending of a spiritual worldview which endures persecution and death for the sake of belief.[7]

Richard Land was a key figure in a broader constituency of Evangelical leaders and organizations that saw Christians as the world's most widely persecuted religious group in the new post-Cold War era. Such persecution was particularly egregious, Evangelicals argued, in what was defined as the "10/40 Window," a geographic area spanning across North Africa, the Middle East, and Central, Southern, and Eastern Asia, which included most of the world's Muslim-majority countries and Communist regimes. The 1983–2005 Sudanese civil war between the Muslim-majority North, seen as the aggressor, and the Christian-majority South, seen as the victim, became a particularly important rallying cry for Evangelical leaders seeking to draw attention among their religious constituencies and political figureheads in Washington, DC to the plight of what they defined as the "persecuted Church" abroad.[8] Along with Land, this constituency included the National Association of Evangelicals (NAE), who in 1996 had released a Statement of Conscience Concerning Worldwide Religious Persecution; major advocacy groups associated with the Christian Right, such as Pat Robertson's Christian Coalition, James Dobson's Family Research Council, and Beverly LaHaye's Concerned Women of America; and a wide range of missionary organizations founded both during the Cold War (such as Voice of the Martyrs, Open Doors, Christian Solidarity International, and Campus Crusade for Christ) and in its aftermath (such as International Christian Concern, Persecution Project Foundation, Christian Freedom International, and Compass Direct).

---

[7] Land (1997).
[8] There are multiple, detailed accounts of Evangelical mobilization on behalf of the "persecuted Church" in the case of Sudan and the "10/40 window," which refers to an area lying between the 10th and 40th degrees North of the equator. Hertzke (2004; 2001a, 2001b) provides the most sympathetic account of this effort, more critical perspectives are voiced by Castelli (2005), Mahmood (2012), and McAlister (2008). Whether Christians are, in fact, the most persecuted religion in the world is hotly debated, see Alexander (2013), and Jones (2014). Regardless, Castelli (2007a), who traces the genealogy of such a narrative, notes how the story of "persecution" is foundational to Christian identity and its maintenance.

Two important wider shifts in the 1990s contributed to making Protestant Evangelicals a powerful force in Washington, DC advocating on behalf of their coreligionists abroad. The first was the growing politicization of Evangelicals and the emergence of the Christian Right after the late 1970s, the very embodiment of global processes of religious resurgence in the American context.[9] The second shift coincided with Evangelicals becoming increasingly engaged with international issues from the early 1990s onward. Such a shift was spurred mostly by trends exogenous to the emergence of a postsecular world society. The end of Cold War rivalries and greater ease of communication and travel encouraged by globalization allowed for an unprecedented expansion of transnational ties and Evangelical missionary work abroad. All this led to a mounting interest in the fate of Christian communities worldwide.[10]

This "bottom-up" religious effort was accompanied by the mobilization of a constituency of desecularizing experts, mostly conservative Christian and Jewish policy analysts connected to think tanks based in Washington, DC. These included Michael Horowitz, a senior fellow at the Hudson Institute, and Nina Shea and Paul Marshall, at Freedom House, who were penning books and articles for major news outlets denouncing what they saw as the rising and historically unprecedented global intolerance and violence directed toward Christians perpetrated primarily by Muslims.[11] This epistemic community argued that mainstream American elites—whether journalists, human rights advocates, or policymakers—suffered from a secular blind spot, which led them to overlook and discount the plight of Christian individuals and communities worldwide. Such views resonated at the time with a postsecular consciousness that was emerging among certain conservative intellectual milieus who critiqued "end of history" narratives that portrayed the end of the Cold War as a peaceful era marked by the triumph of secular liberal modernity.[12] These perspectives were most clearly represented by Samuel Huntington's seminal 1993 *Foreign Affairs* article "The Clash of Civilizations?," which instead placed religious and civilizational identity in general, and a Judeo-Christian West and Islam in particular, at the center of post-Cold War international relations and conflicts.[13] Not accidentally this theme was picked-up by Horowitz's influential 1995 *Wall Street Journal* article, evocatively titled "New Intolerance Between Crescent and Cross," which sought to raise the issue of Christian persecution to a more general American audience.

---

[9] On the politicization of Evangelicals and the Christian Right see Wald and Calhoun-Brown (2018, ch. 8); Wilcox and Larson (2006). For scholarship placing this phenomenon in the context of wider processes of religious resurgence, see Berger (1999); Casanova (1994); Kepel (1994).

[10] On the globalization of American churches in general and Protestant Evangelicals in particular, see respectively Wuthnow (2009) and McAlister (2018). On their intensifying efforts to influence US foreign policy, see Mead (2006); Rock (2011).

[11] Horowitz (1995); Marshall and Gilbert (1997); Shea (1997); also more recently AEI (2015); Marshall, Gilbert, and Green (2009); Marshall, Gilbert, and Shea (2013).

[12] Fukuyama (1992).

[13] Huntington (1993a).

Conservative experts and Evangelical activists joined efforts around 1996 to put pressure on Congress and the Clinton administration.[14] This coalition and their campaign against the persecution of Christians soon bore some fruits. Religiously and ideologically affiliated Republican members of Congress picked up the issue—some possibly persuaded by the principled arguments of the anti-persecution coalition, others likely motivated by political calculations in order to attack the Clinton administration and gain electoral support from Evangelical constituencies[15]—and advanced the anti-Christian persecution cause from within the halls of power.

The result was the Freedom from Religious Persecution Act, introduced in 1997 simultaneously by Republican Congressman Frank Wolf in the House of Representatives and by Republican Senator Arlen Specter in the Senate. Congressional hearings included testimonies by, among others, Land, Horowitz, and Shea.[16] The Wolf-Specter bill was defined by a number of characteristics. First, the bill was overwhelmingly, in Elizabeth Castelli's words, "Christocentric."[17] That is, it largely focused on the plight of Christians, with some expedient ecumenical gestures toward the persecution of Tibetan Buddhists in China and Baha'is in Iran—two countries on the blacklist of conservative foreign policy hawks. Second, it focused on the "persecution of religious believers" exclusively in "Communist countries" and "Islamic countries,"[18] rather than worldwide. Third, the bill mandated automatic action against any nation found guilty of egregiously persecuting religious communities and employed measures designed to limit the president's ability to waive sanctions against countries found wanting. Fourth, it mandated the establishment in the Executive Office of the President of an Office of Religious Persecution Monitoring.

Universalist Principled Desecularizing Discourse: International Religious Freedom as a Human Right

The Wolf-Specter bill was met with strong criticism by a number of faith-based and human rights advocates, the Clinton administration, and the State Department. These were concerned, to varying degrees, with the bill's bias

---

[14] Most notably during a 1996 conference held in Washington, DC, titled "Global Persecution of Christians," organized by Horowitz and Shea designed to galvanize Evangelicals into political action. It was no coincidence that the NAE's (1996) Statement of Conscience Concerning Worldwide Religious Persecution was issued that same year.

[15] Hertzke (2004; 2001a) stresses principled persuasion, while Gunn (2004; 2013) stresses political expediency.

[16] See House Subcommittee on International Operations and Human Rights, *Persecution of Christians Worldwide*, 104th Cong., 2d sess. (February 15, 1996) and House Subcommittee on International Operations and Human Rights, *Worldwide Persecution of Jews*, 104th Cong., 2d sess. (February 27, 1996). For congressional resolutions, see H.R. 102, 104th Cong. (1996) (Baha'is); S. Con. Res. 71, 104th Cong. (1996) (Christians); and H.R. 515, 104th Cong. (1996) (Christians).

[17] Castelli (2005, 333). The opening lines of the bill explicitly stated that it was concerned with the "Persecution of religious believers, particularly Roman Catholic and evangelical Protestant Christians" (Freedom from Religious Persecution Act, 1997).

[18] Freedom from Religious Persecution Act (1997).

toward the protection of favored religious communities in countries not strategically aligned with the United States, and with the limits it imposed on presidential discretionality in foreign policy.[19] The bill, as it stood, seemed unlikely to make it past the president's desk.

Fearing that the issue of religious persecution was going to be scrapped altogether, a second coalition of desecularizing activists and policymakers "enmeshed in religious life"—as Allan Hertzke puts it—and thus "predisposed to sympathy for the cause" of religious communities worldwide,[20] seized the opportunity of turning the principled, yet particularist, concern for Christianity abroad into a permanent fixture of American foreign policy. This coalition would articulate and rally around a *universalist principled desecularizing discourse* centered on the promotion of international religious freedom as a human rights issue. This included, on the one hand, members of Congress and their staffers across parties with a more moderate and internationalist outlook such as John Hanford in the office of Republican Senator Richard Lugar, William Inboden in the office of Republican Congressman Tom DeLay, and Steve Moffitt in the office of Republican Senator Don Nickles.[21] On the other hand, it counted on a plurality of religious actors with a more liberal persuasion. These included Mainline Protestant churches and organizations, especially the Episcopal Church led in its lobbying efforts at the time by Tom Hart, and the National Council of Churches, as well as advocates from other religious traditions, such as Rabbi David Saperstein of the Religious Action Center of Reform Judaism.[22]

This coalition was responsible for proposing an alternative bipartisan Congressional bill titled the International Religious Freedom Act. The act, also known as the Nickles-Lieberman bill after the Congressional members who cosponsored it (Republican Senator Don Nickles of Oklahoma and Democratic Senator Joseph Lieberman of Connecticut), was animated by a similar intent to contest the secular nature of American foreign policy and its alleged disinterest in the fate of religious actors and communities around the world. "The State Department has an institutional bias against religion," chastises Tom Hart, then Director of Government Relations for the Episcopal Church in Washington, DC.[23] Yet the Nickles-Lieberman bill differed from the Wolf-Spectre bill in a number of ways. It did not identify any particular religions that needed protection nor any countries that needed admonishing, but framed religious intolerance and violence largely as a universal human rights issue. It

---

[19] For an overview of the arguments levied against the Wolf-Specter bill at the time, see Gunn (2004, 131–134).
[20] Hertzke (2001a).
[21] Gunn (2004, 625); also Hackett, Silk, and Hoover (1999).
[22] On Tom Hart's role, see Hertzke (2004, 225–227), and Rock (2011, 82). For a critique of the Wolf-Specter bill by the National Council of Churches, see NCC (1998). David Saperstein's role is amply documented in Hertzke (2004). For Saperstein's critique of the Wolf-Specter bill, see Gunn (2004, 641, fn.87).
[23] Hart (2011, author's interview).

was more sensitive to diplomatic protocols and gave the president greater flexibility when responding to violating countries, rather than requiring automatic sanctions. Lastly, it mandated the creation of a dedicated office to be based in the State Department rather than in the White House.

These desecularizing actors and their arguments also drew strength from the development of a postsecular consciousness among certain American elites and scholars. Peter Berger, a leading sociologist of religion, was by the mid-1990s radically revisiting his belief in the secular character of modernity. His reflections on the subject appeared in a landmark edited volume fittingly titled *The Desecularization of the World* sponsored by the Ethics and Public Policy Center (EPPC),[24] a Washington, DC-based Judeo-Christian-inspired think tank led at the time by Elliott Abrams. The volume was groundbreaking for directly challenging the dominance of secularization theories in the social sciences, and indirectly empowering advocacy efforts to operationalize the International Religious Freedom regime. Abrams recalls:

> The literature on the resurgence of religion, and Peter Berger's work in particular, gave legitimacy to the issue of religion. It showed how secular elites did not understand the world around them, and gave confidence to religious groups that their claims should be taken more seriously in a world that is really religious and not secular.[25]

Strategic Desecularizing Discourse: International Religious Freedom as National Security Priority

A third key constituency championing the cause of religious freedom in American foreign policy emerged largely in the wake of the regime's institutionalization and the tragic events of 9/11. This constituency, which would have important links to earlier principled efforts against persecution and for religious freedom, would articulate and mobilize around a distinct *strategic desecularizing discourse* framing the promotion of international religious freedom as a national security priority. Its proponents have presented religious freedom as a sine qua non condition for advancing democracy and stability, as well as curbing religious-based violence and terrorism in the context of a post-9/11 world and America's war on terror. Once again the foreign policy establishment and the State Department would be criticized for their "secularist habits,"[26] seen as preventing them from appreciating the role of religion and the positive contributions that religious freedom could make to American security. There is a need for "desecularizing diplomacy" in the context of "global desecularization," explains Thomas Farr at Georgetown University, from the pages of *Foreign Affairs*.[27] On the back of growing research making connections

---

[24] Berger (1999).
[25] Abrams (2010, author's interview).
[26] Farr (2008a, 114).
[27] Farr (2008a, 111, 118).

between religious freedom and positive security outcomes,[28] this constituency sought to reframe the narrative around religious freedom with the aim also of raising its profile among American foreign policymakers. "So far international religious freedom has been side-lined as it has been seen only as a soft power human rights issue," laments Chris Seiple of the Institute for Global Engagement (IGE).[29] Seiple's mission has been to counter this trend by advancing, in his words, "an understanding of religious freedom as a hard security interest of the U.S."[30]

Articulating and deploying such a discourse are experts constitutive of a particular epistemic community embedded within emerging forms of postsecular consciousness, housed in universities, research institutions, and think tanks—many religiously based—with close connections to policymakers in Washington, DC. At the university level, experts associated with the Berkley Center for Religion, Peace and World Affairs at Georgetown University play a prominent role. These include Thomas Farr, a former US diplomat and the OIRF's first director, and Timothy Shah, a well-known voice in the literature on religion in world politics,[31] who jointly lead the Berkley Center's religious freedom initiatives.[32] These initiatives, along with a newly founded Religious Freedom Institute in 2016 by Farr, Shah, and others, act as a central node in a broader network of like-minded institutes, scholars, and advocates which includes the Institute for Studies of Religion at Baylor University; Daniel Philpott from the University of Notre Dame; Anthony Gill from the University of Washington; Allen Hertzke from the University of Oklahoma; William Inboden from the University of Texas-Austin; and Brian Grim, the original author of a highly influential series of Pew reports surveying religious restrictions and hostilities worldwide.[33]

Notable voices in the think tank community include those of Elliott Abrams, Senior Fellow at the Council on Foreign Relations (CFR), but also former president of the EPPC, member of the George W. Bush administration, and USCIRF Commissioner; and Nina Shea and Paul Marshall, who in 2007 moved from Freedom House to the Hudson Institute. A leading role in this space is played by the Institute for Global Engagement (IGE), a Christian think-and-do tank founded in 2000 by Robert Seiple, the first ever Ambassador-at-Large for International Religious Freedom as we shall see, and directed from 2003 to 2015 by his son Chris Seiple.[34] Chris Seiple is also among the cofounders of the IRF Roundtable, a Washington, DC-area consortium of faith-based and secular

---

[28] Grim and Finke (2010); Saiya (2015); Seiple and Hoover (2004).
[29] Seiple (2011, author's interview).
[30] Ibid.
[31] See Shah, Stepan, and Toft (2012); Toft, Philpott, and Shah (2011).
[32] These include the Religious Freedom Project which was active between 2011 and 2016. In 2017 the project gave rise to two successor initiatives: the Religious Freedom Research Project, based at the Berkley Center, and the Religious Freedom Institute, an independent NGO.
[33] See Farr (2008a, 2008b); Grim and Finke (2010); Hertzke (2013); Inboden (2012); Pew Research Center (2011; 2009a).
[34] Seiple and Hoover (2013), Seiple, Hoover, and Otis (2013), Seiple and Hoover (2004).

organizations that meet regularly to discuss how best to make international religious freedom a "high priority" in US foreign policy and national security.[35]

To sum up, from the 1990s onward a heterogeneous constellation of desecularizing actors emerged, mobilizing around (a) a particularist principled desecularizing discourse focused on the persecution of Christians in Communist and Muslim-majority states, (b) a universalist principled desecularizing discourse framing religious persecution as a broader human rights issue, and (c) a strategic desecularizing discourse presenting international religious freedom as a means to achieve a range of national security ends. Notwithstanding their different, at times competing, interpretations of how, for whom, and to what purpose the United States should advance religious freedom internationally, this constellation of actors—which often did exhibit important connections and overlaps—all sought to contest the secularity of American foreign policy demanding that greater attention be given to the well-being of religious individuals and communities worldwide. As highlighted throughout, much of this lobbying and lawmaking activity can be seen as embedded and influenced by the emergence of a postsecular world society. This involved processes of religious resurgence, represented by the growth in Evangelical activism in particular and of religious advocacy more broadly at home, and the rising political salience of religious beliefs and identities around the world. It also involved the development a postsecular consciousness among American intellectual elites poignantly reflected in the seminal writings of Huntington and Berger, and novel university and think tank initiatives seeking to raise the profile of global religious persecution and freedom among scholars and policymakers.

As we shall see, each of the constituency and coalition of actors articulating the three distinct desecularizing discourses would play an important role in the creation and evolution of America's first post-Cold War religious foreign policy regime. A caveat is in order before proceeding. I am not claiming here that these are the only networks of actors that have advocated and supported the international promotion of religious freedom in the past decades. Moreover, as time has gone by some individuals and organizations have faded from the scene and new ones have emerged, mobilizing still around one or more of the three broad desecularizing discourses outlined here. For instance in 2000, the International Center for Law and Religion Studies was created at the Mormon-based Brigham Young University adding a novel important voice in legal and normative debates about religious liberty. The Religious Freedom Institute, presided over by Thomas Farr, includes on its Board of Advisors Sheikh Hamza Yusuf, cofounder of Zaytuna College in 2008 (the first Muslim liberal arts college in the United States), who has emerged as a prominent Islamic voice in this space. This said, the particular attention given to the constellation of actors coalescing around the three desecularizing discourses identified here

---

[35] International Religious Freedom Roundtable (n.d.).

is nonetheless especially warranted given their central role in defining the original and evolving contours of the International Religious Freedom regime over the past two decades.

Regime Institutionalization, Structure and Practices

The International Religious Freedom Act of 1998

By the late 1990s, two parallel bills championed by distinct coalitions of desecularizing actors were making their way through Congress. One was the Freedom from Religious Persecution Act, known as the Wolf-Specter bill, supported by a fairly religiously and politically homogeneous coalition of Protestant Evangelical organizations, conservative policy experts, and Republican lawmakers. The other was the International Religious Freedom Act, known also as the Nickels-Lieberman bill, which was backed by a more moderate, religiously diverse, and politically bipartisan coalition of actors. The bills significantly differed over which religions deserved the most attention, which areas of the world America should focus on, and how this policy should be implemented. At the same time, both bills shared the view that American diplomacy needed to shed its secularist biases and pay greater attention to the well-being of religious individuals and communities abroad.

The Nickels-Lieberman bill, through a contentious process of arguing and bargaining between the two coalitions,[36] ultimately became the blueprint for the International Religious Freedom Act that was passed by both houses of Congress in 1998. This event was groundbreaking. The act made the monitoring and promotion of international religious freedom an organized objective of American foreign policy. With it, the first religious foreign policy regime was born. While the anti-Christian persecution coalition was necessary to create the initial momentum for IRFA, it was not, however, sufficient to turn this lobbying effort into law and foreign policy practice. The shift from a particularist Christocentric discourse to a more universalist religious freedom one was pivotal in ensuring that a controversial act—one which mandated the State Department to be systematically involved in global religious matters—would ultimately receive the unanimous backing of Congress and pass President Clinton's desk.

The language of religious freedom was able to generate wider domestic support among a plurality of religious actors, all seeking to carve out more space for their voices and communities in international politics. As Saba Mahmood notes, religious freedom is not a "stable signifier," but a broad conceptual construct that acquires different meanings for different constituencies.[37] Protestant Evangelicals and Conservative Catholics, for example, could use this

---

[36] The tensions between these two constituencies are explored by Gunn (2004, 625–626). A useful source for comparing the trajectory of the two bills is offered by the website ReligiousTolerance.org, at http://www.religioustolerance.org/rt_uslaw.htm (accessed May 29, 2017).
[37] Mahmood (2012, 423).

norm to continue publicizing their concerns about Christian persecution, and claim the right to proselytize globally.[38] Mainline Protestants and more progressive Catholics, sensitive to human rights issues, saw religious freedom as a neglected norm that needed greater attention. Jews saw in religious freedom a way to fight anti-Semitism and defend Israel's right to exist. Christian Copts, Tibetan Buddhists, and Baha'is appropriated it to critique governments in Egypt, China, and Iran. Jehovah Witnesses and Scientologists found the discourse relevant for defending and legitimizing their communities abroad from being attacked as "cults."[39]

The discourse of religious freedom, rather than that of persecution, also helped connect the interests of religious communities to international human rights norms, such as article 18 of the Universal Declaration of Human Rights. This move gave wider legitimacy to the concerns of desecularizing actors and empowered their claims in the context of an important exogenous trend to postsecular processes that was taking place at the time. With the end of the Cold War, human rights rhetoric and norms were increasingly gaining political clout and force globally.[40] The discourse of religious freedom clearly resonated with the post-Cold War euphoria for upholding and promoting—increasingly even through military means in what would be labeled as "humanitarian interventions"—human rights globally.

Furthermore, religious freedom rhetoric connected in powerful ways to American identity and norms. Religious freedom had deep roots in particular narratives of American history and in the principles of the most cherished of American texts, the Constitution.[41] This meant that international religious freedom advocates could draw on multiple arguments to persuade Congress, the White House and the State Department to pass and implement the IRFA. Such persuasion may have been deeper in some cases, entailing a genuine change of mind among lawmakers for example, as well as instrumental in other cases, since few in American politics—whether sitting in Capitol Hill or the White House—would want to be portrayed as not supporting religion, freedom, human rights, and the Constitution.[42]

Despite this convergence toward a religious freedom discourse, substantive differences in worldviews and interests remained below the surface among the multiplicity of actors involved in championing and now executing this policy. First and foremost were the frictions between, on the one hand, the particularist concerns of conservative religious and political figures who had provided the initial momentum and would remain the most ardent backers of

---

[38] On the strategic use of liberal, human rights, frames by Evangelicals and Catholics in American politics see, among others, Castelli (2007b).
[39] This point was especially emphasized to me by Grieboski (2011b).
[40] Ropp, Risse-Kappen, and Sikkink (1999).
[41] The very opening paragraph of the IRFA explicitly makes this identity move, stating: "the right to freedom of religion undergirds the very origin and existence of the United States" (IRFA 1998).
[42] A point also explicitly made to me by a National Security Council (NSC) official from the Bush administration (Former NSC Official 2010).

the International Religious Freedom regime, and, on the other, the proponents of the more universalist ethos embedded within the 1998 IRFA itself. Additionally, there were tensions between the galaxy of actors—at the grass-roots level, in think tanks, and Congress—who mobilized to make the regime a reality, and those in the State Department who continued to hold reservations about promoting religious freedom abroad. Apart from the ever-present tension between upholding principles and pursuing interests when engaging in foreign policy, policymakers remained also concerned about safeguarding norms mandating church–state separation, about duplicating existing work on human rights, and about an agenda which they perceived to be imposed by Congress and driven by partisan political and religious interests rather than the national interest.[43] These underlying differences and frictions would profoundly shape, as I will show in the next section, the institutional and operational structure of the regime.

Institutional and Operational Architecture of the International Religious Freedom Regime

Despite the passage of the 1998 IRFA, the Executive Branch remained reluctant to fully embrace the religious freedom agenda. This hesitance was demonstrated by how it handled the bureaucratization of the regime. IRFA mandated that an Office of International Religious Freedom (OIRF) be created within the State Department headed by an ambassador-at-large, intended to be the "principal adviser"[44] on issues of religious freedom abroad to the president and the secretary of state. However, the IRF ambassador was accorded a lower status than any other ambassador-at-large within State.[45] Moreover, IRFA stipulated the creation of a Special Adviser in the National Security Council (NSC), a position that was briefly filled during the Clinton administration but left vacant ever since.[46]

The act further mandated the establishment, for a discrete period, of an independent Commission on International Religious Freedom (USCIRF), headed by nine Commissioners. USCIRF was largely a product of Congressional skepticism toward the State Department. The Commission was, in fact, designed to

---

[43] Before Congress passed the IRFA, the State Department felt compelled to establish an Advisory Committee on Religious Freedom Abroad in 1996. The Advisory Committee was composed of religious campaigners and leaders, and was tasked with advising the then Secretary of State Madeleine Albright on how to enhance the protection of religious freedom abroad. By 1998 the Committee produced an Interim Report addressed to the secretary and the president focusing on two areas: religious persecution and conflict resolution (US Department of State 1998). In response to a Congressional request, the State Department also issued a report titled *United States Policies in Support of Religious Freedom: Focus on Christians* (US Department of State 1997). "Much of this activity by State," Judd Birdsall (2015, author's interview) argues, "was to gain control over the agenda and avoid that Congress imposed its will on it." See also Gunn (2004); Hertzke and Philpott (2000, 74).

[44] International Religious Freedom Act (1998).

[45] The IRF ambassador is ranked in the State Department's organizational structure as reporting to an assistant secretary. This is unique, since all other ambassadors-at-large are ranked at higher levels and either report directly to the secretary of state or to an undersecretary (GAO 2013, 19–20).

[46] George (2014, 13).

closely mirror the priorities of Congress and its religious constituencies, rather than those of American diplomacy and the OIRF at State. This is apparent as Congress appoints most of the USCIRF's Commissioners, its offices are located in the proximity of Capitol Hill rather than Foggy Bottom where the State Department is headquartered,[47] and USCIRF—compared to a generally marginalized and understaffed OIRF at State—has tended to receive relatively abundant resources by Congress from the start.[48] Unsurprisingly, tensions and frictions between the two institutional hubs of the regime have abounded, as we shall see.

This institutional infrastructure would be assigned to promote religious freedom globally through a range of means and activities. These would largely include: (a) monitoring and reporting; (b) diplomatic and policy actions; (c) foreign assistance programming; and (d) building capacity within the State Department and diplomatic corps.[49]

Monitoring and Reporting

Monitoring and reporting generally occurs through the publication of two parallel, partly competing and partly complementary, annual international religious freedom reports drafted by OIRF at State and by USCIRF. The IRF report prepared by the State Department covers all countries around the world—including increasingly abuses committed by non-state actors (e.g., violent groups or terrorist organizations)—and is based on information collected by a dedicated embassy officer. USCIRF reports do not rely on such a network, and tend to discuss the 20 to 30 countries considered to be the worst offenders of religious freedom. Both IRF reports are also intended to present policy recommendations to the US government, and to set in motion presidential actions and sanctions against countries with a problematic religious freedom record, especially those designated as Countries of Particular Concern (CPCs). CPCs are countries where "systematic, ongoing, egregious violations of religious freedom" are believed to be occurring. Between 1999 and 2016, secretaries of state have categorized, at some point or another, a total of twelve countries or regimes as CPCs, including: Afghanistan under the Taliban, Burma, China, Eritrea, Iran, Iraq under Saddam Hussein, North Korea, Saudi Arabia, Sudan, Uzbekistan, Vietnam, and Yugoslavia under

---

[47] For instance, USCIRF Official 1 (2010) would explain to me that in the context of the "Washington geography of power," USCRIF's location close to Congress was no coincidence.

[48] USCIRF would be assigned a budget of around $4 million a year until 2011 and $3 million since then. Although USCIRF has regularly risked being defunded by Congress, and while its overall budget has indeed decreased over the years, OIRF has tended to operate on considerably less resources (Feddes 2011; also GAO 2013, 7). USCIRF's financial means meant it could immediately hire a staff of approximately twenty people. This considerably outnumbered OIRF staff, which to begin with included only two full-time employees—the ambassador-at-large and his secretary—two part-time State officials, and a seconded US Institute of Peace Senior Fellow (Gunn 2004, 637, 640). By 2001 the OIRF still numbered around five or six staff members (State Department Official 2015), and in 2011 around eleven (Grieboski 2011a).

[49] See also IRFA (1998); OIRF (2011a; 2013).

Slobodan Milošević. USCIRF's list of recommended CPC countries generally far exceeds that of the OIRF.[50]

This discrepancy reveals how labeling (in the case of State Department IRF reports) and recommending (in the case of USCIRF reports) countries as CPCs, responds to a variety of different incentives and partisan interests. Indeed, the process of designating a country as CPC in the State Department's IRF report is often a highly contentious one—a "yearly battle," according to a former member of the Bush administration.[51] This is because the State Department's CPC list requires balancing a number of conflicting agendas. On the one hand, those of the more cautious and diplomatically minded foreign policy establishment who is generally careful not to jeopardize relations with strategic foreign allies, and on the other hand those of the more politically and activist-minded USCIRF, which predominantly responds to Congressional pressures and the concerns of religious constituencies.[52]

Tensions between OIRF and USCIRF extends beyond the process of naming CPCs. That's also because over time USCIRF has come to interpret its mandate more broadly than the 1998 IRFA tasked it to do, namely to assess the state of international religious freedom and make policy recommendations to the Executive Branch of government. In fact, prodded by Congressional and religious advocates, USCIRF has increasingly understood its role as that of an international watchdog. As such it has often not shied away from using its "advisory" capacity to the US government to "critique" the State Department's perceived shortcomings and (in)actions on religious freedom matters.[53] Moreover, in its reporting and advocacy activities the Commission has generally played, as a USCIRF official acknowledges, the role of "bad cop" to the State Department's more diplomatic "good cop" with audiences abroad.[54] Unsurprisingly, this stance has at times created tensions with foreign governments, which the State Department would be called upon to mitigate.[55]

---

[50] In 2015, for instance, the State Department list of CPCs was of nine countries, compared to the recommended CPC list of seventeen countries in USCIRF's Report for that same year; see USCIRF (2015, 6).

[51] Former NSC Official (2010, author's interview).

[52] Despite OIRF reports argued from the start that in Saudi Arabia "religious freedom does not exist" (OIRF 2000), the Gulf kingdom was first listed as a CPC only in 2004. This is considerably later than most other nonallied countries which would be added to the CPC list since the very first report, including Afghanistan, Burma, China, Iran, Iraq, Serbia, and Sudan. Conversely, USCIRF adopts a more cavalier approach. Yet USCIRF's policy to report only on the countries that it deems the worst offenders also regularly exposes it to accusations of bias. Particularly controversial, for instance, have been USCIRF's designation of Turkey as a CPC in 2012, and its lack of any reporting on Israel (see dissent note by James Zogby in USCIRF 2017, 17–20). On the political nature and partisanship, and perceptions thereof, of international religious freedom reporting in general, see Cozad (2005); GAO (2013, 17, 36–37); McAlister (2013).

[53] Gunn (2004, 641) and Grieboski (2011a).

[54] USCIRF Official 1 (2010, author's interview). See also GAO (2013, 28).

[55] GAO (2013, 31–33).

Diplomatic and Policy Actions

The monitoring and reporting on the state of religious persecution and liberty around the world is meant to inform the policymaking process. Here the institutions of the International Religious Freedom regime seek to advise or shame the president, the secretary of state, and Congress into action. These actions would range from taking particular diplomatic initiatives that prod governments around the world to further the cause of religious freedom, or adopting more extreme and coercive practices such as imposing economic sanctions against countries that feature on the State Department's CPC list. The decision to economically sanction a country often reveals underlying tensions between upholding norms or pursuing interests in foreign policy. For example, by the year 2015, only Eritrea was being explicitly sanctioned for religious freedom violations. Some non-US allies such as China, Burma, Iran, and North Korea all had "double-hatted" sanctions instead.[56] US allies on the CPC list, such as Saudi Arabia and Uzbekistan, have instead been spared sanctions, with the president exercising his authority to waive them.

A range of further, less coercive, diplomatic actions are also carried out designed to privately and publicly persuade and pressure foreign governments to adopt norms and policies that support what the regime's institutions and advocates define as religious freedom, tolerance and pluralism. Activities range from meeting with government officials and representatives of religious groups to discuss issues of concern to them; persuading, or naming and shaming, governments to adopt particular legal and policy arrangements which support religious minorities and freedom; raising public awareness through press conferences or newspaper editorials in the United States and around the world of cases of religious freedom violations; or convening through the help of US embassies interfaith dialogues in places where sectarian tensions appear to be on the rise. Instances of such practices—whether in China, Nigeria, Turkey, Saudi Arabia, South Sudan, Pakistan, Vietnam, Morocco, Egypt, Iraq, or Indonesia—are countless and well publicized in the IRF reports by the State Department and USCIRF.[57] Actors and institutions connected to the regime have pressed their case not just at the bilateral level, but also in multilateral forums. These, for instance, have played a central role in a larger international network lobbying, successfully, for the UN Human Rights Council Resolution 16/18. The resolution seeks to protect persons against intolerance based on religion or belief, as opposed to attempts by the Organization of the Islamic Cooperation (OIC) to impose a "defamation of religions" norm internationally.[58]

---

[56] Double-hatted sanctions occur when existing sanctions are redesignated to apply also for other issues. In these cases sanctions that were already in existence on a particular state would be further designated as applying also for religious freedom violations.

[57] Key examples can be found in GAO (2013, 10); White House (2016).

[58] The full name of Resolution 16/18 is "Combating intolerance, negative stereotyping and stigmatization of, and discrimination, incitement to violence and violence against, persons based on religion or belief." On the role played by the US and actors tied to the International Religious Freedom regime in passing the resolution, see GAO (2013, 12); OIRF (2011a); The Economist (2010).

Foreign Assistance Programming

Since 2007, the OIRF has also been allocated funding for programming. Between 2007 and 2010 the office managed over $10 million of the Human Rights and Democracy Fund spread over 15 different programs. By 2013 the amount increased to $16.6 million and the number of projects to twenty-seven.[59] Funding is awarded mostly to a mix of religious and secular US-based NGOs—such as the Institute for Global Engagement, Freedom House, or Common Ground—who then may employ local partners.[60] According to a 2011 OIRF internal document, the great majority of programs are implemented along conventional regional lines—Africa, East Asia Pacific, Europe, Near East Asia, South Central Asia. Such programs support a range of actors and initiatives, including religious minorities, religious organizations and leaders that advocate for religious tolerance, interfaith dialogues and activities intended to reduce sectarian and religious violence, and efforts at reforming education policies and textbooks.[61]

Other initiatives are labeled instead as "global programs." These are specifically targeted to a particular transnational and transcontinental religiously defined entity, the Muslim world and Muslim communities, which does not fit neatly within standard regional geographies. Grants have been awarded to a variety of organizations, some of which work directly with specific professional demographics (such as legal and human rights professionals, or religious and secular leaders) to help them develop legal protections in accordance with religious freedom norms, while other programs have sought to train journalists on how to report in a fair and balanced manner on religious issues in general and on Islam in particular.[62] Since 2011, a rapid response program has been set up to provide emergency assistance to victims of religious persecution.[63]

Building Capacity within the State Department and Diplomatic Corps

The fourth objective of the regime has been to elevate and mainstream this normative and policy issue within American foreign policy. The very fact that the act was passed, and that an institutional infrastructure exists, has by default contributed to religious freedom being put on the radar screen of American foreign policymakers. Accordingly, since the operationalization of the regime in the late 1990s, references to issues such as international religious persecution, tolerance, and freedom started to appear with greater consistency in the Clinton administration's National Security Strategies (NSS).[64] Bush's first

---

[59] See respectively OIRF (2011a) and GAO (2013, 9).
[60] OIRF Official 2 (2015).
[61] I obtained the internal document from one of my interviewees (OIRF Official 1 2011). According to this document, programs carried out on a regional basis amounted in 2011 to a total of roughly $6.6 million.
[62] Programs carried out on a global basis, mostly focused on Muslims, amounted in 2011 to $1.9 million. Interventions directed especially at Islam and Muslims are explored further in chapter 5.
[63] OIRF (2013).
[64] Issues of religious persecution or freedom receive no mention in Clinton's 1994 NSS, while receiving at least one in the 1998 NSS and at least 15 in the 2000 NSS. Clinton's NSSs are available online on the National Security Strategy Archive, at http://nssarchive.us/ (accessed May 29, 2017).

and, especially, second NSS would also emphasize the importance of religious freedom.[65] President Obama likewise addressed these issues in major foreign policy speeches, such as in his famous 2009 Cairo Address to the Muslim world, and in the 2011 State Department speech on the Arab Spring.[66]

OIRF and USCIRF have also sought to build the ability of the State Department and the wider diplomatic corps to advance this policy. The organizational hubs of the regime, for instance, have increasingly integrated and delivered trainings on international religious freedom in the curriculum of the Foreign Service Institute (FSI), the primary training institution for officers and support personnel of the US foreign affairs community.[67] The notion of training on religious freedom now being offered to American diplomats, even if on a voluntary basis, was "unthinkable just a decade ago," notes Dennis Hoover at IGE.[68] Moreover, the regime's institutions have acted as a wider knowledge repository on religious matters for presidents, secretaries of state, and other policymakers to draw upon when required. IRF ambassadors have been consulted, to different degrees, by secretary of states when it came to engaging with religious communities at home or abroad.[69] For example, Ambassador Cook participated in the National Security Council's Interagency Policy Committee meetings when religion was a topic of focus.[70] Secretary of State Hillary Clinton would consult OIRF staff for information regarding the state of religious conflicts and minorities in preparation for her visits to the Middle East during the Arab Spring.[71] When the State Department and the White House started holding *Iftar* dinners with greater regularity in the aftermath of 9/11, OIRF staff were called upon to assist with drafting the list of invitees.[72]

Regime Evolution: Deepening and Broadening amid Continued and Novel Constraints

Over the decades, the International Religious Freedom regime—along with its institutions, mandate, and operations—would grow and broaden since its first inception and original intentions. This evolution did not come without continued tensions, constraining pressures, and new pockets of resistance.

---

[65] Issues of religious persecution or freedom receive 1 or 2 mentions, depending on how these are counted, in Bush's 2002, and at least 7 in the 2006 NSS. G.W. Bush's NSSs are available online on the National Security Strategy Archive, at http://nssarchive.us/ (accessed May 29, 2017).

[66] Obama (2009b; 2011).

[67] For an overview of the topics covered in such trainings, see Appendix E of OIRF reports going back to 2007.

[68] Hoover (2011, author's interview).

[69] See GAO (2013, 11).

[70] Ibid.

[71] I observed this in person during my interview with OIRF Official 1 (2011), as the official had to interrupt for a moment our conversation to answer a call from the Secretary's Office.

[72] State Department Official (2015). *Iftar* is when Ramadan-observing Muslims break their fast and gather together for dinner at sunset.

Despite countervailing forces, particularly present during the transition from the Bush to the Obama administration, two important factors contributed to increase the significance of the regime and to the expansion of its infrastructure: on the one hand, the continued support for the regime by a growing pool of well-organized international religious freedom advocates, and on the other, a series of global crises that contributed to raise religion's profile in world politics.

From the 2000s onward an important constituency of scholars, policy analysts, and pundits—in other words, of desecularizing experts—emerged, one that would be strongly committed to expanding the role and place of the regime in American foreign policy. This epistemic community was, and still is, connected to a range of novel hubs of scholarly and policy knowledge production focused on examining the role of religion in world affairs, such as the Institute for Global Engagement (IGE) (created in 2000), the Pew Forum on Religion (established in 2001), the Georgetown University's Berkley Center (created in 2006), the Council on Foreign Relation's (CFR) Religion and Foreign Policy Initiative (launched in 2006), the Center for Religious Freedom at the Hudson Institute (since 2007), and the Religious Freedom Institute (established in 2016). Many individuals within this network of organizations would exhibit close ties to the bureaucracies of the International Religious Freedom regime including, for instance, Thomas Farr and Timothy Shah at Georgetown University and cofounders of the Religious Freedom Institute, Elliot Abrams at CFR, Brian Grim at Pew (before going on to found the Religious Freedom & Business Foundation in 2014), Robert and Chris Seiple of IGE, and Nina Shea at the Hudson Institute.

Importantly, this epistemic community formed in the context of a post-9/11 world in which the United States became increasingly drawn into the Middle East and adjacent regions. Whether it was transnational terrorism or the civil wars that were tearing the region apart following the 2003 Iraq war or the Arab Spring of 2011, these experts saw religion as being deeply entangled in and often responsible for much of the ongoing violence in the region and directed at the United States. They also viewed the promotion of international religious freedom as an antidote to such violence and labored to further raise the regime's profile in US foreign policy. To this end they articulated and deployed, as was discussed earlier, a strategic desecularizing discourse that presented the advancement of religious freedom as a sine qua non for winning the war on terror and bringing peace to the Muslim world either by fostering democracy, providing a means to resolve sectarian conflicts, or by countering the ideology and theology of religious extremists. By presenting religious freedom as a matter of national security, rather than solely a normative aspiration, these experts sought to raise the stakes and profile of the regime. Furthermore, this epistemic community would importantly provide the international religious freedom agenda—widely perceived to be a religiously and politically partisan issue—with the intellectual weight and scholarly legitimacy it often lacked in many policy and diplomatic circles.

The impact of this expert community on the evolution and, in many ways, expansion of the regime would be threefold. First, it would succeed in progressively turning the promotion of religious freedom into a national security matter in American foreign policy. In Bush's 2006 National Security Strategy (NSS), religious freedom became tightly woven into the president's "freedom agenda" of promoting democracy in the Muslim world. This was no coincidence, since Elliot Abrams and William Inboden, who were among the National Security Council (NSC) staff drafting the NSS at the time, had been involved in religious freedom advocacy and institutions.[73] With President Obama, religious freedom was seen as relevant to "national security" to the extent that it helped counter "extremism" and "civil strife," a 2011 OIRF factsheet explained.[74] Under the new administration, attention would thus be given to initiatives designed to "advance curriculum reform to promote religious tolerance and combat violent extremism" in *madrasahs,* and assist "foreign governments [with] review[ing] textbooks, curricula, and teacher training materials" to remove "content that is biased, intolerant, and inflames sectarian tension."[75] The influence played by desecularizing experts in turning religious freedom into a security, rather than solely principled, issue is lucidly captured in the following statement by an OIRF official I spoke to in 2011:

> If you read Grim and Finke's book, the *Price of Freedom Denied,* you realize that religious oppression is a problem, it causes extremism and undermines stability . . . Before we treated religious freedom as a human rights issue, now we are trying to make it more about national security. We are turning religious freedom from an end into a means.[76]

Second, around 2013 this epistemic community joined forces also with longstanding religious liberty advocates, many of whom were the original supporters of the 1997 Freedom from Religious Persecution Act. Together, they stressed once again the suffering and possible "genocide" of Christians and other religious minorities in Muslim-majority countries.[77] At this time, the Middle East was in turmoil and plagued by conflict in the wake of the Arab Spring. Islamist movements, like the Muslim Brotherhood, were winning elections in Egypt while the so-called Islamic State of Iraq and the Levant

---

[73] William Inboden (2011) explained during our interview that he actively worked to raise the profile of international religious freedom during the drafting of the 2006 NSS. Inboden, previously to joining the NSC in 2004, had been a special advisor to the OIRF and before that he was involved in the passage of IRFA as a Congressional staffer. USCIRF Official 1 (2010) argues that thanks to Elliot Abrams, USCIRF would have access to the NSC. Elliott Abrams, before joining Bush's NSC in 2002, had been USCIRF Commissioner between 1999 and 2001 and president of the EPPC before that.

[74] OIRF (2011b); see also Obama (2014a).

[75] OIRF (2013).

[76] OIRF Official 1 (2011, author's interview).

[77] Markoe (2015); NAE (2015). This coalition, for instance, featured desecularizing experts such as Thomas Farr and Chris Seiple, individuals who in the 1990s articulated the particularist principled desecularizing discourse on Christian persecution, such as Congressman Frank Wolf and Nina Shea, as well as organizations like Open Doors and Baha'is of the United States; and some Democratic members of Congress, such as Congresswoman Anna G. Eshoo.

(ISIS) was wreaking havoc across the region. This coalition succeeded in persuading Congress to pass the Near East and South Central Asia Religious Freedom Act of 2014. The act mandated the appointment of America's first ever State Department Special Advisor for Religious Minorities in the Near East and South and Central Asia. Knox Thames, then USCIRF's Director of Policy and Research, was selected to fill this position and tasked with coordinating the work of OIRF staff focused on the Near East and South and Central Asia region, with ensuring that the needs of religious minority communities were taken into account in US military and humanitarian planning, and with assisting religious communities who had been displaced because of conflicts—such as Assyrian Christians or the Yazidis—with returning to their "ancestral homes."[78]

Third, desecularizing experts from the likes of Georgetown University, Pew, or IGE have worked in tandem with OIRF and USCIRF staff to promote the operationalization of similar regimes across other international contexts. From the 2010s onward, this network of governmental and civil society actors has systematically organized workshops at home and attended events abroad,[79] penned reports and journal special issues,[80] and led transnational networks,[81] aimed at purposively sharing and promoting the American experience among interested foreign partners. Through these activities, capacity-building efforts reached a new level. These would no longer be confined to the realm of American foreign policy, but would increasingly target international audiences as well.

This broadening of the regime's agenda and institutional architecture between 2001 and 2016 has taken place against the backdrop of pre-existing and new forms of cultural, political, and bureaucratic constraints, which religious freedom supporters would repeatedly lament about. For instance, they have argued that more could have been done to include religious freedom norms in the new constitutions of Afghanistan and Iraq in the aftermath of America's interventions,[82] or in raising the ranking of the IRF ambassador to that of other ambassadors-at-large in the State Department.[83] Certain regime supporters have faulted the Obama administration for prioritizing engagement with the Muslim world at the expense of upholding religious freedom norms, and for the long-winded appointment process and diplomatically inexperienced nature of its first IRF ambassador, Suzan Johnston Cook.[84]

---

[78] Sapersteine (2015).
[79] A number of Wilton Park conferences in the UK, since 2011, have been among the most important venues for the transatlantic diffusion of international religious freedom policy and norms.
[80] See for instance Thames (2012); *Review of Faith & International Affairs* (2014).
[81] Such efforts include the International Panel of Parliamentarians for Freedom of Religion or Belief, created in 2014 and the International Contact Group on Freedom of Religion or Belief.
[82] Inboden (2011); Philpott (2014).
[83] Farr and Hoover (2009, 19); also Farr (2010a).
[84] For an exemplary critique of President Obama's approach to international religious freedom see Farr (2010b). For a more positive appraisal, see Birdsall (2012); also Birdsall (2014b).

The shift from the Bush to the Obama administration did, in effect, mark a period of reappraisal and uncertainty for the regime. First, in the wake of the highly inflammatory rhetoric and practices of President Bush's war on terror, Obama abandoned the previous administration's controversial "freedom agenda." Unilateral and aggressive democracy-promoting initiatives took a back seat as the Democratic president sought to rebuild America's flailing standing and alliances in the world in general and among Muslims in particular.[85] This context, coupled with the perception—not completely unfounded, as we shall see—that the regime was grounded in a pro-Christian and anti-Muslim bias, led the administration to prioritize policies concerned with reaching out to Muslims, while downplaying policies which appeared to seek to export "freedom" (whether political or religious) to others. Second, a concerted effort was made to limit the influence of conservative Christians and of Congress over the regime's institutions. Obama appointed the first non-Evangelical Christian as IRF ambassador, the Mainline Protestant Susanne Johnston Cook, followed by the first non-Christian ambassador, Rabbi David Saperstein, a longstanding advocate on religious freedom issues abroad. Curbs on USCIRF's budget and Commissioners' tenures were introduced by a Democratically controlled Congress.

Overall, despite continued or new forms of resistance, the promotion of international religious freedom has nonetheless become a fixture of US foreign policy over the decades. New domestic constituencies of desecularizing experts have emerged providing further strategic rationales and greater intellectual legitimacy to the regime in the context of a post-9/11 world. The regime's institutional architecture, resources, and operations have evolved and progressively grown since its inception. This is notable, for instance, with the addition of a Special Advisor for Religious Minorities, the greater resources OIRF has been given to conduct programs since 2007, a shift in thinking toward an approach that views religious freedom increasingly as a security issue rather than a principled one, and the expansion of capacity building efforts to the international level. Furthermore, by the end of the Obama Presidency, Congress passed in December of 2016 the Frank R. Wolf International Religious Freedom Act which amended, by deepening and expanding, the original 1998 act. Among others, the 2016 act now unequivocally presented international religious freedom promotion as a strategic priority of the US government, demanded the institution of a "Special Watch List" for countries falling short of qualifying for CPC status, introduced the designation of "Entities of Particular Concern" and "Designated Persons List" for religious freedom violating non-state actors, expanded protections to include more explicitly nontheistic beliefs, set minimum OIRF staffing requirements, and suggested ways for empowering the ambassador's role.

---

[85] On this grand strategic shift between the Bush and Obama administrations see Drezner (2011); Dueck (2011).

Presidents and secretaries of state would acknowledge this changing reality over the years. "Compared to the past, there is a higher-level focus on the issue of religious freedom all the way up to President Obama and certainly Secretary of State Clinton," an USCIRF official observed in 2011.[86] Cultural and normative barriers, although not necessarily strategic and institutional ones, have considerably decreased within the State Department. Hence international religious freedom advocates like Thomas Farr, who have long lamented the regime's marginalization, started to concede that this agenda was becoming increasingly "respectable" in foreign policy circles.[87] A measure of the regime's success in establishing itself in the American foreign policy panorama can be gauged, paradoxically, by the growing critiques levied against the proliferation of such policies coming from particular academic milieus.[88]

Foreign Policy Desecularization

The emergence of the International Religious Freedom regime has been achieved through the contestation and redefinition of the boundaries between the religious and the secular in American foreign policy. These changes amount to processes of institutional, epistemic, ideological, and state-normative desecularization, which this section will consider in more detail.

First, processes of institutional desecularization are evident as religious actors have become ever more entangled with the making and implementation of American foreign policy through the regime. Of the four IRF ambassadors appointed between 1998 and 2016, all are people with an explicit religious background and role in their faith communities: two Protestant Evangelicals (Robert Seiple and John Hanford), one Mainline Protestant (Suzan Johnson Cook), and one Jewish (David Saperstein).[89] Similarly, USCIRF Commissioners have generally—although not exclusively—been drawn from the ranks of religious institutions,[90] faith-based advocacy and policy

---

[86] USCIRF Official 1 (2011, author's interview). For a list of statements by President Obama and Secretaries Clinton and Kerry on religious freedom, see White House (2016).
[87] Berkley Center (2014a).
[88] In the field of comparative politics and IR, Hurd (2015; 2012b) has probably been the most vocal and well-known critical voice. *The Immanent Frame*, a blog, is a key venue for the articulation of similar critical voices across the social sciences more broadly (*The Immanent Frame* 2012/2013; 2010/2011).
[89] The resume of Robert Seiple, ambassador between 1999 and 2000, includes president of Eastern College and Eastern Baptist Theological Seminary, president of World Vision, and founder of IGE. The resume of John Hanford, ambassador between 2002 and 2009, includes serving in pastoral ministry on the staff of West Hopewell Presbyterian Church in Hopewell, Virginia, and Congressional fellow on the staff of Senator Richard Lugar (R-IN) closely involved with passing the 1998 IRFA. The resume of Suzan Johnson Cook, ambassador between 2011 and 2013, includes founder and president of Wisdom Women Worldwide Center, Senior Pastor of the Bronx Christian Fellowship Baptist Church in New York City, and policy advisor to President Bill Clinton. David Saperstein, ambassador between 2014 and 2017, is the former director of the Religious Action Center of Reform Judaism.
[90] Including, among others, Don Argue, National Association of Evangelicals (NAE); Richard Land, Southern Baptist Convention; William J. Shaw, National Baptist Convention; Cardinal Theodore McCarrick; and Imam Talal Y. Eid.

organizations,[91] or theologians and scholars of religion.[92] Indeed, an underlying consensus exists that to conduct and implement international religious freedom policy, "it is useful to have people that understand faith, and people of faith generally understand faith," an OIRF official explains.[93]

On the implementation side, the distance between the foreign policy apparatus and religious actors is likewise being reduced. This occurs as OIRF, USCIRF, or embassy officials purposely interact with religious leaders and communities worldwide in ever-more structured and sustained ways. Evidence for this growing entanglement include: the monitoring of international religious freedom, the organization of public and private meetings and events between American policymakers and religious communities and actors, and, not least, the direct funding of religious institutions and faith-based organizations for the implementation of international religious freedom-related programs.

This institutional desecularization is tied to parallel processes whereby secularist ideas and norms held by foreign policymakers are disputed and revisited in ways that no longer dominate the policy space. The existence of the International Religious Freedom regime is, in fact, premised on the very notion that religion matters and thus on a degree of epistemic desecularization. As an OIRF official notes, "there is a growing recognition in the State Department that religion is important."[94] Epistemic desecularization can lead to a range of outcomes, from a more middle of the road position that is attentive to religion in relation to other forces or a more extreme one that instead singles out religion above all other factors. Within this spectrum, the regime consistently tends toward a position whereby religion is reified as the most important factor in determining identities, causes, behaviors and events.[95] An OIRF official admits that when in doubt on whether religion matters or not, the policy has been to be "inclusive."[96] That is, the official clarifies, "if it is not clear whether religion is a motivator, but nevertheless an element in the cases we examine, we include it."[97] More often than not the result of this inclusive—or what Castelli also labels "maximalist"[98] —approach is that in international religious freedom discourse religion appears everywhere and explaining everything. In parallel the often complex interplay of historical, cultural, political, economic,

---

[91] Including, among others, Rabbi David Saperstein, former Director of the Religious Action Center of Reform Judaism; Nina Shea, Director of the Center for Religious Freedom at the Hudson Institute; Elliott Abrams, former president of the Ethics and Public Policy Center; Laila Al-Marayati, former president of the Muslim Women's League.
[92] Including, among others, Robert P. George, McCormick Professor of Jurisprudence at Princeton University; Elizabeth H. Prodromou, former Assistant Professor at Boston University; Firuz Kazemzadeh, Professor Emeritus of History at Yale University.
[93] OIRF Official 2 (2015, author's interview). A similar perspective was voiced to me by Marshall (2011).
[94] OIRF Official 1 (2011, author's interview).
[95] This conclusion is based on an analysis of the executive summary and introductions of OIRF reports between 1999 and 2013 and USCIRF reports between 2003 and 2015.
[96] OIRF Official 2 (2015, author's interview).
[97] Ibid.
[98] Castelli (2005, 330).

and social factors that constitute and shape identities, meanings, interests, conducts, events, and outcomes in world politics are then often overlooked.[99]

For example, while authoritarian governments in Burma, Vietnam, or Egypt abuse the rights of their citizens across the board, their actions or inactions are invariably read and presented by the International Religious Freedom regime as instances of "religious persecution," when they could just as plausibly be based on ethnic, racial, economic, or political factors. Violence in Iraq, Syria, Sudan, Nigeria, or the Central African Republic is consistently reported as "sectarian" as if religious difference were its main—and sole—cause rather than other struggles for political power or economic resources. The paradox of an approach that portrays contexts, actors, and causes as primarily religious becomes apparent if the tables are turned on the foreign policy of the United States. If one were to follow the maximalist approach to religion deployed by the regime to explain American military interventions in the Middle East, Castelli suggests, these would appear as instances of persecution of Muslims, discrimination of Islam, and as an upsurge in civilizational conflict.[100] This is of course a narrative which many Islamists, who themselves tend to reify religious causes and factors above all else, would endorse.[101] But one that is likely to be disputed by actors tied to the International Religious Freedom regime instead.

It must be noted, in fairness, that American foreign policy more broadly is careful not to represent world politics exclusively along the religious lines often adopted in religious freedom rhetoric. The International Religious Freedom regime represents a deep pocked of epistemic desecularization, in the context of a wider bureaucracy that often continues to function according to its secular logics. Staff and policymakers in the White House and State Department more broadly have appeared weary of using religious labels for fear of unduly politicizing religious factors and reifying religious differences. When an ISIS-affiliated group in Libya executed 21 individuals in 2015, the White House Press Secretary's Office labeled them "Egyptian citizens."[102] This characterization nonetheless provoked the ire of international religious freedom advocates like Frank Wolf, who claimed—following ISIS' logic—that the attack was and had to be characterized first and foremost as against "Christian Copts."[103] Likewise, not all policymakers operating within the International Religious Freedom regime are oblivious to the analytical and political problems inherent in an epistemic desecularized approach that singles out religion. This said, moments where any such nuance is introduced remain few and far between.[104]

---

[99] For a similar perspective on the reification of religion in international religious freedom discourses, see Adcock (2014); Hurd (2012c); Zogby (2018).

[100] Castelli (2005, 330).

[101] On the reification of religious identities and causes in Islamist discourses see, among many, Halliday (2003, ch.7).

[102] Office of the Press Secretary (2015).

[103] Wolf interviewed by Fox News (2015, 3:20–3:39).

[104] As OIRF Official 2 (2015, author's interview) admits: "In our reports we are now adding some disclaimers about religion as part of more complex dynamics." A dissenting note by Commissioners

Processes of ideological desecularization have taken place as well. When it comes to ideological desecularization the pendulum can swing from a middle of the road stance that treats religion as ambivalent, toward one that positively essentializes it. The regime tends to reproduce a positive essentialization of religion whereby what gets to be labeled as good religion is invariably understood to be true religion, while bad religion must necessarily be false, incorrect, or hijacked religion. Indeed the very regime is built on a view that freed and flourishing religion constitutes a good in its own right, a source of human morality and virtue, and a means to achieve a range of American foreign policy objectives. Such natural goodness of religion when allowed to be free is thus viewed as the foundation (the "first freedom" as it is often referred to by regime advocates) on which to build other freedoms such as democracy and human rights, and a force capable of undermining the supposedly incorrect interpretations of religion that aliment sectarian violence and terrorist activity.

Finally, state-normative desecularization is occurring too as stringent separationist interpretations of the Constitution's First Amendment Establishment Clause are being rethought and relaxed in the context of the regime. Resistance to operationalizing the religious freedom agenda in the 1990s was often framed in terms of concerns around preserving what Thomas Jefferson famously referred to as "a wall of separation between church and state." These sentiments have been contested by and have given way to the more accommodationist interpretations of state–religion relations held by supporters of the regime. "In 1990s those skeptical of the IRFA cited separation of church and state"—a USCIRF official explains—"today, instead, people are more on board."[105] A more accommodationist perspective toward religion can hardly ever be completely neutral and often does lead to some religions and religiosities being accommodated—hence legitimized and supported—more than others. In the context of the International Religious Freedom regime, as we shall see in more detail in the next section, this means that some forms and understandings of religion are deemed more worthy of protection than others.

Effects on Global Religious-Secular Landscapes

The activities of the regime—from reporting to programing, from advocacy to sanctioning—are leading the United States to increasingly and explicitly intervene abroad with a view of shaping religious affairs and dynamics globally.

William Shaw and Azizah Al-Hibri in the 2013 USCIRF report explicitly calls for such an approach. Shaw and Al-Hibri argue in the note that the inclusion of Turkey in the report's CPC list with regards to the mounting tensions between Northern (Turkish-controlled) and Southern (Greek-controlled) Cyprus is problematic, since, they contend, that these tensions are: "more rooted in historical political developments between the South and North regions than in real religious tensions between peoples" (USCIRF 2013, 278). See also the dissenting note by Commissioner James Zogby, in the 2017 USCIRF report (USCIRF 2017, 17–20).

[105] USCIRF Official 1 (2011, author's interview).

The extent to which America's international religious freedom foreign policy is able to do so—as supporters of this agenda wished it could, or as its critics fear it does—is an open question that certainly requires further probing.[106] Moreover, whether such a project simultaneously promotes a wide range of social and political goods—peace, democracy, de-radicalization—as international religious freedom supporters claim, or rather encourages multiple ills—imperialism, violence, and the hardening of religious divides—as its critiques contend, remains unclear and needs further empirical research.[107]

Be this as it may, having the weight of the world's superpower monitoring or intervening on the grounds of promoting religious freedom and in favor of this or against that state, law, social practice, group, or individual is likely to have consequences of some kind, with either intended or unintended outcomes. An example, heralded as a success for international religious freedom policy, is Vietnam. Following its designation as a CPC country in 2004, negotiations with American diplomats, assisted by IGE, led the Vietnamese government to take action to reduce religious persecution against ethnic minority Protestants and independent Buddhist groups.[108] The prospect of striking trade deals with the United States undoubtedly influenced Vietnam's calculations. By 2006 Vietnam's CPC designation was dropped. There are many other cases cited in OIRF and USCIRF reports whereby direct US diplomatic pressure would lead countries to adopt legal arrangements supportive of religious freedom, accord certain religious groups official recognition, or release incarcerated believers from prison. USCIRF and OIRF reports also have indirect effects, including empowering religious groups and organizations around the world vis-à-vis their governments by drawing attention to the former's plight.[109]

While some religious communities gain from America's interest in their condition, for others the outcome may be more ambiguous. America's actions to promote international religious freedom are often profoundly political, with constant tensions having to be negotiated and trade-offs being made between the pursuit of foreign policy interests, the universal aspirations of the norm, and the particularist understandings given to religious freedom by the complex constituency supporting the regime. This can fuel the perception that "religion . . . is being used to promote . . . political interests," Abdolkarim Soroush an Iranian intellectual and reformer explains,[110] thus creating suspicion toward America's international religious freedom policy in numerous

---

[106] Pew Research Center (2009a; 2011; 2014b) reports have identified an increase in religious restrictions and hostilities over the past decade. If these findings are correct, one is to conclude that the International Religious Freedom regime has not been able to achieve much, as its supporters worry, or has possibly been counterproductive, as some of its critics argue.

[107] For a clear statement in support of international religious freedom policies, see Philpott and Shah (2016). For an exemplary critical voice, see Hurd (2015).

[108] GAO (2013, 16, 39); also Seiple (2011).

[109] GAO (2013, 36).

[110] Soroush in Berkley Center (2008, 1:05:32–1:07:51).

constituencies around the world. While Soroush mostly refers to the views that certain Iranians hold about America's outspoken support for the Baha'is, seen by Tehran as Israeli proxies, the case of Christian Copts in Egypt is particularly emblematic.

The status of Christian Copts in Egypt is high on the religious freedom agenda. Well-organized American-based Copts, concerned about their coreligionists abroad as well as what they see as the Coptic Church's leadership collusion with Egypt's military regimes, make their voices clearly heard in the halls of American power. Important sections of the local Coptic community in Egypt do not, however, see these outside interventions as unambiguously helpful. Some Copts toe the governmental line by expressing their skepticism toward foreign meddling in the domestic affairs of a sovereign state, even if apparently in their support. Others fear that international backing jeopardizes local Copts by giving the impression, often with fatal consequences, that autochthonous Christian communities which predated even the arrival of Islam in Egypt—or across the Middle East more broadly—are foreign to their societies or a fifth column of the West.[111] These concerns were on display when, for instance, the Coptic community greeted a 2001 USCIRF mission to Egypt with great suspicion and little cooperation.

In short, American attempts to promote religious freedom may engender different types of responses from each targeted government and religious community abroad, at times improving and at other times exacerbating the problems. Locally, some may welcome and harness foreign interventions for their own agendas as a means to legitimize their particular religious community's status and grievances, while others may resist them for fear of being delegitimized as pawns in the global politics of today's superpower. In the remaining part of this section, I explore in greater depth how the International Religious Freedom regime is producing the three hypothesized effects I outlined in the introduction: shaping religious realities along American norms and interests, religionizing world politics, and diffusing similar regimes in international policy.

Shaping Global Religious Realities Along American Norms and Interests

To the extent that the International Religious Freedom regime intervenes to shape global religious landscapes in multiple ways by claiming to uphold a universal human right, it will likely do so nonetheless according to particular American understandings of religion and religious freedom. Lorenzo Zucca, for example, notes how religious freedom actions are often "guided not by an international-universal understanding of the Human Rights to Freedom of Religion, but rather by a very domestic one."[112] Or, as Jose Casanova puts

---

[111] Ferrara (2013b, 62); Hurd (2013b); Mahmood (2012).
[112] Zucca in Annicchino (2013a, 6).

it, America's "universalism is particularist and irremediably so."[113] It is particularist in the sense that America's norms and interests, I suggest, play into (a) what counts as religion, (b) what types of religiosities are allowed to be free, and (c) which religious communities stand to benefit the most from the institutionalization of the regime. These three claims will be explored in turn.

What Counts as Religion

If the United States is to promote international religious freedom, it is inevitably forced, Hurd notes, to "make determinations about what constitutes religion" and "who qualifies as a religious subject or association."[114] The United States works with an understanding of religion influenced by a powerful political tradition grounded in liberalism, and a religious culture shaped both by Protestant Christianity as well as a tradition of religious pluralism and disestablishment. Religious pluralism and disestablishment lead to a bottom-up, rather than top-down, approach to recognizing religions based on a group's self-definition as religious rather than the state's a priori regulation. Protestant Christian influences are detectable in what are generally understood to be the core characteristic of a religion, which privileges individually held faith and belief over communal rituals and belonging.[115] Once all of this is married with a liberal philosophical tradition, Americans tend to view and experience religions ultimately as "voluntary associations, confessions, or denominations," in Casanova's words, which one can freely choose to adhere to or abandon depending on individual conscience.[116] Thus the ways in which Americans view religion embodies simultaneously a particular kind of *radical pluralism* joined at the hip to a certain type of *Protestant particularism*. This ambivalent take on religion becomes immediately apparent as we start to examine a number of tensions that religious freedom advocacy generates as it encounters different understandings and practices of religion around the world.

One tension arises from the radical pluralist view of faith, which is embedded in the very broad list of religions and religious groups the regime claims are religions and which, as such, ought to be protected, freed, and recognized. This list includes groups that in other parts of the world are often not perceived as legitimate religions and thus are more likely to be labeled as "cults," "sects," or "heresies." Examples include Baha'is for Iranians, Ahmadiyyas for many Muslims, Scientology for certain European states, or the Unification Church, the Church of Latter Day Saints (Mormonism), and Jehovah's Witnesses for peoples and states in various parts of the world.[117] I am not suggesting here that any such groups should be defined one way or

---

[113] Casanova (2010, 15).
[114] Hurd (2012b, 954).
[115] See also Beaman (2003); Castelli (2016); Sullivan (2005).
[116] Casanova in Berkley Center (2010a, 36:02–36:05).
[117] Many of these groups are categorized in OIRF's reports between 1999 and 2013 either as "nonapproved religions" (i.e., nonapproved by other states), religions "wrongfully associated with dangerous 'cults' or 'sects'," or "minority religious groups."

another; rather, I am underlining that the categorization of such groups as legitimate *religions* is often deeply contested around the world, whether for religious, social or political reasons—indeed at times also within American society itself.[118] The following statement by an OIRF official clearly exemplifies this logic and the tensions it creates: "We do not define religions, but let groups to self-define. Hence while some countries and people around the world would define Scientology or Mormons as sects or cults, we do not."[119] In its attempt to free religions, the regime ultimately frees what Americans define as religious groups contra what other states and societies do.

The notion of an "autonomous subject who chooses beliefs,"[120] which underpins the radical pluralist cum Protestant particularist understanding of religion embedded in international religious freedom policy, generates a second tension. The freedom to choose and, thus, change one's beliefs is adamantly defended and promoted by IRF advocates and reports. It is often understood as including the right to proselytize; that is, "efforts taken by individuals or groups to seek the conversion of another."[121] While actively seeking converts is seen as a relatively uncontroversial practice in the context of what is often referred to as America's "religious market-place," in which spiritual customers freely select from a wide range of faiths the religious product that best suits their needs, it is extremely contested internationally for legal, religious, and political reasons.[122]

Legal scholars argue that the right to engage in missionary activity is "perhaps the most controversial component of religious freedom."[123] Those favoring proselytism generally support their arguments by appealing to international human rights norms granting the "freedom to change religion or belief" and "freedom of opinion and expression."[124] Rights to religion and religious expression are however not absolute, as John Witte points out, and human rights regimes have clauses that impose certain limitations on the way religions are permitted to manifest themselves—for reasons of public safety, order, health, and morals—and on the kind of proselytizing tactics that are used, for example concerning the targeting of minors or indigenous peoples who have the right to protect their culture and religion.[125] "The individual's right to leave his or her

---

[118] The Billy Graham Evangelistic Association's website removed references to Mormonism as a "cult," for instance, as recently as 2012—coincidentally during Mitt Romney' presidential campaign (Wang 2012).
[119] OIRF Official 2 (2015, author's interview).
[120] Hurd (2012a).
[121] Witte (2001, 625–626).
[122] On controversies surrounding religious freedom and proselytism, see Berger (2014); Berkley Center (2010b); Hackett (2014); Witte (2001). For authors using economic analogies to talk about America's religious landscape as a marketplace, see Finke and Stark (1992; 1998). A recent Pew Research Center (2015) survey found that the share of Americans who had a religious identity as adults different from that of childhood was as high as 42 percent.
[123] Johan van der Vyver quoted in Hackett (2014, 3).
[124] Quotes are respectively from Article 18 and 19 of the Universal Declaration of Human Rights.
[125] Witte (2001, 625–628) draws this list of limitations mostly from The International Covenant on Civil and Political Rights.

religious community," Casanova adds, "does not necessarily entail the right of outsiders to enter that community in order to encourage others to exit."[126] In sum, international norms leave important margins for competing claims and interpretations of proselytism.

These legal disputes reflect deeper religious and political fissures that exist in the world. Actively seeking converts is a duty for certain evangelizing religions—such as Christianity, Islam and some strands of Buddhism—but not for other religions. After a long history of interconfessional violence and inquisitions, Protestant and Catholic Christians, in particular, have developed views about religious conversion that have been described as "easy-in/easy-out religion."[127] These views collide with other conceptions of religion that tie religious identity and practice to blood, soil, family, and community, notably in Judaism, Hinduism, and Confucianism, as well as in many Asian and African folk religions and traditions. In most Muslim milieus, while conversion into the faith is encouraged, conversions out of it are heavily discouraged. These understandings of what constitutes a religious person and community are hardly reconcilable with views of religion as easily, rightfully, and freely changeable individual belief.

Lastly, proselytism and conversions are often deeply political moments. If in Israel, for instance, all Jews were to convert to Christianity, there would no longer be a "Jewish state."[128] Political tensions come particularly to the fore in a wider geopolitical context often marked by profound power asymmetries. In Afghanistan, for example, the suspicion toward Christian converts, who are often reported in the Western Media as being abused, cannot be divorced from a local environment marked by the presence of Western forces whose militaries have burned Korans,[129] allowed Christian missionaries to operate alongside them,[130] and have been seen wearing patches identifying themselves as "infidels" and "pork eating crusaders."[131] Power disparities also flourish at the intersection of humanitarian work and proselytizing activities. Many Christian faith-based organizations have brought much needed material aid around the world. However, in many instances evangelizers have used these activities to exploit the needs of the vulnerable in order to gain converts.[132] As resentment has grown around the world toward certain Christian charities and missions because of such practices, Christian organizations are feeling increasingly the need to pen voluntary codes of conduct to guide their humanitarian aid work in order to minimize such tensions.[133]

---

[126] Casanova (2010, 16).
[127] Witte (2001); also Casanova (2010, 17).
[128] That is also why important sections of the American Jewish and Israeli population view Protestant Evangelicals in general and Christian Zionists in particular with a degree of suspicion (Borschel-Dan 2014).
[129] Agha and Schifrin (2012).
[130] MRFF (2008).
[131] Ricksmay (2014).
[132] This issue will be discussed in greater detail in chapter 4.
[133] Singh et al. (2005).

A careful reading of religious freedom reports drafted by the OIRF, however, reveals little or no evidence that religious conversions and proselytism are fraught with such legal, religious, and political controversies.[134] The reports largely portray such activities—when not forcefully pursued by governmental officials—as a self-evident international right, a standard religious custom, and an apolitical practice, and thus overwhelmingly criticize attempts made to curb conversions and proselytism as infringements of religious freedom. Hardly if ever, aggressive forms of proselytizing activities, especially when carried out by Christian groups, are mentioned. The reading of conversions and proselytism as relatively uncontroversial practices that emerges from the OIRF reports is thus particularist rather than universally shared, one that—in Witte's words—"largely accept[s] the religious voluntarism common among libertarian and Western Christian groups."[135] All of this shows how in its promotion of religious freedom, America is implicitly operating within and diffusing *its* radical pluralist and Protestant particularist understanding of the sacred, which overlooks or conflicts with other context-specific ways of being religious.

What Types of Religiosities Are Allowed to Be Free

The regime is based on the notion that allowing religions to be free globally is a valuable end in itself, as well as a means to achieve a number of other useful political and security outcomes. As argued in the previous section, this view is based on a positive essentialization of religion as inherently good. Look closely at the regime's practices and discourses, though, and what appears evident is that some kinds of religion produce goods that are of greater value to American foreign policy than others, and thus deserve greater protection and freedom than others. "The project of promoting religious freedom," Elizabeth Castelli notes, "is also a project that involves the construction and support of certain forms of religion."[136] Namely, religious freedom is mostly for those religions, and interpretations and practices thereof, that are compatible with America's immediate security interests and longer-term attempts to build a liberal international order.

As an example, the regime's campaign against the OIC's religious defamation norm underscores an understating of religion that ought to be at best doctrinally pluralist or at least tolerant of criticism, dissent, blasphemy, or heresy. Calls to promote religious freedom as an antidote to extremism and terrorism, for instance, are premised on the idea that religion ought to be moderate, tolerant, and peaceful, not fundamentalist, intolerant, and violent. Yet

---

[134] This conclusion is reached following a survey of the executive summaries of OIRF reports from 2000 to 2013. I came across only one recorded case where proselytism was mentioned as problematic, which involved Christian NGOs in Sudan using "their services to pressure persons to convert to Christianity" (OIRF 2002). OIRF reports do take a stronger stance on issues of forced conversions by individuals that hold government positions, with a number of cases of forced conversions to Islam by government officials in Muslim-majority countries being reported across the years and one episode involving an Evangelical Police Commissioner in Fiji (OIRF 2009).
[135] Witte (2001, 622); also Cozad (2005).
[136] Castelli (2016).

within most religions—Christianity, Islam, Judaism, Buddhism, and others—important traditions exist that oppose criticism and heterodoxy, that are literalist, and that legitimize violence in the name of "holy" or "just" wars. Within the International Religious Freedom regime's framework, religions are asked to marginalize or even to renounce these traditions. These examples should, obviously, not be read as supporting the view that intolerant or violent religion should deserve to be free and protected, but rather to highlight a paradox at the heart of religious freedom activism. This contradiction is aptly captured by Winnifred Fallers Sullivan as follows:

> Religion is not always, in fact, absolutely free. . . . The right kind of religion, the approved religion, is always that which is protected, while the wrong kind, whether popular or unpopular, is always restricted or even prohibited.[137]

Which Religious Communities Stand to Benefit the Most from the Institutionalization of the Regime

There is a perception that in the American foreign policy context, international religious freedom is a euphemism for the promotion and protection of Christianity and Christian interests globally. This perception is generally sustained by the historical origins of the 1998 IRFA, rooted as it is in a movement initially concerned with the safety of Christian missions and minorities in Communist and Muslim countries.[138] Such a view rests also on the fact that in the United States, domestic campaigns for "religious freedom" are generally waged by (conservative) Christians seeking to protect or advance their own religious, social, and political claims in the context of America's culture wars.[139]

Most contemporary actors directly involved in the execution of international religious freedom policies, and those who are supportive of them, would think of these perceptions as either wrong or outdated. Some, for instance, point out that the 1998 IRFA is grounded in universal human rights rather than Christian particularist discourses.[140] Others explain that an effort to recruit policymakers from a wider pool of religious backgrounds, rather than Christian and Evangelical, has taken place and that the appointment of Rabbi David Saperstein to IRF ambassador should be read in this light.[141] It is likewise undeniable that regime actions—also driven by America's radical pluralist understanding of religion highlighted earlier—frequently express apprehension for the conditions of an extremely diverse range of religious communities and traditions, not solely Christian.

Yet while historical circumstance and present political battles may linger on in the perception of a Christian-bias within the International Religious

---

[137] Sullivan (2005, 154).
[138] Cozad (2005).
[139] Castelli (2007a). For an example of the links between domestic and international threats to religious freedom made by Christian intellectuals, see Farr (2017).
[140] Cassidy (2013, 52); Gunn (2004, 636); Philpott and Shah (2016).
[141] OIRF Official 2 (2015).

Freedom regime, a range of further factors contribute—I would argue—to make Christianity nonetheless a central focus of the regime. Some of these factors are cultural. As already pointed out, the International Religious Freedom regime functions in the context of an underlying, tacit understanding of religion and what it means to be religiously free which is based to an important extent on a Protestant Christian template that more readily accommodates the religious needs, practices, and experiences of proselytizing religions—such as Christianity—than those of nonproselytizing faiths.

Domestic institutional, social, and demographic factors are further reasons that sustain this Christian-bias. The democratic and open structure of the American political system allows interest groups to direct American foreign policy in support of their more narrow concerns.[142] In this context, the issue of international religious freedom is often put forward by domestic religious groups interested in mobilizing on behalf of their coreligionists abroad. As a Pew report highlights, "one common mission among denominational groups that engage in global advocacy is protecting or defending fellow believers."[143] Among the very diverse constellation of actors who historically as well as to this day continue to vigorously champion the regime—be it religious institutions and organizations, experts housed in think tanks and universities, or members of Congress—and those charged with its implementation—USCIRF commissioners and staff, and IRF ambassadors and staff—the majority and most influential ones are generally Christian.

Within think tank milieus, a run through the publications and events of the Center for Religious Freedom at the Hudson Institute reveals, for instance, a nearly unique concern for Christians.[144] IGE, one of the most prominent faith-based think-and-do tanks in this space, is founded by Christian Evangelicals.[145] Some of the most active and publicly visible scholarly initiatives focused on international religious freedom are housed at Georgetown University (Catholic), Baylor University (Southern Baptist), and Brigham Yung University (Mormon). In 2015, Notre Dame's Center for Civil and Human Rights Program key project on Global Religious Freedom—in collaboration also with the Religious Freedom Project at Georgetown University—focused on Christians (*Under Cesar's Sword: Christian Responses to Persecution*).[146] The most prominent

---

[142] Baumgartner and Leech (1998).

[143] Pew Research Center (2012, 49). As Baroness Elizabeth Berridge, a working peer in UK's House of Lords and advocate for international religious freedom, also candidly admits: "[International religious freedom] has suffered from what I call global identity politics . . . Christians speak on behalf of Christians, the Baha'is come to you on behalf of the Baha'is, the Ahmadis come for the Ahmadis, *etcetera*" (Berridge in Berkley Center 2015, 19:35–20:06).

[144] See, among many, Marshall, Gilbert, and Shea (2013).

[145] In the past years, for instance, IGE launched the Cradle Fund to help—in the context of Middle Eastern conflicts and the rise of ISIS—"rescue, restore, and return Middle Eastern Christians and other religious and ethnic groups to a home where they can live and practice their faith free from fear." Information and quote were retrieved from the IGE website, at https://globalengage.org/support-ccf (accessed June 2, 2017).

[146] Philpot, Farr, and Shah (2017).

political figure in Congress promoting the international religious freedom cause has been former Congressman Frank Wolf, who self-describes as a "follower of Jesus."[147] Between 1999 and 2016 three out of four IRF ambassadors have been Christian. During the same period a Christian (whether Protestant, Catholic, or Mormon) has acted as USCIRF Commission Chair twelve times, a Jew five, and a Hindu once.[148] Unsurprisingly, USCIRF has regularly been at the center of controversies for its alleged bias in favor of Christians.[149]

This strong Christian presence, which is itself influenced by a wider American demographic and social context weighted toward Christianity, often translates into a sustained concern for the well-being of Christians worldwide. For instance, pivotal events in recent years in the Middle East—state failure, civil wars, and the rise of Islamist movements—are often read by those in the international religious freedom space through the lens of the threats posed to religious minorities in the region, especially to Christian ones.[150] In 2014 Congress passed the Near East and South Asia Religious Freedom Act mandating the appointment of a Special Advisor for Religious Minorities in the Near East and South/Central Asia in the OIRF. Despite the neutral terminology of the act and the special advisor's title, it is the status and safety of Christian minorities in Muslim-majority countries that the champions of the act were mostly concerned with. The act's intent, Congressman Wolf explained, was "to set up a special envoy to advocate on this issue for *Christians and other religious minorities* in the Middle East [emphasis added]."[151] It was not a coincidence that the official announcement of Knox Thames, a Christian, as special advisor occurred during Pope Francis' visit to the United States in 2015.

Cultural, social, and organizational dynamics within the international religious freedom space that may favor Christians in the Middle East and elsewhere intersect with claims arguing that Muslims and their concerns are ignored. Once again, the boundary between reality and perception is often blurred. On the one hand, USCIRF has come repeatedly under fire for allegedly holding a bias against Muslims when hiring staff or reporting on matters of religious freedom abroad.[152] Yet on the other hand, it is evident that IRF reports—especially by the State Department—do commit considerable space to detailing the restrictions, abuses, or violence toward Islamic practices or organizations in places such as Russia, Uzbekistan, Burma, China, or France, for instance.[153]

---

[147] Pershing (2013).

[148] This figure was obtained consulting the biographies of USCIRF commissioners, between the years 1999–2000 and 2016–2017. List of Commissioners can be found on USCIRF's website, at http://www.uscirf.gov/about-uscirf/former-commissioners (accessed July 24, 2018).

[149] Boorstein (2012); Grieboski (2011a).

[150] See also Hurd (2013a).

[151] Wolf quoted in Clyne (2015). In fairness, the status of Christians in the Middle East is increasingly a concern also of more progressive-oriented outlets (e.g., Katulis, deLeon, and Craig 2015).

[152] Boorstein (2012); Zogby (2018).

[153] Countries like Burma, Uzbekistan, and China are on the official CPC list partly because of the mistreatment of Muslim minorities or restrictions imposed on Islamic organizations.

Having said this, it is also evident that international religious freedom advocacy and policy do not take place in a historical, geopolitical, and cultural vacuum. To Middle Eastern ears the focus among religious liberty advocates on the "minority problem" in the Muslim world today, Saba Mahmood has argued, is often reminiscent of Western European colonial interventions and patronages on behalf of Christians, including the Ottoman capitulations.[154] "While those in the West might prefer to forget the past," Michael Barnett similarly highlights, "those outside the West have longer memories."[155] Thus while international religious freedom advocates are quick to point out the power imbalances that exist between Christian minorities and non-Christian majorities in the Middle East, so too Muslim religious leaders, political figures, and scholars are acutely aware of another set of power asymmetries. They see today's claims for international religious freedom in a global context in which Christianity takes the rank of the world's largest religion and where America, the most powerful state in the international system, is heavily involved in the Middle East.[156]

An event—and the reactions it prompted—neatly captures some of these underlying biases and interpretive tensions. In 2010 Christian missionaries accused of proselytizing at a Moroccan orphanage were expelled by the country's government. In Morocco, Christians and Jews are generally allowed to practice their religion openly, while active proselytization is viewed as a controversial issue and unlawful practice, particularly when targeted at vulnerable populations such as children. Republican Members of Congress closely connected to the regime, including Frank Wolf and others, quickly took up the cause of the expelled missionaries and insisted that Morocco allow their return.[157] Urged by Congress, USCIRF sent a delegation, whose report largely sided with the missionaries.[158] The State Department's 2010 IRF report refers to the incident as an example of "decline in some respects" of Morocco's religious freedom environment.[159] Moroccan government officials, however, came to hold a very different opinion about the incident. In the words of one of its diplomats:

> As Morocco is becoming more open, Evangelicals think they can exploit this to proselytize. There is in fact an explicit desire to target Muslims. After the expulsion of the missionaries, many in America said that Morocco was against Christians. Muslims have come to perceive this as an American Evangelical crusade to convert them.[160]

---

[154] Mahmood (2012).
[155] Barnett (2015, 23).
[156] Berkley Center (2008).
[157] In this circumstance, along with Frank Wolf, other particularly vocal Republican Members of Congress included Chris Smith and Trent Franks (Rosensaft 2010).
[158] USCIRF (2011, 350–353).
[159] OIRF (2010).
[160] Moroccan Diplomat (2011, author's interview). Not all supporters of this regime sided with the Western missionaries. Eliot Abrams (2010, author's interview) acknowledges that "missionaries having orphanages is more sensitive than just building a school or providing health. Morocco was right to get angry about the issue."

I am not suggesting here that the International Religious Freedom regime is a ploy for the advancement of Christianity globally at the expense of all other religions, particularly Islam. Nor am I suggesting that Christian communities are not being targeted, often deliberately, in the context of the violence that is gripping the Middle East in the past decades. I am arguing, though, that a number of domestic and international factors fuel the perception, as well as the reality in some cases, that international religious freedom advocacy and policies reflect the values, and support the interests of, Christian denominations more so than those of other religious traditions.

Religionizing World Politics

The regime, as a USCIRF official explains, is rooted in the notion that religion is "an important variable in international affairs."[161] Yet a religious foreign policy regime does not merely reflect a reality in which religion matters, but it can also be complicit in producing one where religion matters even more. In other words, the regime can contribute to processes of religionization in world politics, both through mechanisms of *elevation* and *categorization*.

First of all, religionization through elevation is in many respects a central objective of the regime. As Elizabeth Prodromou argues, while international religious freedom "is not really about promoting religion," its intent is nonetheless to "create the possibility for religious outcomes, fostering the institutions and regulatory frameworks which create an enabling environment for religion."[162] The regime is certainly facilitating the presence of religious perspectives and interests in the making and implementation of American foreign policy. Whether it is also generating an enabling environment for faith globally remains to be seen, given its patchy success record.

In parallel, the regime actively contributes to religionizing world politics through mechanisms of categorization. Its institutions, discourses, and practices regularly (re)present and (re)produce a world dominated by religious categories and realities: one in which actors, identities, motives, causes, cleavages, conflicts, or abuses are overwhelmingly framed as religious, thus overlooking what are often multiple nonreligious identities that actors may hold and the complex underlying political, social, and economic dimensions which can explain events in world politics. Through the lenses of the regime we appear to live in a world made exclusively of Christians, Muslims, Sunnis, Shia's, Jews, Baha'is, Alevis, and Buddhists, among others, who act and participate in public life or who are freed, tolerated, incarcerated, and killed primarily because of their religious beliefs or identities.

The interesting question, which needs further probing, is whether this process of religionization through categorization by the International Religious Freedom regime amplifies existing narratives and identities employed in the

---

[161] USCIRF Official 1 (2010, author's interview).
[162] Prodromou (2011, author's interview).

world from the bottom-up, or whether it produces new religious ones from the top-down. Probably both. In some instances, the regime does reflect and elevate religious categories already employed by actors on the ground, whether it is groups claiming to be persecuted qua religious groups, say Baha'is in Iran, or whether it is the narrative employed by extremist Islamist organizations—such as Al Qaeda or ISIS—who regularly frame their social and political reality along religious lines and divides. In other instances, though, this foreign policy regime may be incentivizing or socializing some actors to adopt and present themselves through religious categories. Melani McAlister notices for instance how—in a slightly different context—Sudanese refugees in Egypt have found it useful to claim to be "a persecuted Christian" to obtain "asylum status or help from UN programs."[163]

Regime Diffusion in International Policy

International religious freedom policy and the constellation of actors tied to it have contributed to the diffusion and proliferation of similar initiatives and regimes among allied, mostly Western, countries and multilateral institutions. It may well be that the multiple arrangements which have sprung up to promote religious liberty globally since the 2000s in places like Canada, Italy, the United Kingdom, or the EU are themselves the product of similar forces that have brought about change in the American context—chiefly, macro-level postsecular processes and micro-level desecularizing agents and discourses. This said, there is also evidence that the American experience and its actions are playing an important role in this process.

In the United Kingdom, the Foreign and Commonwealth Office (FCO) has issued since 2010 a series of guidelines and toolkits on promoting "freedom of religion or belief" abroad.[164] In 2012, British Parliamentarians launched an All Party Parliamentary Group on Freedom of Religion or Belief.[165] These initiatives have gained momentum in the context of sustained transatlantic interactions between American and British advocates, experts, and policymakers concerned with international religious freedom policies.[166] Canada, mirroring its southern neighbor, established during the conservative government of Stephen Harper its own Office of Religious Freedom in the Department of Foreign Affairs and International Trade between 2013 and 2016. When Italy's Ministry of Foreign Affairs briefly operated an Oversight Committee for Religious Freedom between 2012 and 2014, a press statement specified that the country was "following the lead of the United States, Canada and other

---

[163] McAlister (2013).
[164] For example, FCO (2015).
[165] More information on the All Party Parliamentary Group on Freedom of Religion or Belief is available at https://freedomdeclared.org/ (accessed June 5, 2016).
[166] Birdsall (2014a); Petito et al. (2016); Warsi (2013). See also FCO-sponsored conferences at Wilton Park such as "Promoting Religious Freedom around the World" held in July 2011 and "Developing a Multilateral Approach to Freedom of Religion or Belief: a European Perspective" held in February 2015.

countries."[167] The European Union (EU) would publish its own Guidelines on the Promotion and Protection of Freedom of Religion or Belief in 2013.[168] In 2014 an International Panel of Parliamentarians for Freedom of Religion or Belief was launched as the result of a partnership between the British All-Party Parliamentary Group and USCIRF, and in 2015 America's IRF ambassador and its Canadian counterpart spearheaded the International Contact Group on Freedom of Religion or Belief, which included over twenty-five governments working on similar issues.

Two general pathways of American influence are discernible: a direct (push) and an indirect (pull). The former pathway involves American advocates, experts, and policymakers purposively acting as international religious freedom norm entrepreneurs. They share their experience and coordinate networks to advance similar arrangements abroad. In the latter pathway, the American International Religious Freedom regime acts as a blueprint that advocates and policymakers in other states seek to mimic, or refer to in order to legitimize and expand similar activities in their own foreign policies. The extent and type of influence exercised by the institutions and actors tied to this religious foreign policy regime across different international contexts remains to be further empirically explored and assessed.

Interestingly, with the global and comparative spread of similar religious foreign policy regimes, general tendencies inherent to international religious freedom policies and those more specific to the US case have become increasingly discernible. A revealing common denominator across the Western world, for instance, is that Christian actors, interests, and concerns dominate this policy space. In Canada, similar perceptions of a Christian-bias in the staffing and agenda of its international religious freedom office existed.[169] When announcing Italy's Observatory, the only religious individuals and communities of concern mentioned in the foreign ministry's communiqué were Christian.[170] The EU's first-ever Special Envoy for the Promotion of Freedom of Religion or Belief—Jan Figel, a former head of the Slovak Christian Democratic party—was officially presented in an atmosphere caustically described by *The Economist* as overwhelmingly "Catholic."[171] On the other hand, compared to the United States, Europeans speak about these issues in terms of freedom of religion and belief (FoRB). In the context of Europe's strong secular tradition, the focus also on *belief* has meant that nonreligious voices (atheists, humanists, and secularists) are given greater recognition and, as Jocelyne Cesari further notes, greater latitude to "criticize religion."[172]

---

[167] Ministero degli Affari Esteri (2012, author's translation). On the Italian experience more generally, see Annicchino (2013b), Ferrara (2013a).
[168] Council of the European Union (2013). For an engagement by USCIRF staff in the European debate around the guidelines see Thames (2012).
[169] Bjornson (2013).
[170] Ministero degli Affari Esteri (2012).
[171] *The Economist* (2016).
[172] Cesari (2015, author's interview); also Petito et al. (2016).

Conclusion

In the space of two decades, systematic attention to religious freedom internationally has substantially grown in US foreign policy. The promotion of religious freedom abroad, once mostly an ad hoc practice, now boasts a budding institutional, policymaking, and normative infrastructure. The International Religious Freedom regime also counts on a well-organized network of religious advocates and experts outside of government relentlessly working to raise the profile of this foreign policy and of international religious freedom issues more broadly. This constellation of actors has organized itself around three—at times competing, other times overlapping—desecularizing discourses which articulate either a *particularist principled* concern for the persecution of Christians and other minorities by Communist regimes or Muslims, a *universalist principled* concern for religious freedom as a broader human rights issue, or a *strategic* understanding of religious freedom as a means to achieve a range of national security ends.

Critiques of this foreign policy regime argue that religious freedom has become "the civilizing discourse of our time" with often negative far-reaching social, political, and religious consequences.[173] This may be an exaggeration, given the continued constraints—institutional, resource, cultural, and strategic—the international religious freedom agenda faces in American foreign policy that I have highlighted throughout. Nonetheless, the regime can no longer be said to be, as Thomas Farr once put it, just a "boutique issue" in "one of the more secular departments of government."[174] Thinking about, reporting on, and advancing religious freedom has become part and parcel of America's approach to promoting human rights as well as a constant presence in security debates concerning the fight against terrorism and strife in the Middle East. While certain curbs have been put on the resources and manpower of USCIRF, OIRF staff and responsibilities have consistently grown over time. Compared to the early 2000s, the office now manages a continuously expanding pool of resources and programs, counts a novel Special Envoy for Religious Minorities, and its roles and responsibilities have been both broadened and deepened thanks to a 2016 Congressional act named after Frank Wolf.

In the process, the boundaries between the religious and the secular in American foreign policy have been redrawn. Processes of institutional, epistemic, ideological, and state-normative desecularization that underpin the International Religious Freedom regime are opening up greater spaces for the organized and sustained inclusion, reification, positive essentialization, and normative accommodation of religious actors, concerns, and voices in US foreign policy.

---

[173] Hurd (2014a).
[174] Farr (2016).

It still remains to be seen whether the world will become religiously free as envisioned by international religious freedom advocates and policymakers. What is evident, though, is that through this regime US foreign policy is increasingly intervening in global religious and secular dynamics in a number of specific ways. First, despite concerted attention made by the regime to align itself to international norms and standards, American values and interests exercise a profound influence on what the regime counts as religion and which religiosities are deemed as deserving to be free. In short, the regime includes multiple—at times contradicting—perspectives. It adopts a radically pluralist view of religion which is inclusive of an extremely broad range of religious minorities and any group claiming to be one. It is informed by Protestant particularist and liberal notions of belief which overwhelmingly treat conversions—and attempts at promoting these—as an uncontroversial right. It embeds liberal notions of politics which influence what kind of religious traditions are especially allowed to be free. Along with certain ideational features, the historical, institutional, and demographic makeup of the regime tend to favor the interests and perspectives of Christian individuals, groups, and communities relatively to others.

Second, the regime contributes to religionizing world politics. It does so by seeking to protect and open up greater spaces for the presence of religious actors and perspectives in US foreign policymaking and in the public sphere of countries around the globe, as well as by adopting discourses and practices that (re)produce religious categories in and explanations of the world. Lastly, it is promoting—directly and indirectly—the diffusion of similar foreign policy regimes across Western and multilateral partners.

What does the future hold for the International Religious Freedom regime? It is very likely that the regime will continue into the foreseeable future given its Congressional mandate. Despite elements of path dependency, which shape the regime's institutional infrastructure and its core competences in important ways since its inception in the 1990s, the regime is clearly capable of growing and evolving over time. As this chapter showed, changes can be driven by new international and security circumstances, the emergence of novel domestic constituencies, and by shifts in the direction imposed on American foreign policy by different presidents.

Under the current Trump presidency, as of late 2018, international religious freedom issues appear to be receiving particular attention by the administration. A novel IRF ambassador-at-large was appointed relatively quickly, in the figure of a political heavyweight like Sam Brownback—a former (Republican) Senator and Governor, and among the key sponsors of IRFA in 1998. The president and vice president themselves have spoken out repeatedly on the issue of religious freedom at home and abroad. Secretary of State Mike Pompeo held the first ever Ministerial to Advance Religious Freedom in July 2018, a major three-day meeting that brought together foreign ministers, international organization representatives, religious leaders, and civil society representatives to the State Department to share experiences and coordinate efforts.

Trump's National Security Strategy stresses its commitment to this issue by emphatically stating, in a section titled "Champion American Values": "The United States also remains committed to supporting and advancing religious freedom—America's first freedom."[175]

What has been evident as well is the administration's shift toward embracing more explicitly than in past decades a perspective that largely reflects the particularist principled desecularizing discourse concerned with the persecution of Christians, along with its anti-Islamic undertones, articulated most prominently by Religious Right desecularizing actors and certain Republican political figures. Indeed, conservative Evangelicals have been among the staunchest backers and most important allies of President Trump. These include Vice President Mike Pence, who defines himself as "a Christian, a conservative, and a Republican, in that order."[176] Pence is a vocal supporter of international religious freedom, especially for Christians in the context of ongoing violence taking place in the Middle East.[177] Sam Brownback, like Pence, has often sided with (conservative) Christian causes at home, including opposition to abortion and LGBTQ causes. So far, he has done little to alleviate concerns from multiple sources that his primary interest as IRF ambassador would be for the welfare of Christians around the world.[178] The tilt toward a religious-freedom-for-Christians approach has been matched by a parallel rise in anti-Islamic sentiments within the administration and by policies restricting similar rights for Muslims; most notably in the context of President Trump's "travel ban," otherwise also commonly known as the "Muslim ban."[179]

---

[175] USG (2017, 41).

[176] Pence (2017).

[177] See, among others, Pence's (2017) speech delivered in occasion of the 2017 World Summit in Defense of Persecuted Christians organized by Franklin Graham, an Evangelical pastor and son of the famous Billy Graham (also Green 2017).

[178] *The Economist* (2017).

[179] On Islamophobic statements by Donald Trump and members of his administration, see Gjelten (2018); Hirsh (2016). For a critique by supporters of international religious freedom policy of the pro-Christian and anti-Muslim approach adopted by the Trump administration, see Henne (2018).

CHAPTER 4 | Faith-Based Foreign Aid

In every instance where my Administration sees a responsibility to help people, we will look first to faith-based organizations, to charities, and to community groups.

—presidential candidate George W. Bush, 1999[1]

THE ROOTS OF THE modern-day humanitarian and development sector, some suggest, can be traced back to the colonial era when European Christian missionaries were treading the globe intent on saving souls as well as meeting the physical needs of non-Europeans.[2] More fundamentally, at the heart of most religious traditions rests an impulse to assist the least fortunate among us— codified in the practice of *zakat* in Islam or the parable of the Good Samaritan in the New Testament for example—which is often at the core of contemporary humanitarianism.[3] And yet faith has not featured large in America's postwar foreign aid activities.

Two factors are important to note here. First, the modern aid sector, which largely emerged in the twentieth century out of the ashes of two World Wars and in the context of the Cold War, has tended to be inimical toward religion. When the US Agency for International Development (USAID) was created in the early 1960s, development approaches were rooted in the secularist assumptions of modernization theory.[4] This paradigm posited religion as a hindrance, at best, or as the very antithesis to human progress, at worst.

Second, between the 1940s and 1990s, US government support to religious organizations for service provision was increasingly viewed as problematic. During this time, the Supreme Court adopted an increasingly strict separationist interpretation of the Establishment Clause of the Constitution's

[1] Bush in White House (2008).
[2] Barnett (2011, especially Part I); Thaut (2009, 322).
[3] Barnett and Stein (2012).
[4] Barnett (2011, especially ch. 6); Clarke (2007, 79); Deneulin and Bano (2009, especially ch. 2).

First Amendment, declaring the funding of religion as, by and large, unconstitutional. The Court distinguished between "pervasively religious" organizations, which systematically mixed religion and service provision, and those that were merely religiously affiliated but delivered social services along secular lines. Being perceived as pervasively religious significantly curtailed an organization's chances of receiving government funding.[5] These two factors together alimented a view where religious actors where scarcely seen as valuable partners and where faith-based organizations faced substantial restrictions in accessing federal resources for delivering aid abroad.

Faith-based organization (FBO) is a general term for an organization that engages in humanitarian and development work, which "derives inspiration and guidance for its activities from the teachings and principles of the faith or from a particular interpretation or school of thought within the faith."[6] FBOs greatly vary in size, scope, objectives, worldview, theology, and in their relationship with established religious structures. Based on the extent to which religious identity, goals, values, and practices—including worship, prayer, and proselytization—permeate an FBO's institutional structure and humanitarian activities, these organizations can be ranked on a continuum that stretches from less to highly pervasively religious.

On the lower pervasively religious end of the spectrum are what some call "synthesis humanitarian agencies" or "secular Christian" non-governmental organizations (NGOs).[7] In the United States these are mostly Catholic, Mainline Protestant, and ecumenically minded FBOs, such as Catholic Relief Services, Episcopal Relief and Development, Lutheran World Relief, or Mercy Corps. While these FBOs are religiously inspired and motivated, their primary goals are overwhelmingly humanitarian and developmental in nature. Accordingly, they do not overtly and publicly infuse their assistance programs with religious messages nor engage in missionary and proselytizing work. In their hiring practices and frontline operations these organizations tend to mirror secular NGOs, from which they are at times indistinguishable.

On the highly pervasively religious end of the spectrum are what some label "Evangelical humanitarian agencies" or "Militant Christian" NGOs.[8] These FBOs are generally rooted in more theologically conservative Protestant Evangelical denominations. Two factors distinguish these FBOs from the rest. First, they tend to hire according to religious belief and belonging. Second, as Gerard Clarke explains, "they combine humanitarian and development activities with a fervent commitment to winning converts to the faith."[9] Many put proselytizing—that is, "efforts taken by individuals or groups to seek the

---

[5] Pew Research Center (2009c, 2). See also DiIulio (2007, especially chs. 1, 2); Rogers and Dionne (2008).
[6] Clarke and Jennings (2008b, 6).
[7] See, respectively, Thaut (2009) and Benedetti (2006).
[8] See, respectively, Thaut (2009) and Benedetti (2006).
[9] Clarke (2007, 83).

conversion of another"[10]—and humanitarianism and development work on the same plane. Such proselytizing may take different forms, from more explicit and coercive attempts, which may involve the use of material inducements, to more indirect approaches that many FBOs call "witnessing," namely acting out a Christian ethic of care and sharing one's faith only upon being asked about it.[11] The most pervasively religious FBOs may even see their religious commitments and duties as the main purpose of their humanitarian work.[12] As a country director for Samaritan's Purse, a major Evangelical FBO, explains, "we are first a Christian organization and second an aid organization."[13]

While USAID has not completely shied away from partnering with FBOs, prior to the 1990s such partnerships were overwhelmingly entered into with the less religiously pervasive organizations. Mark Brinkmoeller, interviewed in 2011 while at the ONE Campaign, frames USAID's history with FBOs as follows:

> When it comes to USAID's engagement with FBOs, Catholics and Episcopal groups have always been involved to some degree, Evangelicals less so. That's because Catholic and Episcopalians . . . can speak in secular terms about religious issues. Evangelicals instead speak in an explicitly religious language . . . and are less inclined to use secular terminology. Catholics and Mainline Protestants are comfortable not to do "God speak," Evangelicals are not.[14]

Moreover, notwithstanding a few exceptions, American foreign aid institutions and practices would scarcely admit the importance of the sacred as an aspect of human development and flourishing. In fact, for much of its modern history, the relationship between America's foreign aid policy and religion could be safely described as "fragile and intermittent at best, critical and confrontational at worst."[15]

From the 2000s onward, however, a progressive movement from "estrangement to engagement" between US foreign aid policy and religion started to take place.[16] As soon as George W. Bush entered the White House in 2001, he made good on campaign promises to "look first to faith-based organizations" when seeking to help those in need.[17] He did so by using his executive powers

---

[10] Witte (2001, 625–626).

[11] Lynch and Schwarz (2016, 4–6).

[12] See Bornstein (2002, 9); Hearn (2002, 34); Kniss and Campbell (1997, 100); Thaut (2009, 349). Jonathan Agensky (2013) warns however against conflating all too readily Evangelical agencies with the contemporary missionary enterprise. In his view FBOs have actually become a key pillar of the wider global humanitarian governance architecture, with its in-built technical-rational secularizing pressures.

[13] Cottle (2003).

[14] Brinkmoeller (2011, author's interview). For a similar perspective, see also King (2012, 927).

[15] Marshall and Keough (2004, 1). While Marshall and Keough discuss the relationship between multilateral donors (e.g., UN and World Bank) and religion, their insights apply as well to the relationship between faith and bilateral donors like USAID.

[16] Clarke (2007, 79). While Clark discusses changes occurring in the wider aid sector, I find that these apply as well to the US foreign policy context.

[17] Bush in White House (2008).

to launch what was then labeled the Faith-Based and Community Initiative. The initiative's intent was, among other things, to "level the playing field" between secular NGOs and religious FBOs,[18] and give greater opportunities to religious organizations—including highly pervasively religious ones—to access US government resources for the delivery not just of domestic services but also of international aid. Partnerships between the federal government and religious organizations received a further boost with a $15 billion President's Emergency Plan for AIDS Relief (PEPFAR) in 2004. In some cases, PEPFAR requirements even tilted the playing field in favor of FBOs over NGOs.

With this step-change, what I call the *Faith-Based Foreign Aid regime* was born. Under President Obama, the regime's infrastructure and operations would be deepened and broadened overall. Within the space of just two presidencies, partnering with religious organizations—including with pervasively religious FBOs—would become increasingly seen as acceptable and desirable. As Melissa Rogers, a scholar of religion and policymaker in the faith-based aid space, tellingly argued in 2011:

> There has always been a level of engagement between government and religious groups. Today, however, this relationship is even more intentional, visible to the public, and widespread.[19]

The emergence under President Bush and continuation with President Obama of the Faith-Based Foreign Aid regime raises some puzzling questions. Republicans and conservatives are notoriously skeptical of spending government resources on social services and foreign assistance. How is it possible, then, that the Bush administration's legacy would be defined in significant ways by its commitment to developmental and humanitarian causes, especially thanks to the Faith-Based and Community Initiative and PEPFAR?[20] Moreover, why did the Faith-Based Foreign Aid regime not wither away with the arrival of Barack Obama? Indeed, many on the left were surprised and disconcerted to see President Obama expand, rather than curb, the presence of religious actors in the delivery of social services at home and aid abroad.[21]

The next section begins to answer some of these questions by outlining the constellation of desecularizing actors, clustered around specific discourses, supporting the operationalization and continuation of America's Faith-Based Foreign Aid regime. Here I further show how the various actors are embedded in a wider macro social and historical context marked by postsecular dynamics, as well as benefitting from particular post-Cold War exogenous trends such as globalization and the expansion of the aid sector. The subsequent two sections trace the causal process that led to the institutionalization

---

[18] White House (2001).
[19] Rogers (2011, author's interview). In 2013 Rogers would be appointed Executive Director of Obama's White House Office of Faith-Based and Neighborhood Partnerships.
[20] Robinson (2012).
[21] Berlinerblau and Salmon in Berkley Center (2009, 4:44–5:33); Sullivan (2009).

of the regime under President Bush and its subsequent evolution under the Obama administration. They show how the institutions and operations of the regime evolved over time, reflecting the interests of distinct religious and political coalitions within the heterogeneous constellation of desecularizing actors championing the regime, and their ideological affinities with the two different administrations. The chapter then unpacks the types and degrees of foreign policy desecularization that sustain and are in turn promoted by the Faith-Based Foreign Aid regime. The section that follows focuses on the ways in which the regime may be shaping religious and secular realities globally. The conclusion summarizes the chapter's findings, compares key elements of the regime to the International Religious Freedom one, and considers ongoing developments under the Trump administration.

Desecularizing Actors and Discourses in Context

From the late 1980s onward, a heterogeneous constellation of desecularizing actors would emerge with the intent of pushing for greater attention to religion and support for religious organizations by the US federal government when seeking to provide relief to those in need. This constellation of actors can be subdivided into four more coherent groupings and their desecularizing discourses. Two emerged chiefly in conservative religious, expert, and political milieus advocating that conservatives pay greater attention than in the past to the poor and the sick, and that religion would provide a valuable resource for alleviating their suffering and improve their lives. Another set of principled and strategic desecularizing discourses emerged among more progressive milieus, urging Democrats as well as humanitarian and development experts to pay greater attention to the important role of religious ethics and organizations in assisting the poor and the sick they cared about. To begin with, much of the focus of desecularizing actors was on opening up government resources to FBOs for service provision at the domestic level. It is on the back of such efforts that attention and energies were then devoted to foreign aid institutions and practices. In other words, to understand changes in foreign policy, as this section will show, we also need to consider developments in domestic policy.

Religious Principled Desecularizing Discourse: Ending the Discrimination of FBOs

A key development in American politics over the past decades was the emergence of the Christian Right, a movement—as argued also in chapter 2—embedded within processes of religious resurgence. Many conservative Protestant Evangelicals and Catholics saw religion as being pushed aside in the public sphere by secular forces throughout the twentieth century, especially through court cases that made prayer in school illegal, allowed the teaching of evolution, and legalized abortion. For many conservative Christians, reclaiming what Father Richard John Neuhaus caustically labeled the "naked public square"[22] became a social and political priority.

This agenda took multiple paths during the 1980s and 1990s. One particularly well-known path was to engage in the so-called culture wars over issues of gender, family, and sexuality.[23] Another was to advance claims that religious organizations who did not want to give up their explicitly religious character were being unjustly barred from accessing federal funds to deliver domestic social services to support those in need—whether youth, prisoners, or addicts. "In the religious milieu there is a sense of grievance that religion has been unfairly squeezed out of the public sphere," Mark Brinkmoeller explains, "as a reaction there are strong voices pushing for a less strict separation and greater access to government resources."[24] By the early 1990s, a process of contestation from below of strict separationist interpretations of the Establishment Clause thus began. This would be expressed through the articulation and deployment of a principled desecularizing discourse that demanded "equal treatment" for religious organizations compared to secular NGOs, and an end to "discrimination" in accessing governmental resources for the provision of services and welfare.[25]

In parallel, an exogenous trend was taking place that facilitated this process of contestation. During the 1990s the federal government gradually rolled back its involvement in social service provision. "The emergence of a neoliberal consensus across the political spectrum," Elizabeth Prodromou highlights, "brought Democrats to think that government 'could not' and Republicans that it 'should not' provide welfare services."[26] This shift in thinking and policy, Prodromou continues, "opened a vacuum that faith-based organizations stepped in to fill."[27]

It is in this context—marked by religious resurgence, principled discourses contesting the exclusion of religious actors, and exogenous neoliberal trends—that steps were taken toward the creation of the first federally sanctioned faith-based initiative. In 1996, a Charitable Choice provision was introduced in Congress as part of a larger welfare reform bill, the Personal Responsibility and Work Opportunity Reconciliation Act, proposed by two Republican Senators, John Ashcroft, a devout Pentecostal, and Rick Santorum, a devout Catholic. Passed by a Republican-controlled Congress and signed into law by President Clinton, the provision along with the act were designed to reduce the government's direct role and encourage the participation of civil society

---

[22] Neuhaus (1984).
[23] Hartman (2015).
[24] Brinkmoeller (2011, author's interview).
[25] An extensive list of statements, reports, and publications by faith-based actors mobilizing around such discourse are available on the Center for Public Justice's website, at http://www.cpjustice.org/content/resources (accessed May 16, 2017).
[26] Prodromou (2011, author's interview).
[27] Ibid.

organizations, especially religious ones, in service delivery. Religious organizations receiving state or federal funding were now being allowed to "carry out their missions consistent with their beliefs."[28] This meant that they could deliver services in a religious environment and hire according to religious preferences. While organizations of all religious denominations were intended to benefit, the highly pervasively religious ones—mostly Evangelical—were among the bill's biggest beneficiaries.[29]

Charitable Choice, passed by a Republican-majority Congress and signed into law by a Democratic president, heralded an emerging bipartisan consensus on the desirability of closer state–religion cooperation for aiding the needy. It is in this context that two further principled desecularizing discourses emerged on the right and on the left emphasizing the necessity and virtue of expanding Charitable Choice into a more structured faith-based initiative at the domestic as well as international level.

Conservative Principled Desecularizing Discourse: Compassionate Conservatism

Among conservative intellectual and political elites, a principled desecularizing discourse emerged around the 1990s known as the compassionate conservative agenda. Marvin Olasky, an Evangelical intellectual, was among its most articulate proponents.[30] According to a former Chief of Staff to Republican Senator Rick Santorum, compassionate conservatism "was fundamental for opening up space among conservatives to talk about poverty."[31] This agenda married neoliberal ideas of small government with Evangelical ones seeking a bigger role for religion in society. It argued that conservatives should follow Jesus in caring for the poor and downtrodden, and that the best way to deliver care was not through big government but through civil society and religious organizations who were closer to the needs of their communities. Government's role was to support religious organizations, not to replace them.

Compassionate conservatism became a central theme in the 2000 presidential campaign of the then Texas Governor George W. Bush. Bush was an enthusiastic supporter of Olasky, a longtime friend and advisor, and of Charitable Choice, which he implemented in Texas. Bush's receptiveness to the cause sprung from a mix of religious affinities, personal convictions, and electoral incentives. Key to this was his own born-again faith journey, inspired by "America's pastor" Billy Graham. For Bush, this religious experience was transformative, enabling him to defeat his alcoholism and undertake

---

[28] White House (n.d.).

[29] Rebecca Sager (2010, 17) similarly suggests that Charitable Choice came about through a combination of two forces: "desecularization" (i.e., "the increasingly prominent role of religion in politics and policy") and "devolution" (i.e., "the growing devolution of government social services to the nonprofit and private sectors").

[30] Olasky (1992; 2000).

[31] Rodgers (2011, author's interview). Similar ideas were expressed to me by Hart (2011).

the journey that would lead him to the presidency.[32] Campaign strategist Karl Rove furthermore encouraged Bush's explicitly religious rhetoric, artfully penned by his Evangelical speechwriter Michael Gerson.[33] "Rove believed that in a context where Evangelicals were becoming a growing political force," the Evangelical intellectual Michael Cromartie argues, "the compassionate agenda could do much to mobilize the vote."[34] Making electoral inroads into poorer and religiously vibrant African-American communities entered these calculations too.[35]

Desecularizing experts who spearheaded thinking on these issues included Marvin Olasky himself, John DiIulio, and James Wilson, all of whom were invited during the campaign to give policy guidance on how to translate the compassionate conservative agenda into a nationwide faith-based initiative.[36] It was thus no coincidence that candidate Bush's first major policy address, from which this chapter's opening quote is drawn, was delivered to a church audience in Indianapolis on July 22, 1999. The speech, titled "Duty of Hope," included promises to expand the role of faith-based charities through the relaxation of norms mandating a strict separation of church and state, and the introduction of new funding streams for religious organizations.[37]

Progressive Principled Desecularizing Discourse: Faith-Based Progressivism

While the faith-based initiatives received chequered support among liberals, some sections of the Democratic establishment embraced them more enthusiastically. After all, President Clinton had signed the Charitable Choice laws in 1998 and presidential candidate Al Gore in 2000 explicitly welcomed a more faith-friendly government.[38] Such positions, however, were met with considerable resistance by important sections of the Democratic Party: progressive activists and liberal intellectuals remained skeptical about the role of religion in public life—especially in the context of the culture wars.[39] Yet as religious

---

[32] Bush (2010, 31–34).

[33] *Time* magazine nominated Gerson, in 2005, among the most influential Evangelicals in America (*Time* 2005). In his speechwriting career Gerson is credited for adding much of the religious language that characterized President Bush's speeches, including coining the famous "axis of evil" expression referring to Iraq, Iran, and North Korea.

[34] Cromartie (2011, author's interview).

[35] The importance of this tripartite relationship—between the compassionate conservative movement, Bush's own faith, and Rove's political calculations—in setting the grounds for Bush's faith-based initiative, was also emphasized to me by Hart (2011). For similar perspectives, but with differing emphases on each of these factors, see DiIulio (2007); Kuo (2006); Sager (2010).

[36] Cromartie (2011); DiIulio (2007).

[37] See Brownstein (1999).

[38] DiIulio (2007, 85).

[39] Commentary on the "secular left vs. religious right" divide in American society and politics, often polemic in character from either side, abounds. For a reference connected to the topic of this chapter see DiIulio (2007, especially ch. 1). For scholarly explanations of this divide, see Hout and Fischer (2014); Putnam and Campbell (2010).

voters were increasingly flocking to the Republican Party, particularly in the election and then re-election of George W. Bush, some Democrats became ever more concerned with their party's so-called "God gap".[40]

Enter Barack Obama, then Senator with close connections to African American churches and a former community organizer with church-based groups in Chicago. More than any other Democrat in generations, Obama was comfortable speaking in public about his faith and acknowledging the positive contribution of religion to social and political life. Obama appeared determined to reclaim faith for progressive causes—such as social justice, curbing inequality, or reforming immigration laws—and revitalize America's Religious Left.[41] In a seminal 2006 speech delivered at a Sojourners conference, a Progressive Evangelical outlet led by Jim Wallis, then-Senator Obama chastised fellow liberals for "dismiss[ing] religion in the public square as inherently irrational or intolerant" and "abandon[ing] the field of religious discourses" to conservatives. "The problems of poverty and racism . . . are not simply technical problems" that government can fix, Obama explained, but "require changes in hearts and a change in minds" that religious groups can uniquely bring about. "Secularists are wrong when they ask believers to leave their religion at the door before entering into the public square," Obama continued, suggesting that great American reformers from Abraham Lincoln to Martin Luther King "repeatedly used religious language to argue for their cause."[42]

By 2008, presidential candidate Obama was investing considerable energy in closing the party's God gap. Not only did the then Senator happily speak about his faith during the campaign, but invested heavily in reaching out and courting Evangelical leaders and voters themselves.[43] According to some, Obama had built the "largest religious outreach team of any Democrat by a magnitude of four or five."[44] Advising and leading this effort were Evangelicals of a more progressive bent such Joshua DuBois and Mara Vanderslice, as well as Mainline Protestant scholars and theologians such as Shaun Casey. That Democrats were keen on making inroads among religious publics became even more evident when, in a campaign speech titled "Faith in America," then-Senator Obama "stunned"[45] liberal elites by promising to substantially strengthen America's engagement with FBOs.

---

[40] Steinfels (2006).
[41] Olson (2007); Pally (2013).
[42] Obama (2006). For commentary on the speech's historical and political importance see Dionne (2006).
[43] Pew Research Center (2008). Of high symbolic value was, among others, candidate Obama's appearance on the *Civil Forum on the Presidency* hosted by Rick Warren, an Evangelical pastor. The Forum was presented as the first major "debate"—although in the format of back-to-back interviews—between presidential candidates John McCain and Barack Obama and largely focused on matters of faith and morality.
[44] Shaun Casey in CAP (2009, 30:41–30:55).
[45] Berlinerblau in Berkley Center (2009, 4:44–5:13).

International Strategic Desecularizing Discourse: Limits of Secular Aid, Advantages of Faith-Based Approaches

While the previous three discourses were mostly articulated by and intended for domestic constituencies, a fourth, more internationalist desecularizing discourse emerged around the same period. This desecularizing discourse was mostly articulated by a network of actors from two distinct constituencies: by certain religious figures and leaders embedded within processes of religious resurgence, and by humanitarian and development experts who were representative of an emerging postsecular consciousness in the sector.

This desecularizing discourse was predominantly strategic, rather than principled, stressing the limits of secular aid practices and the advantages of faith-based approaches within the wider global humanitarian and development field. The humanitarian and development sector's secular blind spot, the discourse went, hampers the effectiveness of its standard operations for two reasons. First, they overlook the important role that religious belief, belonging, practices, and organizations play in local realities across the developing world. Second, they discount the unique contributions that FBOs, compared to secular NGOs and governmental counterparts, make in helping the vulnerable. These contributions include a more "holistic" understanding of humanitarian and development assistance that goes beyond the mere fulfillment of material needs,[46] and a distinctive set of tangible and intangible resources that religious actors and organizations possess and mobilize. These, the argument goes, include enjoying high levels of trust and legitimacy in local communities, global networks, and infrastructures that reach the poorest and remotest parts of the world, and important advantages in terms of human and financial resources including highly motivated staffers, vast pools of volunteers, and access to considerable funds from private citizens.[47]

The religious constituency mobilizing around such a discourse was overwhelmingly comprised by Christian—often Evangelical—organizations who were starting to pay greater attention to issues of global poverty.[48] By the turn

---

[46] Religious actors and desecularizing aid experts, respectively, tend to understand "holism" in different ways. For religious humanitarians, nonmaterial assistance includes providing spiritual support and growth, promoting faith-inspired morality and behaviors, forwarding ethical visions in the pursuit of a just society, and saving souls through conversions. For aid experts, holism is a way to critique neoliberal thinking in the humanitarian and development space, which privileges technical fixes and economic growth, and to recognize that the well-being of individuals and societies rests also on the fulfillment of a host of other values. An example of this approach is the notion of *human*, rather than solely *economic*, development (Sen 1999; see also Narayan et al. 2000).

[47] For faith-based voices making these claims, see Mugabi (2003); Steinitz (2006); Warren (2015). See also the *Practitioners and Faith-Inspired Development Interview Series* published online by Georgetown University's Berkley Center, available at http://berkleycenter.georgetown.edu/projects/practitioners-and-faith-inspired-development-interview-series (accessed May 16, 2017). For policy reports articulating the international strategic desecularizing discourse on the limits of secular aid, see Belshaw, Calderisi, and Sugden (2001); Green (2003); Marshall and Keough (2004). For scholarship highlighting the limits of secular aid, see Deneulin and Bano (2009); Thomas (2004); Tomalin (2013).

[48] See Huliaras (2008); King (2012); Mead (2006, 37–39).

of the millennium, pervasively religious Evangelical FBOs were emerging as energetic newcomers in a humanitarian and development field long dominated by secular NGOs and less pervasively religious Christian organizations such as Catholic Relief Services or Mercy Corps. Occasionally branded as "new Evangelicals,"[49] these religious actors saw government differently. No longer solely as the embodiment of everything "evil," argues Tom Hart at the ONE Campaign, and former Episcopal Church lobbyist, but also as a potential partner, "with its big money it could now be used to do big charity."[50] In 2004, for instance, the National Association of Evangelical's (NAE) was releasing a document titled *For the Health of the Nation: An Evangelical Call to Civic Responsibility*. The document became a "turning point" for Evangelicals' engagement on issues of global poverty, according to Brinkmoeller.[51] In it, Evangelicals were exhorted to actively engage not solely in time-honored conservative battles, like abortion, but on global social justice and humanitarian issues as well, including caring for the poor, the sick, the environment, fair trade, human rights, and peace. Evangelicals were invited to make these issues "a central concern of American foreign policy" and support "international aid agencies."[52]

The internationalization of American Evangelicals' outlook occurred in the context of a dramatic growth in global missionary activity, which itself took place against the backdrop of exogenous globalizing trends. This development was so monumental that it led some to argue that "the beginning of the new millennium marks not the end of the missionary era but its high point."[53] Missions around the world, and the progressive globalization of the Evangelical movement itself, contributed to raise awareness among Evangelicals back home in the United States of the desperate needs of people in far-flung places.[54] It is thus that HIV/AIDS became a major concern for instance. Christian leaders and organizations long ignored or stigmatized the disease, which they saw as God's punishment for the "sinful" behavior of prostitutes, homosexuals, and drug addicts. Attitudes started changing as the flocks and pastors of churches across Africa became infected too, and as orphanages—often church-based—started swelling with HIV-positive children. Since HIV/AIDS involved issues of sexuality, some in

---

49 Pally (2013).
50 Hart (2011, author's interview).
51 Brinkmoeller (2010, author's interview).
52 NAE (2004, 9).
53 Hearn (2002, 32). By the late 1980s, roughly nine out of ten American Protestant missionaries were from an Evangelical (including Pentecostal) congregation, displacing Mainline denominations who had dominated the field (Hearn 2002, 39). Robert Wuthnow (2009, 23) estimates that in 2001, the number of Americans who traveled abroad as volunteer missionaries was 350.000 for those who stayed between two weeks to one year, and a further 1 million for those who stayed less than two weeks. By the late 2000s, American churches were spending nearly $4 billion annually on overseas ministries, almost a 50 percent increase over the previous decade (Wuthnow 2009, 1). Asteris Huliaras (2008, 162) reports that in 2002, for example, the Southern Baptist Convention spent $290 million abroad, mainly in Asia and Africa, establishing more than 8,000 churches and baptizing more than 421,000 converts.
54 On the globalization of American Evangelicals, see McAlister (2018).

the Evangelical community saw interventions in this space as an opportunity to promote their views on religion, sex, and family.[55]

Whether this emerging interest in the well-being of the poor and sick worldwide is genuine or instrumental for the purposes of proselytizing remains hotly debated.[56] What is evident, though, is that Evangelical agencies carrying out international humanitarian and development work have grown exponentially. In 2004, American Evangelical FBOs accounted for 48 percent of the total number of religious humanitarian agencies and 33 percent of all relief and development agencies, compared to only 8 percent of Catholic organizations.[57] By 2012, according to some estimates, Evangelical organizations accounted for around 80 percent of all Western-based Christian FBOs.[58]

Evangelical FBOs vary in size and scope, ranging from a multitude of smaller "invisible,"[59] mostly church-planting operations to larger professionalized agencies, like World Vision. World Vision, for instance, is currently one of the largest providers of international relief and development assistance in the world. Its total annual operating revenue was around $1billion yearly between 2011 and 2015.[60] With over 40,000 staff in nearly a hundred countries, it has more staff members than CARE, Save the Children, and USAID combined. Other major Evangelical FBOs include Franklin Graham's Samaritan's Purse, Pat Robertson's Operation Blessing, and Food for the Hungry. Prominent figures, particularly in the HIV/AIDS space, include Rick Warren and his Saddleback Church, and Bishop Charles Blake of the Church of God in Christ, the largest Pentecostal church in the United States, who founded Save Africa's Children (SAC) in 2001 specifically to support children affected by HIV/AIDS and poverty.

The other important constituency mobilizing around an international strategic desecularizing discourse in foreign aid included humanitarian and development experts who represent a developing postsecular consciousness in the sector. With the end of the Cold War in the 1990s, the international donor and NGO sector went through an exponential growth.[61] In many parts of the developing world, the retreat of the state—due to the loss of Cold War patronages in some cases, and to neoliberal economic reforms in others—was opening up a vacuum in service provision that civil society would increasingly seek to fill. Unexpectedly, in the eyes of secular international aid experts, religious civil society actors were among those who most consistently stepped forward.[62]

---

[55] Burkhalter (2004); Epstein (2005); Prince, Denis, and van Dijk (2009).
[56] See debates held at the 2015 conference "Sharing the Message? Proselytism and Development in Pluralistic Societies" organized by Georgetown University's Berkley Center available at http://berkleycenter.georgetown.edu/events/sharing-the-message-proselytism-and-development-in-pluralistic-societies-a-public-dialogue (accessed May 16, 2017).
[57] Thaut (2009, 323).
[58] Barnett and Stein (2012, 5).
[59] Hearn (2002).
[60] World Vision (2015).
[61] Barnett (2011, especially Part III).
[62] See Deneulin and Rakodi (2011, 46–48); Lipsky (2011, 31).

Humanitarian and development experts increasingly started to recognize that religions were not withering as predicted by secularization theories, but were actively engaging in the social, economic and political life of the societies they sought to aid. Drawing on the work of prominent scholars who challenged secularization theory, such as Casanova, Berger, and Habermas, voices calling for the humanitarian field to "rewrite its secular script," to "reconsider secularism as a norm," and to "revisit religion" would become ever more common.[63]

By the late 1990s several seminal initiatives emerged seeking to bridge the secular–religious divide in the humanitarian and development fields, which reflected this growing convergence of interests between religious actors and postsecular aid experts. In 1998 World Bank President James Wolfensohn together with Archbishop George Carey of Canterbury launched the World Faith Development Dialogue (WFDD).[64] The Jubilee 2000 campaign—which drew heavily on religious themes—saw faith leaders partnering with U2's Bono and other music and Hollywood celebrities to lobby G8 countries to cancel the debt of the world's poorest countries. Among the faith-based voices, Protestant Evangelicals became particularly active and important political players in the campaign since, as Tom Hart recalls, "Evangelicals had an ease of access to the Bush administration that others did not enjoy as much."[65]

Overall, by the 1990s and 2000s, then, a range of desecularizing discourses were being articulated by a complex constellation of actors advocating on principled and strategic grounds for a closer relationship between faith and aid. On the one hand, religious voices—generally of Protestant Evangelical origin—were pushing conservatives to care more about the needs of the poor and sick. On the other, parallel forces were calling on more progressive and liberal milieus—whether in the Democratic Party or across the humanitarian and development field—to recognize the positive contribution that religious perspectives and organizations could make to those in need. Starting from different premises, ultimately these multiple constituencies, coalitions, and networks of actors all converged toward a consensus that a greater and more structured nexus between religion and service provision at home and aid delivery abroad would be desirable and necessary.

President Bush's Faith-Based and Community Initiative

The election to the presidency of George W. Bush, who had campaigned on a compassionate conservative platform, provided an important opening—a

---

[63] Expressions in brackets are taken from the titles of seminal works in the field, respectively Deneulin and Bano (2009), Carbonnier (2013), and Deneulin and Rakodi (2011). See Deneulin and Rakodi (2011, 49–50) for an explicit reference to postsecular thinking by Jürgen Habermas and others.

[64] The initiative led to a number of seminal reports on the religion-development nexus, including Belshaw, Calderisi, and Sugden (2001), Marshall and Keough (2004), Marshall and Van Saanen (2007). The WFDD continues to this day (as of 2018), based at Georgetown University's Berkley Center.

[65] Hart (2011, author's interview). See also Busby (2007); Huliaras (2008, 165).

critical juncture—for the institutionalization of America's Faith-Based Foreign Aid regime. As soon as President-elect Bush stepped into the White House in January 2001, he signed a series of executive orders that led to the creation of a new Office of Faith-Based and Community Initiatives in the White House—which I will call with the general title of White House Office of Faith-Based Initiatives or WHOFBI—along with partner Centers for Faith-Based and Community Initiatives across a number of domestically oriented departments.[66] Through the revolving door practice, scholar and compassionate conservative advocate John DiIulio was brought in the White House to coordinate the initiative, becoming—as he would put it—the nation's first "faith czar."[67]

Bush's remarks at the time closely reflected both the desecularizing discourse against religious discrimination advanced by conservative Christians as well as themes put forward by the compassionate conservative narrative:

> When we see social needs in America, my administration will look first to faith-based programs and community groups, which have proven their power to save and change lives. We will not fund the religious activities of any group, but when people of faith provide social services, we will not discriminate against them.[68]

While the initiative's main focus was initially domestic, it nonetheless provided a key platform for its subsequent expansion to the international realm. This came about in response to pressures by actors, especially the "new Evangelicals," mobilizing around the international strategic desecularizing discourse on the limits of secular aid. This internationalization occurred along two overlapping, but somewhat distinct, lines: first, by building the institutional and normative capacity within USAID to include religious perspectives and actors in its assistance programs; and second, by launching a new major, faith-friendly aid initiative such as PEPFAR. These two developments would lie at the core of America's new religious foreign policy regime.

The Faith-Based Initiative Goes Global

In December 2002, Bush established through executive order a Center for Faith-Based and Community Initiatives (CFBCI) within USAID.[69] According to Tom Hart, this development showed how "Evangelicals were capable of using their political voice to get greater access to foreign aid."[70] The initiative was officially designed to "level the playing field" between religious and secular organizations,[71] a technical term that hinted at lessening what

---

[66] These were the Departments of Health and Human Services, Housing and Urban Development, Justice, Education, and Labor. This infrastructure emerged thanks to Executive Orders 13198 and 13199.
[67] DiIulio (2007, 1).
[68] Bush (2001b).
[69] In particular Executive Order 13280.
[70] Hart (2011, author's interview); also Huliaras (2008).
[71] White House (2001).

Evangelicals claimed were a range of discriminatory barriers preventing them from accessing government resources.

The playing field was to be leveled in a number of ways. First, the initiative sought to give FBOs, even to the most pervasively religious ones, greater access to existing USAID resources. This especially required making normative adjustments to reduce the regulatory hurdles that religious agencies and institutions faced in accessing federal funds. Crucial here was the introduction in 2004 of the Final Rule on Participation by Religious Organizations in USAID Programs. The rule was intended to align USAID's understanding of Establishment Clause issues with interpretations that favored an accommodationist, rather than a separationist, stance toward religious actors. Supporting these normative changes was Bush's Attorney General and former Charitable Choice-champion John Ashcroft.

According to this rule, USAID could not exclude organizations from competing for funding on the basis of their "religious character or affiliation."[72] This mostly included two provisions sympathetic to FBOs, especially to highly pervasively religious ones. First, USAID could fund organizations that hired on the basis of religious belief and identity, a practice considered discriminatory outside the religious realm. FBOs would not be allowed, however, to discriminate for or against beneficiaries according to their religious beliefs. Second, USAID could not exclude organizations that engaged in "inherently religious activities" such as worship, religious instruction, or proselytization. FBOs were expected to fund these types of activities through private channels and to undertake them separately from USAID-funded activities. Overall, the rule was intended to allow FBOs to substantially retain their religious character even in the face of growing financial support by and entanglement with the state.

Second, the initiative sought to engender a cultural shift away from longstanding secularist habits of thought that overlooked and dismissed religion in the aid field. The push toward a more religion-friendly USAID was encouraged through the preparation of a range of reports, guidelines, and briefs that highlighted the role of religious leaders, communities, and organizations as valuable and indispensable partners in humanitarian and development efforts.[73]

Third, within the context of these normative and cultural shifts, USAID's Faith-Based Center would become the key interface between USAID and FBOs. The Center operated as a hub for sharing knowledge and information through events and newsletters with FBOs about USAID initiatives and funding opportunities. In order to broaden the pool of FBO partners, the Center would provide training, capacity building, and technical assistance to religious organizations—many of them Evangelical—wishing to receive

---

[72] Quote retrieved from the USAID website, at https://www.usaid.gov/faith-based-and-community-initiatives/usaid-rule-participation (accessed April 4, 2016).

[73] Green (2003); USAID (2008; 2009a, 2009b).

2001	2002	2003	2004	2005	2006	2007	TOTAL
247	260	420	419	375	552	586	2,859

[a]Marsden (2012, 964). See also Hasdorff (2006).

USAID funding for the very first time. Overseeing these developments was USAID Administrator Andrew Natsios, former vice president of World Vision. As Natsios explained to me in 2010, "you simply cannot work in societies around the world which are religious without involving religious groups on the ground."[74]

These normative and institutional developments contributed to generating a broader engagement and more structured interface between USAID and religious organizations than had previously existed. As a result, USAID resources started flowing increasingly to FBOs. The *Boston Globe* found that while in 2001 USAID assigned 10.5 percent of its resources to religious groups and agencies, this had nearly doubled to 19.9 percent by 2005.[75] The USAID's Office of Inspector General (OIG) calculated that between 2006 and 2007 the amount of USAID funds awarded to faith-based groups rose from $552 million to $586 million, counting 512 assistance agreements with 136 faith-based organizations.[76] Using these reports, Marsden compiled a table—reproduced here as Table 4.1—showing the growing sums allocated annually to FBOs during President Bush's two terms.

From fiscal year 2001 to 2005, the largest recipient of USAID was Catholic Relief Services, which received funding in excess of $638 million. Evangelical FBOs were among the larger beneficiaries too. World Vision received approximately $374 million; the Adventist Development and Relief Agency, $85 million; Food for the Hungry, $49 million; Franklin Graham's Samaritan's Purse, $31 million; NAE's World Relief, $22 million; and Pat Robertson's Operation Blessing, $390 thousand. Smaller organizations—mostly church-planting missions rather than humanitarian agencies—received funding for the very first time, including Christian Mission Aid, $2.7 million; Voice of the Martyrs, $305 thousand; and Evangelistic International Ministry, $290 thousand.[77]

PEPFAR: The Single Biggest Program of the Faith-Based Initiatives

A second component of the emerging Faith-Based Foreign Aid regime was a new presidential initiative, launched in 2003, which focused on HIV/AIDS: PEPFAR. DiIulio would describe it as "the single biggest program to

---

[74] Natsios (2011, author's interview).
[75] Kranish (2006).
[76] OIG (2009, 3).
[77] *Boston Globe* (2006).

result from born-again President George W. Bush's push . . . for faith-based initiatives."[78] Through PEPFAR, Bush's faith-based initiative firmly established itself at the international and not just domestic level. PEPFAR would be a five-year, $15 billion program spread across fifteen countries, mostly in sub-Saharan Africa, which sought to prevent 12 million new infections, treat 3 million people living with AIDS, and care for 12 million people including vulnerable children and orphans. PEPFAR was reauthorized in 2008 with an additional $48 billion over five years (2009 to 2013), and its pool of beneficiary countries was broadened.

Unlike most other institutional and policy configurations of the religious regimes in this book, PEPFAR is not explicitly religious. Most obviously, its title does not mention "religion" or "faith." Yet a number of features make it a key component of the Faith-Based Foreign Aid regime. A coalition of faith-based activists and postsecular actors tied to the international strategic desecularizing discourse on the limits of secular aid and advantages of faith-based approaches played a key role in persuading law- and policymakers within the halls of power to take action. This coalition included Christian actors from across denominations, spearheaded by World Vision, joining efforts with rockstars like Bono of U2, all of whom pressured in the early 2000s Congress and the Bush administration to create a major HIV/AIDS initiative. This coalition managed to secure the backing of coreligionists in the Senate, most notoriously that of ultra-conservative and well-known aid skeptic Jesse Helms, of President Bush's Evangelical speechwriter Michael Gerson, and finally of the president himself.[79]

This faith-inspired activism would shape so profoundly the initiative's institutional, normative, and operational structure that PEPFAR would come to take on a substantial religious dimension in all but its name. As Melinda Cooper puts it, "both in its design and implementation, PEPFAR heralded the arrival of a distinctly theological style of emergency relief."[80]

First, the program focused overwhelmingly on HIV/AIDS treatment and care. Around 80 percent of the budget was assigned to these activities, with President Bush speaking with Biblical references about the "Lazarus effect" of anti-HIV drugs in saving AIDS patients from the brink of death. The remaining 20 percent of the budget were allocated to the more religiously controversial prevention activities, such as those which incentivized the use of contraception.

Second, religiously inspired requirements would be demanded of organizations implementing PEPFAR programs. For example, prevention activities needed to be carried out following the ABC approach: Abstinence, Be Faithful, use Condoms. One third of the total resources for prevention would be

---

[78] DiIulio (2007, 263).
[79] For the role of Evangelical FBOs, Bono, Jesse Helms and Michael Gerson, among others, in President Bush's decision to launch PEPFAR, see Busby (2007); DiIulio (2007, 263); Gerson (2014).
[80] Cooper (2015, 55).

assigned exclusively to abstinence-related programs. When such constraints were later lifted with PEPFAR's 2008 reauthorization, given the controversial nature of promoting prevention practices that did not include the use of condoms,[81] FBOs who wanted to carry out abstinence-focused prevention activities were still allowed to apply for funding, thanks to PEPFAR's "conscience clause."[82] Other values-related clauses included the "anti-prostitution pledge," requiring organizations receiving PEPFAR resources not to work with sex workers, a high-risk group, because of fears of encouraging prostitution and sex-trafficking.

Third, PEPFAR would be a standalone initiative managed by a newly created Global AIDS Coordinator Office in the State Department. "Religion and faith played a crucial role, among others, in creating PEPFAR as a separate entity," argues Mark Brinkmoeller.[83] The intent, in fact, was to circumvent other ongoing health programs and donors over which religious organizations had little influence. "USAID was seen as too secular," Tom Hart explains, "not favorable to funding non-abortion, non-condom initiatives."[84] Another key donor in this space, the UN's Global Fund to Fight AIDS, Tuberculosis, and Malaria, was seen as a multilateral initiative beyond America's direct control, and too friendly to family planning programs.[85]

PEPFAR opened up a substantial stream of funds for FBOs, from more experienced Evangelical FBOs in the field of HIV/AIDS, such as World Vision and Samaritan's Purse, to others with little or no experience, such as Food for the Hungry. In certain circumstances the playing field was not only leveled but tilted in favor of religious organizations. Funds ear-marked exclusively for abstinence-inspired prevention programs, and tied to various religious-inspired clauses (like the anti-prostitution pledge), meant that limited funding was available for organizations that carried out condom distribution or worked with high-risk groups. Similar clauses, such as the Mexico City Policy/Global Gag Rule, were being applied to USAID programming more generally in order to curb funding of organizations that supported abortions and condom use in their family planning programs. The organizations mostly hit by this "theological turn in US foreign aid"[86] were secular NGOs such as CARE, Planned Parenthood, Marie Stopes International, and Population Services International (PSI).

---

[81] For critiques of abstinence-focused HIV/AIDS prevention activities see McNeil (2015); OIG (2011); Santelli, Speizer, and Edelstein (2013). For a dissenting voice, stressing especially the counterproductive nature of relying overwhelmingly on encouraging the use of condoms in the context of the HIV/AIDS epidemic in Africa, see Green (2011).

[82] The clause permits FBOs that employ only A (abstinence) and B (be faithful) prevention methods, but do not wish to use C (condoms) because of their religious perspective, to equally qualify for PEPFAR funding.

[83] Brinkmoeller (2011, author's interview); also Hart (2011).

[84] Hart (2011, author's interview).

[85] Hart (2011); also Kaplan (2004).

[86] Cooper (2015, 65); also Clarke (2007, 83); Kranish (2006).

President Obama and the Broadening of the Faith-Based Foreign Aid Regime

By the time that President Bush had left the White House in 2008, the foundations and contours of the Faith-Based Foreign Aid regime had been set in place. Its institutional architecture revolved around two new offices in the White House and USAID, and initiatives such as PEPFAR. Cultural and normative shifts were under way, encouraging and authorizing greater partnerships with religious organizations, including the most pervasively religious ones. A structured and growing interface between the American government and FBOs had been created.

All of this was not without controversy. First of all, these developments entailed an important redefinition of existing boundaries between state and religion toward greater entanglement between the two. Second, the turn to faith in development and humanitarian policy was generally perceived—by opponents and supporters of President Bush alike—as a political payback by the president to his Evangelical supporters.[87] Finally, while reports were showing that programs like PEPFAR were successfully providing life-saving antiretroviral treatment and other forms of care to millions of people,[88] questions nonetheless abounded on the overall effectiveness of developmental and healthcare approaches informed more by what progressive critics saw as conservative religious values rather than by research-based evidence.[89] Much of the regime's institutional and normative infrastructure had not been codified in legislation, but came into being through executive orders. This meant that it could have been easily undone by a new Democratic, politically unaligned, administration. Yet this did not happen.

Against the prevailing wisdom in liberal and progressive milieus that saw Bush's faith-based initiative as anathema and wished it gone, Barack Obama— a junior Democratic Senator from Illinois running for president in 2008— appeared particularly supportive of it. During his presidential campaign, Obama explicitly promised to reform Bush's faith-based initiative, given the controversies swirling around it, but also to substantially widen and deepen it. In his speech "Faith in America," Obama deployed a desecularizing discourse that made the case for growing cooperation, rather than separation, between the state and religions when it came to aiding the most vulnerable. "Few are closer to the people than our churches, synagogues, temples, and mosques," Obama remarked, "That's why Washington needs to draw on them." "The challenges we face today—from saving our planet to ending poverty—are simply too big," he continued, "for government to solve alone."[90] Obama

---

[87] This critique was made both by nonsupporters (Sager 2010) and supporters (DiIulio 2007; Kuo 2006) of the initiative alike. The fact that the WHOFBI was placed under the direction of the White House's political wing, headed by Karl Rove, was a further giveaway.

[88] White House (2009).

[89] Evertz (2010).

[90] Obama (2008).

promised a "broader role" for the WHOFBI, which would now "help set our national agenda." Compared to his predecessor's office in the White House, which was "underfunded" and pursued "partisan interests," Obama argued, the new one would become both a critical part of the administration and more pluralist in character. The then-Senator insisted, however, that his administration would seek to support "programs that actually work," and regulate more decisively against government money used to proselytize and FBOs' hiring practices based on religious preferences, both of which were in tension with church–state separation norms.

Obama was likely motivated by a mix of personal belief in the power of religion, derived by his past experience as community organizer, and electoral calculations, namely the desire to close the Democrat's God gap. This said, other self-reinforcing and path-dependency mechanisms were at play too. The regime was exciting a wide range of religious constituencies across denominational, theological, and ideological lines that came to hold an interest in seeing it continue. As an enthusiast Obama administration White House staffer in the faith-based initiatives space put it to me in 2010:

> There are few gifts that the Bush administration left behind. The faith-based infrastructure is one of those. It is great and we are planning to expand on it. It is especially a gift for us folks interested in the progressive movement of faith-based organizations. It allows us to have a voice and carry forward our ideas in the policy process.[91]

Within a month from his inauguration, President Obama issued Executive Order 13498 reconstituting Bush's White House office into a newly named Office of Faith-Based and Neighborhood Partnerships (which I will continue to call White House Office of Faith-Based Initiatives, or WHOFBI). Religious advisers and activists working on faith-based outreach during Obama's campaign—such as Joshua DuBois and Mara Vanderslice—were brought in through the revolving door practice to manage and lead the office and its initiatives.[92] As promised on the campaign trail, the WHOFBI's scope was now broadened.

First, the office was given greater policymaking responsibilities. It was placed under the Domestic Policy Council, rather than under Political Affairs, and empowered with a new twenty-five-member-strong Presidential Advisory Council. The council was composed largely of religious figures from a plurality of backgrounds—including Christian, Jewish, Muslim, and Hindu—as well as some nonbelievers. This reflected Obama's intent to work with a wider range of religious groups compared to the Bush administration's focus on conservative Evangelicals and Catholics.

---

[91] WHOFBI Official (2010, author's interview).
[92] DuBois would also become known as Barack Obama's "spiritual adviser" for the daily devotionals he send the president while serving in his administration. See DuBois (2013).

Second, the revamped office and the new council were tasked with focusing increasingly on a broad range of foreign policy matters. These included developing thinking on the future direction of the Faith-Based Foreign Aid regime, as well as devising policy solutions that could feed directly into an expanding range of religious foreign policy regimes emerging at the time.[93]

Finally, Obama backtracked on electoral promises to curb some of the regime's more controversial aspects, namely supporting organizations that actively proselytized and hired on a religious basis. Once the administration began reflecting upon the constitutionality of these aspects of the regime, it came under pressure from a wide range of religious leaders and organizations wishing to maintain the new accommodationist status quo.[94] Ultimately the Obama administration clarified the norms governing federal partnerships with FBOs, without however substantially altering them from what had been put in place during the Bush years.[95]

USAID and the Faith-Based Initiatives 2.0

A renewed commitment by the Obama administration to the regime meant a step-change for USAID and its faith-based center. An official in USAID's CFBCI explained to me in 2010 the regime's evolution as follows:

> With Obama, we have moved from faith-based initiatives 1.0 to faith-based initiatives 2.0. This office's initial focus was mainly on "leveling the playing field," ensuring that FBOs are treated equally to secular organizations. Today we also actively seek new ways of engaging and partnering with organized religious groups and NGOs across different faiths. What we are doing is broader than the Bush years.[96]

Faith-based initiatives 2.0 meant a number of things. First, the USAID's CFBCI would commit itself to including an ever-wider range of religious organizations, big and small, across most new major international assistance initiatives launched by the administration. For example, USAID organized an event in January 2011 bringing together its Administrator, Rajiv Shah, with over thirty religious leaders and activists to discuss President Obama's new signature program to alleviate global hunger, Feed the Future.[97] Similar efforts, often scheduled in the context of the Easter and National Prayer Breakfasts,

---

[93] White House (2010).
[94] The backbone of the coalition included a diverse range of Evangelical organizations, as well as Mainline Protestant, Catholic, Jewish, and ecumenical voices. See for instance the signatories to an August 2010 letter urging members of Congress not to amend laws regarding hiring practices, which is posted on the website of World Vision and available at: www.worldvision.org/resources.nsf/main/ religious-hiring-rights/$file/RHR-letter.pdf (accessed August 28, 2015). Notable among the signatories are Richard Stearns of World Vision and Jim Wallis of Sojourners, who were also members of Obama's Presidential Advisory Council at the time.
[95] Rogers (2010); also Posner (2009).
[96] USAID CFBCI Official 1 (2010, author's interview).
[97] Alexander (2011).

took place for other initiatives such as the Global Health Initiative, Child Survival, and Counter-Trafficking in Persons.[98]

Second, new ways of partnering with religious groups and leaders on the ground were pursued. A case in point was the 2010 Haiti earthquake. During this incident, USAID's faith-based initiatives office sought to be at the heart of the wider USAID humanitarian response by coordinating with religious organizations that were playing an active role in the emergency. During the operation, USAID as a whole capitalized and built upon the CFBCI's network of local religious contacts in Haiti. This experience was used to expand and institutionalize these relations more widely within USAID by creating a list of local FBOs for future operations.[99]

Likewise, USAID's CFBCI explored avenues for reaching out to the ever-expanding "invisible"[100] world of smaller, often church-planting, American FBOs engaged in poverty reduction and health activities. A CFBCI official explained the policy to me as follows:

> American churches, especially Evangelical ones, are in droves establishing branches in developing communities to provide among other things poverty assistance. However, these churches, except larger ones such as Saddleback, know very little about development. Hence there is a lot of scope for us at USAID to partner with them and help them improve their poverty reduction activities on the ground.[101]

Third, further steps were taken in an attempt to shift culture and norms in favor of religion. Papers and events designed to raise the profile and role of faith in foreign aid activities proliferated.[102] In 2011, attempts were made to further relax USAID rules to allow funding for the "acquisition, construction, or rehabilitation of structures that are used, in whole or in part, for inherently religious activities"; that is, churches, synagogues, or mosques for example.[103] With these words, a CFBCI official explained the strategic rational behind this move:

> We need to be pragmatic about how things work in the field. Religion is a pervasive presence in civil societies worldwide. Over-restrictive interpretation of the Establishment Clause ties our hands in certain cases and we cannot meet our humanitarian and development objectives. It is important that we both clarify and update our understanding of the law; this needs to mirror world reality.[104]

The proposal marked an evolution in thinking. Most administrations had adhered, at least publicly, to the understanding that the Constitution did not

---

[98] USAID (2013; 2012; 2011).
[99] USAID CFBCI Official 1 (2011). On the role of religious actors in Haiti's recovery, see Wallin (2011).
[100] Hearn (2002).
[101] USAID CFBCI Official 1 (2011, author's interview).
[102] See for instance the event "Faith Works: Partnering to Advance Peace, Prosperity, and Development Around the World" hosted by USAID in parallel to Pope Francis' visit to the US in September 2015.
[103] Federal Register (2011).
[104] USAID CFBCI Official 1 (2011, author's interview).

permit taxpayer money to be spent on buildings devoted to religious use.[105] The proposal appears to have been thereafter dropped, yet such practices may have been taking place nonetheless. An audit found, for instance, that $325,000 in USAID funding was used to rehabilitate four mosques and adjoining community centers in Fallujah, Iraq, in 2007.[106]

Fourth, under President Obama's Faith-Based Foreign Aid regime, funding would continue to flow to religious organizations. Whether in growing amounts or possibly to a wider pool of FBOs is hard to tell, since detailed studies from 2008 onward have not been made public. According to an estimate by the former USAID Administrator Shah, USAID's partnerships with religious groups during Obama's first term had increased by more than 50 percent.[107]

Diluting PEPFAR's Theology

PEPFAR would continue during the entire Obama presidency, having been reauthorized until 2018 by Congress with the PEPFAR Stewardship and Oversight Act of 2013. While the operationalization of religion flourished in the context of USAID's activities, with respect to PEFPAR religion's role in foreign aid policy would be diluted during the Obama years instead. Candidate Obama promised that he would focus more consistently the faith-based initiatives on "what worked."[108] This meant two important changes to the program.

First, some of the more religiously driven approaches to HIV/AIDS were reconsidered. In an otherwise extremely faith-friendly 2012 PEPFAR report titled *A Firm Foundation*, suggestions were made to hold religious organizations more accountable when "ineffective" or when using "religion to promote stigma and shame," especially of commercial sex workers and of lesbian, gay, bisexual, and transsexual individuals.[109] The use or application of faith-friendly policies and clauses would be less stringent too. For instance, while in theory the "conscience clause" would remain in place during the Obama years, in practice the administration recognized the limits of prevention programs exclusively based on abstinence and would thus reduce their funding.[110] The Mexico City Policy/Global Gag Rule was revoked by the administration and by 2013 the Supreme Court would declare the "anti-prostitution pledge" unconstitutional.

Second, the attention to global health issues would gradually move beyond PEPFAR, which would no longer be a stand-alone program but a component, however major, of a wider Global Health Initiative. Moreover, and to the chagrin of religious conservatives, the administration progressively shifted

---

[105] See ACLU (2011).
[106] OIG (2009).
[107] Shah in PBS (2012).
[108] Obama (2008).
[109] PEPFAR (2012, 33).
[110] Prince, Denis, and van Dijk (2009, xi).

resources away from bilateral programs like PEPFAR in favor of multilateral initiatives such as the Global Fund.[111]

Interest in partnering with FBOs and local religious leaders for health-related purposes would, nevertheless, remain high. The overall tone of PEPFAR's *A Firm Foundation* report suggests that FBOs ought to become more, rather than less, involved in health programs given their "unique contributions."[112] Elements of path dependency existed with funding still being awarded during the Obama presidency to religious operations whose work would not always be in line with public health science consensus or liberal values on issues of gender and sexuality. Journalistic reports, for instance, detail how sexual education material and condoms were not available, in 2012, in a Catholic Relief Services clinic in Uganda receiving PEPFAR funding and yet they were still tasked with implementing HIV prevention programs that included such approaches.[113] In 2013 Samaritan's Purse was still being awarded $1.3m for implementing abstinence-only-until-marriage programs and HIV/AIDS prevention activities in Mozambique that excluded information about condom use.[114]

Foreign Policy Desecularization

The emergence of the Faith-Based Foreign Aid regime was achieved through, and accompanied by, a contestation and redefinition of the perceived secular arrangements that govern US foreign aid policy. This contestation has opened the way for different processes of foreign policy desecularization. Institutional desecularization has occurred as religiously inspired actors have become ever more entangled in the making and implementation of aid policy. More and more religious leaders, scholars, advocates, and activists have been brought in government, through the revolving door practice, to oversee humanitarian and development policies in general or to staff the regime's institutional infrastructure that would grow considerably between 2001 and 2016. This infrastructure would come to include a dedicated office for faith-based initiatives in the White House and at USAID, and a novel bureaucratic architecture dedicated to PEPFAR in the State Department.

In the Bush years, devout Catholics and faith-based advocates John DiIulio and Jim Towey would lead what was then called the White House Office of Faith-Based and Community Initiatives, while key posts in the administration with direct influence on the regime's fortunes went to individuals tied to the Christian Right, such as John Ashcroft, Michael Gerson, and Andrew

---

[111] Reports suggest that between 2010 and 2013 the administration increased support for the Global Fund by $600 million while decreasing funding for PEPFAR by $543 (Collins 2013). For overall funding trends during the Bush and Obama administrations, see Kaiser Family Foundation (2017, 3).
[112] PEPFAR (2012, 34); also USAID (2009a, 2–5).
[113] Kopsa (2014).
[114] Kopsa (2013).

Natsios. President Obama's administration may have been less outwardly and publicly religious, concentrating faith-friendly voices within the broadening architecture of the regime instead. In charge of his White House Office of Faith-Based and Neighborhood Partnerships were first Pentecostal minister Joshua DuBois, and then Baptist scholar and policy analyst Melissa Rogers, while Jewish and Catholic faith-based advocates like Ari Alexander and Mark Brinkmoeller headed USAID's faith-based center.

A further step in bringing religion more closely into the state's policymaking structures came with the creation of Obama's twenty-five-member Presidential Advisory Council in the White House. The significance of this move was evident by the contrasting reactions it engendered at the time by supporters and critics of the regime. Progressive Evangelical voices, like those of Jim Wallis, enthusiastically noted: "There has been an incredible amount of outreach to the faith community from this administration. I've never seen so much before."[115] Secular civil rights organizations like the American Civil Liberty Union (ACLU) saw the council in quite a different light:

> What we are seeing today is significant—a president giving his favored clergy a governmental stamp of approval. There is no historical precedent for presidential meddling in religion—or religious leaders meddling in federal policy . . . Although former President George W. Bush gave prominence to his faith-based initiative and informally consulted with individual religious leaders, even he never formed a government advisory committee made up primarily of clergy.[116]

Moreover, during the Obama administration religious leaders and FBOs would be invited on an increasingly regular scale to participate in USAID and government-wide consultations about aid. In the realm of foreign policy implementation, growing entanglement has taken place as an ever-greater proportion of humanitarian and development funds started to be awarded to both non- and highly pervasively religious American and local FBOs.

In parallel to institutional desecularization, changes in understandings and norms would take place as well. Processes of epistemic desecularization in foreign aid thinking have become noticeable. The whole regime is indeed premised on giving greater attention and importance to the role of religious perspectives and actors in devising and delivering aid programs.

Likewise, ideological desecularization has taken place as longstanding generalized views of religion as antithetical to modernization and development have been contested and weakened. The Faith-Based Foreign Aid regime has tended toward a position that positively essentializes religion's contributions to human flourishing. Actors and institutions tied to the regime do acknowledge that a number of controversial issues exist surrounding the use of FBOs,

---

[115] Wallis cited in PBS (2009).
[116] ACLU (2009).

especially when these are pervasively religious. Apart from more obvious concerns regarding proselytization, this includes the adoption of development approaches informed more by faith than by research-based evidence, the potential for stigmatizing vulnerable groups, or lack of professionalism and capacity.[117] Yet these problems do tend to be downplayed or ignored in the context of an overall regime discourse that presents religious perspectives and actors not simply as on the par with, but often superior to, secular ones in the humanitarian and development space.

Moreover, as Rebecca Sager highlights, faith-based initiatives seek to promote a cultural shift "away from an understanding that state and religion are in conflict or at odds with one another, toward one which views the relationship more in terms of partnership and cooperation."[118] This shift sustains and reinforces an ongoing process of state-normative desecularization whereby norms governing state–religion relations are reframed in more accommodationist terms away from strict separationist interpretations. These normative changes, described by both regime advocates and critiques as unthinkable just decades ago,[119] manifest themselves in the context of the Faith-Based Foreign Aid regime with USAID's 2004 rule (i.e. Final Rule on Participation by Religious Organizations in USAID Programs) and proposals around 2011 to relax these norms further. "Once we used to focus on establishment clause issues domestically," an ACLU attorney explained to me, "today we are branching out into foreign policy issues. There are worrying debates in Washington that the Establishment Clause does not apply abroad."[120]

Greater formal accommodation can also turn into informal support for religion in some cases. An independent audit, for instance, found that during an investigation of the constitutionality of USAID funding for religious activities, USAID lawyers would question the "applicability of the Establishment Clause overseas, especially in light of compelling foreign policy priorities."[121] This included instances where funds would be used for the rehabilitation of mosques and adjoining community centers in the context of counterinsurgency efforts in Iraq, and where an USAID-funded HIV/AIDS program integrated lesson plans containing Biblical applications and discussions. In other words, an accommodationist interpretation of the Establishment Clause can and does lead to greater state entanglement with and some degree of support for religion. In some cases, like the initial phases of PEPFAR, a range of religiously inspired clauses even benefited religious FBOs over nonreligious NGOs, thus even tilting – rather than simply leveling – the playing field toward the former against the latter.

---

[117] See, for example, Olivier et al. (2015).
[118] Sager (2010, 8).
[119] See, respectively, Kuo and DiIulio (2008), and Sullivan (2009).
[120] Weaver (2011, author's interview).
[121] OIG (2009, 6). It is likely that the audit underestimated the extent to which USAID funds religious activities and institutions since it relied mostly on self-reporting by FBOs.

Effects on Global Religious-Secular Landscapes

There is a vibrant debate on whether the Faith-Based Foreign Aid regime makes positive or negative contributions to humanitarian and development goals. Nowhere is such debate more vehemently fought out than over health issues in general and the legacy of PEPFAR in particular.[122] PEPFAR has been widely praised across the political and religious spectrum for its remarkable achievements, which have included bringing antiretroviral treatment and care to millions of people in some of the poorest parts of the world.[123] Yet the program has as well been critiqued for its embrace of religion and its theologically infused approaches to HIV/AIDS interventions.[124] While these debates are important, this chapter, and the book more broadly, focuses less on policy outcomes and more on how religious foreign policy regimes and their constitutive processes of desecularization potentially contribute to molding global religious and secular dynamics in particular ways. And it is to these that I will now turn.

Shaping Global Religious Realities Along American Norms and Interests

Compared to the International Religious Freedom regime, which explicitly seeks to regulate religious landscapes around the world, the Faith-Based Foreign Aid regime does not have such a mandate. Its stated objective is to mobilize religious resources—tangible and intangible alike—to reach those in need of humanitarian and development assistance.[125] Moreover, rulings do require that if government-funded FBOs wish to engage in explicitly religious activities—such as worship or proselytization—these should be funded privately and separately from USAID activities in both time and location. The declared secular objective to focus on needs and governmental regulations, aim to ensure that in *theory* the state is not directly involved in religious affairs. In *practice*, however, funding and partnering with religious organizations does contribute indirectly to the shaping of global religious realities as the Faith-Based Foreign Aid regime involves a transfer of significant resources—especially monetary—from the superpower to religious leaders, institutions and communities around the world.

The main religious beneficiaries of US governmental resources, supplied either through USAID or PEPFAR, are American-based FBOs. By 2012, for example, only 14 percent of USAID's grant funding was given to groups based outside the United States.[126] These organizations are also likely to be in the

---

[122] For a thoughtful and sober perspective that stresses the lack of sufficient research and data to assess the relative strengths or weaknesses of faith-based healthcare, see Olivier et al. (2015).
[123] For some of the most recent statistics see Kaiser Family Foundation (2017).
[124] Epstein (2005); Evertz (2010); Kopsa (2014; 2013).
[125] White House (2008, 1).
[126] Piccio (2013).

context of America's faith-based humanitarian and development landscape, for the most part Christian in orientation. The *Boston Globe*, for instance, found that Christian FBOs were given the lion's share of the regime's resources, receiving 98.3 percent of all funding for religious actors between 2001 and 2005.[127] It is highly probable, as we shall see, that this percentage did not change substantially over the years.

The reasons for this are multiple and complex, and certainly cannot be reduced to some kind of "hidden" Christian agenda. First, because if there is a Christian agenda, this is not that hidden after all. Much of the impetus behind the institutionalization of the regime came precisely from the desire of Evangelicals to gain greater access both to making and implementing America's foreign aid policy. Second, given America's religious demographics and Christianity's long and organized tradition of charitable work, American-based Christian organizations are likely to be the most well established, with the greatest capacity to run large government-funded programs, and adept at applying for funding. Finally, as we shall see later, further domestic and security-related factors may be hampering the ability of organizations from other faith traditions—especially Muslim—from accessing resources for development and humanitarian activities.[128]

The result is that the Faith-Based Foreign Aid regime shapes international religious landscapes by supporting, often indirectly, the global growth and presence of Christianity in general, and of certain types of Christianity in particular. Such support occurs through three channels. First, and most obviously, religious realities are shaped when the regime supports highly pervasively religious FBOs, which are usually Protestant Evangelical (including Pentecostal) in nature. These organizations generally seek to provide for both the material and the spiritual well-being of the people they target. In other words, winning souls is an important element of much of their work. Highly pervasively religious FBOs vary quite substantially in the way they seek converts. Some are more direct and explicit in their attempts to evangelize, even using coercive tactics and offering inducements, while others adopt a more indirect approach generally referred to as "witnessing," living out one's faith by helping others and sharing one's beliefs upon being asked.[129]

Erika Bornstein explains, for example, how for World Vision staff in Zimbabwe bringing economic development meant also to Christianize.[130] The view that material and spiritual needs go hand in hand is what the organization calls "holistic development." Bringing people to Christianity is done through what Bornstein calls "lifestyle evangelism" and setting up

---

[127] Kranish (2006).
[128] Other factors may be at play too. Some studies have found, for instance, that an aid-recipient country's religion is a significant determinant of individual-level foreign aid preferences, which in the case of Americans—especially when Christian—generally expresses itself in a preference for giving to Christian-majority countries in contrast to Muslim- or Buddhist-majority countries (Blackman 2018).
[129] Lynch and Schwarz (2016, 4–6).
[130] Bornstein (2002, 17).

evangelism committees at project sites.[131] For World Vision in Zimbabwe, Bornstein concludes, "the discourse of conversion was also the discourse of development."[132]

Among those FBOs that most openly seek converts is Samaritan's Purse. Its founder Franklin Graham explains how the organization operates when receiving public funds:

> Of course you cannot proselytize with tax dollars, and rightfully so. I agree with that. But it doesn't mean that we can't build buildings, we cannot provide housing and buy bricks and mortar. The proselytizing or the preaching or the giving out of Bibles, people [i.e., private donors] give us funds for those.[133]

A case in point was Samaritan's Purse's activities in the wake of Haiti's devastating 2010 earthquake. On this occasion, the organization received millions in USAID funding to provide shelters, medical care, food distribution, clean water, sanitation, and education. Journalistic reporting found that in parallel to these activities, missionary doctors or chaplains privately supplied by the Billy Graham Evangelistic Association would carry out their religious duties in Samaritan's Purse premises that displayed USAID logos. By 2011 a Billy Graham Evangelistic Association's deployment manager in Haiti proudly acknowledged that thanks to the work of its chaplains nearly 2,000 Haitians had "come to Christ" within Samaritan's Purse clinics, including 1,500 "first time salvations" and 154 "re-dedications for Christ."[134]

For Samaritan's Purse staff, relief and development in Haiti is understood as inseparable from changing the local religious landscape by taking people away from local religious traditions and into the Christian fold. A medical missionary explains on the webpages of Samaritan's Purse:

> I think about the future of Haiti. Will voodoo continue or will this be a time for Christ? . . . In the Samaritan's Purse clinics, many patients become first-time believers. I believe the work we are doing here—food, shelters, water and latrines, medical—is making a difference. I believe Haiti is on the verge. I believe we have one chance in time to change this nation. I believe now is the time for these people to connect with God.[135]

Food for the Hungry, another highly pervasively religious FBO, received a $10.9 million grant in the early 2000s to provide training in hygiene, childhood illnesses, and clean water in remote mountainous parts of Kenya. The

---

[131] Bornstein (2002, 13–14) explains lifestyle evangelism as follows: "Instead of providing access to Christianity through preaching or publishing Bibles, World Vision employees introduced Christianity through a style of life encompassing material and religious ideals embodied in development . . . Key to the process was the ability to respond to the questions 'how come you love us?' and 'how come you serve us?' with the response: 'Well, God cares about you. God loves you, and Jesus has sent us here. We're serving him and we want to serve you'."

[132] Bornstein (2002, 27).

[133] Graham in Kranish (2006).

[134] Sauer (2011). See also Beeson (2010).

[135] Furman (2010). Beyond Haiti, see Canellos and Baron (2006).

organization "has brought all that, and something else that increasingly accompanies US-funded aid programs," a report by the *Boston Globe* finds, namely "regular church service and prayer."[136] Indeed, at the organization's outpost in Lakartinya, staff members spoke openly about how they preached about Jesus while teaching breast-feeding and nutrition. According to local staff and villagers, over the seven years that Food for the Hungry was operating there, it converted almost the entire area to Christianity.[137]

Samaritan's Purse and Food for the Hungry similarly received millions in PEPFAR funding. Reports from the field in the 2000s found that much of these organizations' health programs were so infused with religious messages that the two—"preventing AIDS" and "saving souls"[138]—were virtually indistinguishable. Upon visiting a Samaritan's Purse PEPFAR-funded operation in Africa in 2013, Andy Kopsa reports that "abstinence-only . . . programs seem to have less to do with HIV/AIDS . . . prevention and more with the promotion of Christianity, degrading of homosexuals and providing opportunities for conversion."[139] Food for the Hungry was awarded in 2005 an $8.3 million grant through PEPFAR's Abstinence and Health Choices for Youth Program. Upon inspection, a reporter found that the "manual that the organization uses to teach the classes relies on biblical references and stories."[140] On its website, Food for the Hungry would describe its HIV work as "Biblical training on abstinence and faithfulness, medical support, outreach, supporting orphans, and HIV/AIDS victims."[141] A 2009 USAID audit found that the agency was knowingly funding an HIV/AIDS program for African youth that provided curriculums on abstinence and behavior change containing Biblical stories and religious messages.[142]

Certain Evangelical FBOs are keen to reach out to and convert Muslims.[143] World Witness is the foreign missionary agency of the Associate Reformed Presbyterian Church whose "primary focus," the organization's website states, "is the Muslim world."[144] The *Boston Globe* reported in 2006 that the organization ran a hospital in Pakistan with top-of-the-line medical equipment—computers, machinery, lecture theatres—all emblazoned with USAID stickers, while hospital patients learned about the gospel from missionary nurses whose salaries were not paid by USAID. "I want Muslims to become Christians," the hospital director explained when interviewed.[145]

---

[136] Kranish (2006).
[137] Kranish (2006).
[138] Epstein (2005).
[139] Kopsa (2013).
[140] Evertz (2010, 21).
[141] Ibid.
[142] OIG (2009).
[143] See also Cottle (2003); McAlister (2012).
[144] Quotes are taken from World Witness' website, at http://worldwitness.org/about (accessed September 9, 2018).
[145] Quoted from Milligan (2006).

These examples reveal the complex entanglements that emerge between American aid efforts and attempts by certain FBOs to promote Protestant Evangelical Christian beliefs and practices worldwide. At best, American aid indirectly assists in the spread of Evangelical Christianity by allowing proselytizing FBOs to free up resources collected from Churches and private donors to be deployed for religious, rather than humanitarian and development related, activities and materials. At worst, Evangelical FBOs divert government funds for religious purposes. More often than not, it remains rather difficult—as the examples here suggest—to clearly disentangle where the humanitarian and development activity ends (to be funded with public money) and where the religious one begins (to be funded with private money).

Entanglements—real and perceived—between US foreign policy and the advancement of Evangelical Christianity are enabled by two further factors. On the one hand, there is generally little consistent oversight of whether FBOs actually comply with rulings seeking to keep aid and faith distinct.[146] "As a Government over the past decade we have turned a blind eye towards Christian proselytization," an official in Obama's White House faith-based office admitted to me in 2010.[147] Similarly, Andrew Natsios acknowledges that under his leadership, USAID was not able to keep a close eye on whether groups were using money to proselytize.[148] On the other hand, vulnerable people on the ground may have little time and interest to understand which parts of an FBO's activities are funded by the US government and which are not. Given the ways in which the lines between aid and faith become blurred in such instances, it is not surprising that a perception is emerging across localities—whether in Kyrgyzstan, India, El Salvador, or Haiti—that the United States is promoting Evangelical Christianity through its foreign aid.[149]

Second, the shaping of global religious realities and the support for Christianity abroad occurs even as the Faith-Based Foreign Aid regime partners with organizations that do not have such overt and explicit religious missions. Take Catholic Relief Services, which is assiduous in separating itself from evangelization and generally operates in a nonsectarian way that stresses the suffering and needs of those served, not their faith. This organization would likely not be as wealthy and powerful if it did not receive US government funding. Catholic Relief Services' annual budget has gone from $250 million in 1992 to $850 million budget in 2010. "Increasing ties between the government and these FBOs," Amy Beeson notes, referring also to Catholic Relief Services, "account for a significant proportion of their expansion."[150] As of 2012, out of a list of top USAID-funded grant implementers, most of which are secular NGOs, Catholic Relief Services came in second place with awards

---

[146] For an exception that proves the rule, see OIG (2009).
[147] WHOFBI Official (2010, author's interview).
[148] Natsios in Kranish (2006).
[149] Gonzalez (2001); Pelkmans (2009); Sauer (2011); Subramanya (2015).
[150] Beeson (2010).

amounting to $172 million.[151] These synergies and resources are important for Catholic FBOs—as well as Mainline Protestant ones—since they allow these organizations to maintain a presence and possibly expand their operations across the developing world.

Third, through the regime, the United States intervenes in religious landscapes abroad not just by funding American-based—often Christian—FBOs, but also when it supports the capacity, infrastructure, and authority of local religious partners or institutions.[152] Health interventions in general and PEPFAR in particular have injected substantial resources into local religious and social realities in Africa, for instance. In Uganda the US government sought since the early 2000s to build the capacity of the Inter-Religious Council of Uganda (IRCU), a council bringing together the country's five main religious traditions: Catholics, Anglican Protestants, Seventh Day Adventists, Orthodox Christians, and Muslims. Thanks to USAID and PEPFAR funding, IRCU grew over the years into a nationally accredited coordination mechanism for faith-based HIV/AIDS interventions,[153] providing its own prevention, care, and treatment services as well as subgrants and technical assistance to hundreds of FBOs in the country. Controversies around IRCU's support for Uganda's anti-homosexuality laws led the Obama administration to withdraw its support for the organization in 2014, which has since dramatically shrunk in size and capacity.[154]

More broadly, multiple studies find that the substantial injection of funds through PEPFAR at times outstripped the health budget of the poorest African states. This money would often empower local churches and Christian organizations, not just more established Catholic or Anglican but also Evangelical and Pentecostal ones, making them indispensable conduits of healthcare in many parts of the continent. By doing so, these resources would contribute to institutionalizing and amplifying these religious institutions' presence and influence across the social fabric of African societies. In the process, Melinda Cooper tellingly remarks, " 'Africans' religiosity itself has come to be refigured by the politics of international foreign aid."[155]

While Christian organizations and institutions of different kinds and sizes have been major beneficiaries of the faith-based turn in foreign aid, certain realities are preventing other religious traditions from receiving comparable support. This particularly appears to be the case with Muslim and Islamic-based organizations. By 2016, President Obama's final year in office, few large Muslim-based relief organizations—such as Islamic American Relief Agency, Islamic Relief USA, and Islamic Aid—had received consistent funding or any major direct USAID grant to deliver aid (and possibly promote Islam)

---

[151] Piccio (2013).
[152] A USAID (2009a) brief details many examples of capacity building activities aimed at religious leaders and communities.
[153] According to Terri Hasdorff (2006), then director of USAID's faith-based center.
[154] Dionne (2014); Kaaya (2014).
[155] Cooper (2015, 58); see also Dilger (2009); Prince, Denis, and van Dijk (2009).

worldwide. There are of course some exceptions, which include grants disbursed to the Aga Khan Foundation of the USA,[156] or instances where Mosques are rebuilt in Fallujah to win over the hearts and minds of Iraqis.[157] Yet the general lack of support for Muslim charities is particularly striking, considering that much US-funded humanitarian and development work is carried out in Muslim-majority countries such as Egypt, Iraq, Afghanistan, Pakistan, and Indonesia, as well as many African countries with large Muslim populations.[158]

Why is this so? A number of domestic religious and international security factors play a key role. On the one hand, Muslim Americans form a small portion of the overall population. Their organizations, moreover, often lack the organizational capacity and well-established institutional ties that are necessary to secure donor resources.[159] On the other hand, wider geopolitical issues are at play too. Since 9/11, the funding of Muslim charities has been a concern in the US foreign-aid sector for fears of financing terrorism and radicalization activities.[160]

The regime's particular support for certain international and local religions and FBOs—mostly Christian—and the neglect of others—often Muslim—raises a number of thorny questions. It is hard to know whether, for instance—as Melani McAlister ponders—such imbalances can be fixed or are instead the product of a project which is "inherently flawed and unsalvageable" from the outset.[161] What seems to be occurring, though, is that these dynamics may aliment wider narratives of religious biases and conflicts. "Sometimes this issue of proselytism, of religious charitable giving when it is preferential for one group over another," Salam Al-Marayati, president of the American-based Muslim Political Action Committee argues, "reinforces [the myth of] the clash of civilizations."[162] Such perceptions have real consequences on the ground as Western-based aid organizations, faith-based or otherwise, are increasingly being seen and targeted as foreign colonial agents in places like Somalia, Afghanistan, or Iraq.[163]

---

[156] Marsden (2012, 965) calculated that as of 2012, the Aga Khan Foundation had received 37 USAID grants totaling $37.8 million.

[157] OIG (2009, 5–6).

[158] The website USASpending.org provides a list of all grants and loans awarded. The list of the major US aid recipient countries can be found on the website of USAID at https://explorer.usaid.gov/aid-trends.html. My own research shows that as of 2017, Islamic Relief received a $200.000 subgrant in 2014 from a prime USAID grant awarded to World Vision for humanitarian assistance projects in Sudan. It is important to emphasize that when it comes to initiatives and programs that are more clearly security oriented, there is a great deal of interaction between state and "mosque" in American foreign policy (something that chapter 5 of this book explores in greater detail).

[159] USAID Official (2015, author's interview).

[160] Danan and Hunt (2007, 19). For a wider discussion on Muslim organizations and Islamic charities, and the adversities these face in a post-9/11 international context, see Barnett and Stein (2012, 6–7); Benedetti (2006); Ghandour (2003).

[161] McAlister (2013).

[162] Berkley Center (2013, 1:19:21–1:19:41).

[163] See De Cordier (2009, 668, 675–677); Thaut (2009, 324–325).

Religionizing World Politics

The Faith-Based Foreign Aid regime contributes to the religionization of world politics by emphasizing and promoting the role and place of religion in international relations. Such processes of religionization have largely taken place, in the case of the present regime, through dynamics of *elevation* rather than *categorization*. Religionization via categorization has hardly occurred since the regime's discourses and practices—despite some obvious references to religious idioms in President Bush's compassionate conservatism rhetoric, for instance—have not overtly (re)produced religious subjects or realities in and onto the world. The regime, in fact, has tended to mirror the wider secular humanitarian and developmental discourse focused on reducing poverty and sickness through the provision of humanitarian relief or developmental assistance. Countries and populations would be overwhelmingly identified not according to religious categories and identities, but rather according to their needs.

In terms of mechanisms of elevation, though, the regime has contributed in substantial ways to the empowerment of religious actors and voices in US foreign policy and in localities around the world. The regime itself has been based on an evolving and expanding institutional infrastructure—spanning the White House, USAID, and State Department—clearly designed to provide greater space for faith-based perspectives to influence the making and implementation of US foreign aid policy.

On the ground, religionization through elevation is particularly notable in the case of health and HIV/AIDS interventions in Africa through faith-friendly programs like PEPFAR, which have put into circulation "new ideas of health, sexuality, gender relations and morality, human rights, and activism."[164] Programs such as these have been infusing health practices and discourses with religious ethics and mores. There are critics and supporters of such shifts, but of shifts we are talking nonetheless.

Melinda Cooper, for example, notes how behaviors—such as extramarital relationships, homosexuality, prostitution, and drugs use—in populations "at risk" became increasingly framed as "sinful" or "immoral."[165] PEPFAR, she suggests, "served to institute a Christian morality of prohibition and sinfulness as a legitimate prism through which to address the issue of public health crisis."[166] Others, like Ruth Prince and colleagues, similarly argue that funding outlets like PEPFAR have led to the "Christianization of public discourse and debate about AIDS" across African societies since the 2000s.[167] In some instances, Christian values would literally replace prevention messages emphasizing condom use in public spaces. In Uganda, billboards advertising

---

[164] Prince, Denis, and van Dijk (2009, vii).
[165] Cooper (2015, 54).
[166] Ibid.
[167] Prince, Denis, and van Dijk (2009, v).

condoms were substituted in 2004 with new ones promoting religious messages of abstinence and fidelity.[168] If a religious or Christian ethic is what is necessary to promote behaviors that can reduce risk, including abstinence before marriage or being faithful rather than engaging in multiple concurrent sex partnerships, such a route should not be discarded a priori, scholars like Edward Green have instead argued.[169]

Moreover, the HIV/AIDS epidemic and the accompanying health interventions promoted by Christian organizations have started to shape wider societal moralities and debates too. On the more positive side, the empowerment of religious perspectives in public health discourses is contributing to elevating in these societies "values of love, brotherhood, equality, and honesty," Prince et al. argue.[170] These values may not be "specific to Christianity" but, nevertheless, the authors admit, they "offer the possibility of rising above what African publics see as an increasingly immoral public sphere," riven by huge inequalities and widespread corruption.[171] On the more controversial side, others note, conservative FBOs receiving PEPFAR funding are exporting to Africa America's domestic "culture war" with its battles over family values and sexuality.[172]

We should be careful, however, in viewing conservative religious and Christian perspectives as simply being transplanted to African societies through American funds and FBOs. African Christianity and societies do have and retain considerable agency.[173] Certain conservative or traditional attitudes, especially when it comes to issues of sex before marriage and homosexuality, are often already present on the ground. Uganda's First Lady Janet Museveni, a born-again Christian, played an active role in lobbying Congress for PEPFAR and advocating for the inclusion of clauses stressing prevention through abstinence and fidelity methods.[174] Ultimately, though, the regime has been contributing to processes of religionization in local contexts through mechanisms of elevation by giving both international as well as domestic religious organizations greater opportunities to influence healthcare practices and societal debates in line with their faith-based ethics and perspectives.

The Regime in the Context of Parallel International Policy Changes

When America's Faith-Based Foreign Aid regime started to emerge in 2001, it appeared in a global environment already experiencing a generalized interest and parallel developments toward bridging the secular and religious gap in the

---

[168] Ibid., ix.
[169] Green (2011).
[170] Prince, Denis, and van Dijk (2009, ix).
[171] Ibid.
[172] Evertz (2010, 22–29); Kaoma (2014); Kopsa (2014).
[173] Cooper (2015, 56, 69); Epstein (2005); Prince, Denis, and van Dijk (2009, ix).
[174] Cooper (2015, 69).

humanitarian and development fields. These included the World Bank's World Faith Development Dialogue of 1998, the United Kingdom's Department for International Development (DIFID) launch of a faith and development interface in 1997, the Jubilee 2000 Campaign which successfully mobilized faith-based and secular actors for the cause of debt relief, and growing efforts by the UN around the year 2000 to reach out to religious communities when formulating the 2015 Millennium Development Goals.[175]

It is this wider context, the chapter argues, which to some extent propelled what was initially an American domestically oriented faith-based initiative onto the international aid arena. Nonetheless, the United States may be leading among Western and global donors in at least one respect. This is the extent to which it funds—compared to other Western donors—the most pervasively religious FBOs who infuse their aid work with faith and actively seek converts around the world. This is mostly a speculative claim, and greater research is certainly needed that compares different multilateral and bilateral donor approaches to religion and FBOs in order to identify more systematically their similarities, differences, and relationships.[176]

Conclusion

American humanitarian and development efforts abroad, and religion, tended to inhabit separate worlds during much the post-World War II period. This state of affairs started to change in important ways with the creation of the Faith-Based Foreign Aid regime in the early 2000s. The regime has unquestionably generated a more structured interaction and entanglement between America's foreign aid sector and religious perspectives and actors. Created under the leadership of George W. Bush with the intention of expanding access to governmental resources for pervasively religious FBOs—often Protestant Evangelical—the regime was mostly broadened and deepened under the new Democratic presidency of Barack Obama. This took many by surprise, especially within more liberal circles that saw the regime as a one-off initiative influenced by Bush's born-again faith and political payback to his Christian Right supporters.

The chapter showed how the emerging religion and foreign aid nexus is not just the product of one particular event or president, but part of the new status quo. This can only be explained in the context of pressures exerted by multiple desecularizing actors—whether activists, experts, or policymakers—tied to an emerging postsecular world society. Such pressures include the growing political clout exercised by Evangelicals who were becoming ever more interested

---

[175] Clarke (2007).
[176] Despite mounting scholarship exploring the nexus between aid donors and religion (e.g. Carbonnier 2013; Clarke and Jennings 2008a; Deneulin and Bano 2009; Haynes 2014), few engage in the comparative work called for here.

in helping the least fortunate, the continued and increasing relevance of religious organizations as service providers across the developing world, and a novel recognition among conservative and progressive political milieus as well as among humanitarian and development experts of the role that religious leaders and organizations can play in helping the needy and vulnerable.

The extent and value of the growing entanglement between religion and American foreign aid policy has been the object of much contention and debate. At one extreme, the original advocates and supporters of the regime have lamented how Bush's faith-based initiatives turned out to be a politically expedient façade rather than a real step-change in governmental partnership with FBOs.[77] Similarly, some have described Bush's initiative as heavy on symbolism, but light in substance.[78] At the other end of the spectrum, critics of the current changes tend to present the regime as a governmental "takeover" by religions,[79] possibly constituting a perilous slide toward "theocracy."[80]

The reality is likely to lie somewhere in between. There is certainly greater willingness and capacity, driven by multiple processes of desecularization, toward partnering with religion. The Faith-Based Foreign Aid regime is built on an even deeper process of institutional desecularization than the International Religious Freedom regime, for instance. Its institutional architecture is designed to create structured channels for the direct inclusion of and engagement with religious perspectives in the making of American foreign aid policy. Most importantly, the regime contributes to opening up vast and growing amounts of American foreign aid resources to religious organizations that seek to live out and possibly promote their faith through humanitarian and development work around the world.

The religious character of an organization is, in fact, no longer considered to constitute a reputational or normative obstacle to receiving governmental support. The regime embodies and promotes across the foreign aid sector, an ideologically desecularized view which challenges understandings of religion as inimical to progress, modernization, and thus development. It is grounded in a perspective that positively essentializes religious approaches and actors, instead, as offering uniquely important humanitarian and developmental resources, compared to secular viewpoints and organizations. In parallel it simultaneously tends to overlook the more controversial aspects of delivering aid through faith-based channels, including issues of proselytization and theologically informed approaches to healthcare and HIV/AIDS prevention. Processes of state-normative desecularization, which reveal a shift away from separationist to more accommodationist interpretations of the Establishment Clause, have even allowed the support of religious over nonreligious organizations, especially under the Bush administration.

---

[77] Kuo (2006).
[78] Sager (2010).
[79] Clarkson (2014).
[80] Phillips (2006).

Previous secular settlements have been revisited and the boundaries between the religious and the secular have been clearly redrawn in favor of the latter in American foreign aid policy. Nonetheless I am far from suggesting that American foreign assistance is today completely driven by religious interests and logics. Data show that despite increased partnerships with FBOs, the lion's share of USAID funds still go to secular organizations, for example.[181] Most development programs and initiatives are not designed around theological imperatives but follow other nonstrictly religious logics (standard development theories, economic principles, or national security interests). Rules exist that maintain, at least in theory, a separation between government-funded aid and privately funded religion. Under President Obama the more controversial theologically driven aspects of PEPFAR would be diluted or repealed.

This being said, the regime is leading American foreign policy to increasingly intervene in and potentially shape global religious realities and landscapes in two particular ways. First, it is important to specify that unlike the International Religious Freedom regime, the Faith-Based Foreign Aid regime is not designed to produce a particular—intended or not—religious outcome. Its aim is humanitarian and developmental. Yet as it does so by drawing on religious perspectives and actors, the regime has provided an interface whereby US foreign policy is becoming progressively intertwined with the support and expansion of Christianity globally. This is not an explicit objective of the regime, but the consequence of a number of domestic, historical, institutional, and international factors which favor Christian—often American-based—actors and organizations, compared to those of other religions as the regime facilitates a more structured and cooperative relationship between faith and state. As a result we may be witnessing, some have argued, the emergence of an ever more structured nexus between America's aid sector and the most energetic elements of the Christian missionary enterprise at the dawn of the twenty-first century.[182] This observation is particularly poignant when considering how pervasively religious proselytizing Evangelical FBOs are increasingly being relied upon to deliver humanitarian and development assistance abroad.

The second important effect relates to processes of religionization. Unlike the International Religious Freedom regime, the Faith-Based Foreign Aid regime does not generate an official discourse that privileges and (re)produces religious categories in world politics. The regime nonetheless can contribute

---

[181] For example, USAID's top 5 vendors (governments excluded) for FY 2011 were: the World Bank Group, Chenomics International, World Food Program, Partners for Supply Chain Management, and John Snow. See transition.usaid.gov/policy/budget/money (accessed July 25, 2012).

[182] Cooper (2015); Hearn (2002). For a note of caution see Agensky (2013). Certainly more research is needed to fully understand this phenomenon, especially the extent to which the faith-aid nexus may be contributing to the global spread of Christian traditions and groups that are originally or most prominently American—such as Southern Baptists, Pentecostals, Prosperity Churches, or Mormonism—which are thriving today in parts of Latin America, Africa, and Asia (Jenkins 2011).

to processes of religionization by elevating religious perspectives and actors in US foreign policy as well as on the ground around the world. Reports suggest that health programs like PEPFAR are empowering international and local Christian institutions in many parts of Africa, thus contributing to a gradual Christianization and moralization of health-related discourses as well as wider societal and political debates.

What does the future hold for the Faith-Based Foreign Aid regime? The regime is built on the back of executive orders which could be quickly overturned. As this chapter has shown, though, processes of path dependency and the rise of multiple domestic religious constituencies with a vested interest in faith-based approaches to aid means that the regime is unlikely to disappear without some form of major resistance. And indeed, we are seeing its continuation under the new Trump presidency. During the 2018 National Day of Prayer, Donald Trump announced the launch of his own faith-based initiative. As the president put it on the day: "we know that in solving the many, many problems and our great challenges, faith is more powerful than government, and nothing is more powerful than God."[183]

Yet amidst an element of continuity, two broad changes seem to be taking place as well. First, President Trump's initiative and the institutions in the White House and at USAID bearing its name, would now be called Faith-Based and Opportunity Initiative. This change in form relates to a deeper change in substance. The regime appears to being retailored—in ways that are similar if not even more pronounced than under the Bush administration—to the concerns of Donald Trump's Christian Right supporters and desecularizing actors, among whom Franklin Graham of Samaritan's Purse stands out in particular. In January 2017, upon taking over the presidency, Trump quickly reinstated the Mexico City Policy/Global Gag Rule. With the Faith-Based and Opportunity Initiative, rules demanding that FBOs clearly separate their operations from their faith commitments are being relaxed and issues of religious freedom and persecution are being given greater consideration.[184]

These latter concerns, especially as they are defined by the conservative religious backers and members of the Trump administrating, mean that an important part of development and humanitarian resources will likely be directed toward Christians. Vice President Mike Pence, for instance, has assiduously labored to renegotiate and reduce funding for UN programs and increase bilateral aid to support religious minorities—including Christians—in Iraq and Syria suffering from conflict and the advance of ISIS in past years. In June 2018, USAID Director Mark Green proudly announced that "help is on the Way for Middle Eastern Christians."[185] Estimates published by the *Washington Post* suggest that through different channels, total US aid to assist Christian

[183] Trump (2018).
[184] White House (2018). For a critique of these changes, see Rogers (2018).
[185] Green (2018).

and Yazidi communities in Iraq has been in the order of $100 million for the 2018 fiscal year.[186]

At the same time, a second important change may be under way. Overall, the current administration appears to have a generally negative or transactional view of humanitarian and development assistance. Important cuts to the foreign aid budget—whether destined to the UN, USAID, or even PEPFAR—are being made. It remains to be seen how far these will go and the extent to which the Faith-Based Foreign Aid regime in general and the resources made available to FBOs in particular will be affected by the cuts.

[186] Morello (2018).

CHAPTER 5 | Muslim and Islamic Interventions

The war on terrorism is not a clash of civilizations. It does, however, reveal the clash inside a civilization, a battle for the future of the Muslim world. This is a struggle of ideas and this is an area where America must excel.
—the National Security Strategy of the United States, 2002[1]

The relationship between Islam and the West includes centuries of coexistence and cooperation, but also conflict and religious wars. . . . I've come here to Cairo to seek a new beginning between the United States and Muslims around the world, one based on mutual interest and mutual respect, and one based upon the truth that America and Islam are not exclusive and need not be in competition.
—President Barack Obama, 2009[2]

FOR MOST OF THE twentieth century, neither a major world religion, nor the people or countries defined by one, featured as key American security concern. During the Cold War period, for instance, America's chief geopolitical rival, the Soviet Union, and its ideological nemesis, Communism, were profoundly anti-religious forces. The immediate post-Cold War moment was marked by liberal optimism and views of the "end of history."[3] These shaped in multiple ways America's foreign policy, especially its efforts in the 1990s to consolidate and enlarge international organizations such as the North Atlantic Treaty Organization (NATO) or the World Trade Organization (WTO), promote democracy and human rights around the world, or supporting economic globalization.[4]

The attacks of September 11, 2001, conducted on American soil by individuals tied to Al Qaeda, an organization claiming to act in the name of *Allah* and in

---

[1] USG (2002, 31).
[2] Obama (2009b).
[3] Fukuyama (1992).
[4] Ikenberry (2011).

the defense of all its believers, brought about a dramatic change in views and policies. In the aftermath of 9/11 presidents and high-level policymakers increasingly saw—as the chapter's introductory quotes suggest—America's national security as deeply dependent on the internal dynamics of Islam and the "Muslim world," and on how Islam and "Muslims" would relate to the West in particular and to liberal modernity more broadly.[5] Under the banner of America's war on terror, an extensive range of foreign policies would be put in place to govern, reform, and pacify the world's second largest religion, and a disparate range of peoples and countries chiefly identified with it. These policies, and the normative and institutional architecture supporting them, would come to form America's third religious foreign policy regime: *the Muslim and Islamic Interventions regime.*

The Muslim and Islamic Interventions regime was born under the Bush administration, evolving thereafter during the presidency of Obama. The regime has been on the whole structured along two main components. One component has revolved around initiatives targeting particular people and countries defined primarily by their religious identity, the Muslims and the Muslim world. These interventions would be largely designed to address political, economic, social, and cultural issues affecting Muslims and the Muslim world. Under the Bush administration such policies would appear mostly in the form of the president's "freedom agenda" in the "Broader Middle East," while under the Obama presidency they appeared in the form of "global Muslim engagement" policies.

The regime's other component has revolved around initiatives targeting Islam itself. The intent here has been to steer religious education, practices, teachings, and beliefs away from theological and political interpretations articulated by extremist and jihadist groups, and toward more moderate, pietist, liberal, or even fundamentalist but nonviolent understandings of Islam. Religious and public opinion leaders willing to speak out—on satellite TV, through *fatwas*, or in mosques and local communities—against the religious credentials, political theology, and violent acts of the likes of Al Qaeda, the Islamic State of Iraq and the Levant (ISIS) and their affiliates, would be sought and supported. With Bush, such initiatives were framed in terms of engaging in a "war of ideas" against "Islamic fundamentalists," while under the Obama administration they were reframed as Countering Violent Extremism (CVE). Different labels, as we shall see, also mark some important differences in substance.

Only a decade or two ago, the very existence of foreign policies designed to intervene in the political, economic, social, and religious lives of more than a billion Muslims worldwide would have struck anyone as unimaginable.

---

[5] I refer here to "Muslims" and the "Muslim world" by using apostrophes because I do not see these as ontologically real categories independent from the labels that we—individually and collectively—assign to particular actors and geographies (see also Aydin 2017). Given though that these religious categories are increasingly used and naturalized in American foreign policy discourses and practices, as this chapter will show, I will omit the apostrophes from hereon.

"It was unheard of," a State Department official explains referring to such policies, "that U.S. diplomacy singled out a discreet religious group as an object of its foreign policy."[6] To be sure, from the 1970s onward, presidents and policymakers had started to assess the role played in world politics by Islam in general and Islamism in particular.[7] These forces would on occasion be seen as rivals of the United States, as in the context of the surprising 1979 Iranian revolution, but on other occasions they were considered its closest partners, particularly when fighting "Godless" Communism in Afghanistan or secular nationalist Arab forces in the Middle East during the Cold War.[8] As Islamists gained ground following the end of the Cold War in many Muslim-majority countries and as they increasingly attacked American targets and interests in the region, the Bush Sr. and Clinton administrations were forced to engage in early attempts to understand and respond to this phenomenon.

In 1992 Edward Djerejian, President George Bush's Assistant Secretary of State for Near Eastern Affairs, delivered what is considered the "first thorough statement given by any US administration on the Islamist question."[9] In his Meridian House Address, Djerejian hinted that the United States should approach Islamist movements on a country-by-country basis, support the moderate elements in the region, aid its economy, promote conflict resolution measures, and above all undermine ideas of a coming confrontation between "Islam and the West."[10] Similarly, the Clinton administration would repeatedly emphasize—in speeches,[11] symbolic gestures,[12] national security strategies,[13] and policy planning activities[14]—that America found itself increasingly at odds with autocrats and terrorists in the Middle East, but not in conflict with Islam as such.

Yet until the events of 2001, much of this activity was sporadic, ad hoc, and chiefly confined to speeches. Winning the hearts, minds, and souls of Muslims in an institutionalized and organized manner was simply not what American foreign policy was designed to do. Indeed, what is now often labeled without much second thought as the Muslim world, before 9/11 hardly if ever featured as a cultural or geographical space in the mind, discourses, and practices of American foreign policymakers. Today's Muslim world, for instance, was mostly divided along the lines of ethnicity (Arab, Persian, etc.), geography (the Middle East, Central Asia, etc.), or ideology (nonaligned countries, Third

---

[6] Policy Planning Official (2011, author's interview).

[7] For example, see Graham (2017).

[8] Gerges (1999, 60); Halliday (2003, ix).

[9] Gerges (1999, 78).

[10] Djerejian (1992).

[11] Clinton (1994).

[12] In 1996, then-first lady Hillary Clinton hosted the first ever *Eid al-Fitr* dinner at the White House to celebrate the end of Ramadan.

[13] USG (1998, 16, 54); see also USG (1999, 45).

[14] Policy planning exercises were being carried out in the State Department—which included the participation of Warren Christopher, then Secretary of State, and Madeleine Albright, then ambassador to the UN—with the scope of building an appropriate understanding and response to Islamist movements (Gerges 1999, 89).

World, etc.). Before the events of 9/11, belief in Islam or knowledge of Islamic history, traditions, and texts were hardly if ever attributes explicitly sought-after in foreign policymakers.

Why and how did all this change? Clearly—as emphasized thus far— the 2001 terrorist attacks on American soil were a turning point. Yet these events also needed to be interpreted as instances where religion played an important role. The next section does precisely that, by mapping how from the 1990s and then accelerating after 9/11 a heterogeneous constellation of desecularizing actors came forward within American intellectual and advocacy milieus articulating a variety of discourses that laid down the intellectual foundations of the regime. The two sections that follow trace how the events of 9/11 acted as a critical juncture in the development and inclusion of such discourses in American foreign policy, thus giving rise to the Muslim and Islamic Interventions regime. I show, first, why and how more conservative and conflictual desecularizing discourses about Muslims and Islam shaped the Bush administration's foreign policy in general and the religious regime in particular, and then why and how more liberal and cooperative desecularizing discourses molded Obama's foreign policy approach and regime.

The chapter then highlights the processes of institutional, epistemic, ideological, and state-normative desecularization that have taken place as American foreign policy would increasingly seek to target, pacify, and reform Muslim politics and Islamic traditions, in the context of the war on terror. The section that follows explores the regime's actual and potential effects on global religious and secular realities as Islam and Muslims increasingly would become an explicit subject and object of US foreign policy. The conclusion summarizes the findings of the chapter, compares the Muslim and Islamic Interventions regime with the regimes examined in the previous two chapters, and considers changes that have been taking place under the Trump presidency.

Desecularizing Actors and Discourses in Context

With the fall of the Berlin Wall, American foreign affairs analysts were left wondering what the future of world politics would hold without the threat of Soviet Communism. Some were celebrating the forward march of an American-led liberal, capitalist, order.[15] Others were instead warning of a return to the nineteenth-century balance of power politics between great powers.[16] Against the backdrop of a debate that largely discounted the role and place of religion, an ever-growing constellation of expert voices—scholars, pundits, and faith-based leaders—argued otherwise. This heterogeneous epistemic community embodied elements of an emerging postsecular consciousness. It would articulate multiple desecularizing discourses suggesting that for better or for

---

[15] Fukuyama (1992).
[16] Mearsheimer (1990).

worse, international peace and security in the post-Cold War era depended very much on the theological, political, economic, and social trajectory of one particular religion, Islam, and more than 1.6 billion people singularly defined by it, the Muslims and the Muslim world. As these desecularizing actors claimed, American foreign policymakers would discount this religious and cultural reality at their peril.

These discourses appeared in the context of a series of trends endogenous and exogenous to the emergence of a postsecular world society. Endogenous to a postsecular world society would be the growing political salience that Islam and Muslim identity would acquire for people and societies in Muslim-majority countries from the 1970s onward. Since that decade, Islamic figures and Islamist movements claiming a religious inspiration and legitimation for their actions burst onto the political scene—on many occasions violently—in the Middle East, North Africa, and Central and South Asia.[7] In parallel, from the 1990s onward, globalizing processes were increasingly undermining the centrality of the territorial state and national identities, while simultaneously empowering transnational forms of religious identities and non-state Islamist actors.[8]

In parallel, during the decades preceding the end of the Cold War and in the one immediately following it, the United States had become ever more involved—diplomatically and militarily—in the politics of Middle Eastern and neighboring countries. During the 1970s and 80s, America was active in Afghanistan against Soviet and Communist forces, in Iran during the Islamic revolution and the hostage crisis, in the Iran-Iraq conflict, and in Lebanon's civil war. The 1990s brought among other things, the first Gulf War and with it a heavy presence of American troops on the ground and their permanent stationing in the region. Along the way, the United States was also deeply involved in facilitating multiple peace agreements between Israel and its neighbors.

As the United States became ever more entangled in the Middle East and adjacent Muslim-majority countries, the values and interests of Islamist actors—whose influence and power was growing in the region—increasingly tended to conflict with America's. None did more so than those of Osama Bin Laden and his associates, who—turning against their former American backers in the context of the Soviet-Afghan war—claimed the mantle of defender of Islam and all Muslims against "Crusader" aggression.[19] The tragic events of 9/11, as shocking and unexpected as they were, were the culmination of a series of earlier attacks by Al Qaeda on American targets abroad and at home.[20]

[7] I understand political Islam and Islamism along Katerina Dalacoura's (2011, 15) definition of a "political ideology which employs an interpretation of Islam as a blueprint for building the ideal society."
[18] Mandaville (2001); Roy (2004).
[19] Bin Laden (1996).
[20] Including the World Trade Center in New York in 1993, US embassies in Kenya and Tanzania in 1998, and the USS Cole warship stationed in Yemen in 2000.

TABLE 5.1 Desecularizing Discourses on the Muslim World and Islam

	CONFLICTUAL LENS	COOPERATIVE LENS
Muslim world	Clash of civilizations	Dialogue of civilizations
Islam	Clash within a civilization	Islam as a resource

Against the backdrop of these trends—the mounting political salience of Islam and American foreign policy's growing focus on the Middle East—desecularizing experts in the United States arrived at considerably divergent interpretations of the role played by Islam and Muslims in world politics in general, and in relation to Islamist violence in particular. Attitudes can be divided into two broad camps split along the lines of those discursively presenting Islam and the Muslim world through a conflictual lens, and those adopting a more cooperative lens. These perspectives would themselves be divided between discourses that concentrated more broadly on the political, economic, social, and cultural dynamics affecting the Muslim world, and those more narrowly focusing on religious   dynamics within Islam. In total, four distinct—yet at the same time partly overlapping—desecularizing discourses would thus emerge (see Table 5.1).

Conflictual Desecularizing Discourse: Clash of Civilizations

Where a conflictual lens meets an interest in the Muslim world, we find the *clash of civilizations* desecularizing discourse. This discourse emerged in the early 1990s, articulated most prominently by scholars such as Bernard Lewis at Princeton and Samuel Huntington at Harvard, whose ideas were being published on the pages of important policy-oriented journals such as *The Atlantic* and *Foreign Affairs*.[21] Lewis and Huntington presented the Muslim and Islamic world as distinct cultural entities historically contraposed to the West and Christianity. The rise of Islamic fundamentalism and Islamism, they argued, were the most visible expression of a wider and deeper Islamic animosity and Muslim "rage" against the West.[22] Fundamentalism and Islamism revealed that something had gone awfully "wrong" within Islam and the Muslim world,[23] seen as representing the most visible symptoms of a whole religion and civilization frustrated by its weakness, stunted by a lack of freedom, and unable to reform in the face of liberal modernity. This discourse foresaw an impending confrontation of religions and civilizations between, on the one hand, a liberal, Judeo-Christian, Western world and, on the other, an Islamic and Muslim world—a confrontation that would replace the Cold War's ideological struggle between Western Capitalism and Eastern Communism.

---

[21] See respectively Lewis (1990) and Huntington (1993a). Also Lewis (2002d; 2001; 1997) and Huntington (1996; 1993b).
[22] Lewis (1990).
[23] Lewis (2002d).

While Lewis and Huntington would be among the most articulate proponents of this discourse, other constituencies deployed similar narratives of religious and civilizational clash. These included Christian Right milieus, spearheaded by notorious televangelists like Jerry Falwell, who would label Muhammad a "terrorist,"[24] and Pat Robertson, who has repeatedly described Islam as "a political system . . . intent on world domination."[25] Others include a multitude of far-right organizations, generally referred to as the counter-Jihad movement, such as David Horowitz's Freedom Center, Robert Spencer's Jihad Watch, and Pamela Geller's American Freedom Defense Initiative.[26]

What is to be done to fight fundamentalism, cure the Muslim malaise, and prevail in the clash of civilizations? Huntington and Lewis would offer diametrically opposite solutions to these questions. Lewis suggested, in increasingly explicit ways following 9/11, that Islamist terrorism and Muslim rage could be fought by actively and vigorously promoting democracy and other liberal norms across the Muslim world in general and in Iraq in particular.[27] Samuel Huntington struck a very different note. If the West wanted to avoid worsening intercivilizational hostilities, it should abandon any attempt to universalize its liberal take on politics, economics, and culture to other civilizations. At the same time, it should focus on putting its own house in order, including: stemming its "moral decline," represented by increases in antisocial behavior, family decay, or the weakening of the work ethic; avoiding "cultural suicide," represented by the rise of multiculturalist ideology which supported growing immigrant populations of Muslims in Europe and Hispanics in the United States who refused to assimilate; and stemming "political disunity," represented by emerging rifts in the transatlantic relation and the potential dissolution of NATO.[28]

Conflictual Desecularizing Discourse: Clash within a Civilization

Where a conflictual lens meets a focus on Islam, we find the *clash within a civilization* discourse. This largely emerged following the events of 9/11 and especially in the context of America's war on terror. The clash within a civilization discourse does not present Islamism as the modern reincarnation of Islam's long-time struggle against Christianity and the West. Rather, Islam and the Muslim world are framed as entities marked by an internal conflict between two main warring camps pitting "good" against "bad" Muslims.[29] Those articulating and deploying such a discourse are, for the most part, individuals

---

[24] Falwell (2002).
[25] Pater Robertson quoted in Hanson (2015).
[26] For an overview of the movement and its rhetoric, see CREST (2016).
[27] On democracy promotion in the Muslim world in general see Lewis (2001; 2002d); on democracy promotion in Iraq see Lewis (2002a, 2002b, 2002c). See also Dassa Kaye et al. (2008).
[28] Huntington (1996, ch. 12).
[29] For a critique of the good/bad Muslim dichotomy, see Mamdani (2002).

and institutions tied to the neoconservative movement,[30] including policy analysts with the American Enterprise Institute (AEI),[31] RAND Corporation,[32] the Hudson Institute,[33] and the Middle East Forum.[34]

In the clash within a civilization discourse, good Muslims and Islam would generally be labeled as "moderate." The category of moderate would be quite capacious and applied to a diverse range of actors seen to be aligned with American interests, secular ideologies, or having a de-politicized view of religion. Hence, despite their vast differences, the secular Arab government of Hosni Mubarak in Egypt, the Conservative Religious Kingdom of Saudi Arabia, and mystic Islamic traditions such as Sufism are all considered "moderate" in such a discourse.

On the other hand, those identified as bad Muslims and Islam are generally Islamists of all shapes and forms, who despite their substantial differences are presented as a coherent bloc within Islamic civilization that cuts across countries, societies, and religious traditions. Within this category are included transnational terrorist networks, such as Al Qaeda; more domestically oriented movements, such as the Egyptian Muslim Brotherhood and Hezbollah in Lebanon; or entire states and regimes, such as Iran. This galaxy of actors is generally labeled with broad-brush terms such as "Islamic fundamentalism," "Islamofascism," or "radical Islam," and deemed evil on a par with Communism and Nazism. Islamists are portrayed as locked into a "war of ideas" fought against two fronts: first moderate Islam and Muslims, to determine the future direction of their religion and civilization; and second against the West, to determine the future direction of Middle Eastern politics and world order more broadly.[35]

Policy-wise, neoconservatives would exhort the United States to engage and take sides in this war of ideas. The strategies they proposed would differ, but their common denominator would be to promote an Islam favorably disposed to America's interests and values as well as supporting moderates— whether "secularists, liberal Muslims, and moderate traditionalists, including Sufis" as a RAND report put it[36]—against fundamentalists. Such a mission would be formidable, another RAND report humbly acknowledged:

> It is no easy matter to transform a major world religion. If "nation-building" is a daunting task, "religion-building" is immeasurably more perilous and complex.[37]

---

[30] Podhoretz (2007).
[31] Muravchik and Szrom (2008); also Frum and Perle (2003); Glassman (2008b).
[32] Benard (2003),.; Rabasa et al. (2007); Rabasa et al. (2004); Rosenau (2006).
[33] See for instance the series *Trends in Islamist Ideology*, available at http://www.currenttrends.org/ (accessed September 17, 2018). Also see Baran (2004).
[34] For example, Pipes (2002).
[35] For an overview of neoconservative thinking on Islam and political Islam, see Lynch (2008).
[36] Rabasa et al. (2007, 70).
[37] Benard (2003, 3).

Cooperative Desecularizing Discourse: Dialogue of Civilizations

Where a cooperative lens meets an interest in the Muslim world, we find the *dialogue of civilizations* discourse. Situated in diametric opposition to the clash of civilizations narrative, the dialogue discourse would emerge in the 1990s and gain further momentum in the aftermath of 9/11. The dialogue discourse is articulated by a complex and ever-growing set of actors located in more liberal oriented milieus, with considerable presence in foreign policy debates in Washington, DC.

These actors include the voices of mainstream sections of the Middle East and Islamic studies scholarly community, such as those of John Esposito and John Voll, founders in 1993 of the Prince Alwaleed Bin Talal Center for Muslim-Christian Understanding at Georgetown University;[38]Akbar Ahmed, Ibn Khaldun Chair of Islamic Studies at American University and former Pakistani High Commissioner to the United Kingdom and Ireland;[39] Peter Mandaville, professor and codirector of the Ali Vural Ak Center for Global Islamic Studies at George Mason University;[40] or Mustapha Tlili, director of the New York University Center for Dialogues: Islamic World-US-The West.

A second site articulating and mobilizing around such a discourse extends to the think-tank milieu, especially liberal-leaning and nonpartisan institutes such as the Brookings Institution with its Project on US Relations with the Islamic World, launched in 2002; and Gallup's Center for Muslim Studies, first directed by Dalia Mogahed.[41] Here we also find a range of research and advocacy institutes explicitly founded to address the concerns of Muslims and Muslim-Americans, such as the Center for the Study of Islam and Democracy (CSID) founded in 1999 by Radwan Masmoudi, the Institute for Social Policy and Understanding (ISPU) founded in 2001, and the World Organization for Resource Development and Education, better known as WORDE.

A third locus of dialogue of civilizations discourses can be found in a variety of prominent interreligious and intercultural dialogue initiatives promoted by Muslim and Muslim-American religious leaders, intellectuals, or advocates. These include Fethullah Gulen's Rumi Forum, created in 1999; Imam Feisal Abdul Rauf Cordoba Initiative, launched in 2002; Eboo Patel's Interfaith Youth Core, established in 2002; and the Washington, DC-based Buxton Initiative, cofounded in 2004 by Akbar Ahmed at American University and Douglas Holladay, an Evangelical businessman.

Many of these voices from academia, research institutes, and Muslim-based advocacy organizations would come together in 2007–2008, in a major initiative called the Leadership Group on US-Muslim Engagement. Led by former Secretary of State Madeleine Albright, who by that time had increasingly

---

[38] Esposito (2002, 1999); Esposito and Voll (2000; 1996).

[39] Ahmed (2010; 2007; 2003); Forst and Ahmed (2005).

[40] Peter Mandaville (2010a; 2001). Mandaville (2010b), though, would become with time more critical of the reification of Muslim identity in such discourses.

[41] Esposito and Mogahed (2007).

begun to turn her attention to the role of religion in world politics,[42] the group produced a seminal report titled *Changing Course: A New Direction for U.S. Relations with the Muslim World*. The report was intended to inform the foreign policy of a potential Democratic administration in the aftermath of the 2008 presidential elections.[43]

Overall, the dialogue of civilization discourse argues that the essence of Islam and Muslims is peace, and that their beliefs are perfectly compatible with modernity, democracy, and American/Western values. Rather than essentializing Islam and Muslims as inherently violent, the religion and its more or less faithful adherents are portrayed instead as innately tolerant, compassionate, and just. Violent Islamist groups like Al Qaeda are thus seen neither as an inevitable phenomenon nor representative of Islam or Muslims as a whole but rather as an exception, constituted by a vociferous minority who are hijacking the religion by distorting its history and teachings to serve their political interests. Ultimately terrorists are viewed as the product of political and socioeconomic forces—namely a history of Western interventions in the Middle East and economic stagnation and miss-management—rather than culture or religion. This discourse is a desecularizing one nevertheless because those articulating it do not make simply the distinction between terrorists and civilians, but seek to engage instead in a conversation about what "true" Islam is and who "real" Muslims are.

Scholars, pundits, institutes, and initiatives articulating the dialogue discourse propose a range of policies intended both to improve America's relations and ties with Muslims worldwide, and undermine narratives and perceptions of civilizational clashes. These would include interfaith and intercultural initiatives and exchanges, designed to promote greater knowledge and appreciation of Islam among Americans and of America among Muslims; policies aimed at rectifying the political and economic grievances that poisoned US–Muslim relations and upon which Islamists thrived on; or programs intended to strengthen educational and economic partnerships and opportunities for Muslims around the world.[44]

Cooperative Desecularizing Discourse: Islam as a Resource

Finally, where a cooperative lens meets an interest in Islam, we encounter the *Islam as a resource* discourse. This desecularizing discourse views terrorism

---

[42] Albright (2006).
[43] US-Muslim Engagement Project (2009). Notable scholarly voices in the project included those of Mustapha Tlili and Vali Nasr. Among Muslim-based researches and advocates featured Dalia Mogahed, Ahmed Younis, and Imam Feisal Abdul Rauf. Along with Albright, other notable policymakers include Richard Armitage, and Dennis Ross. The group further counted on individuals from the business community, Christian churches and Israeli interest groups. The full list of participants can be found at www.usmuslimengagement.org (accessed April 27, 2016).
[44] See especially Esposito (2007); Esposito and Mogahed (2007); Forst and Ahmed (2005); Mandaville (2010a); US-Muslim Engagement Project (2009).

as a marginal, not central, phenomenon within Islam. As a Brookings report puts it, the conflict is not between the West and Islam, but between "terrorist elements in the Muslim world and Islam."[45] Unsurprisingly, then, many actors and sites articulating this discourse have tended to overlap with those promoting the dialogue of civilizations discourse.

Proponents of the Islam as a resource discourse include, first, mainstream Middle East and Islamic studies scholarly voices, such as those of John Esposito, as well as others like Marc Lynch, professor of political science at George Washington University, and Quintan Wiktorowicz, former scholar turned policymaker and consultant.[46] Second, experts from across liberal-leaning think tanks including Rashad Hussain, William McCants, and Shadi Hamid, all tied, more or less formally, to the Brookings Institution;[47] Ed Husain with the Council on Foreign Relations (CFR);[48] and reports by USIP's Religion and Peacemaking program.[49] Third are faith-based voices such as those of Douglas Johnston's International Center for Religion and Diplomacy (ICRD),[50] or Hedieh Mirahmadi at WORDE.

What distinguishes the *Islam as a resource* discourse from the *dialogue of civilizations* one is its timing and conceptual focus. First and foremost, the former discourse would develop largely as a set of policy recommendations following the events of 9/11, and in the context of the war on terror. Second, this discourse concentrates on the theological and ideological relationship between Islam, political Islam, and violent Islamist groups, rather than on wider social, political, or economic dynamics of Muslim civilization as such, and its relationship to the West.

The Islam as a resource discourse shies away from generalizations while highlighting instead the complex relationship between Islam, Islamism, and violence. Islam is not presented here as a monolith (as clash of civilizations discourses tend to do) or simply split into two broad camps of "moderates" and "radicals" (as clash within a civilization discourses generally do). Rather, it is seen as a religion with a long illustrious history of tolerance and accomplishments, as well as open to multiple and contradictory interpretations which can even stress violence, depending on geographic, political, and historical context. With Islam viewed as complex, so are Islamists. Islamists are not all lumped together into one single "Islamofascist" entity, but their evolving characteristics and differences are highlighted. Distinctions are hence made between global or local, violent or peaceful, fundamentalist or reformist, intolerant or tolerant Islamist voices and groups. Importantly, this

---

[45] Hussain and Madhany (2008, ix).
[46] Esposito (2002); Lynch (2010); Mandaville (2005); Wiktorowicz (2004).
[47] Hussain and Madhany (2008). See also the 2016 Rethinking Political Islam initiative at the Brookings Institution led by Shadi Hamid and William McCants, at https://www.brookings.edu/research/rethinking-political-islam/ (accessed June 5, 2017).
[48] Husain (2013).
[49] Smock (2004); Smock and Huda (2009).
[50] Johnston (2011b, especially ch. 13).

perspective treats Islamism as a modern political ideology that draws from religion, rather than as a predominantly religious phenomenon with profound roots in Islamic history.

These premises lead to particular policy conclusions. American foreign policymakers are invited to recognize the nuances within Islamism and think of Islam more broadly not as a cause but as a solution to, and an ally against, violent groups that use terrorism. Policymakers should find ways to intervene in the religious and theological arena to undermine and delegitimize the Islamic credentials and politico-religious interpretations of violent Islamists. Multiple avenues are proposed for pursuing such a strategy. A first step involves abandoning a national security language that provides a religious legitimization to organizations such as Al Qaeda or ISIS by referring to them as "Islamic" or "*Jihadist.*" The central effort, though, involves supporting and promoting so-called credible or mainstream Muslim voices online, via satellite TV, in mosques, community centers, university campuses, or prisons. These voices would be those of religious, cultural, and political leaders—reformists as well as nonviolent fundamentalists—who put forward theological and political arguments that counter or provide alternatives to violent interpretations of Islam and clash of civilizations narratives mobilized by specific Islamist groups.[51]

This discourse suggests that religious actors and theological responses should constitute a key element of a broader set of security, intelligence, and community-based policies designed to prevent radicalization and fight the ideological battle against terrorists targeting America and its allies. The umbrella term for these policies would become that of Countering Violent Extremism (CVE), a terminology that is profoundly influenced by the Islam as a resource perspective. First, the term "countering" replaces the more conflictual language of "war" used for instance in the neoconservative notion of a war of ideas. Second, the generic category of "violent extremism" replaces any references that explicitly connect Islam to violence (e.g., "Islamic terrorism"). Third, by focusing on "extremists" that are "violent," it signals a narrower focus on specific Islamist organizations that use terrorist tactics against the United States and its allies, rather than the whole galaxy of Islamist actors, movements, parties or regimes as such.

Lastly, it should be noted that while the Islam as a resource perspective has had a profound influence over the CVE label and its practices, it would not monopolize this policy space entirely. Over the years thinking around CVE has evolved and varied considerably. Most notably, a second perspective would emerge tied in part to dialogue of civilizations thinking. This perspective, while considering Islam an important asset, has however stressed the need to move "beyond theology."[52] Rather than focusing on the ideological dimension of counter terrorism, this alternative view of CVE has emphasized instead the

---

[51] These claims are advanced, to different degrees, by Husain (2013); Hussain and Madhany (2008); Johnston (2011b, especially ch. 13); Lynch (2010); Mirahmadi, Farooq, and Ziad (2012); Mirahmadi et al. (2015); Smock (2004); Smock and Huda (2009).
[52] Mandaville and Nozell (2017, 11).

need to confront the social, economic, and political dynamics—also with the help of religious leaders—that provide a fertile ground for Islamist extremists and their narratives to emerge and spread.

The Bush Administration, 9/11, and Regime Emergence

As planes were flown into the symbols of American economic and military power at the shout of *Allahu Akbar* on September 11, 2001, the nation anxiously asked itself, "why do they hate us?" At this critical juncture, desecularizing discourses on Muslims and Islam and the heterogeneous epistemic community articulating them stepped in to fill a generalized lacuna of knowledge about Islamism. Desecularizing discourses, especially those of civilizational clashes and dialogues, were already circulating among certain scholarly, expert, and policy-oriented milieus before 9/11, and became important meaning-making frameworks from the earliest phases of the war on terror. They provided much sought-after answers to who exactly *they* were, *why* they hated America, and *how* the United States should go about addressing the root causes of a terrorism seemingly inspired by religious fervor that went beyond the more immediate military-focused reaction against Al Qaeda.

President Bush initially adopted a dialogue of civilization perspective on the attacks. In a symbolic gesture of outreach, the president visited a famous mosque in Washington, DC on September 17 where he would unequivocally praise "Islam" while singling out "terrorists" as the source of America's troubles. "These acts of violence against innocents violate the fundamental tenets of the Islamic faith," Bush explained on this occasion, "The face of terror is not the true faith of Islam. That's not what Islam is all about. Islam is peace."[53] Embracing this discourse seemed to come naturally to a president who had a deep appreciation of religion. It also followed in the footsteps of similar moves adopted by earlier American foreign policymakers in response to the growing number of terrorist attacks in the 1990s during the Bush Sr. and Clinton administrations.

However, it was the conflictual desecularizing discourses of the *clash of civilizations* and the *clash within a civilization*, articulated by conservative scholars and neoconservative pundits, which mostly resonated with the Bush administration soon thereafter. In fact, neoconservatives, like Lewis "Scooter" Libby, Richard Perle, Paul Wolfowitz, Elliot Abrams, and Zalmay Khalilzad, and their conservative allies, like Vice President Dick Cheney and Secretary of Defense Donald Rumsfeld, all occupied key positions in the administration at the time.[54] Their voices became ever more prominent and influential in the insecure and ideologically charged post-9/11 climate. It was, as Fukuyama described it, the "neoconservative moment."[55]

---

[53] Bush (2001a).
[54] All were signatories to the Statement of Principles of the Project for a New American Century, a neoconservative foreign policy think tank in Washington, DC between 1997 and 2006.
[55] Fukuyama (2004); also Halper and Clarke (2004).

As this occurred, their conflictual views of the Muslim world and Islam increasingly defined the administration's understanding of 9/11, its framing of the war on terror, and a number of more specific policies which constituted the budding elements of America's Muslim and Islamic Interventions regime. In the process, voices that took a more realpolitik view of international relations within the administration were increasingly sidelined, along with their own take on the 9/11 events. A State Department official recalls:

> People like Colin Powell and Brent Scowcroft worked outside cultural frameworks. These touted a more Realist line, which ignored religion and focused on assessing strategic interests rather than painting Islam or Islamofascism as the new existential threat to the United States.[56]

Bush's Freedom Agenda as the Solution to the Clash of Civilizations

To neoconservatives and their friends in the Bush administration, the theories of Bernard Lewis and Samuel Huntington about civilizational clashes seemed prophetic in the wake of 9/11. Between the two scholars, though, it would be the former who would exercise the greater intellectual influence on the administration. In contrast to Huntington's skepticism of liberal views of politics and historical progress, Lewis' diagnosis of the freedom deficit plaguing Muslim civilization and Islam, and his advocacy for democratization as a solution to Islamism and the clash of civilizations, resonated with the liberal interventionist foreign policy views of neoconservatives.[57] Lewis also benefited from longstanding ties to important neoconservative members of the administration, including Libby, Perle, Wolfowitz, and Abrams.[58] Dick Cheney was also a self-confessed admirer of the Princeton-based scholar.[59]

In the wake of 9/11, Lewis would thus be invited on multiple occasions to the White House to speak to members of the administration and to President Bush himself.[60] Ian Buruma reported that Lewis's book *What Went Wrong?* became "in some circles . . . a kind of handbook in the war against Islamist terrorism."[61] While the clash of civilization rhetoric was hardly adopted publicly,

[56] Policy Planning Official (2011, author's interview).
[57] On neoconservative's "liberal interventionist" or "muscular Wilsonian" view of foreign policy, see Fukuyama (2004). For a first hand statement of neoconservative foreign policy principles, see Kristol and Kagan (1996).
[58] Waldman (2004); also Buruma (2004).
[59] Cheney (2006).
[60] Waldman (2004); also confirmed by Cheney (2006).
[61] Buruma (2004); also confirmed by Policy Planning Official (2011).

also probably because of its inflammatory character,[62] Lewis' thinking squarely underpinned the Bush administration's "freedom agenda." This consisted of attempts to promote democracy and human rights across the so-called Broader Middle East—through both forcible and nonforcible means—as an antidote to the apparent malaise afflicting the Muslim world.

President Bush and his supporters thus presented the 2003 Iraq war as the military linchpin of an aggressive American strategy—alongside ongoing efforts in Afghanistan—to "inspire [democratic] reforms throughout the Muslim world."[63] Less coercive measures were also deployed to advance freedom. Palestinians were being urged to hold elections, which they did in 2006. In 2002 the Middle East Partnership Initiative (MEPI) was launched. MEPI was described by the then Director of Policy Planning in the State Department, Richard Haas, as an attempt to "expand political participation, support civil society, and fortify the rule of law [in] Muslim nations."[64] While MEPI focused mostly on Middle Eastern countries, in 2005 the Broader Middle East and North Africa Initiative (BMENA) was created to foster, as a Congressional report put it, "economic and political liberalization in a wide geographic area of Arab and non-Arab Muslim countries."[65] Along with the trillions spent on Iraq, these initiatives disbursed further hundreds of millions of dollars with the objective of democratizing Muslim lands.[66] This was the beginning of the Muslim-centered initiatives side of the regime. Policies focused more specifically on interventions within Islamic traditions and debates were developing in parallel, as the next section will show.

Winning the War of Ideas within Islam

In the aftermath of 9/11, neoconservative-friendly think tanks and research institutes—such as the RAND Corporation, the AEI, and the Hudson Institute—were generating a parallel conflictual desecularizing discourse about Islam and the Muslim world. This was the clash within a civilization discourse, which framed the terrorist attacks and the Islamist phenomenon as the product of an ongoing "war of ideas" within Islam, between good (pro-American) Muslims and bad (anti-American) Muslims. The ideological and personal connections between these policy research outlets and ever-more influential neoconservatives in the administration facilitated, once more, the circulation and adoption of this discourse by the White House.

By 2002, Bush's National Security Strategy (NSS) would explicitly frame the rise of Al Qaeda and the war on terror as elements of a wider "clash inside

---

[62] Elliot Abrams (2011) conveyed this point to me as follows: "The Cold War was easier! Marxism was a secular ideology, it was not a religion, and we could explicitly say that it was bad and wrong. With religion we cannot say that, that Islam is bad and wrong."

[63] Bush (2002). See also Lewis (2002b).

[64] Haass (2003, 144).

[65] Sharp (2010, 19–20).

[66] On the costs of the Iraq war, see Bilmes and Stiglitz (2008). By 2009 MEPI had contributed over $530 million to implement more than 600 projects in 17 countries and territories (Spirnak 2009).

a civilization, a battle for the future of the Muslim world. This is a struggle of ideas."[67] Reorienting American foreign policy to intervene in what was seen as the religious civil war between "moderates" and "Islamofascists"— neoconservative terms that started also to permeate President Bush's rhetoric[68]—proved conceptually and bureaucratically challenging. "We saw that within the Muslim world there were violent as well as peaceful Muslims"— recalls William Inboden, a scholar and policymaker in the Bush administration at the time—"We wanted to reach out to the peaceful Muslims, but the State Department was tone deaf on religion and on how to engage with Muslims."[69] Elliott Abrams similarly recalls the difficulties he and others in the National Security Council (NSC) faced at the time:

> In the administration some of us were wondering how does a state like the U.S. deal with a religion? Who is in charge? Our national security bureaucracies, such the NSC, State and Defense Departments, dealt with countries and regions, but were not adept to coming up with a strategy that tackled the war of ideas going on within Islam.[70]

In response to this dilemma, Abrams explains, "we formed an interagency group which sought to understand how to deal with religion and the transnational threat posed by Islamic ideology."[71] In 2002 the first such interagency group linking the White House to other departments was created in the form of the Strategic Communications Policy Coordination Committee (PCC). By 2004 it had morphed into the Muslim World Outreach PCC and in 2006 became the Public Diplomacy and Strategic Communication PCC. It is here that the budding elements of the Islamic-focused interventions part of the regime came into being. A U.S. National Strategy for Public Diplomacy and Strategic Communication was then released in 2007.[72] Its intent was to give greater direction to an increasing number of what a governmental report would call "Muslim-specific initiatives," that had developed in the aftermath of 9/11 to win the battle for Muslim hearts and minds worldwide.[73]

These initiatives largely consisted of promoting America's image and culture, and supporting the so-called moderates within the Muslim world and Islam. Overseeing the implementation of these activities were, between 2001 and 2003, advertising executive Charlotte Beers, and from 2005 to 2007, Karen Hughes, a long-time Bush communication advisor. Media campaigns were launched to convey American messages to Muslim audiences on satellite TV, newspapers and radio. In 2002, for example, the $15 million Shared Values Initiative was launched during the month of Ramadan, portraying

---

[67] USG (2002, 31); also USG (2006, 9).
[68] *BBC* (2006).
[69] Inboden (2011, author's interview).
[70] Abrams (2011, author's interview).
[71] Ibid.
[72] Policy Coordinating Committee (2007).
[73] GAO (2005); also Johnson, Dale, and Cronin (2005, 7–8).

America as a religiously tolerant country where moderate Muslims thrived. The Broadcasting Board of Governors (BBG), a US government agency responsible for overseeing Voice of America and Radio Free Europe, developed similar Muslim-focused media outlets such as Radio Sawa in 2002 and the Al-Hurra TV channel in 2004 which would broadcast in Arabic across the Middle East.

Another integral part of the strategy comprised an expanding range of exchange programs and interfaith activities directed at a broad range of people targeted because of their Muslim-*ness*—whether youth, students, academics, business people, and religious leaders.[74] In 2005 Karen Hughes undertook a much-publicized tour across the Muslim world—including Indonesia, Malaysia, Saudi Arabia, Egypt, and Turkey—reaching out to youth and women's organizations, and participating in events to explain that "faith" was also an "important part of life for so many Americans."[75] A program called Citizen Dialogue, for instance, would increasingly send American Muslims—clerics, youth leaders, or musicians—to represent their country and brand of supposedly moderate Islam among Muslims worldwide. Multimillion education programs seeking to reform *madrassas* (religious schools), seen as hotbeds of anti-American Islamist ideology in places like Pakistan, Afghanistan, and Indonesia, were created. Such programs focused on revising the religious content of textbooks and promoting a broader curriculum to ensure that subjects such as mathematics, science, and literature were taught in addition to religious studies.[76]

The strategy further considered ways of supporting Sufi traditions,[77] and tarnishing Al Qaeda's image. Reports at the time showed that the CIA was revitalizing Cold War-era programs of covert action to target Islamic media, religious leaders, and political parties.[78] "Some of our operations were modeled on the Cold War's CFF [Congress for Cultural Freedom]," Elliot Abrams acknowledges.[79] "Because of her background in Soviet studies," Abrams continues, "Condoleezza Rice was very receptive to the idea that we needed something like a CCF for Islam."[80] A *US News* report calculated that in 2005 the American government was spending around $1.26 billion on these kinds of activities.[81] A more conservative figure estimated that in 2006 the United States was spending at least $437 million on public diplomacy programs "targeting Arab and Muslim populations."[82]

---

[74] Amr (2009, 8).
[75] Hughes quoted in Danan and Hunt (2007, 11).
[76] Pease (2009, 8, 15); also Pipes (2011).
[77] Baran (2004).
[78] Kaplan (2006; 2005a, 2005b).
[79] Abrams (2011, author's interview). The CCF was a CIA financed initiative during the Cold War that brought together left leaning and former-communist intellectuals, scholars, and artists from the West and, where possible, from the East to denounce and expose Communist ideology and Soviet practices.
[80] Ibid.
[81] Kaplan (2005b).
[82] Amr (2009, 8).

An Emerging Regime in Flux

By 2006–2007 the neoconservative moment was coming to an end. America's liberal interventionist foreign policy was in tatters. The Iraq war was a "fiasco."[83] Afghanistan was similarly descending into chaos. After Hamas, an Islamist organization, had won the Palestinian elections in 2006, the administration started backtracking on its democratization commitments. Reports were detailing the scandalous abuse and torture of prisoners in Guantanamo and Abu Ghraib. By framing the war on terror in terms of the forces of freedom against Islamofascism, the administration was "closely reproducing the narrative of a clash between the West and Islam," Inboden admits, "by legitimizing Osama Bin Laden as a serious although misguided representative of Islamic civilization."[84] Anti-Americanism was rampant across the world and especially among Muslims, polls showed.[85]

As President Bush increasingly sidelined neoconservatives and their close allies in his administration,[86] the emerging Muslim and Islamic Interventions regime—until then largely based on a conflictual reading of the Muslim world and Islam—entered a period of flux. While the element of the regime centered on Islamic interventions remained anchored to a neoconservative war of ideas paradigm, some important changes were made to it. In 2008 James Glassman, senior fellow at the AEI, was appointed as the new Under Secretary for Public Diplomacy. In what he labeled "Public Diplomacy 2.0," the focus of the war of ideas shifted from a direct approach to communicating America's message, to a more indirect one which sought to support pro-American or anti-Islamist Muslim third parties instead.[87] As to the Muslim-focused side of the regime, the freedom agenda inspired by the clash of civilizations discourse was shelved. Greater emphasis was placed on a more dialogical approach, similar to that which characterized President Bush's initial reaction to 9/11. Symbolic gestures of a cooperative nature toward Muslims, which in fairness the administration never entirely abandoned,[88] were now however expanded and increasingly publicized. Embassies around the world were encouraged to host annual *Iftar* dinners as the White House did. Sada Cumber, a Pakistani-born American, was appointed as America's first-ever Special Envoy to the Organization of Islamic Conference/Cooperation (OIC). The core of Cumber's mission, Bush argued, was to reach out and "explain to the Islamic world that America is a friend . . . that we value religion."[89]

---

[83] Ricks (2006).

[84] Inboden (2011, author's interview); also Lynch (2010, 16).

[85] Pew Research Center (2006).

[86] By the end of 2006, for instance, Paul Wolfowitz, Donald Rumsfeld, and Scooter Libby were no longer members of the administration.

[87] Glassman (2008a).

[88] For instance, President Bush hosted annual *Iftar* dinners in the White House during his presidency. In 2005 a copy of the Koran was added to the Presidential Library, and further visits to mosques were conducted in 2002 and 2007.

[89] Bush (2008, 00:32–00:56).

By the time President Bush left the White House, the notion had gained ground that America's post-9/11 war on terror necessitated more than just a military solution, and required a broader focus on pacifying Islam and governing a complex array of people and countries singularly defined by it. A range of institutional arrangements, strategies, and policies specifically devoted to this task had been developed. These took many shapes and forms, waxing and waning over time, but generally coalesced around the "freedom agenda" and "war of ideas" frameworks. These constituted the emerging elements of a distinctive Muslim and Islamic Interventions regime structured on a conflictual view of the Muslim "other," based on two desecularizing discourses—the clash of civilizations and the clash within a civilization—which were being articulated in conservative and neoconservative intellectual milieus at the time. Indeed, James Glassman was proud to report in 2008 to a departing President Bush that unlike in 2001, when there was "no war-of-ideas infrastructure, no strategy, and few programs," the United States could now count instead on "a platform, a strategy, and many programs."[90]

President Obama: Changes and Continuities in the Regime

Barack Obama's presidential campaign slogan "Change," which propelled him to the White House, also applied in important ways to America's foreign policy conduct in the war on terror. Obama's electoral victory represented a major opening for reconsidering the wisdom and direction of America's Muslim and Islamic Interventions regime. One approach the administration could have pursued was to dismantle the whole regime. For instance, some hoped that the United States would return to a pre-9/11 state of affairs where the religious categories of Muslims and the Muslim world were no longer key frames of reference in American foreign policy discourses and practices.[91] Likewise, budding attempts to intervene, reform, or pacify Islam in the context of war of ideas policies could have been abandoned in light of mounting concerns about state entanglement with religion.[92]

Yet this did not happen. In fact, the Muslim and Islamic Interventions regime would persist, but in a modified form. By 2009 the idea that America's war on terror could not be conducted without taking into consideration the wider state of the Muslim world and Islam, and America's relation to these entities, had in fact gone from a marginal to a mainstream international affairs discourse. A State Department official recalls:

The new Obama administration internalized the idea of the "Muslims." Members of the administration would look at polling data out there and see that

---

[90] Glassman (2008a).
[91] See for instance Mandaville (2010b); Roy and Vaisse (2008).
[92] Kaplan (2006; 2005b).

"Muslims" hate us, and that there was a "global Muslim" problem that needed to be addressed.[93]

In this context, however, it was desecularizing discourses of a more cooperative nature on Muslims and Islam articulated within liberal intellectual milieus that resonated most with the incoming Obama administration. Experts voicing both dialogue of civilizations and Islam as a resource discourses—whether at Georgetown University, the Brookings Institution, Muslim-American organizations, or the Leadership Group on US-Muslim Engagement—counted on close ties to Democratic political circles and State Department policymakers. These voices were adamant that the new administration should redouble its efforts to improve relations with, and the lives of, Muslims, while simultaneously approaching and mobilizing Islam and religious leaders in more nuanced ways to counter the narratives and delegitimize the violent tactics of Islamist groups.

From *Dialogue of Civilizations* Discourse to Global Muslim Engagement Policies

Repairing the seemingly deteriorating relationship between the United States and Muslims worldwide became a pressing task for newly elected President Obama. The administration soon came up with a policy framework generally referred to as "global Muslim engagement" whose scope was to build greater understanding, respect, partnerships, and networks between America and a wide range of actors singularly defined by their Muslim religious identity. A State Department official aptly captures elements of regime continuity and change as follows:

> We saw the carrying over from one administration [Bush's] to the next [Obama's] of the category of the Muslims. While the Bush administration saw Muslims as a danger, the Obama one wants to reach out and engage with them.[94]

Such engagement would be based on a three-pronged strategy: (i) using high profile symbolic acts of a dialogical nature toward Muslims, (ii) addressing widely held political grievances against the United States, and (iii) launching a whole range of economic, social and cultural initiatives targeting Muslims worldwide. Such a strategy was built directly on the analysis and policy recommendations provided by the 2008 report *Changing Course: A New Direction for US Relations with the Muslim World,* drafted by the Leadership Group on US-Muslim Engagement and led by Bill Clinton's former Secretary of State Madeleine Albright.[95] The White House and State

---

[93] Policy Planning Official (2011, author's interview).
[94] Policy Planning Official (2011, author's interview). For a similar view emphasizing both elements of continuity and change between the administrations, see Lynch (2010).
[95] US-Muslim Engagement Project (2009). For a detailed comparison of Obama's strategy and the report, see Zaharna (2009).

Department brought in, through the revolving door practice, scholars, and analysts mobilizing around similar dialogue of civilizations discourses to advise and devise policy. Dalia Mogahed, a member of the Leadership Group on US-Muslim Engagement, and Eboo Patel, a Muslim interfaith activist, for instance, were among those invited to join President Obama's new White House Faith-Based Advisory Council and contribute to its working group on "inter-religious cooperation."[96] Rashad Hussain, the coauthor of a Brookings Institution report titled *Reformulating the Battle of Ideas: Understanding the Role of Islam in Counterterrorism Policy*, was appointed to the role of deputy associate White House counsel.[97]

The first element of President Obama's global Muslim engagement strategy was to reach out to Muslims everywhere through dialogical symbolic gestures. The president repeatedly used his oratory qualities and personal story to underscore the common values that united Americans and Muslims everywhere, while confronting lingering narratives of civilizational clashes. The most powerful moment in this process came with the president's 2009 "New Beginning" address, delivered in Cairo and widely referred to as Obama's speech to the Muslim world.[98] The speech, peppered with quotes from the Quran and references to Islam's historic accomplishments, was in fact intended to reach an audience far beyond Egypt, and the highly emblematic Al-Azhar University and center of Islamic learning, where it was delivered. Obama had come to Cairo, he explained, to "seek a new beginning between the United States and Muslims around the world."[99]

The president's second approach focused on addressing contentious political issues—notably the Israeli-Palestinian conflict, torture and Guantanamo, and the war in Iraq—that were perceived to be aggravating relations with those of Muslim identity. Within the first month of his presidency, Obama quickly moved to appoint a special envoy to the Israeli-Palestinian peace process, and signed executive orders to shut down Guantanamo and curb torture. He also committed to withdrawing America's military operations from the unpopular "war of choice" in Iraq, refocusing on the less controversial "war of necessity" in Afghanistan. While these policy shifts had national security merits in their own right, they did not occur in a vacuum of meaning. The urgency with which changes were pursued was part and parcel of a wider strategy to ease tension

---

[96] White House (2010, 69–93).

[97] For an insight into the roles of Dalia Mogahed, Eboo Patel, and Rashad Hussain in the administration and their influence in shaping the direction of the Muslim and Islamic interventions regime, see Goldberg (2010); Pew Research Center (2009b).

[98] Before Cairo, Obama made similar conciliatory overtures toward Muslims and Islam for instance during his inaugural address and a state visit to Turkey. Later efforts include a notable visit and speech delivered at a Baltimore mosque in 2016. In his attempts to connect to Muslims, President Obama would often mention his time spent as a child in Indonesia and explain that his middle name of Hussein was a gift from his Muslim Kenyan father.

[99] Obama (2009b).

between the United States and Muslims, as Obama also hinted at in his Cairo address.[100]

The third component of President Obama's global Muslim engagement strategy involved the creation of new social, economic, and cultural partnerships and programs, on top of those already put in place during the Bush era. These programs were seen, at least implicitly, as essential to deterring terrorist sympathizers and recruits in the Muslim world. They also importantly shifted the emphasis of State Department assistance away from more contentious democracy promotion activities.[101] An institutional infrastructure was put in place and empowered—partly by confirming older appointees, partly by creating new positions and offices—to devise, manage, and implement this programmatic side of the Muslim engagement strategy. Similarly to the Bush administration, these institutional developments appeared necessary to complement a foreign policy bureaucratic architecture unaccustomed to engaging categories of peoples and countries singled out for their religious identity.

In a gesture of continuity with the previous administration, this infrastructure included a reappointed special envoy to the OIC. President Obama publicly nominated Rashad Hussain to this position in 2010 in a video message delivered at a Brookings-sponsored US-Islamic World Forum—a key venue for actors engaged in dialogue of civilizations thinking. What made Rashad Hussain stand out as a candidate for the position, Obama explained, was the fact that he was a *hafiz*, someone who had memorized the Quran.[102] An entirely new position was then created within the State Department, that of Special Representative to Muslim Communities. Farah Pandith, an American of Kashmiri origin, was first appointed to this position, having held similar Muslim-focused roles in the NSC under Elliott Abrams during the Bush years. In 2009, a Global Engagement Directorate had also been created in the NSC— led by Pradeep Ramamurthy, a Washington, DC policy insider—in order to coordinate global Muslim engagement initiatives from the White House.

Policies in this space included multimillion dollar initiatives promoting science, technology, entrepreneurship, education, and economic opportunities, as well as interfaith and intercultural exchanges targeting young people, women, and religious leaders across Muslim-majority countries.[103] Special Envoy Hussain would regularly intervene in matters of religion, whether by calling on Islamic religious leaders to theologically denounce terrorism and violence,[104] or by condemning the targeting of Christians and other minorities in Muslim-majority countries.[105] Under the leadership of Special

---

[100] Obama (2009b).
[101] Programs like MEPI or BMENA's Foundation for the Future, however, were not completely abandoned by the Obama administration and in some instances even expanded (McInerney 2011, 3; Sharp 2010, 17).
[102] *Reuters* (2010).
[103] Ramamurthy (2010); US Department of State (2010).
[104] Hussain (2010).
[105] Hussain (2012).

Representative Pandith, embassies worldwide would be asked to regularly connect with local Muslim leaders and communities, and host *Iftar* dinners. Hussain, Pandith, and Ramamurthy would all repeatedly travel to Muslim-majority countries and places with large Muslim minorities, to "address concerns and misperceptions about American attitudes towards Islam and Islam in America," as a diplomatic cable reporting on one such activity in Indonesia explains.[106]

Through the global Muslim engagement framework, Obama would place an even greater emphasis on targeting particular peoples and countries because of their religious identity. "Having worked on this issue for many years now and especially in the context of a post-9/11 world," Farah Pandith enthusiastically noted in 2010, "[at] no other time in our history have we seen the kind of attention over the course of the last year and a half on the issue of engagement with Muslims around the world."[107] In time, the two ambassadorial posts to the Muslim world, held by Hussain and Pandith respectively, would be filled by other American Muslims and brought together within a newly emerging Office of Religion in Global Affairs in the State Department (more on this in the next chapter). As the following section will show, the focus of the White House Directorate for Global Engagement increasingly shifted toward the Islamic interventions side of the regime.

From *Islam as a Resource* Discourse to Countering Violent Extremism

Processes of change and continuity also marked the Islamic interventions element of the regime. Obama substantially built on the regime infrastructure and knowledge inherited from the previous administration's neoconservative-inspired war of ideas, while reorienting America's ideological and theological battle against religious-based terrorism toward a new framework called CVE.[108] CVE gathered particular momentum in US foreign policy in the aftermath of the Arab Spring of 2011, and especially with the rise of ISIS around 2014. It further crystallized into a distinct policy framework around 2015 following a major White House CVE summit.

It is difficult to pinpoint with accuracy the individual actors responsible for championing the adoption of CVE policies within the administration. It is clear, however, that the CVE framework would be profoundly influenced by the Islam as a resource desecularizing discourse, and partly by the dialogue of civilizations one, given that so many experts articulating such discourses would be called upon to formulate policy in this area during the Obama presidency. These included Quintan Wiktorowicz, who in 2011 would replace Ramamurthy as head of the Global Engagement Directorate on the NSC; William McCants,

---

[106] *WikiLeaks* (n.d.); see also US Department of State (2010).
[107] Pandith in CSID (2010).
[108] See also Lynch (2010, 13).

who served between 2009 and 2011 as a State Department senior advisor on CVE; Rashad Hussain, who would be appointed in 2015 to be US special envoy for strategic counterterrorism communications following his stint as ambassador to the OIC; and Peter Mandaville, as policy planning staff member in the State Department between 2011 and 2012, and then as senior advisor in the Secretary of State's Office of Religion and Global Affairs, between 2015 and 2016.

The administration's approach to addressing the religious dimension of violent Islamist extremism was twofold. The first element was both discursive and symbolic. It consisted of the president and his administration regularly emphasizing the peaceful nature of Islam, and that of the majority of Muslims, by drawing from particular Islamic textual references, traditions, and histories.[109] In parallel, the administration de-emphasized the relationship between terrorism and Islam in order to delegitimize violent Islamist organizations as spokespersons for, and defenders of, their religion. Al Qaeda and other violent Islamist groups would thus no longer be labeled in official discourse as Islamofascists or Islamic fundamentalists, but as a "network of violence and hatred" and "violent extremists."[110] The president frequently stressed how Islamist organizations like ISIS, for instance, were "not Islamic" nor "religious leaders,"[111] and thus America's fight was not against Islam but against terrorists who perverted Islam.

Second, the new strategy would bring about a change in practices. The Bush-era war of ideas was framed around a grand struggle against an all-encompassing global Islamist ideology, to be won by promoting the American brand or seeking to bolster so-called moderate Islam across the Muslim world. Islamic interventions under CVE involved a shift toward more indirect, often localized and targeted initiatives. These were designed to support a disparate range of "peaceful" and "credible" Muslim and Islamic actors, whether religious or lay, moderate, or fundamentalist, to speak out against the theology and ideology of violent groups such as Al Qaeda, ISIS, and their affiliates. Such mobilization would occur by reaching out and working with Muslim communities; generating or amplifying alternative religio-political narratives to those of violent Islamists; reforming madrassas and revising school textbooks; disseminating fatwas and religious statements against intolerance, violence, and terrorism;[112] or promoting interfaith dialogues and initiatives to discredit ideas of a West at war with Islam. All of this would occur across multiple global and local sites, such as mosques, *madrassas*, community centers, university campuses, prisons, online platforms, satellite TV, and print.[113]

---

[109] See, for example, Hussain in *Al Jazeera* (2012, 05:00–06:36).
[110] See respectively Obama (2009a), and USG (2010, 19–22).
[111] See respectively Obama (2014b), and Obama (2015).
[112] Among the most popular *fatwas* and declarations feature: the Amman Message (2004), the North American Muslim Scholars' Fatwa Against Terrorism (2005), Muhammad Tahir-ul-Qadri's Fatwa on Terrorism and Suicide Bombings (2010), and Shaykh Abdallah Bin Bayyah's Fatwa Against ISIS (2014).
[113] For an overview of these activities, see Miller and Higham (2015); McKenzie (2016); also White House (2015).

Guiding thinking on many of these policies was the White House strategy Empowering Local Partners to Prevent Violent Extremism released in 2011. With time an even more expansive understanding of CVE would emerge, captured in a new strategy titled Department of State & USAID Joint Strategy on Countering Violent Extremism, released in 2016. This joint strategy is notable because it showed how CVE thinking would come to be influenced by dialogue of civilization perspectives articulated over the years, among others, by scholars like Peter Mandeville, who between 2015 and 2016 served as a senior advisor in the State Department. These development meant that increasing emphasis was given, along with policies that focused on the ideological battle against terrorism, also to community-based efforts and social and developmental issues in the fight against extremism.

These changing strategies were to be implemented by a constantly evolving bureaucratic infrastructure across departments. Within the State Department, for instance, key sites would include the Bureau of Counterterrorism, revamped in 2016 as the Bureau of Counterterrorism and Countering Violent Extremism, and the Center for Strategic Counterterrorism Communications, created in 2011 and reorganized as the Global Engagement Center in 2016.[114] In the Department of Homeland Security, the Office for Community Partnerships—newly created in 2015—would become a pivotal center of CVE policies. Not only, but thanks to US leadership, CVE initiatives and the institutional infrastructure supporting them increasingly acquired a global dimension. In 2011, for instance, the Global Counterterrorism Forum (GCTF) was launched by the United States and Turkey. The Forum supported the creation of *Hedayah* in 2011, the first-ever multilateral center for CVE activities housed in the United Arab Emirates. GCTF is also involved in the Geneva-based Global Fund for Community Engagement and Resilience, which was created in 2014 and first proposed by Ed Hussain in a 2013 Council of Foreign Relations Memo.[115]

By the end of President Obama's second term, then, a complex and evolving web of policies and institutional arrangements designed to win the war on terror was in place seeking to govern, reform, or pacify Muslim communities and Islam. These constituted the evolving contours of a third explicitly religious foreign policy regime, the Muslim and Islamic Interventions regime which originated in the Bush Jr. administration's assessment of and reaction to the events of 9/11. Despite some continuities between the Bush and Obama administrations, important differences existed in the regime's orientation. Under Bush the regime was shaped predominantly by conflictual desecularizing discourses about Muslims and Islam that emanated from conservative intellectual milieus. The arrival of Obama, however, was a critical juncture that opened a window of opportunity for cooperative desecularizing

---

[114] For a detailed summary of these changes see Hudson (2016).
[115] Husain (2013).

discourses, and the more liberal actors who articulated them, to influence and redirect the regime's infrastructure and policies.

Foreign Policy Desecularization

The emergence of the Muslim and Islamic Interventions regime both sustains and promotes multiple processes of desecularization. Institutional desecularization is occurring as a category of people and organizations identified primarily by their religious identity and beliefs are being brought into the making and execution of American foreign policy. In terms of policymaking, high-level positions within the regime are generally, though not exclusively, occupied by individuals chosen because of their cultural or religious Muslim-*ness*, such as Sada Cumber, Farah Pandith, Rashad Hussain, Dalia Mogadeh, and Eboo Patel.[116] When it comes to policy implementation, a sprawling range of initiatives and partnerships are widening and deepening America's interactions with Muslims in the United States and around the world. This aspect of the regime—whether in the context of Bush's freedom agenda or Obama's Muslim engagement framework—encompassed a wide range of measures from symbolic gestures (hosting *Iftar* dinners or visiting mosques) to specific programs designed to promote democracy, economic opportunities, social and educational reform, or cultural exchange in the Muslim world. Islamic intervention policies under both the Bush-era war of ideas and Obama's CVE framework have seen substantial sums of money expended on mobilizing and supporting—whether directly or indirectly—Muslim and Islamic actors at home and abroad, delivering political narratives and religious interpretations against those offered by Islamists, especially the most violent among them.

The progressive bureaucratization of the relationship between the United States and *Muslims* is itself sustained by a series of ongoing cultural and normative shifts. These include processes of epistemic desecularization within foreign policy milieus, where notions of religion's irrelevance to international relations are contested. The regime is in fact based on an understanding of world politics that oscillates between either *appreciating* or *reifying* the role that religion—in this specific case Islam—plays in shaping the identity, beliefs, interests, and behaviors of particular actors and communities. The reifying of religious categories is most evident in the context of a regime whose institutional and policy architecture is structured around an understanding of American security as dependent upon how a primarily religiously defined set of people (i.e., the Muslims), interpret and practice their faith (i.e., Islam), and

---

[116] Beyond the Muslim-*ness* of a particular individual, other important characteristics for occupying positions or gaining access to policymakers within the regime include national security expertise (e.g., Eliot Abrams or Pradeep Ramamurthy) or knowledge of Middle Eastern affairs and political Islam (e.g., Bernard Lewis or Peter Mandaville).

how they act politically across a geo-cultural space that stretches from Indonesia to Morocco, from Saudi Arabia to Paris or Los Angeles (i.e., the Muslim world). This singling out of religious factors over others appears most explicitly, for instance, in the case of appointees such as that of the Special Representative to Muslim Communities, but it is also implicit in CVE initiatives, which have overwhelmingly been targeted to violent extremists that are Muslim. The regime, in fact, emerged precisely as an effort to move beyond the secular themes or geographic silos that the foreign policy bureaucracy was more accustomed to work around.

Processes of ideological desecularization are evident too, with the regime oscillating between positions of *ambivalence* or *positive essentialization* of Islam. An ambivalent view of Islam was notable in the Bush era, neoconservative-inspired, war of ideas framework. This policy was very much premised on an understanding of Muslims and Islam as divided into two broad blocks of "good/moderate" and "bad/fundamentalist" Muslims. In contrast, Obama's regime has tended toward the positive essentialization of Muslims and Islam, that is, starting on the basis that they are inherently good, rather than a source of problems. In this view, organizations like ISIS cannot possibly be Islamic.[117] The Islam as a resource discourse that underpins in important ways CVE activities is premised on an understanding of violent extremists as distorting, hijacking, and violating the religion's true, and peaceful, essence.

Established norms mandating a strict separation of religion and state have repeatedly frustrated policymakers in the Muslim and Islamic Interventions regime space. Members of the Bush administration, for instance, did recognize that engaging in the war of ideas was going to drag "Washington into a battle involving mosques, mullahs, and Scripture [that] went against 200 years of U.S. church–state relations."[118] Douglas Johnston's ICRD, which around 2004 started to operate a *madrassa* reform program in Pakistan, received little support for many years from the US government. "Messing around with Pakistani religious schools," Johnston argues, was seen by US diplomats as running into "church and state" issues, and as being "politically too hot."[119] Quintan Wiktorowicz found that the United States often could not "directly address the warped religious interpretations of groups like ISIL [ISIS] because of the constitutional separation of church and state."[120] Likewise, William McCants recalls how during his time at the State Department his proposal to fund a "small Muslim nongovernmental organization overseas to compile Islamic Scriptures that promoted tolerance," was seen by the Department's lawyers as government promoting "one interpretation of a religion over another."[121] And thus it was axed.

---

[117] Obama (2014b).
[118] Kaplan (2005b).
[119] Johnston in Berkley Center (2014b, 30:03–30:52).
[120] Wiktorowicz quoted in Gertz (2014).
[121] McCants (2015).

Notwithstanding such barriers, signs of state-normative desecularization driven by the strategic logic of fighting terrorism are evident. A *US News* report found that in spite of early concerns, the Bush administration still pressed ahead with initiatives supporting moderate Islamic education, movements and actors.[122] McCants recalls how the rejection of his proposal was unexpected, since the State Department "had funded a similar program elsewhere."[123] Despite earlier resistance, the State Department would start to support ICRD's *madrassa* program in 2012.[124] An accommodationist attitude toward Islam seems to have emerged, one that may be blurring into state support in many instances. In fact, as the American state would intervene ever more consistently in Islamic affairs, a 2014 petition signed by civil liberties and community-based organizations admonished that "in choosing partners, CVE programs could have the constitutionally impermissible effect of advancing a particular set of religious beliefs and suppressing others."[125]

Effects on Global Religious-Secular Landscapes

What are the international effects of the Muslim and Islamic Interventions regime? Heated discussions revolve around whether the regime's policies are making America more or less safe. These include highly contentious debates around the promises or pitfalls of Bush's freedom agenda in the Middle East,[126] on the progress or lack thereof in US–Muslim relations following Obama's Cairo "New Beginning" address and Muslim engagement policies,[127] or on the efficacy of decades-long public diplomacy and strategic communication campaigns as violent Islamist groups would continue to proliferate—from ISIS to *Boko Haram*—with their ideological appeal remaining high.[128] While these are important policy debates, the book's theoretical framework directs the attention instead to how religious foreign policy regimes and their constitutive processes of desecularization interact with global religious and secular dynamics. It is to these that I will now turn.

Shaping Global Religious Realities Along American Norms and Interests

A sizable component of the regime has been designed to intervene and shape the course of the world's second largest religion, Islam. Interventions have taken many forms either explicit or implicit, public or covert, direct or indirect, intended or unintended. One of the most visible, explicit, and direct forms

---

[122] Kaplan (2005b).
[123] McCants (2015).
[124] Johnston in Berkley Center (2014b, 30:03–30:52).
[125] ACLU et al. (2014, 4).
[126] Carothers (2007).
[127] POMED (2010).
[128] Miller and Higham (2015); Zaharna (2009).

of intervention is when—as David Graham puts it—presidents and high-level officials seek to "explain Islam to Muslims."[129] Whether by engaging in debates about the true nature of Islam and Mohammad's teachings, about Islam's relationship and compatibility with other religions, and around who counts as a religious moderate, a fundamentalist or a *jihadist*. Thus, President Bush's well-intentioned observation that "Islam is peace" or Obama's contention that ISIS is "not Islamic," for example, turn presidents into theologians-in-chief as they enter contested religious waters on what Islam is and what it is not, what counts as Islamic and what not, who is a true believer and who is not.[130]

Less public and generally more indirect forms of interventions have taken place through a proliferating and wide-ranging set of activities carried out in the context of Bush's war of ideas and Obama's CVE policies. An important, although not exclusive, component of these policies is to advance particular Islamic interpretations and traditions, co-opt certain religious communities and leaders, and promote specific Muslim voices with the aim of countering the theology and political narratives of violent Islamist groups. Much of this effort is undertaken by third parties in Muslim majority countries—whether religious leaders, faith-based organizations, institutes of learning, or specifically dedicated regional CVE centers—which the American government seeks to "support," "empower," or "amplify" by providing funds or other forms of assistance and resources; including infrastructure, technology, training, and so on. US foreign policymakers would become over the years increasingly aware and careful not to be seen as explicitly supporting particular interpretations of Islam. Assistance to Muslim partners for CVE activities generally comes "with no visible USG [US government] stamp," a State Department official in the Obama administration explains.[131] The intent is to avoid delegitimizing and discrediting such voices, given the stigma associated with being tainted as "Islam's scholars for dollars" in the region.[132] Indeed, organizations like ISIS prey on such perceptions, aiming to buttress their own Islamic and resistance credentials by framing inimical Muslim voices as Western stooges.[133]

Overall, as the regime intervenes in ways that could "change the very face of Islam,"[134] as a news outlet once put it, the kind of face the United States is attempting to give this centuries-old religion is hard to discern. First, a variety of vague and unspecified labels are generally applied to the kind of Islam and Muslims that America seeks to support. To use the regime's jargon they can be "moderate," "peaceful," or "credible," although it is often unclear whether these terms refer to political or religious moderation, whether moderates and fundamentalists alike can be peaceful, or in whose eyes they are deemed

---

[129] Graham (2017).
[130] Wood (2015) offers a critique of Obama's theological stance on ISIS. For an overview of the contentious debates around the "Islamic," or lack thereof, character of ISIS, see Emon (2015).
[131] OIRF Official 2 (2015). See also Mandaville and Nozell (2017, 12).
[132] Moghul (2013). See also Nozell and Hayward (2014).
[133] See, for example, issue no. 7 of ISIS's magazine *Dabiq* (1436).
[134] Kaplan (2005b).

credible. Hence, unsurprisingly, a Congressional report found that the Obama administration employed no clear criteria when selecting Muslim partners.[135] Second, when moving from labels to practices, the United States appears to be supporting a huge variety of individuals, organizations, and groups that apparently have little in common—whether American Muslim organizations and leaders, Sufis around the world, established government-backed religious authorities in Egypt, the Ulema council of Kandahar in Afghanistan, Shia clerics in Iraq, or nonviolent Salafis in Pakistan. Third, given the nonpublic nature of most CVE operations and the general absence of any consistent monitoring and evaluation efforts, information regarding the precise range of actors and activities America supports is hard to come by.[136]

Despite this lack of clarity, I would argue that the regime is broadly designed to promote Muslims and Islamic interpretations that are compatible with American interests and identity. First, American foreign policymakers are generally drawn to support what they believe and recognize, explicitly or implicitly, to be "good" or "safe" as opposed to "bad" or "dangerous" Islam. Good or safe Islam is, at best, an Islam that embraces liberal values such as pluralism, tolerance, human rights, gender equality, democracy, and religious disestablishment.[137] At worst, if illiberal, it is an Islam that at least is aligned with American security priorities in its war against Al Qaeda, ISIS, and affiliates.

Second, at a deeper level, American foreign policymakers' interpretations bear the hallmarks of a Christian, especially Protestant, view of the historical and theological trajectory that religions should undergo before they can become compatible with liberal modernity. Indeed, the underlining premise of the war of ideas and CVE policies is that the United States should nudge the Muslim and Islamic world toward some kind of Protestant-like religious reformation. The assumption being that the reformation was good for Christianity and the West. "We need an Islamic reformation, and I think there is real hope for one," Paul Wolfowitz spoke on the eve of the 2003 Iraq war.[138] Obama similarly admitted how, through his 2009 Cairo address, he wished to

> trigger a discussion . . . for Muslims to address the real problems they are confronting . . . that some currents of Islam have not gone through a reformation that would help people adapt their religious doctrines to modernity.[139]

This Protestant bias is critiqued in several quarters. These voices, for instance, question whether all religions do and should follow the same path as Christianity, and whether the reformation is an unambiguously good model to follow anyway.[140]

---

[135] Bjelopera (2014, 24). Bjelopera mostly focuses on domestic CVE activities. Similar conceptual vagueness plagues international programs too, according to Hudson (2016); also Cesari (2015); OIRF Official 2 (2015).

[136] Bjelopera (2014, 28); also Schmid (2013, 43, 54).

[137] See also Cesari (2017).

[138] Wolfowitz quoted in Ignatius (2003).

[139] Obama quoted in Goldberg (2016).

[140] Hamid (2016); Zubaida (2016).

Ultimately, it is hard to determine the extent to which the world's superpower is actually changing the course of one of the world's greatest religious traditions, intentionally or unintentionally, as it intervenes publicly and directly or covertly and indirectly in its midst. Religious change may be extremely slow to occur and possibly will be detectable only with hindsight in the not so near future. Also, it may well be that US foreign policy interventions pale in comparison to the enormity of the task of (re)making a religion,[141] or may simply be ineffective.[142] This said, more research is needed to explore the kind of changes that may or may not be occurring on the ground, as America seeks to direct, govern, and possibly reform Islam to fit its national security concerns, liberal views of modernity, and its understanding of the positive role of the Protestant Reformation in the history and evolution of Christianity.

Religionizing World Politics

The Muslim and Islamic Interventions regime is grounded on an understanding of world politics, especially post-9/11, where religious identities, beliefs, practices, and sites matter. Given this premise, we can see how the regime further sustains and amplifies this logic in and onto the world through processes of religionization, both through mechanisms of categorization and elevation.

The religious category of the Muslim—applied to a range of wildly diverse individuals, institutions, communities, states, and worlds—was hardly a significant identity marker in American foreign policy before 9/11. Today it is constantly normalized and (re)produced in world politics through the regime's institutional architecture, the people and geographies that the regime's policies are designed to target and influence, symbolic gestures and travel itineraries of presidents and high-level policymakers, as well as through their discourses and rhetoric.[143] As Justin Vaisse points out,

American policymakers over time have come to address the "Muslim world" rather than the "Arab World." Muslims exist only in representations. Representations however do matter. Representations become reality when taken into consideration in research, analysis and policies.[144]

Under Bush a process of categorization of terrorism as Islamic—evident in the use of terminology such as "Islamofascism" or "militant Islam"—permeated the rhetoric and practices of the Islamic interventions side of the regime. With Obama the link between religion and terrorism would be discursively de-emphasized in the context of the CVE framework, yet it has largely

---

[141] Benard (2003, 3).
[142] For instance, the lack of resources and coordination plaguing CVE efforts has been a recurrent theme (GAO 2017; Hudson 2016; Wiktorowicz 2014).
[143] See also Bettiza (2015). For an intellectual history of the idea of the Muslim world, see Aydin (2017).
[144] Vaisse (2011, author's interview).

persisted in practice since it was mostly *violent extremism* among Muslims that the policy generally sought to *counter.*[145]

Countries around the world have themselves also started to pick up on the categories and narratives used by desecularizing actors and US foreign policymakers. States like Jordan and Morocco, for example, have sought to present themselves to the international community as moderate Muslim voices and the supporters of moderate Islam; notably also by sponsoring initiatives like the Amman message in 2004 or the Marrakesh declaration of 2016. The reasons for pursuing such efforts are likely to be multiple, including—as Stacey Gutkowski argues—using the "moral authority of religion" to "deepen political trust with the United States."[146]

Along with categorizing people, communities, states, and regions along religious lines, the regime is further contributing to religionizing world politics through mechanisms of elevation. This is occurring as American foreign policy seeks to empower and create platforms for the diffusion of the voices of what it deems to be good or true Muslims and Islam in the fight against extremists. Theological debates become a matter of high politics, with presidents themselves repeatedly entering religious discussions seeking to position America as an arbiter of what real Islam or moderate Muslims are or should be.

The Regime in the Context of Parallel International Policy Changes

Many elements of the Muslim and Islamic Interventions regime are not unique to the American case. Neither has the United States been consistently at the forefront of religiously based counterterrorism and counterradicalization solutions.[147] There is much to suggest that the United Kingdom's post-9/11 counterterrorism strategies had an important influence on America's domestic CVE strategy.[148] In many countries the level of religious interventions, at least at the domestic level, exceeds that of the United States. In France, for instance, the French Council of the Muslim Faith was established in 2003 by the government to formalize relations with French Muslims and to explicitly encourage a "French Islam."[149] De-radicalization programs in Saudi Arabia contain a substantial component of state-funded religious re-education.[150] Algeria, Morocco, Pakistan, Russia, and the United Kingdom have likewise sponsored Sufism as an alternative to politicized Islam.[151]

---

[145] ACLU et al. (2014); Patel and Koushik (2017).
[146] Gutkowski (2016, 206). See also Sheline (2017).
[147] For comprehensive global overviews, see Nasser-Eddine et al. (2011), and Schmid (2013).
[148] Quintan Wiktorowicz, had a prominent role in drafting America's CVE strategy Empowering Local Partners to Prevent Violent Extremism (White House 2011). He joined the Obama White House in 2011 following a senior advisory role in the US Embassy in London, at a time when the UK government was releasing its own counterradicalization strategy Pursue, Prevent, Protect, Prepare: The United Kingdom's Strategy for Countering International Terrorism (HM Government 2010).
[149] Fernando (2005).
[150] Porges (2010).
[151] Muedini (2015).

This said, there is little in the way of systematic comparative studies, let alone research, that traces and explains processes of policy learning, borrowing, mimicking, and diffusion from one case to another.[152] Despite these limits, some preliminary inferences can nevertheless be made about the American case. Due to its size, power, and pivotal role in the war on terror, America's Muslim and Islamic Interventions regime is likely to have greater breadth, global reach, and international resonance than similar activities pursued by other, Western, countries. When President Obama speaks to the world's Muslims from Cairo, everyone stops to listen. The United States also appears to be leading in promoting a growing range of multilateral arrangements, such as the Global Counterterrorism Forum and the Trans-Sahara Counterterrorism Partnership, which actively engage in the ideological and theological battle against violent Islamists. The proliferation of such arrangements is a fairly recent phenomenon that further expands—by coordinating efforts across countries—the field of global interventions into the secular and religious lives of Muslims. How far these initiatives reflect overwhelmingly American understandings and concerns, or combine in creative (and possibly contradictory) ways approaches pursued by different states, remains to be understood and empirically investigated.

Conclusion

In contrast to the two regimes presented in the previous chapters—the International Religious Freedom and the Faith-Based Foreign Aid regimes—the Muslim and Islamic Interventions regime did not emerge under pressure from domestic processes of religious resurgence. While the growing political salience of religion certainly played a part, these forces were mostly external to the United States, represented by the rise of Islamism and the dramatic attacks of 9/11 carried out by an organization claiming to act in the name of *Allah* and the defense of all Muslims. For the regime to be created, however, such processes and events needed to be interpreted as "religious."

Competing with those voices that would frame 9/11 and the wider phenomenon of Islamism in nonreligious terms,[153] a constellation of experts enmeshed in postsecular ways of thinking would come forward and articulate a range of desecularizing discourses. These discourses shared some important features. They were responding to the growing political salience of Islam and of Muslim identity in post-Cold War global politics; they were skeptical of liberal, secular, triumphant narratives of the "end of history"; and they highlighted the importance of understanding Islamism and Islamist organizations that used

---

[152] A recent exception is Chowdhury Fink and Bhulai (2016).

[153] As the chapter argued, realist policymakers like Colin Powell tended to operate outside any religious or cultural frame. Likewise, for instance, religious-based framings and policies are hardly considered in an overview of global CVE activities commissioned by the Australian government (Nasser-Eddine et al. 2011).

violence and terrorism in the context of Muslim politics and Islamic history. Despite these similarities, discourses importantly differed according to their focus on either Muslims, as a religiously defined set of people and countries, or on Islam, as a major world religion; and on their assessment of Muslims and Islam's relationship and compatibility with liberal modernity and the West. Such divides ran generally between conservative and liberal intellectual and policy milieus. Among the former a conflictual view of Muslims and Islam dominated, framed in terms either of a *clash of civilizations* or a *clash within a civilization*. In more liberal milieus instead, a cooperative approach dominated which developed around the discourses of *dialogue of civilizations* and *Islam as a resource* .

This constellation of desecularizing actors was able over time to shape American foreign policy on the basis of the assumption that the war on terror also required winning and reforming the hearts, minds, and religious beliefs of Muslims. Given their ideological and personal ties, conservative experts gained particular resonance within the Bush administration in the aftermath of 9/11. These experts' discourses laid the foundations of a Muslim and Islamic Interventions regime with conflictual characteristics, based on an ambitious "freedom agenda" in the "Broader Middle East" and engaging in a "war of ideas" against "Islamofascism." The regime survived the Bush years, but in altered form. The arrival of President Obama provided a critical opening for liberal experts and voices close to the administration, who were articulating cooperative desecularizing discourses about Muslims and Islam, to reorient the regime. These processes of change and continuity materialized in the form of Obama's "global Muslim engagement" initiatives and the CVE policy framework.

Unlike the two regimes explored in previous chapters, the Muslim and Islamic Interventions one has been characterized by a more decentralized and relatively uncoordinated institutional and policy architecture. The regime is essentially split into two, somewhat distinct yet still complementary and overlapping, components. One making Muslims the subject and object of American foreign policy interventions and the other making Islam the target instead. The process of devising and implementing policy has been scattered across a range of institutional centers, rather than a few clearly defined ones, which just in the case of the State Department, included by the end of President Obama's second term: the Bureau of Near Eastern Affairs, the Bureau of Counterterrorism and Countering Violent Extremism, the Global Engagement Center, the Special Representative to Muslim Communities, and the Special Envoy to the OIC. Homeland Security and the White House developed their own infrastructure focused on both domestic as well as international counterterrorism efforts. This architecture is very much a function of contested understandings about what Islamism is, how it relates to violence and religious dynamics, and the multiple desecularizing discourses through which explanations and solutions to this transnational phenomenon have been put forward.

This sprawling architecture would also start to constitute and contribute to the emergence of the wider American foreign policy regime complex on religion. For instance, parts of the infrastructure originally intended for the Faith-Based Foreign Aid regime, namely the Bush-era White House Office of Faith-Based and Community Initiatives, would be tasked by President Obama with an advisory role on global Muslim engagement matters. America's "ambassadors" to the OIC and Muslim communities would be progressively folded from 2013 onward into the institutions of a fourth distinct regime on Religious Engagement (explored in chapter 6).

The regime is grounded in and emerges out of a contestation of secular perspectives, habits, and practices in American foreign policy in the wake of the 9/11 attacks. In this context, the Islamic and Muslim Interventions regime is generating, like the regimes that emerged before it, processes of foreign policy desecularization. Institutional desecularization is apparent as the regime facilitates the inclusion of religious perspectives into the making and especially the implementation of American foreign policy, as substantial resources are directed to pacifying Muslim communities and reforming Islam. The regime is sustained by an epistemically desecularized outlook that reifies Muslim identity and tends to associate terrorism with Islam (especially during the Bush administration). Unlike the previous two regimes which are mostly grounded on a positive essentialization of religion in world politics, this chapter's regime has displayed an ambivalent position toward Muslims and Islam's role in world politics over time, seeing it mostly as a problem under the Bush administration and a force for good under Obama. Norms demanding a strict separation between state and mosque are likewise being revisited, although mostly informally, toward more accommodationist interpretations in order to support certain Muslims and forms of Islam over others.

When it comes to interventions in global religious and secular landscapes, the Muslim and Islamic Interventions regime displays important differences as well as similarities to the other regimes. What is most distinctive about it is its explicit focus on one particular religious tradition and religiously defined community, compared to regimes like the International Religious Freedom and Faith-Based Foreign Aid ones which are—in theory—religiously neutral. Like the other regimes, though, as the Muslim and Islamic Interventions regime attempts to manage, shape, and pacify the societies, politics, economics, and religiosity of Muslims, it does so following three particular American logics: first, America's national security priorities in the war on terror; second, its liberal views of modernity and order; and third, its prevalently Christian and Protestant understanding of religion. These three factors all play important roles in framing the kind of "moderate" and "good" Muslims and the "peaceful" and "true" Islam the regime seeks to support and thus promote. Whether the United States is actually successful in achieving these goals remains unclear.

The Muslim and Islamic Interventions regime furthermore contributes to the religionization of world politics both through processes of categorization as well as elevation. Regime institutions, policies, and discourses consistently normalize and (re)produce onto world politics the category of the Muslim, and at times of terrorism as predominantly a byproduct of Islam. Much of the Islamic interventions component of the regime is dedicated—either in the context of the war of ideas or CVE policies—to opening up space and elevating Muslim voices and Islamic interpretations in local and global politics that are alternative or in direct opposition to those of Islamists in general and violent groups in particular. In other words, more Islam rather than less is brought into the public sphere through the regime.

The Muslim and Islamic Interventions regime has formed and evolved in a wider context where comparable policies designed to govern Muslims and reform Islam have come to the fore. This suggests that like the United States, other states and international organizations may be responding—in their own ways—to similar domestic and international pressures brought by the emergence of a postsecular world society. What remains to be explored, though, is how America's war on terror policies directed at Muslims and Islam compare and relate to those of other countries and multilateral institutions, what processes of diffusion and knowledge circulation exist across these different sites, and, ultimately, what effects they may cumulatively be having on the life of more than 1.6 billion people identified as Muslims and on the trajectory of Islam, the world's second largest religion.

What does the future hold for the regime under the presidency of Donald Trump? The administration has made the fight against terrorism one of its top priorities. The regime is thus poised to continue, while also reverting to a more conflictual stance on Muslims and Islam however. In 2018, at the time of writing, multiple members of the Trump administration—whether current or past—have expressed anti-Muslim and anti-Islamic sentiments, including Michael Flynn, Steve Bannon, Jeff Sessions, John Bolton, Mike Pompeo, and Donald Trump himself.[154] Trump's campaign pledge for a "total and complete shut down of Muslims entering the United States,"[155] which materialized in a series of executive orders seeking to temporarily block travel to the United States from a selected number of Muslim-majority countries, is largely rooted in a clash of civilizations view of world politics.[156] President Trump's discourses and policies in this instance appear more in line with a Huntingtonian rather than Lewisian view of civilizational clashes, one where the West secures itself by protecting its borders, culture, and demographics rather than by attempting to reshape the Muslim world and Islam along liberal lines.

Unsurprisingly, Muslim engagement activities—underpinned by dialogue of civilizations thinking—have been scaled back. The two State Department special appointee positions to Muslim communities and the OIC remain vacant. For the first time in decades no White House *Iftar* dinner was held in

---

[154] Gjelten (2018); Hirsh (2016).
[155] Trump (2016).
[156] See also Haynes (2017).

2017. Reinstated in 2018, the dinner proved controversial since it largely catered to foreign diplomats with little attendance by American Muslim organizations.

Likewise, Donald Trump's insistence in lumping al Qaeda, ISIS, the Taliban, and other actors under the generic, broad rubric of "radical Islamic terrorism"— a label that explicitly links terrorism to Islam—signals a parallel shift back to a clash within a civilization discourse.[157] It seems unlikely that the administration will rebrand CVE efforts as "countering Islamic extremism" or "countering radical Islamic extremism," as it first suggested. Yet that Muslims are considered more so than ever the primary violent extremists that need to be countered is apparent in the multiple security-oriented plans the administration has been devising aimed at increasing surveillance of Muslim communities and immigrants.[158] Once again, squarely at the center of the attention, is the view that ideology and theology—rather than other social and political factors—is the main driver of terrorism and that moderate Muslims and Islam are thus its solution. Noticeable in this respect has been President Trump's support for Saudi Arabia's Global Center for Combating Extremist Ideology (*Etidal* in Arabic), whose stated mission is "fighting extremist ideology" and "spreading the principles of tolerance and moderation."[159]

---

[157] Trump (2017). For a perspective similarly suggesting a return to Bush-era "war of ideas" thinking on Islam, see Mandaville (2017).

[158] Patel and Lindsay (2018). Likewise the new National Strategy for Counterterrorism of the United States of America opens with the following statement: "our principal terrorist enemies are radical Islamist terrorist groups . . ." (USG 2018, 1).

[159] Quotes are taken from *Etidal's* website, at https://etidal.org/en/about-etidal/ (accessed July 30, 2018).

CHAPTER 6 | Religious Engagement

We ignore the global impact of religion . . . at our peril.
—Secretary of State John Kerry, 2013[1]

WITH THIS DIRE WARNING, President Obama's then newly appointed Secretary of State John Kerry launched the State Department's Office for Faith-Based and Community Initiatives in 2013. That same year saw the release of the first ever US Strategy on Religious Leader and Faith Community Engagement. Together the new strategy and office—later renamed the Office of Religion and Global Affairs (RGA) in 2015—marked the beginning of America's fourth explicitly religious foreign policy regime: the *Religious Engagement regime*. Its stated purpose was to build greater capacity in US foreign policy to understand the role of religion in world politics and, based on such understanding, to engage and mobilize religious actors and voices in the pursuit of American values and interests globally. Such values and interests would be described by the religious engagement strategy primarily in terms of providing effective development and humanitarian assistance, promoting human rights and religious freedom, and advancing peace and security.

The operationalization of the regime can be seen as representing both a moment of continuity as well as change in American foreign policy. Practices that could go under the rubric of religious engagement have been a staple of US foreign policy across history. Washington regularly looked to the expertise of protestant missionaries for advice on China, for instance, when they were among the few Americans, up to the mid-twentieth century, with any direct knowledge of China—even recruiting them on occasion as ambassadors to Beijing.[2] During the Cold War, in an effort to stem the advancement of "Godless" Communism and erode the power of the Soviet Union, the United States often turned to religion for help. It is in

---

[1] Kerry in Kerry, Casey, and Rogers (2013).
[2] Inboden (2010, ch. 4); Preston (2012, 194–195).

this context that successive US administrations from Truman to Reagan sought to form diplomatic alliances with Pope Pius XII and John Paul II, or supported religiously inspired actors from Christian Democratic parties in Western Europe to Catholic trade unions such as *Solidarność* in Poland, and the *Mujahidin* in Afghanistan.[3]

The 2013 strategy explicitly recognized such history, stating that "U.S. officials have long engaged religious leaders and institutions."[4] Yet it also noted that more than ever before, the Obama administration was now working "to elevate those efforts."[5] A tension, though, would bedevil this regime. On the one hand, religious engagement was thought of as a fourth stand alone policy area whose scope was to mobilize religions in line with US foreign policy goals as they were set out by any one particular administration. In this view, the Religious Engagement regime was understood as complementing a range of other religious foreign policy regimes with more specific mandates—stemming religious persecution, promoting humanitarian and development goals, or curbing Islamist terrorism—that were already in existence. On the other hand, as the US Strategy on Religious Leader and Faith Community Engagement revealed, the new regime was also thought of as a central hub for coordinating a sprawling set of offices, appointees, policies, and initiatives that had emerged since the end of the Cold War explicitly designed to target religious issues and actors across a range of issue. Ultimately, as we shall see, by the end of the Obama presidency the Religious Engagement regime never quite managed to achieve either, whether acquiring a distinctive identity or becoming an umbrella under which other regimes would be fully nested.

Regardless of this ambiguity at the core of the Religious Engagement regime, a step-change had clearly occurred with its operationalization represented most explicitly by the new strategy and RGA office. Why this change, and why in 2013? The next section shows how, like with the other regimes, the intellectual origins of this particular regime can be traced back to a range of actors coalescing in more or lesser organized ways around certain desecularizing discourses emerging with the end of the Cold War and gaining further momentum in the aftermath of 9/11. The two sections that follow trace how these discourses influenced the thinking, institutions, and practices of the first and second Obama administrations. They furthermore show why, despite strategic desecularizing discourses promoting religious engagement in American foreign policy had been circulating since at least the mid 1990s, the operationalization of the regime occurred only in 2013—a relatively late arrival compared to other religious foreign policy regimes. The chapter then assesses the multiple processes of foreign policy desecularization that the regime is both a product of and, by its very existence, itself contributing to. In

---

[3] Inboden (2010, ch. 3); Preston (2012, Part VII).
[4] White House (2013).
[5] Ibid.

the subsequent section, the chapter teases out the particular ways in which the regime intervenes in and affects religious and secular landscapes worldwide. In the conclusion, I summarize the chapter's findings and compare elements of the Religious Engagement regime to the previous three regimes. I then consider ongoing developments under the presidency of Donald Trump and the regime's future prospects.

Desecularizing Actors and Discourses in Context

For most of the twentieth century, the conventional wisdom among cultural elites in the United States—as well as in many other parts of the world—was that progress and modernization would spell, for better or worse, the death of God and the disenchantment of the world.[6] By the 1980s and 1990s, however, the first signs of a postsecular consciousness started to emerge in the American academy as ever more persistent questions were being raised about the supposedly secular or inevitably secularizing character of modern times. Indeed to a small but growing number of scholars, the world increasingly appeared in the thralls of a religious resurgence affecting most faiths and regions around the globe.

In the early 1990s, Marty Martin and Scott Appleby, for instance, were highlighting the modern character of religious fundamentalism, a phenomenon that was gaining ground across all major traditions including Christianity, Islam, Judaism, Buddhism, and Hinduism.[7] In 1993, Samuel Huntington predicted a post-Cold War-era marked, rather than by the triumph of secular liberal modernity, by rising intercivilizational and interreligious conflicts instead, with Islam at its forefront.[8] In 1994 José Casanova would advance one of the first, and most articulate, critiques of standard secularization theory.[9] By 1999 William Connolly was explaining why he was "not a secularist,"[10] while Peter Berger was repudiating his earlier belief in secularization theory and suggesting that the modern world was actually experiencing a process of "desecularization" rather than secularization.[11]

What is notable about this scholarly production was its frequently close connection to institutions seeking to influence public debates and policy. Huntington's theory appeared on the pages of *Foreign Affairs*, the leading journal among American foreign policy elites. Peter Berger's statement about desecularization was published under the auspices of the Ethics and Public Policy Center (EPPC), a Washington, DC-based think tank which self-describes

---

[6] Smith (2003).
[7] Marty and Appleby (1991–1995).
[8] Huntington (1993a).
[9] Casanova (1994).
[10] Connolly (1999).
[11] Berger (1999a, 2). It is important to highlight that such perspectives have not been confined only to the American academy (e.g., Eisenstadt 2000; Kepel 1994).

as conservative and Judeo-Christian in orientation. Scott Appleby would become a leading figure of the policy-oriented Kroc Institute for International Peace Studies at the University of Notre Dame, while José Casanova would become a faculty member of Georgetown University, the training ground for America's diplomatic and national security elites.

It was no coincidence, then, that the production of scholarly knowledge in the American academy about the limits of secularization theory and the need to bring religion back into the social sciences soon started to inform similar critiques contesting the secularity of the American foreign policy establishment and advocating the benefits of paying greater attention to religion in the making and implementation of US foreign policy itself. It is in this global context of resurging religions and domestic intellectual dissatisfaction with secularization theory and paradigms that a constellation of desecularizing experts—constituted by scholars, analysts, and former policymakers housed in leading universities and think tanks—would form around the 1990s–2000s. This loosely knit network of experts exhibited a particular interest in the nexus between religion, world affairs, and American foreign policy, and would articulate two strategic desecularizing discourses on the virtues and necessities of religious engagement abroad.

One discourse would present religious engagement in more narrow terms as a means of promoting peace and security; the other would present it more broadly as necessary to the advancement of international order and progress. Despite their different thematic focus, these two discourses would share several common features. First, both would present a world "heavily influenced by religion," if not even "abuzz with religious fervor."[12] Second, these discourses would identify a profound mismatch between what they perceived as a religiously fervent international reality and an American foreign policy establishment that suffered from a "religion avoidance syndrome" often rooted in a particular secular "bias" or "myopia."[13] This secular baggage, the discourses would argue, limited the effectiveness of American diplomacy in various ways. It blinded foreign policymakers to the worldwide role of religion and thus prevented them from anticipating history-making events such as the 1979 Iranian revolution, the 1989 fall of the Berlin Wall, or the terrorist attacks of September 11, 2001. In the rare instances when the power of the sacred was acknowledged in world politics, it would all too often be viewed in negative terms, as a problematic force that needed marginalizing rather than as a positive influence that could be harnessed. Secular lenses further sustained a separationist understanding of church–state relations that impeded attempts to systematically partner with religious actors worldwide in the service of American interests. Third, and finally, both desecularizing discourses would advance a wide range of solutions intended to obviate the secular shortcomings

---

[12] Quotes are respectively from Danan and Hunt (2007, 1) and Appleby and Cizik (2010, 21).
[13] See, for instance, Birdsall (2013); Appleby and Cizik (2010, 21); Danan and Hunt (2007, 3); Farr (2008a, 114); Mandaville and Silvestri (2015, 3); Seiple (2007).

of US foreign policy. The next two subsections explore in greater detail the main moments, networks, and actors articulating and advocating both the narrow and the broad understandings of religious engagement.

Narrow Strategic Desecularizing Discourse: Religious Engagement for Peace and Security

Huntington's concern in 1993 about an impending clash of civilizations was countered at the time by scholarship highlighting instead the peacemaking power of faith in world politics. Seminal here was a 1994 edited volume suggestively titled *Religion: The Missing Dimension of Statecraft*.[14] The volume forcefully advocated a paradigm shift in the way that America's foreign policy establishment thought about religion. Articles throughout complained that American foreign policy suffered from an "enlightenment prejudice"[15] or "dogmatic secularism,"[16] which blinded it to a post-Cold War world inflamed with religious fervor as well as to the power of religion to resolve conflicts and advance peace. A cultural change was necessary and with it also an institutional one. Edward Luttwak, a contributor to the volume, proposed that "religious attachés" be assigned to embassies in "countries where religion has a particular salience, to monitor religious movements and maintain contact with religious leaders."[17]

The brainchild of the project was Douglas Johnston, an Evangelical then at the Center for Strategic and International Studies (CSIS), a notorious Washington, DC-based think tank. The perception of a global resurgence of religion was pivotal to the inception and realization of Johnston's project:

> I had thought about such a book back in the 1980s. During the Cold War security environment, however, it was very difficult to think about religion and politics and we could find scarce funding for the project. But after 1989—with Communism crumbling, having seen the role of the Polish Pope and Walesa in the process, and ethnic conflicts blossoming everywhere—five foundations came forward and we were able to move ahead with the book.[18]

The volume was forwarded by former President Jimmy Carter and published under the auspices of CSIS, an institution, Johnston explained, "devoted to hardnosed strategic issues and known for its realist Cold War mentality."[19] The intent was clear: reach the broadest possible foreign policy audience to make the case that religion was anything but a dying or a problematic force globally. In a world where religion appeared increasingly tied to dynamics of violence and peace, addressing these issues head-on had become of paramount

---

[14] Johnston and Sampson (1994).
[15] Luttwak (1994, 9).
[16] Burnett (1994, 286).
[17] Luttwak (1994, 16).
[18] Johnston (2011a, author's interview).
[19] Ibid.

strategic importance, a matter of "realpolitik," as Johnston ever more forcefully suggested.[20]

Johnston left CSIS in 1999 to found the International Center for Religion and Diplomacy (ICRD), and put into practice what he was preaching. ICRD was revolutionary in that it was one of the first faith-based think-and-do tanks in the Washington, DC intellectual panorama entirely dedicated to researching and programing at the nexus of religion, security, and American foreign policy. Explicitly nonproselytizing, ICRD's mission has been, as its website states, to "bridg[e] religious considerations with the practice of international politics in support of peacemaking."[21]

Described as the "father" of "faith-based diplomacy,"[22] a cognate term for religious engagement, Johnston and his organization have sat at the intersection of an emerging and expanding epistemic community devoted to practicing and advancing the case of religious peacemaking in world politics and American foreign policy. This network includes, within more religiously based milieus, people like Doug Coe, head of the Evangelical-based Fellowship Foundation and the organizer of the yearly National Prayer Breakfast in Washington, DC; and William Vendley, of Religions for Peace International. Leading figures in academic milieus include Scott Appleby and Daniel Philpott,[23] both at the University of Notre Dame; and Andrea Bartoli and Marc Gopin, both at George Mason University.[24] Among think tanks, the US Institute for Peace (USIP) would become, since the launch in 2000 of its Religion and Peacemaking Program, a particularly influential voice articulating the narrow peace and security-oriented desecularizing discourse on religious engagement.[25]

A pivotal moment in the circulation and diffusion within the foreign policy establishment of this discourse came in 2007. In the context of a post-9/11 world, with US forces mired in conflicts in Iraq and Afghanistan, CSIS turned its gaze once again to religion. It did so with a 92-page-strong report, led by Liora Danan, titled *Mixed Blessings: U.S. Government Engagement with Religion in Conflict-Prone Settings*. The report, which tellingly opened with a quote by Peter Berger, set out to explore how US foreign policy was adapting and responding to an "age of explosive, pervasive religiosity."[26] The report noted how despite some positive changes—by 2007 in fact the International Religious Freedom,

---

[20] Johnston (2003); also Johnston (2011b).
[21] Quote is taken from ICRD's website, at http://icrd.org/ (accessed December 22, 2016).
[22] Moll (2008).
[23] Appleby (2000); Philpott (2012; 2007); Cox and Philpott (2003). Among other things, Philpott has also taken part in faith-based reconciliation projects in places like Kashmir under the auspices of ICRD.
[24] Andrea Bartoli has been involved in many conflict resolution activities as a member of the Catholic faith-based organization Community of Sant'Egidio. Among his publications, see Nan, Mampilly, and Bartoli (2011). Marc Gopin, Director of the Center for World Religions, Diplomacy and Conflict Resolution at George Mason University, is the author of a number of seminal books on religious peacemaking (see especially Gopin 2002; 2000; 1997).
[25] See, for example, Smock (2006).
[26] Berger quoted in Danan and Hunt (2007, 1).

Faith-Based Foreign Aid, and Muslim and Islamic Interventions regimes were already in place—it still found these developments wanting. Secular resistance within the foreign policy establishment, the report argued, led to "poor conflict anticipation, counterproductive policies and missed opportunities for religion-related solutions."[27]

Broad Strategic Desecularizing Discourse: Religious Engagement for International Order and Progress

A second strategic desecularizing discourse on religious engagement would emerge from the 2000s onward, this time oriented toward broader issues of international order and progress rather than solely focused on security matters. This discourse was articulated and deployed by a network of scholars, policy analysts, and policymakers—some explicitly faith-based—which often connected and included other networks of desecularizing actors with an interest in religious peacemaking, international religious freedom, faith-based humanitarianism, and Islamic and Muslim world issues.

Three moments were particularly important in the development and deployment of the broader discourse on religious engagement. The first coincided with a critique, gathering pace in American scholarly milieus in the aftermath of 9/11, of the secular underpinnings of IR theories and American foreign policy practices. For some in this scholarly milieu, such as Elizabeth Shakman Hurd, the critique of the secular represented an aspect of a more general critique of any attempt by the state to govern religion.[28] For others, however, it represented a means for subsequently articulating elements of the broad discourse on religious engagement. Exemplifying this latter strand of scholarship is Monica Duffy Toft, Daniel Philpott, and Timothy Samuel Shah's 2011 book, *God's Century: Resurgent Religion and Global Politics*. The book combines research by three leading scholars in the emerging field of religion and IR, and notably concludes with a list of recommendations to American foreign policy analysts and practitioners on how to "survive" God's century.[29]

A second consequential moment came with the publication in 2006 of Madeleine Albright's autobiographical reflections on how the "almighty" had become surprisingly relevant to world affairs and as a result also to America's national interest at the dawn of the twenty-first century. "To anticipate events rather than merely respond to them," Albright reasoned, "American diplomats will need to . . . think more expansively about the role of religion in foreign policy and about their own need for expertise."[30] The fact that such a prominent former Secretary of State would so forcefully, and repeatedly,[31] appeal to the foreign policy establishment to take religions

---

[27] Danan and Hunt (2007, 5).
[28] Hurd (2008). See also Hurd (2015).
[29] Toft, Philpott, and Shah (2011); also Patterson (2011).
[30] Albright (2006, 99).
[31] See, for example, Albright (2015); and US-Muslim Engagement Project (2009).

seriously would have a considerable galvanizing and legitimizing effect on the religious engagement agenda.

A third pivotal moment in the articulation and mobilization of the broad discourse on religious engagement occurred with the release in 2010 of the report *Engaging Religious Communities Abroad: A New Imperative for U.S. Foreign Policy.*[32] The report was notable for a number of reasons. First, it was explicitly intended to inform the foreign policy of the newly established Obama administration and was released under the auspices of a think tank, the Chicago Council on Global Affairs (from hereon Chicago Council), with important connections to the Obamas.[33] Second, on the back of America's arguably unsuccessful military experiences in Iraq and Afghanistan, the report assembled in one place multiple leading voices calling for greater attention, across issues and areas, to religion in American foreign policy. The report's task force was led by the University of Notre Dame scholar Scott Appleby and the Evangelical lobbyist and advocate Richard Cizik, and included prominent policy and faith-based voices championing religious peacemaking, religious freedom, faith-based aid, and Muslim engagement.[34] Finally, the report laid out some of the most extensive normative, institutional, and policy recommendations for making religious engagement "an integral part of [American] foreign policy."[35] Suggestions included building capacity in the National Security Council (NSC) for addressing the role of religion in world affairs, providing mandatory training on these matters to government officials, and clarifying that the Establishment Clause did not bar policymakers from engaging religious leaders and communities abroad.[36]

These three publications—Toft et al.'s *God Century*, Albright's *Mighty and the Almighty*, and the Chicago Council's report—emerged in the context of a rapidly expanding infrastructure within universities, think tanks, and research institutes designed to produce foreign policy-relevant knowledge about religion, and connect the faith-based, scholarly, and policymaking worlds. Within the walls of academia, for instance, Georgetown University's Berkley Center would become a major force in this field. Launched in 2006, the Berkley Center has been organized around an ever-expanding number of programs carrying out research, organizing conferences, educating students, and training policymakers on the intersection between religion and a host of issues including globalization, US foreign policy, human rights, democracy and

---

[32] Appleby and Cizik (2010).
[33] Michelle Obama sits on the Chicago Council's board of directors and it was here that then-Senator Barack Obama gave the first major foreign policy speech of his presidential campaign on April 2007.
[34] These included José Casanova, Thomas F. Farr, Ken Hackett, William Inboden, Martin Indyk, Douglas Johnston, Katherine Marshall, Radwan A. Masmoudi, Dalia Mogahed, Eboo Patel, Rabbi David Saperstein, and Timothy Samuel Shah.
[35] Appleby and Cizik (2010, 13).
[36] In a dissenting note, Jean Bethke Elshtain, Thomas Farr, William Inboden, David Neff, and Timothy Samuel Shah would go as far as suggesting that the Establishment Clause should not be applied to foreign policy matters at all, especially when national security concerns were involved (Appleby and Cizik 2010, 84).

religious freedom, development, conflict and peace, and Islam in world politics. The center hosts prominent names in these fields such as José Casanova, Timothy Samuel Shah, Thomas Farr, Katherine Marshall, and Jocelyne Cesari. Other noteworthy initiatives in the academic space include Harvard University's Initiative on Religion in International Affairs (2007–2012) directed by Monica Duffy Toft, and the Global Politics and Religion Initiative in Johns Hopkins' School for Advanced International Studies (SAIS) (2012–2014). Both were especially designed to promote greater understanding of religion among foreign policy practitioners.

In the world of think tanks, the Institute for Global Engagement (IGE), an Evangelical-based think-and-do tank founded in 2000, has become a leading voice in this space. While IGE's programmatic interest has tended to be around promoting religious freedom, its intellectual presence in Washington, DC has mostly focused on exploring the nexus between religion and international affairs and advocating for a broad conception of religious engagement in US foreign policy. It has done this directly through the normative entrepreneurship of its then President Chris Seiple, but also in more indirect ways, for instance by launching in 2002 the *Review of Faith & International Affairs*, the first peer-reviewed journal entirely dedicated to issues of religion and global politics. The *Review's* mission, its editor Dennis Hoover explained to me, has been to "bridge the academic, policymakers and religious worlds."[37] Although Chris Seiple and IGE can be said to epitomize the broad discourse on religious engagement, while Doug Johnston and ICRD epitomize the narrower one on peace and security, collaboration between the two institutes has, in fact, not been uncommon.[38]

One innovation that stands out in the more conventional, and scarcely faith-friendly, think-tank community is the Council on Foreign Relations' (CFR) Religion and Foreign Policy Initiative. By 2016, the initiative's Advisory Committee boasted the presence of Madeleine Albright and other prominent analysts of religion, theologians, religious leaders, and faith-based advocates.[39] The initiative was created in 2006, Irina Faskianos of CFR explains, in "reaction to the growing presence of religious voices in foreign policy debates" and with the desire to provide a structured "forum to deepen the understanding of issues at the nexus of religion and US foreign policy."[40] It does so particularly effectively through, among other means, its *Religion and Foreign Policy Conference Call* series designed to give "religious and congregational leaders, scholars, and thinkers the opportunity to participate in nonpartisan, cross-denominational conversations on global issues."[41] Numerous other think tanks

---

[37] Hoover (2011, author's interview).
[38] Hoover and Johnston (2012).
[39] These include Bryan Hehir, Richard Land, Eboo Patel, Feisal Abdul Rauf, David Saperstein, Chris Seiple, Richard Stearns, and Jim Wallis.
[40] Faskianos (2011, author's interview).
[41] The quote is taken from CFR's website, at http://www.cfr.org/events/series.html?id=85 (accessed April 24, 2017).

and research institutes have joined the religion bandwagon. The Pew Research Center on Religion and Public Life, launched in the immediate aftermath of 9/11, has become a key site for the extensive production of practitioner-friendly research on religion in global affairs. The Brookings Institution has been particularly active in this space too.[42]

To summarize: starting from the early 1990s and accelerating exponentially in the aftermath of 9/11, a loosely knit epistemic community, carrier of a postsecular consciousness, emerged among international affairs scholars, analysts, and policymakers in the United States. This network of experts articulated and mobilized two strategic desecularizing discourses on religious engagement. One presented religious engagement more narrowly as a means of promoting peace and security, and the other presented it in more ambitious and broad terms as a means of promoting international order and progress. These discourses proposed a range of solutions to what they perceived as the problematic gap existing between the global vibrancy and resurgence of religion, on the one hand, and the secularity of American foreign policy, on the other. This intellectual effort was necessary although not entirely sufficient, as we shall see in the next section, to the institutionalization of America's fourth explicitly religious regime.

The First Obama Administration: Mobilizing from Within to Operationalize Religious Engagement

Early Obstacles to Regime Operationalization

Since the mid-1990s, when religious engagement discourses first emerged, there were a number of occasions when the religious engagement agenda could have become official US foreign policy. Yet this did not occur. One occasion presented itself around the mid-1990s. Both issues of religious freedom and Doug Johnston's notion of faith-based diplomacy were then receiving growing attention within the State Department. In 1996, Secretary of State Warren Christopher established an Advisory Committee on Religious Freedom Abroad, with some members of the commission focused on religious freedom and others on matters of religious peacemaking and reconciliation, Johnston recalls.[43] By 1998, however, the religious freedom agenda was being institutionalized, while attention to religious peacemaking fell by the wayside. A second occasion for operationalizing religious engagement would come in the aftermath of 9/11. Yet while the terrorist attacks acted as a critical juncture for the operationalization of the Muslim and Islamic Interventions regime, they did not provide the same opening for the religious engagement agenda.

---

[42] See, for instance, Hehir (2004), and Mandaville and Silvestri (2015).
[43] Berkley Center (2014b, 18:04–18:09). For the Advisory Committee's report see US Department of State (1998).

In each instance, religious engagement faced several important obstacles. First, compared to the international religious freedom agenda, religious engagement could not count on the same broad-based and grass-roots political and faith-based mobilization expressed in the passage of the 1998 International Religious Freedom Act (IRFA) by Congress.[44] Religious engagement has been mostly promoted by an elite group of experts with little connection to American political movements or official religious institutions. Second, the nature of the 9/11 events conducted by a group claiming to act in the name of Islam and Muslims lent particular urgency to the desecularizing discourses focusing on Islam and the Muslim world, rather than on religious engagement more generally. Moreover, the conciliatory and diplomatically flavored concept of engagement lacked resonance with a Republican administration whose security-focused reaction to 9/11 was heavily tilted toward a conflictual view of Islam and Muslims, and a militarized and unilateral approach to foreign policy.[45] Judd Birdsall, a key proponent of religious engagement, recalls these hurdles as follows:

> By pushing through the IRFA, Congress took up all the religious space in the 1990s. 9/11 securitized thinking on religion. To the extent that engaging religion was important, the [Bush] administration was thinking of engaging Islam. It was hard at the time to broaden and put forward a more ecumenical agenda.[46]

The election of Barack Obama changed much of that. Two important factors—exogenous to postsecular processes—came together at this critical juncture, opening up space for and giving impetus to the religious engagement agenda. First, President Obama promoted a strategic shift in American foreign policy toward an approach that favored multilateralism and diplomacy over unilateralism and militarism.[47] The Obama administration often deployed the very same concept of engagement to capture this change in its overarching strategy, whether in launching a new era of engagement with disaffected European allies or longstanding rivals such as Iran and Russia.[48] Second, President Obama exhibited an equal enthusiasm to that of his predecessor toward the operationalization of religion in foreign policy. This was apparent once he kept, but also elevated and broadened, the mission of the Bush-era White House Office of Faith-Based Initiatives (WHOFBI) – a general name I use for an office that has been changing title from one administration to the next.[49] Obama's inclination toward a foreign policy of engagement on the one hand, and his openness to religion on the other, crystallized

---

[44] See this book's chapter 3.
[45] See this book's chapter 5.
[46] Birdsall (2015, author's interview).
[47] Nau (2010).
[48] See, for example, USG (2010).
[49] Named White House Office of Faith-Based and Community Initiatives during the Bush administration, it would then be called White House Office of Faith-Based and Neighborhood Partnerships during the Obama presidency.

most explicitly at the start of his administration in the president's famous 2009 "New Beginning" address in Cairo and the "global Muslim engagement" policy framework that took shape around it.[50]

Championing Religious Engagement from Within Government

In this context, officials already tied to the existing religious foreign policy regime infrastructure—most notably in the WHOFBI and in the State Department's Office for International Religious Freedom (OIRF)—either saw an opportunity for or were even directly invited by the president to advance the religious engagement agenda from within the foreign policy bureaucracy.[51] Regime champions within the halls of power were not alone, though, as they could count on, and draw from, the intellectual and expert resources outside of government who had been promoting both the narrow and broad conceptions of religious engagement. During the first Obama administration, a number of initiatives and sites within the foreign policy bureaucracy soon became pivotal in forming networks with external experts and pushing for the operationalization of a fourth explicitly religious foreign policy regime.

One such site was the Religion and Global Affairs Forum launched in 2009 by Judd Birdsall, an official in the State Department's OIRF who also exhibited important links to the faith-based think-and-do tank IGE. The forum was designed as a venue for sharing ideas, generating discussions, and inviting speakers with the objective, Birdsall explains, to "foster collaboration on religious engagement and socialize the Department to the growing salience of religion in international relations."[52] Connections with the external epistemic community championing the cause of religious engagement were soon made. The forum's first two invited speakers, for instance, were Douglas Johnston and Chris Seiple, leading voices respectively advocating both the narrow (peace and security) and broad (international order and progress) understanding of religious engagement.[53] The forum's guiding principle was to contest a State Department culture seen as inimical to taking religion seriously. As Birdsall saw it, "if you were a strict church–state separationist," as most officials in the State Department were, "there would be large swathes of the earth that you just couldn't engage at all."[54]

The WHOFBI would become a second important site championing the operationalization of religious engagement. From the start of Obama's presidency it had been given a wider mandate—compared to the one mostly focused on assisting the poor and vulnerable under Bush—to think more expansively about the role of religion in world politics and American foreign policy. An official in President Obama's White House explained to me the thinking at the time:

---

50 On global Muslim engagement policies, see chapter 5.
51 Birdsall (2012); Frykholm (2013).
52 Birdsall (2012, 35).
53 Birdsall (2015).
54 Birdsall in Frykholm (2013).

Although it is in our national interest to have a better grasp of religious dynamics internationally, we have done a poor job at it so far. People at the State Department have a secular bias. They lack an appreciation of the importance and power of religion [in world politics], because they also lack an appreciation for religion in their own lives, and see religion as inherently regressive. In many places the only civil society that works effectively is religious. We as government need to understand this and work with them better. President Obama gets it and he's moving in the right direction by expanding the White House office's responsibilities.[55]

One way in which the WHOFBI's responsibilities were expanded was by constituting a twenty-five-strong Advisory Council to think more broadly about the role of religion in America's domestic and foreign policy. The Council's 2010 report called for a "new era of partnerships" with religious actors and communities.[56] Partly in response to this call, a White House-led Interagency Working Group on Religion and Global Affairs was created in 2010 connecting the WHOFBI to members of the National Security Council (NSC), the Center for Faith-Based and Community Initiatives (CFBCI) at USAID, and OIRF in the State Department. The working group's objective was to bring together different parts of the foreign policy bureaucracy with an interest in religion, and find ways to better coordinate ongoing activities and further integrate religious considerations in American foreign policy. A *Religious Engagement Report* was being compiled with the help of colleagues at USAID and the State Department to survey and assess what was "already going on within the U.S. Government in terms of our interaction and engagement with religious leaders abroad," explained Joshua DuBois, director at the time of Obama's WHOFBIs.[57]

The report's findings highlighted that religious engagement was often "sporadic and ad hoc."[58] That's because foreign policymakers, the document argued, lacked an understanding of what was permissible under the Constitution's Establishment Clause, knowledge about religion itself, and the expertise required to best engage with religious actors. The report also provided multiple examples—from places like Nigeria, Tanzania, Israel, India, and the Philippines—which showcased the contributions that religious actors and existing partnerships with them were making to American foreign policy objectives.[59] The whole exercise provided argumentative ammunition to religious engagement champions in the administration to press the case for greater systematization, strategizing, and capacity-building in this policy space.[60]

Within the State Department, a Religion and Foreign Policy Working Group would be created in 2011. This working group would become a third key

---

[55] WHOFBI Official (2010, author's interview).
[56] White House (2010).
[57] DuBois (2010).
[58] DuBois (2010); also Birdsall (2012, 36).
[59] WHOFBI Official (2010); also Frykholm (2013).
[60] WHOFBI Official (2010); also Birdsall (2012, 36); DuBois (2010).

bureaucratic site for advancing the religious engagement agenda from within government. The working group emerged in response to two trends. On the one hand, it followed on from the momentum being generated by the OIRF's Religion and Global Affairs Forum and the activities and reports coming from the White House. On the other hand, it developed in the context of Secretary of State Hillary Clinton's push to broaden American diplomacy beyond standard state-to-state interactions toward greater engagement with non-state and civil society actors as well.[61]

The State Department's Religion and Foreign Policy Working Group brought together a range of people that exemplified the multiple forces at play championing the religious engagement agenda from within and outside government. The working group counted on two governmental representatives: one from OIRF, in the figure of Ambassador-at-Large for International Religious Freedom Suzan Johnson Cook; and the other from the WHOFBI, in the figure of its director Joshua DuBois. These were joined by two civil society advisors, each representing a different facet of the religious engagement discourse: William Vendley of Religions for Peace International, who mostly subscribed to the narrower discourse on engagement for peace and security; and Chris Seiple of IGE, who had mostly been articulating the broader discourse on engagement for international order and progress.

Unsurprisingly, the working group's White Paper reproduced much of the language of both the narrow and broad desecularizing discourses on religious engagement. The paper called on the State Department to abandon a "culture" that views religion as "anachronistic" and as a "source of conflict and division," and to recognize instead that "four out of five people on the planet believe in something greater than themselves" and that religion is often a "force for peace, human rights, democracy, and development."[62] Following on these premises, the report recommended that guidance be sought on the "applicability of the Establishment Clause . . . overseas."[63] It further suggested that capacity be built within the foreign policy bureaucracy—through trainings, improved coordination across religious regimes, a purposely drafted strategy, and a dedicated office for religious engagement—in order to better understand and mobilize religion worldwide in the pursuit of American interests.[64]

A fourth institutional site where progress was being made in terms of moving the religious engagement forward, was in the realm of training. Around 2010 new trainings on religion started to be offered to State Department officials and diplomats. Building on the findings of the White House-led *Religious Engagement Report*, for instance, Judd Birdsall and colleagues organized in

---

[61] The Religion and Foreign Policy Working Group was part of a larger Strategic Dialogue with Civil Society initiative launched by Secretary Clinton in 2011.
[62] Religion and Foreign Policy Working Group (2012, 5, 3).
[63] Ibid., 4.
[64] Ibid., 7–10.

2010 a symposium hosted by USIP with officials, scholars, and activists titled "USG Religious Engagement Overseas."[65] Drawing from expertise and knowledge accumulated by the International Religious Freedom and the Muslim and Islamic Interventions regimes, the Foreign Service Institute launched in 2011 a new stand-alone three-day elective course titled "Religion and Foreign Policy." "A yawning gap in diplomat training has begun to be filled," an enthusiastic Judd Birdsall remarked at the time.[66]

Overall, by the end of President Obama's first term, considerable intellectual and bureaucratic momentum had been built from a range of sources for the operationalization of religious engagement in US foreign policy. All that was missing was a clear mandate and an institutional home—arguably both important. The opportunity arrived on the back of Barack Obama's re-election and the appointment of a new secretary of state.

The Second Obama Administration: Operationalizing the Religious Engagement Regime

The momentum that had been building around the religious engagement agenda during Barack Obama's first term bore its fruits upon the president's re-election. In the summer of 2013 the Religious Engagement regime became a reality with the simultaneous launch of the first ever US Strategy on Religious Leader and Faith Community Engagement by the White House and the creation of an Office for Faith-Based and Community Initiatives in the State Department by Secretary of State John Kerry. The presence and mobilization of an existing religious foreign policy regime infrastructure would be pivotal in making all this happen. It obviated the lack of widespread grass-roots mobilization efforts which plagued the religious engagement agenda, while also providing a supportive platform and bureaucratic environment to build upon and institutionalize yet another religious foreign policy regime.

The White House strategy signaled that promoting greater and more coordinated engagement with religious actors and issues was of central concern to the president. It laid out three overarching objectives for the newly emerging regime: promote development and effective humanitarian assistance; advance pluralism and human rights, including religious freedom; and prevent, mitigate, and resolve violent conflict and contribute to stability and security.[67] The strategy was developed in the context of the White House Interagency Working Group on Religion and Global Affairs under the leadership of Shaarik Zafar, then-director of Global Engagement in the White House National Security Council.

---

[65] Birdsall (2012, 36).
[66] Ibid.
[67] White House (2013).

The new office in the State Department was charged with turning the strategy into action and, as Secretary Kerry explained during its inauguration, to "expand our understanding of religious dynamics and engagement with religious actors."[68] At first the office was named along the lines of similar centers created in the context of President Bush's faith-based initiatives. In 2015, however, it would be renamed as the Office of Religion and Global Affairs (from hereon, RGA). The new title mirrored those of the eponymous State Department Forum and White House Interagency Group. This change further signaled how the new State Department entity would focus on religious engagement as a distinct policy issue, constituting a separate regime, rather than being strictly tied to the Bush-era faith-based initiatives architecture.

The office, Kerry acknowledged, was in fact the product of multiple forces that had been pushing for some time for the operationalization of the religious engagement agenda. These included the State Department's Religion and Foreign Policy Working Group, supportive staff in the White House, and the role of out-of-government desecularizing experts, such as Madeleine Albright.[69] Kerry's own leadership and role as a desecularizing policymaker was pivotal too. Indeed, despite multiple calls over the years, Secretary Clinton never came round to establishing an institutional home for religious engagement. "Of the different streams which led to the creation of the office, the most important is that of Secretary Kerry," an official in the RGA told me.[70] The issue of religious engagement seems to have resonated particularly with the former Massachusetts Senator also thanks to Kerry's own postsecular conversion. "If I headed back to college today," Kerry has often been fond of saying, "I would major in comparative religions rather than political science."[71]

Secretary Kerry's address during the launch of the RGA closely reproduced most of the themes in the desecularizing discourses on religious engagement. First, the statement "we ignore the global impact of religion, in my judgment, at our peril" emphasizes the strategic need for American diplomacy to realize that religion matters, and increasingly so, in world politics. Second, with his claim that "all of these faiths are virtuous" he raises the importance of recognizing that religion is mostly a force for good, rather than a source of problems. Third, when suggesting the "need to partner with [faith communities around the world] to solve global challenges," he clearly articulates the imperative of finding ways to mobilize religion's positive force in the pursuit of America's foreign policy goals. Finally, Kerry recognizes that such a policy can take place within the confines of existing constitutional norms on church–state separation, as all of these things "can be done without crossing any lines whatsoever."[72]

---

[68] Kerry (2015).
[69] Kerry in Kerry, Casey, and Rogers (2013).
[70] RGA Official (2015, author's interview); see also Willard (2014).
[71] Kerry (2015).
[72] Kerry in Kerry, Casey, and Rogers (2013).

The RGA would be given three overarching tasks.[73] The first was to advise the secretary of state and other elements of the bureaucracy on policy matters as they related to religion. For this purpose, the RGA would be strategically positioned within the Secretary's Bureau and physically placed on the State Department's notorious seventh floor where the secretary and his immediate staff are located. Along with formal structures, having informal and personal access to the secretary of state is often of vital importance too. Shaun Casey, then a professor of Christian ethics at Wesley Theological Seminar in Washington, DC, was appointed to lead the office. Described as a "friend" by Kerry himself, Casey—who had acted as an advisor on religious issues and outreach to the former Massachusetts Senator since the mid-2000s—could clearly count on having the secretary's ear.[74]

Second, the RGA would be tasked with a range of capacity building efforts. Most importantly, these would concentrate on building the competence of the State Department, its bureaus, and embassies to assess religious dynamics and engage with religious actors. To do so, the RGA actively leveraged in-house State Department expertise as well as faith-based and scholarly perspectives from outside of government. In September 2016, for instance, in partnership with Georgetown University's Berkley Center and others, the RGA convened the first ever "Religion and Diplomacy Conference" hosted by the State Department. Government officials, scholars, religious practitioners, and community activists were invited to showcase approaches on how to assess religious dynamics, share experiences of religious engagement and identify success stories, and deepen and expand networks between government, experts, and religious actors. The RGA would seek to promote knowledge about faith communities and religious engagement by providing training opportunities to fellow State Department colleagues as well as by expanding the courses offered by the Foreign Service Institute. On the back of these efforts, Secretary Kerry issued numerous invitations to American diplomats, explicitly encouraging them to connect with religious leaders and communities around the world.[75] Along the way, Kerry, Casey, and other prominent officials in the office such as Peter Mandaville, a well-known scholar of political Islam and RGA special advisor, would participate in numerous roundtables, events, and workshops designed to explain the value and activities of the Religious Engagement regime to domestic constituencies and international audiences.[76]

---

[73] US Department of State (2016a).

[74] Kerry in Kerry, Casey, and Rogers (2013); also Willard (2014).

[75] For example Kerry in Kerry, Casey, and Rogers (2013). In March 2015, Kerry also sent a letter to all US embassies urging them to connect with religious leaders and groups.

[76] On domestic events see for instance, Kerry (2016), and Berkley Center (2016b). Foreign conferences that members of Obama's RGA participated in, include "Religion, Foreign Policy and Development: Making Better Policy to Make a Bigger Difference," Wilton Park, UK, February 5–7, 2014; "International Politics, Diplomacy and Religion Scientific Coordinators," European University Institute, Florence, Italy, May 4–5, 2015; "Making Democracy One's Own: Muslim, Catholic and Secular Perspectives in Dialogue on Democracy, Development, and Peace," Notre Dame Global Gateway, Rome, Italy, May 30–June 1, 2016.

The third objective of Shaun Casey's office would be to serve as a first point of contact for external faith-based actors interested in engaging the State Department on matters of concern as they relate to religion and world politics. Casey has claimed that within the first months of the office's creation, "over 400 domestic religious groups, actors or NGOs" had knocked at his door.[77]

Aside from these tasks, what kind of religious knowledge and engagement would the regime actually produce, and for what purpose? The institutional structure, policy ideas, and practices of the RGA during President Obama's second term reveal a hybrid at best or amorphous at worst regime that struggled to define its role and identity within the foreign policy bureaucracy and in relation to other regimes. The reasons for this are complex. I would suggest, though, that these could be traced to the regime embodying a combination and an uneasy cohabitation of the broad international order-oriented and the narrow security-focused conceptions of religious engagement.

The broad view of religious engagement was on display in the RGA's implicit designation as the main institutional hub for religious matters as they pertained to American statecraft. For instance, the office was seen as the custodian of the US Strategy on Religious Leader and Faith Community Engagement, despite the strategy also focused on matters pertaining to other regimes such as international religious freedom, and humanitarian and development assistance.[78] Moreover, the RGA would mobilize religious resources and actors on a wide range of issues. For instance, it harnessed the growing environmental consciousness among religious communities and movements—epitomized for instance by Pope Francis' 2015 encyclical *Laudato Si* on the environment and human ecology, and the 2015 Islamic Declaration on Global Climate Change—to pressure for an agreement in the 2015 Paris Climate Change Conference. Other initiatives focused on the Syrian refugee crisis, anti-corruption efforts in Nigeria, and combating Islamophobia and anti-Semitism in Europe.[79] In parallel, the office was designed to act as a bureaucratic hub for consolidating a variety of pre-existing special appointees with a religiously related mandate, including the Special Envoy to the Organization of Islamic Cooperation (OIC), the Special Representative to Muslim Communities, and the Special Envoy to Monitor and Combat Anti-Semitism.

This said, political, bureaucratic, and strategic factors would also limit the RGA's ability to pursue a broad understanding of the religious engagement agenda, and become the umbrella under which other religious foreign policy regimes would be nested. Judd Birdsall, for instance, would argue that "ideally we should see the religious freedom office folding into

---

[77] Casey in Belfer Center (2016, 6:42–6:46).>
[78] The strategy was available online only through the RGA's website.
[79] For an extensive overview of RGA activities, see Casey in Berkley Center (2016b, 05:56–18:30). Also US Department of State (2017).

the RGA."[80] This did not occur, however, largely due to countervailing pressures from different fronts. "Congress will not want and allow it [folding OIRF into RGA] to happen," an OIRF official would explain to me, "given that there are important political pressures making sure that the OIRF remains independent."[81] Likewise within the RGA, many did not want to associate the more diplomatically oriented religious engagement agenda with the normative commitments, watchdog functions, and politicized reputation of the International Religious Freedom regime. Thus the two regimes would be seen as complementary at best, or perceived as rivals at worst. The RGA did certainly bring under its roof America's special representatives to Muslim communities and the OIC, and would be involved in Countering Violent Extremism (CVE) activities. Yet the office's tasks constituted only a part of the wider ongoing foreign policy effort to win the hearts and minds of Muslims and shape theological, legal, and political debates within Islam (which where explored in chapter 5).

Moreover, the narrow-security focused understanding of religious engagement appeared to shape in important ways the identity and focus of the regime as well. Of the three overarching objectives laid out by the US Strategy on Religious Leader and Faith Community Engagement—international development and humanitarian assistance, human rights and religious freedom, and peace and security—only the last one did not already have a specifically dedicated office across the foreign policy bureaucracy. Not surprisingly, then, a sizable part of the RGA's energies and high-level staff would be dedicated precisely to tackling security issues. Shaun Casey's chief of staff Liora Danan, the lead author of the land-mark CSIS report *Mixed Blessings*, joined the RGA from the Bureau of Conflict and Stabilization Operations, where she was managing the religion and conflict mitigation portfolio. RGA Special Advisor Peter Mandaville not only advised on efforts to counter ISIS and violent extremism, but also focused on sectarian tensions in the Middle East. The Israeli-Palestinian conflict and the issue of gender and security would be on the RGA's agenda, as well as carrying out engagement activities with leaders in Orthodox-majority countries such as Ukraine and Cyprus to promote social and political stability and security.

Overall, then, with the second Obama presidency and under the leadership of Secretary Kerry, years if not decades of patient advocacy finally yielded results as the religious engagement agenda obtained its own White House-sanctioned strategy and its institutional home in the State Department. The importance given to this agenda was noticeable by the place the RGA was assigned in State's bureaucracy, namely among the bureaus/offices reporting directly to the Office of the Secretary. Likewise, by the end of the Obama presidency, the

---

[80] Birdsall (2015, author's interview). Similarly, Jocelyne Cesari (2015, author's interview) notes that "the long term goal of the RGA, would be to absorb the OIRF."

[81] OIRF Official 2 (2015, author's interview); also Birdsall (2015).

RGA reached within just a few years the count of thirty staff members, as many as those of OIRF which instead had a much longer history.[82] Yet the regime would struggle with carving out a specific identity and mandate; either as an entirely different regime among others—within a larger, loosely connected regime complex—focused on a clearly defined set of issues (especially in and around religious peacemaking and conflict-resolution), or as a capacious space for understanding and engaging religion in the pursuit of a wide range of diplomatic, humanitarian, human rights, and security objectives, thus also becoming the central hub around which all other regimes would be reorganized to form a larger and clearly structured nested regime.

Foreign Policy Desecularization

The operationalization of the Religious Engagement regime was made possible by the contestation and successful redefinition of the boundaries between the religious and the secular in American foreign policy. This contestation has led, in turn, to different parallel processes of desecularization. Processes of institutional desecularization have occurred as the regime brought about greater entanglements between religious actors and perspectives, and the institutions that make and execute American foreign policy. The very concept of religious *engagement* is premised on the need to establish a sustained interaction between state and religion. Thus theologians, like Shaun Casey, have been invited to lead the RGA. Likewise, "the knowledge and expertise of religious scholars, leaders, practitioners, activists, representatives from civil society, and the rank and file," Casey explains, would be highly sought after in order to "enrich the U.S. foreign policymaking process."[83] In terms of foreign policy implementation, the regime has likewise sought to generate, in the words of Secretary Kerry, "wider and deeper ties" with religious leaders and communities.[84] In this case, however, institutional entanglements with religion have not been as substantial as those generated by other regimes, since the RGA would not—for the most part—facilitate or channel funds to faith-based actors.

Religious engagement has also been part and parcel of a wider cultural shift that has seen an erosion of epistemic and ideological secularist assumptions among members of the foreign policy establishment. In the words of Secretary Kerry:

> Historically the State Department has tended to downplay the role of religion [i.e., epistemic secularism] or pay attention only when religion is deemed a problem, a threat, a challenge [i.e., ideological secularism]. The department has not traditionally had the resources or made the necessary commitment to systematically

---

[82] Casey in *Desert News* (2018); Seiple in CFR (2018, 0:38:33–0:38:40).
[83] Casey (2016).
[84] Kerry (2016).

analyze the importance that religion holds for the success or failure of our foreign policy. . . . Now that has changed.[85]

Actors and perspectives tied to the Religious Engagement regime under the Obama administration have sought to avoid *reifying* the role of religion in world politics, adopting instead an epistemically desecularized approach that is *attentive* to religion. The RGA, Peter Mandaville has argued, sought to cultivate within the State Department a "right sized" approach to religion. This approach is intended to "flag" religion's role in situations where it is relevant but the State Department is not "sufficiently cognizant" of it, while simultaneously helping "to better contextualize the complex role of religion in cases where [colleagues] may . . . place too much emphasis on religion."[86] "An important part of the office's work is to help the state department understand the imperfections of religion as a category," an RGA official likewise explained to me.[87] "[The] goal is to make sure we approach religion with a critical and sophisticated analytical lens," echoed Secretary Kerry, adding, "We must be careful to not overemphasize the role of religion and to properly understand its intersection with political, economic and other factors."[88]

The ideologically desecularized understanding of religion that the regime would embody and promote, is one that views the sacred as *ambivalent*—both good and bad, violent and peaceful—rather than essentializing it as a uniquely positive force. Indeed, implicit in much of the rhetoric and practices of the regime, would be an intention to harness "good" religion to solve many of the world's worst ills such as climate change or the Syrian refugee crisis, while also combating "bad" religion where this appeared entangled with conflict, terrorism, and violence.

State-normative desecularization would occur as strict separationist views of state–religion relations circulating within the US foreign policy establishment would be challenged and relaxed in conjunction with the operationalization of the regime. To that effect, around 2013–2015 State Department lawyers released official guidelines on the matter of compliance with Establishment Clause norms.[89] While these guidelines do not appear to be publicly available, an analysis of the discourses and practices surrounding the regime do, however, give an indication of the type of normative arrangements being promoted. Policymakers invested in the regime, from John Kerry to Shaun Casey, regularly stressed that constitutional limits did apply and that engaging religions fell squarely within the boundaries permitted by the Establishment Clause.[90] Hence, they would reject the suggestion put forward by some desecularizing experts—most notably expressed in a dissenting note in a Chicago Council Report[91]—that the

---

[85] Ibid.
[86] Mandaville in Berkley Center (2016a, 1:00:31–1:01:00).
[87] RGA Official (2015, author's interview).
[88] Kerry (2015).
[89] Ibid.
[90] Casey (2016); Kerry (2016).
[91] See note 36.

Establishment Clause should not apply to strategic foreign policy matters. Yet Kerry and Casey would also push for a reinterpretation of Establishment Clause norms away from separationist readings toward more accommodationist positions that allowed for greater diplomatic partnerships, cooperation, and entanglements with religion.[92]

Overall, the emergence of the regime occurred in parallel with multiple processes of desecularization. Judd Birdsall has approvingly noted, for instance, how approaching religious issues and partnering with faith-based actors—once considered for the most part irrelevant, marginal, or taboo activities—was now instead "increasingly viewed as part and parcel of American statecraft."[93] Thus an enthusiast RGA official would similarly explain to me in 2015:

> The culture has shifted a lot in the State Department. There is a recognition that religion matters. The issue is no longer that controversial. Particularly for those working in certain regions, such as the Middle East.[94]

Effects on Global Religious-Secular Landscapes

Shaping Global Religious Realities Along American Norms and Interests

The Religious Engagement regime, unlike the International Religious Freedom and the Muslim and Islamic Interventions ones, is not designed to directly produce religious outcomes. In this respect, Religious Engagement is more akin to the Faith-Based Foreign Aid regime, its intent being that of drawing on and mobilizing specific religious networks, entities, and voices in the pursuit of what are ostensibly nonstrictly religious objectives such as conflict-resolution or curbing climate change. In the words of a high-ranking official within the RGA:

> There is a discomfort in the office with the notion and terminology of "religious engagement." None of our engagement is "religious." What we do instead is engage with "religious actors."[95]

Nevertheless, as the United States engages with religious actors—to collect information, devise policy, and summon potential partners and supporters on a particular issue—it would unwittingly intervene in and thus potentially shape religious realities worldwide. Through the process of engagement, social power, legitimacy, and recognition can and do flow in subtle, complex, and diffused ways from the world's superpower to religious actors in general and to some religious voices in particular. As Elizabeth Shakman Hurd puts it:

---

[92] Casey (2016); Kerry (2016).
[93] Birdsall (2013).
[94] RGA Official (2015, author's interview).
[95] RGA Official (2015, author's interview).

Such projects require the government to decide which groups count as religious and worthy of engagement. . . . For the government to decide which groups are in and out grants sanction to some theological understandings and practices over others.[96]

It is important to highlight that religious actors are not merely the passive objects and instruments of American power. Religious leaders, organizations, communities, and followers all have their own agency. They may well exploit America's novel institutional, intellectual, and normative openness toward religious partnerships to their own advantage. And they do so in ways that seek to boost their own standing and their own religious and nonreligious objectives locally or globally. In other words, as American foreign policymakers increasingly and purposefully seek to partner with religious leaders, organizations, and communities—and as these reciprocate by actively seeking the support of the United States for their agendas—those religious actors and traditions who benefit from this access may gain in influence, while those that do not lose out.

Given these dynamics, the question then becomes: which religious traditions and actors would end up benefitting, compared to others, from American foreign policy engagement? In the absence of any data or records of meetings and partnerships with the RGA or embassies published by the State Department, the short answer is that it may be too hard to tell. This dearth of information has not deterred some observers from advancing two plausible, although somewhat disputable, propositions about the kinds of religious actors and traditions that are being engaged, and thus empowered, by the regime.

First, some scholars and church–state separation advocates have suggested that the regime chiefly advances Christian interests and perspectives.[97] Such suggestions are generally based on the observation that many of the regime's most ardent champions, along with those implementing such a policy, can be identified as believing and practicing Christians. At the forefront of religious engagement debates among civil society experts feature, for instance, Doug Johnston and Chris Seiple—both of whom are Evangelicals—and their faith-based think-and-do tanks ICRD and IGE. Equally important in this space is the scholarship and the initiatives coming from two leading American Catholic universities such as the University of Notre Dame and Georgetown University. Within government, Christian voices have been particularly prominent as well, including those of Judd Birdsall and Ambassador Susan Johnston Cook within the OIRF and Joshua DuBois and Melissa Rodgers in the WHOFBI. John Kerry, an avowed Catholic, summed up the RGA's mission during its launch by quoting one of his "favorite passages" from the Gospel of Mark.[98] Shaun

---

96 Hurd (2013a); also Hurd (2015).
97 See McAlister (2013); also Boston in Berkowitz (2013).
98 Kerry in Kerry, Casey, and Rogers (2013).

Casey, a Mainline Protestant Christian ethicist and theologian, would be the RGA's first director.

Despite the evident substantial Christian influence and presence in the making and conduct of the Religious Engagement regime, I would nonetheless argue that this did not appear to translate in substantial ways into support for Christian groups and traditions over others abroad—at least not under the Obama administration. Staff in the RGA office appeared to be particularly attentive to adopting an open and inclusive approach to the religious actors they would seek to engage with.[99] Such openness has been, in a sense, part and parcel of the regime's mission. Compared to religious freedom policy—which is based on an "activist" mindset that includes naming and shaming possible abusers—religious engagement would instead be based on more "diplomatic" premises. Namely, that the United States should reach out to and build relationships even with those religious actors with whom there are major value and interest differences. Moreover, one of the leading forces behind the drafting of the US Strategy on Religious Leader and Faith Community Engagement was Shaarik H. Zafar, a Pakistani-American, who in 2014 would be appointed as Special Representative to Muslim Communities. Institutionally, during the Obama administration the RGA held no specific special appointee for engagement with Christians, for instance, while it would include two focused on Muslims and one devoted to combating anti-semitism.

A second line of argument put forward by scholarly critiques of the operationalization of religion in international policy suggests that those who predominantly were engaged and thus empowered by the regime would be the representatives of "official religion."[100] By official religion, these voices refer to the generally recognized religions around the world and their organized hierarchies or self-appointed spokespersons, most of whom are old and male. Those who are sidelined and excluded from the process of state engagement, these critics suggest, are ordinary followers and grass-roots members of religious communities, women, youth, religious dissenters, and nontraditional or un-recognized religions.

Advocates and policymakers in the religious engagement space, however, did explicitly acknowledge from the very beginning that the risk of focusing on official religion, so to speak, was present and needed to be avoided. The State Department's Religion and Foreign Policy Working Group, for instance, warned early on about the pitfalls of discriminating against, and the importance of partnering with, "women religious leaders" and "other non-traditional religious leaders, particularly youth."[101] Shaun Casey regularly stressed the importance of "lived religion,"[102] a religion that is practiced and experienced

---

[99] See Casey in Berkley Center (2016b, 49:44–49:47). This point was emphasized to me on multiple different occasions, including by Birdsall (2015), and RGA Official (2015).
[100] Badran in *The Immanent Frame* (2013); Hurd (2015).
[101] Religion and Foreign Policy Working Group (2012, 8).
[102] Casey in CIRIS (2015).

everyday by ordinary people rather than official doctrine and hierarchies. Echoing these sentiments, Secretary Kerry emphasized that America's religious engagement should not be about "having meetings almost exclusively with men" or with "designated leaders," but involved reaching out to "much more diverse group of figures" including "women," "activists," "minorities," and the "rank and file."[103] It is evident that an awareness of a potential bias toward official, rather than lived, religion was present. Having said this, how far this potential bias was addressed and overcome in practice remains unclear and in need of further investigation.

To sum up what has been argued thus far: a range of voices have suggested that the Religious Engagement regime has a bias, and thus favors, Christian actors or official religion. Yet we currently have little data and systematic evidence to be able to confidently support these claims. Quite importantly, as well, we have reasons to believe given the structures of the regime and the intentions voiced by key policymakers—including Secretary Kerry himself—that the risks of falling prey to such biases was low or being mitigated. Hence one could reasonably expect that at least in theory, although in practice it remains an open question, efforts were made to be inclusive.

What does seem evident, though, is that despite such inclusivity the types of religiosities which have likely had greater access to the foreign policymaking process and have been mobilized in its execution, would be those faith-based entities and theologies implicitly defined as "good". I would argue that in the context of a regime whose mission—Mandaville reminds us—would be "first and foremost about augmenting the diplomatic toolkit"[104] and whose institutional home would be lodged in the State Department's Office of the Secretary, what would be conceived as good would be a religion that is aligned with America's national interest as defined by any one particular administration and their ideological inclinations. As Melani McAlister frames it, the United States is "likely to directly support groups that promote particular interpretations of their own religion—specifically those that are friendly to US policy."[105] Indeed, as Secretary Kerry explicitly argued about the purpose of engaging religion:

> We don't establish contacts just for the sake of having interesting conversations. We do so to make progress towards our foreign policy and our national security goals.[106]

Under President Obama, religious actors and traditions that shared the administration's thinking on foreign policy issues, and that tended to be of a pluralist, ecumenical, liberal, and progressive nature, were likely to become viable partners. For instance, the Obama administration championed the resolution of the Israeli-Palestinian conflict on the basis of a two-state solution.

---

[103] Kerry (2016).
[104] Mandaville (2017).
[105] McAlister (2013).
[106] Kerry (2016).

The religious actors that the regime has likely cooperate with and thus favored in this effort, would be those who shared such a view. It may have been possible—under such circumstances—for the United States to engage Jewish, Muslim, or Christian voices who viewed the resolution of the conflict along the lines of a one-state solution, either in terms of a greater Israel or historic Palestine. Yet such an engagement, if it occurred at all, would probably have been for the purpose of changing such groups' religious and political stance on the conflict. Curbing climate change, aiding with the resettlement of Syrian refugees in the United States, or countering Islamophobia were other issues which Shaun Casey's RGA was actively involved in and sought to mobilize religious actors around. These are not politically neutral (nor indeed, religiously uncontested) stances, and constitute profound areas of disagreement between liberals and conservatives, Democrats and Republicans, in American society and politics itself.

To bring the point home more clearly, let us consider an alternative scenario. A look at the pronouncements and actions of the current (as of late 2018) Trump-Pence administration, for instance, suggests that a two-state solution to the Israeli-Palestinian conflict, curbing climate change, or resettling Syrian refugees in the United States are not its priorities. It is not far-fetched to assume, then, that if the regime continues under the new Trump administration—which, as we shall see, it appears to be the case but in a much reduced capacity—it would likely be reoriented toward other policy objectives and with it empower other types of religious actors and perspectives.[107] These are likely to be more conservative and possibly, given the influence that Protestant Evangelicals exercise on the administration thanks to Vice President Mike Pence, more Christian.

Overall, then, in light of the empirical evidence we currently have I would caution toward arguing that the Religious Engagement regime had, during the Obama administration, an in-built bias toward Christian communities or official religion. What can be inferred though with quite some degree of confidence is that the regime—given its architecture—has likely generally granted access, sought partners, and empowered those religious actors and traditions viewed as good, and thus potentially influenced global religious realities and landscapes accordingly. As has been noted, what gets to be understood as good religion is very much dependent on a regime structure that prioritizes the foreign policy interests and the ideological orientation of any one particular US administration.

Religionizing World Politics

The Religious Engagement regime contributes to processes of religionization by making faith matter more in the way international politics is discussed and practiced. Officials working under Shaun Casey's RGA have been particularly

---

[107] For a similar argument, see Willard in Berkley Center (2016b, 40:00–41:00).

attentive to not singularly superimpose or reify religious causes and labels onto the world. Nonetheless, religionization through *categorization* does still partly occur. This is particularly the case with actors or issues which, as they get enmeshed and entangled with the regime's institutions and practices, invariably become categorized as religious even though they may have multiple identities or causes.

One notable example is the integration into the RGA of the Special Envoy to Monitor and Combat Anti-Semitism. "Being Jewish cannot be reduced to religion, it is also a cultural and ethnic feature," argues a senior program officer at USIP, adding, "Anti-Semitism is not exclusively a religious issue, yet the Special Envoy is folded into the RGA and given mostly a religious dimension."[108] A Pew poll, for instance, finds that there is great disagreement among Jews in Israel on whether they describe their "Jewish identity" primarily as religious, ethnic, or cultural.[109] The complexity and fluidity of the Jewish and Semitic identity categories is further apparent when comparing American foreign policy practices with European ones. In the context of EU initiatives designed to combat anti-Semitism, these activities are presented in terms of fighting racism and xenophobia rather than viewed as an issue chiefly connected to religious persecution or freedom.

For the most part, though, the regime contributes to religionizing world politics through mechanisms of *elevation*. Indeed, that's exactly one of the regime's key objectives: to provide greater space for listening to and including religious voices and concerns in the making and implementation of American foreign policy, rather than ignoring or marginalizing them. For instance, one of RGA's official missions is to act as a first point of contact for religious groups. This has been met, according to Casey, with a "flurry of activity" by actors who previously had "no door to knock on at the State Department." Since the office's creation, "thousands of these folks," Casey adds, have "come through our door" asking to be connected to any one particular office working on issues of concern to this or that religious group.[110] Although it is difficult to assess with certainty how influential these actors have been in affecting the foreign policy of the world's superpower, there is no doubt however that through such dynamics religious voices have been increasingly and consistently brought out from the cold and into the fold of international relations practices.

Regime Diffusion in International Policy

A surge of interest in religious engagement-type policies has been evident among Western governments and institutions over the past decade, including in France, Italy, the United Kingdom, and Germany. There are multiple drivers underpinning

---

[108] USIP Official (2015, author's interview).
[109] Pew Research Center (2016).
[110] Casey in Berkley Center (2016b, 48:47–49:21).

these developments. For one, in line with this book's theoretical framework, states may be finding themselves increasingly pressured domestically and internationally by the forces and agents constitutive of an emerging postsecular world society. Foreign policy institutions in these states could thus be responding and adapting to these pressures by operationalizing their own versions of a more religiously attentive foreign policy. This seems to be very much the case in France where in 2009—before the creation of the RGA in the State Department—a special division in charge of religious issues (*Pôle Religion*) was created in the Policy Planning Unit of the Ministry of Foreign Affairs. Similarly, the Policy Planning Unit in Italy's Ministry of Foreign Affairs has been sponsoring a yearly international seminar on the theme of religion in international relations since 2009.

A second story that can be told, complementary to the first, is one where the American experience plays a more significant role, either directly or indirectly, in the global diffusion of religious engagement thinking and practices. Indeed, both American epistemic communities and government officials connected to the US Religious Engagement regime have been at the forefront of processes of knowledge circulation and advocacy among Western allies. Notable here are a number of reports published in 2015—by the Brookings Institution and by a partnership between Georgetown University's Berkley Center, the British Council, IGE, and the University of Leeds[111] —replicating at the transatlantic level the American discourse of religious engagement. A Transatlantic Policy Network on Religion and Diplomacy was formed in 2015, to "facilitate communication and collaboration among diplomats from Europe and North America who have a responsibility for religion-related issues."[112] The Cambridge Institute on Religion and International Studies (CIRIS), at Cambridge University, acts as the network's secretariat in partnership with George Mason University. Judd Birdsall, a key champion of the religious engagement agenda in the American context, leads CIRIS' policy-facing activities.

In parallel to these civil society-led efforts, RGA officials have also acted as global regime entrepreneurs. The US Strategy on Religious Leader and Faith Community Engagement explicitly encourages American foreign policymakers to "build . . . the capacity of our international partners to engage religious leaders and faith communities."[113] RGA leadership has been extremely receptive to meeting with, for instance, members of the Transatlantic Policy Network on Religion and Diplomacy.[114] Likewise, Shaun Casey, Liora Danan, and Peter Mandaville have regularly attended European conferences and events connecting scholars and practitioners exploring the nexus between religion and foreign policy in order to share their expertise and champion the religious engagement agenda abroad.[115]

---

[111] See, respectively, Mandaville and Silvestri (2015), and Birdsall, Lindsay, and Tomalin (2015).
[112] Quote taken from CIRIS' website, at http://ciris.org.uk/ (accessed December 18, 2016).
[113] White House (2013).
[114] US Department of State (2016b).
[115] See note 76.

The American experience is also indirectly promoting religious engagement internationally by acting as a powerful example for those actors and governments around the world seeking to advance and legitimize similar policies in their specific contexts. Processes of learning, adaptation, mimicking, and borrowing from the United States are visibly taking place. In Italy, for instance, interest in religious engagement in the Italian Ministry of Foreign Affairs predated the release of the 2010 Chicago Council Report and the creation in 2013 of the RGA in the State Department. Yet both of these events substantially galvanized ongoing efforts and generated further momentum toward religious engagement, as key protagonists in the Italian experience acknowledge.[116]

Conclusion

The Religious Engagement regime shares important parallels with the three regimes that preceded it, but also some noteworthy differences. Like the other regimes, Religious Engagement was first championed by a constellation of civil society actors, embedded in and responding to an emerging postsecular world society in multiple ways. Starting from the early 1990s and accelerating exponentially in the aftermath of 9/11, a loosely knit desecularizing epistemic community, carrier of a postsecular consciousness, emerged among international affairs scholars and analysts in the United States coalescing around two types of strategic desecularizing discourse on religious engagement. These two discourses would share a number of characteristics. They both articulated a range of solutions to what they argued was a problematic gap existing between the global vibrancy and resurgence of religion, on the one hand, and the secular blind spots of American diplomacy, on the other. They differed however in their understandings of what religious engagement was for: one presented religious engagement more narrowly as a means of promoting peace and security, and the other presented it in more ambitious and broad terms as a means of promoting international order and progress.

Out-of-government experts, who were central to the articulation and circulation of both the narrow and broad religious engagement discourses, operated in and out of a thriving infrastructure of initiatives, projects, and centers tied to prominent and well-connected American universities (including Georgetown, Notre Dame, Harvard, and George Mason) and think tanks (including CFR, CSIS, the Chicago Council, Pew, and Brookings). This epistemic community also counted on the energy and foresight of novel faith-based think-and-do tanks, such as Johnston's ICRD and Seiple's IGE. Blessing the whole enterprise by giving it a high-level policy stamp of approval was former Secretary of State Madeleine Albright.

---

[116] See Ferrara (2013a); Petito and Thomas (2015).

The operationalization of the religious engagement agenda came in 2013 with the release of a specific strategy and the creation of a new State Department office, the RGA. The institutionalization of the regime, however, occurred rather late compared to other regimes. That's because its champions encountered a number of stumbling blocks along the way. On the one hand, religious engagement advocacy was mostly confined to expert milieus and, unlike the International Religious Freedom and Faith-Based Foreign Aid regimes, could not count on the propulsive force and political weight of domestic grass-roots religious movements and institutions. On the other hand, the diplomatically oriented theme of religious engagement lacked resonance in the immediate aftermath of the 9/11 events, given in particular the Bush administration's security-oriented and Muslim-focused response to the attacks.

The initial obstacles faced by the regime were overcome at a later stage by two factors. The first was the mounting mobilization—quite unique to the regime—of policymakers within the foreign policy bureaucracy itself championing the religious engagement agenda. Officials connected to other religious foreign policy regimes—most notably in the White House and the State Department—were pivotal in generating momentum for the operationalization of the new Religious Engagement regime. The second factor was the advent of the Obama administration, which provided a critical opening. Religious engagement discourses resonated both with the president's appreciation of the role of religion in social and political life and with his foreign policy approach, which sought to emphasize multilateralism and diplomacy rather than Bush-era unilateralism and militarism.

These disparate forces and circumstances profoundly shaped the strategy, institutional architecture, and policies of the regime. In its various forms and practices, the Religious Engagement regime would turn out to be a hybrid at best or an amorphous regime at worst. It appeared to combine, but also be torn by, different impulses: first, between the narrow conflict-resolution focused and broad international order-oriented views of religious engagement; second, between acting as a separate stand alone regime with a distinct mandate and space of action, or as a hub and umbrella under which other existing religious foreign policy regimes (International Religious Freedom, Faith-Based Foreign Aid, and Muslim and Islamic Interventions) would be nested.

Like other regimes, Religious Engagement has been the product of a process of contestation and redefinition of secular–religious settlements and boundaries in American foreign policy. The regime has generated a growing and structured entanglement between religious issues and actors, and the institutions and practices of American foreign policy. Such a process of institutional desecularization, however, does not go as deep compared to those generated by the other three regimes. That's because, with a few minor exceptions, by the end of the Obama presidency the RGA was not conducting programs or facilitating the funding of religious actors.

The regime has also engendered particular ideational shifts within American foreign policy that I identify with processes of epistemic, ideological and state-normative desecularization. A notable difference compared to other regimes is in the realm of epistemic desecularization. Officials tied to the Religious Engagement regime under the Obama administration adopted an approach that was attentive to the power of the sacred in world politics while being particularly careful not to reify religious categories and causes—something that the International Religious Freedom and Muslim and Islamic Interventions regimes would tend to do instead.

In terms of the regime's international religious and secular effects, parallels and differences with the other three regimes abound as well. First, as with the Faith-Based Foreign Aid regime, Religious Engagement does not seek to directly manage and govern religious landscapes globally. Religions are more or less engaged to the extent that they can contribute to US foreign policy objectives, without any overt attempts being made to restructure global religious realities in any particular or explicit way. However, as the world's superpower has sought to draw from, partner with, and mobilize religious actors through this fourth regime, it has nonetheless supported, and thus empowered, certain religious leaders, groups, perspectives, and interests over others—hence potentially shaping, albeit indirectly, religious realities in the process.

Such shaping would occur especially by empowering what US foreign policymakers in this space would implicitly understand as "good" religion. Given certain structural features of the regime, what would get to be defined—and thus supported and legitimized—as good religion would depend on the foreign policy interests and ideological preferences of any one particular administration. At the time of Barack Obama's leadership in the White House and that of John Kerry's in the State Department, what qualified as good were generally religious actors and traditions of a pluralist, ecumenical, liberal, and progressive kind. Such religious actors and traditions could be counted upon as valuable partners to promote interreligious cooperation and dialogue, address climate change and environmental problems, advance a two-state solution to the Israeli-Palestinian conflict, or fight for social justice and against discrimination (in the case of women or refugees, for example).

Second, similarly to the Faith-Based Foreign Aid regime, Religious Engagement contributes to the religionization of world politics mostly through the process of elevation. This is inherent in its very premise. The notion of engagement is centered on an effort to include, rather than marginalize, religious actors and voices in the making and implementation of US foreign policy and thus, by extension, in the practice of world politics. There is some evidence of the regime contributing to processes of religionization via mechanisms of categorization too, although not to the same degree taking place with the International Religious Freedom or Muslim and Islamic Interventions regimes. Emblematic, for instance, was the inclusion under the RGA of the previously independent Special Envoy to Monitor and Combat Anti-Semitism, a task that can be viewed also from a lens other than a primarily religious one.

Third, like the Faith-Based Foreign Aid and Muslim and Islamic Interventions regimes, the religious engagement agenda is being operationalized in US foreign policy in an international environment where similar policies are emerging across other states and institutions. Compared to these two other regimes, however, the policymakers and the wider epistemic community tied to the Religious Engagement regime occupy a much more prominent and central place in the diffusion of religious engagement policies, particularly across the transatlantic space.

How has the regime evolved, if at all, under the current Trump presidency and what does its future look like? Being so closely tied to the vision and priorities of then President Obama and Secretary Kerry, the fortunes of the regime appear to have dramatically waned under the new Republican administration. As of late 2018, no one has been appointed to replace Shaun Casey. During Rex Tillerson's tenure as secretary of state, ambitious plans were made to substantially restructure and downsize the State Department, which included—according to multiple sources—the closure of the RGA.

Yet although sidelined, the regime does exhibit some signs of life. The RGA webpage on the State Department's website is still active, rather than having being archived, and its Facebook page is being updated. A new secretary of state has been appointed in the figure of Mike Pompeo. Secretary Pompeo has shown a greater interest than Tillerson in religion, although—similarly to President Trump and Vice President Pence—largely on issues of religious freedom and the ideological-theological struggle against Islamists. It may be that, rather than being completely abandoned, the issue of religious engagement and remaining RGA staff are permanently folded under the OIRF in the State Department or tied more closely to counterterrorism and other security operations.

The idea of engagement with religions, although of a less institutionalized kind, is still floating around. This was most notable with Donald Trump's first international trip as president, which included stops in Saudi Arabia, Israel, and the Vatican City, viewed as the symbolic homes of the three Abrahamic faiths. The trip was explicitly presented by the administration as a historic effort by the president to "unite people of all faiths around a common vision of peace, progress and prosperity."[117] In any case, if some kind of religious engagement policy is likely to persist, this will be closely tailored to the priorities of the current administration—which, for instance, has taken a much less balanced approach to the Israeli-Palestinian conflict compared to the Obama administration, especially notable with the controversial decision to move the American embassy from Tel Aviv to Jerusalem.

In parallel, supporters of the Religious Engagement regime as it was operationalized during the Obama years are regrouping themselves to pressure the current administration and reinject energy into this policy space in

---

[117] McMaster (2017, 01.18–01.40).

case a new Democratic administration occupies the White House in the future. Shaun Casey, who now leads the influential Berkley Center at Georgetown University, and Peter Mandaville, through a Brookings Institution report, have chastised the Trump administration's general neglect of the issue.[118] Ultimately, the fate of the regime is up for grabs and only time will tell which direction—given the multiple countervailing pressures that exist at the moment—the regime might take.

---

[118] Casey in *Desert News* (2018), and Mandaville (2017).

| # Conclusion

The US Foreign Policy Regime Complex on Religion

During the Cold War our greatest fear was that someone with his finger on the nuclear button would miscalculate and trigger what technocrats bloodlessly referred to as a "nuclear exchange." Today, perhaps, our worst nightmare is that religion will ignite fears and conflicts that we will be unable to contain.

—Former US Secretary of State Madeleine Albright, 2016[1]

This trip is truly historic, no President has ever visited the homelands and holy sites of the Jewish, Christian, and Muslim faiths all on one trip. And what President Trump is seeking, is to unite people of all faiths around a common vision of peace, progress and prosperity.

—National Security Advisor H. R. McMaster, 2017[2]

FAR FROM THE GODLESS and disenchanted world that Max Weber and secularization theorists in the twentieth century predicted would define our modern era, we are witnessing a revival of religion and of its prominence in world politics at the dawn of the twenty-first century. Opening the century and grabbing most people's attention were the spectacular and tragic attacks of 9/11, conducted by an organization claiming to act in the name of Islam and in the defense of all Muslims. Yet equally momentous and possibly even more consequential in the long run has been the growing institutionalized entanglement between the international conduct of the world's superpower and religious dynamics, actors, and communities worldwide.

Madeleine Albright's words at the beginning of the chapter, uttered by one of America's best known and admired secretaries of states, powerfully capture

---

[1] Albright (2015, 08.08–08.30).
[2] McMaster (2017, 01.18–01.40).

the crucial role that religion has come to occupy not just in world politics, but also in the global imaginary of America's foreign policy establishment since the end of the Cold War. With shifts in understandings and fears of new religious wars being ignited, foreign policy practices have changed too. President Trump's first trip abroad, in May 2017, was immersed in sacred symbolism and presented as a historic religious pilgrimage intended to pay homage and preach a message of unity and peace to all three Abrahamic faiths—as the quote by then National Security Adviser McMaster highlights. These are not just isolated incidents. As this book has shown, religion has progressively and systematically become an organized subject and object of US foreign policy from the 1990s onward.

These changes have been most visible in the emergence, over the space of just two decades, of four distinct religious foreign policy regimes. These regimes are constituted by particular bundles of ideas, practices, and institutions oriented toward managing and harnessing the power of faith globally in support of American interests and values abroad. The first to emerge in chronological order was the International Religious Freedom regime through a Congressional act in 1998, followed by the Faith-Based Foreign Aid regime launched by George W. Bush in the early days of his presidency. Then, in the aftermath of 9/11, we saw the progressive development of the Muslim and Islamic Interventions regime. Finally, the Religious Engagement regime was created in 2013.

My contention is that taken together, these four regimes—which this study explores in depth during a timeframe stretching from the early 1990s to the end of the Obama presidency in 2016—form a larger whole: a foreign policy regime complex on religion. So far, this book has mostly explored the causes, structure, evolution, and international effects of the four regimes separately and, to some extent, comparatively. In the first part of this conclusion I will highlight the commonalities that connect the four different religious foreign policy regimes into one overarching complex. As I delineate more explicitly the contours of America's foreign policy regime complex on religion I will simultaneously provide a summary of the book's main arguments and findings. The second part of this conclusion has a different objective. It seeks to tease out the wider implications of this study for our understanding of religion not just in American foreign policy but also in world politics more broadly, and highlights a number of areas for further research and thinking.

The Foreign Policy Regime Complex on Religion

Six factors tie together the four individual regimes—International Religious Freedom, Faith-Based Foreign Aid, Muslim and Islamic Interventions, and Religious Engagement—into one broader regime complex: (i) a shared focus on religion, (ii) overlapping and interconnected institutional architectures, (iii) parallel histories, (iv) analogous causes, (v) common parallel desecularizing processes, and (vi) the generation of three broadly comparable global religious-secular effects. I will break down and examine these six factors in three distinct subsections focusing first on the causes and shape of the regime complex, then on processes of desecularization, and finally on effects.

Regime Complex Causes and Structure

Even if the formal objectives of each regime are different and at times in tension and competition with one another,[3] all regimes (i) *share a common focus on religious actors, dynamics, and issues.* Policymakers and advocates within and outside of government do recognize that the four regimes inhabit a similar and potentially complementary "religious space" in the foreign policy architecture and as such often champion the need for greater coordination among them.[4] In some instances regime objectives also overlap. For example, the policies of the International Religious Freedom, Muslim and Islamic Interventions, Faith-Based Foreign Aid, and Religious Engagement regimes all address the issue of Islamist violence and terrorism, albeit to a greater or lesser extent and through different means. The US Strategy on Religious Leader and Faith Community Engagement was released in 2013 with the purpose of binding together the objectives of the different regimes into one overarching, and more coherent, strategy.

Moreover, (ii) *the institutional architecture of the four regimes overlaps in multiple ways.* The White House Office of Faith-Based Initiatives—a generic term I use to identify an office whose title has changed across administrations—and its cousin center at USAID were first created by President Bush mostly to oversee and implement faith-based aid policies. Under the Obama administration, for example, the White House Office of Faith-Based Initiatives' mission would be broadened to encompass policy formulation for the Muslim and Islamic Interventions regime, and actively contribute to the operationalization of the Religious Engagement regime.

When the Religious Engagement regime came into being in 2013, one of its stated aims was to provide greater institutional coherence to what, by then, was a sprawling range of explicitly religious foreign policies. Its institutional core, the Office for Religion and Global Affairs, became a hub for consolidating a range of disparate appointees dedicated to religion, including the positions of Special Envoy to the Organization of Islamic Cooperation (OIC), the Special Representative to Muslim Communities, and the Special Envoy to Monitor and Combat Anti-Semitism. This reorganization—in tandem with the publication

---

[3] One such tension exists, for instance, between the International Religious Freedom and Religious Engagement regimes. The International Religious Freedom regime has an explicit advocacy and normative agenda, which also includes coercive or punitive measures aimed at changing the target country's rules and policies. Religious Engagement by contrast has been based on more diplomatic premises, encouraging the United States to reach out and build relationships even with those religious actors whose values and interests do not align with those of the United States.

[4] See US Department of State (2016a).

of the US Strategy on Religious Leader and Faith Community Engagement—appeared to signal the intention of turning a loosely coupled regime complex into a more structured and hierarchical nested regime under the broad umbrella of Religious Engagement. This effort would not prove entirely successful, since key institutional centers of other religious foreign policy regimes—such as the Office for International Religious Freedom in the State Department or the Centre for Faith-Based and Community Initiatives at USAID—remained independent of the Office for Religion and Global Affairs.

A third factor that ties the different regimes together is that in their current institutionalized form, (iii) *all four regimes are historically novel post-Cold War developments.* The Office for International Religious Freedom along with the parallel independent commission (USCIRF) were created in 1998, the White House faith-based office in 2001, and its cousin center at USAID in 2003; appointees and practices focusing on Islam and Muslims have progressively emerged in the aftermath of 9/11, and the Office for Religion and Global Affairs was launched in 2013. Traces of similar policies can undeniably be found in American history, as was argued and shown throughout the preceding chapters. While there is clearly a historical background to the present day regimes, these also mark a decisive shift in terms of the breadth and depth that religion has become a structured and bureaucratized subject and object of US foreign policy. Remarkably, all of this occurred in a relatively short space of time, within a couple of decades since the fall of the Berlin Wall.

Another factor that binds the regimes together is that (iv) *all have come into being through similar processes.* Namely, they came about through the efforts of multiple desecularizing actors who, from the 1990s onward, articulated and mobilized around a range of principled and strategic desecularizing discourses to contest what they viewed as the problematic secular character of US foreign policy. Through such discourses, these actors proposed multiple ways in which policymakers should actively and systematically embrace and manage the power of religion, for good or ill, in world politics.

Desecularizing actors are not all cut from the same cloth, however, but are a rather heterogeneous bunch. They have different backgrounds (grass-roots religious activists, experts housed in think tanks and universities, lawmakers within Congress and policymakers in the Executive Branch), and come together in multiple formations (as constellations, networks, coalitions, and constituencies) often divided along religious, political, theological-ideological, and issue lines. This diversity explains the plurality of religious foreign policy regimes and, to a large extent, their respective structure and trajectories across time and administrations.

Desecularizing actors did not surface in a vacuum, though, but emerged in a particular global, social, and historical context, which they simultaneously are embedded in and responding to. This context has witnessed the emergence of a postsecular world society from the 1970s onward. I conceptualized this postsecular world society as constituted by two main processes occurring both within the United States and around the world. One is represented by the growth in the political salience of religious actors, beliefs, symbols, identities, and practices. The other is a parallel change in knowledge and mentalities associated with the rise of postsecular thinking.

Regime Complex and Desecularization Processes

The turn toward religion in American foreign policy is sustained by, and itself designed to promote across the foreign policy architecture, (v) multiple parallel processes of desecularization. The four regimes and the overall complex emerge as desecularizing actors contest existing secular–religious settlements and boundaries that govern the making and implementation of US foreign policy. I identify four types of desecularizing processes: institutional, epistemic, ideological, and state-normative. These *types* of desecularizing processes are all, in their own way, contributing to the rise of the regime complex. Each regime varies, though, in *degree* of type of desecularization, largely depending—as the case studies showed—on the policy ideas and understanding of religion that different desecularizing actors who champion a particular regime, and a specific understanding thereof, articulate and advance.

Institutional desecularization takes place as religious actors and perspectives are increasingly included in the material structures of American foreign policy such as its bureaucracies and practices. The Faith-Based Foreign Aid regime, for instance, is generating some of the highest levels of religion–state entanglements among all regimes. The regime has two specifically dedicated offices across the executive branch, one in the White House and the other at USAID. Policymakers heading both offices have regularly been individuals connected to various religious communities and faith-based organization (FBOs). Furthermore, the regime facilitates—ostensibly for humanitarian and development purposes—the flow of vast amounts of government funding to religious organizations and institutions.

Epistemic desecularization is the erosion of the view that religion is irrelevant in world politics, replaced by an approach that is instead either *attentive* to religion or that *reifies* it. The International Religious Freedom regime, for instance, generally adopts the latter posture, whereby motivations, identities, and behaviors of actors, or the causes of specific events and dynamics, are nearly exclusively framed in religious terms. A tendency toward reifying religion is also present in the Muslim and Islamic Interventions regime whereby the Muslim-ness of actors, societies, and regions takes precedence over nonreligious criteria of identification, and the association of terrorism with Islam is emphasized over other drivers, for example political ones (especially during the G. W. Bush administration). By contrast, the Religious Engagement and the Faith-Based Foreign Aid regimes have tended toward a religiously attentive position, mixing and balancing faith with other factors.

Ideological desecularization involves a shift away from a secularist understanding of religion as an inherently problematic force, especially when entangled with politics, toward adopting either a view of religion as *ambivalent* or one that *positively essentializes* it. The International Religious Freedom and Faith-Based Foreign Aid regimes tend toward a positive essentialization of religion. In the former case, international religious freedom advocates and policymakers often claim that religious liberty is "the first freedom," foundational to all other freedoms. In the latter case, those championing the Faith-Based Foreign Aid regime generally suggest not only that development and humanitarian efforts need all the hands they can get, including faith-based ones, but that religious voices and organizations can often reach further and delve deeper into solving health and poverty issues than their secular counterparts. The Muslim and Islamic Interventions regime adopts an ambivalent position, which can swing from the poles of ideological secularism that views Islam as the primary source of contemporary terrorism and violence, to a positive essentialization in which Islam is perceived as a valuable resource for promoting peace and combating terrorism. Likewise, a view of religion as a complex force, both good and bad, marked the thinking and practices of policymakers within the Religious Engagement regime space.

State-normative desecularization involves the contestation and relaxation of strict separationist interpretations of the US Constitution's Establishment Clause that governs state–religion relations. Such a process can lead to new normative arrangements ranging from religious *accommodation* to *establishment*. The foreign policy regime complex is the visible manifestation of ongoing shifts toward a more accommodationist interpretation of the Establishment Clause over the past two to three decades. However, accommodation hardly ever is neutral in practice. In one way or another accommodation leads to some kind of support either for certain religions over others, certain ways of being religious over others, or even of religion over nonreligion. For instance, America's Islamic interventions are not geared toward backing and elevating all Muslim and Islamic voices equally, but mostly so-called moderate ones over fundamentalist and extremist perspectives. President Bush's Faith-Based Foreign Aid regime imposed conditions on donors—especially in the case of health-related initiatives such as PEPFAR—that would favor the humanitarian and development practices of (often conservative) religious organizations and FBOs, over those of secular non-governmental organizations (NGOs).

Thus overall we have seen a growing enmeshment of religious actors, communities, and agendas with US foreign policy institutions and practices, and vice versa. Much of this has been facilitated by underlying ideational and normative changes. As Judd Birdsall, an important voice and practitioner in this space, approvingly explains: "the boundaries, although still strong, have been pushed and have shifted quite a bit in the past years, a 'cultural space' has been opened for dealing with religion."[5] Nonetheless, the chapters also showed that as secular–religious settlements have been redrawn and novel and deeper forms of entanglement emerged, the profane (i.e. foreign policy) has not been

---

[5] Birdsall (2015, author's interview).

entirely taken over by the sacred (i.e. religious actors and considerations), as some of the most vociferous critics of the regimes have generally suggested.

Similar to Sadia Saeed's understanding of desecularization as a "historically contingent and instituted" process,[6] the changes observed in the case studies show that while religious norms, practices, and actors have certainly become increasingly entwined with considerable features of US statecraft and diplomacy, the practice of foreign policy has nonetheless retained on the whole its autonomous "secular logic," so to speak. The issue of international religious freedom, while certainly gaining in importance and standing over the years, remains a relatively secondary concern of US foreign policymakers which competes for attention with—and is often trumped by—a wide range of other issues and priorities. Humanitarian and development aid is not exclusively provided to faith-based actors or according to theological logics, but resources are disbursed to a broad set of actors—most of them nonreligious—following a variety of secular logics including material needs of the poor, secular humanitarian norms and development theories, or foreign policy interests. Interventions in Islamic beliefs and theologies are often a discrete—although conceptually quite important—portion of a much broader national security approach to counterterrorism which includes military, intelligence, and financial operations. Religious engagement has generally been presented as a strategy to augment, rather than replace, existing American diplomatic practices.

While it is important to put processes of desecularization into perspective, ongoing secular–religious entanglements are nonetheless considerable. Thus I would also dispute arguments put forward by many regime advocates who lament that current changes are not substantial enough. *Contra* these voices, the post-Cold War emergence of the regime complex constitutes without doubt a remarkable change—unprecedented in size, organization and scope—in America's attempt and capacity to manage and marshal faith in the pursuit of its interests and values abroad. So monumental is this shift—without doubt in symbolism and in many respects also in practice—that we may need to revisit our longstanding assumptions about the type of international order we inhabit in this day and age, as I will discuss later in this conclusion.

Regime Complex and Global Effects

The final factor that constitutes the four regimes into one larger complex is that they all have led, in their distinctive ways, (vi) *to a systematic, organized, and structured intervention by the world's superpower in global religious and secular affairs.* These interventions, I have argued, can potentially bring about three broad types of changes: (a) shaping global religious realities along American interests and norms; (b) contributing to the religionization of world politics; and (c) promoting and diffusing similar religious regimes in international policy.

---

[6] Saeed (2016, 23).

Shaping Global Religious Realities along American Interests and Norms

In line with the theoretical model developed, my case studies have shown how, by intervening in global religious landscapes through its foreign policy regimes, the United States would seek to shape them—directly or indirectly—according to four specific logics. These four logics, which may be at work either alone or in conjunction in the case any of the regimes, include: American short-term security and long-term international order-building interests; its domestic party political and ideological cleavages; the country's religious identity, demographics, and norms; and the priorities of specific religious actors championing a particular regime.

Taken together, these logics have led the overall regime complex to potentially shape global religious realities prevalently in three directions. First, the much-critiqued secular blind spot in American foreign policy has been partly replaced by a Christian soft spot. What I mean by this is that the foreign policy regime complex on religion, predominantly through the International Religious Freedom and Faith-Based Foreign Aid regimes, generates policies that favor—mostly indirectly, implicitly, and unintentionally—Christian understandings and practices of religion, as well as Christian organizations, communities, and traditions globally. To understand and contextualize this phenomenon, it is useful to keep in mind the argument Daniel Philpott makes about religious advocacy and lobbying more generally:

> What is important to understand about religious actors is that religious politics, even when it converges with that of the state, emanates from beliefs, practices, and communities that themselves are prior to politics.[7]

The energy behind the institutionalization of the International Religious Freedom regime came prevalently—although not exclusively—from Christian, particularly Evangelical but also Mainline Protestant and Catholic, milieus. In the specific case of international religious freedom, its most vocal and influential champions have been especially animated by a concern with the state of Christian minorities, and the ability of American missionaries to operate and seek converts, in Muslim-majority and Communist countries. Unsurprisingly, then, as was discussed in chapter 3, by the end of Obama's second term in 2016, it would be overwhelmingly individuals of faith—mostly Christian—who staffed key positions in the regime's architecture, such as that of Ambassador-at-Large for International Religious Freedom, the Special Advisor for Religious Minorities in the Near East and South/Central Asia, or those of commissioners in the US Commission on International Religious Freedom (USCIRF).

Moreover, the very concept of religious freedom as it is generally understood in the context of US foreign policy is based both on America's own domestic historical, political, and legal understanding of this norm, but also quite unreflexively on a general view of religion rooted in a specific Christian

---

[7] Philpott (2009, 193).

and especially Protestant experience.[8] This "Christianized" notion of religion manifests itself—in the discourse of international religious freedom advocates or official reports—in a conception of religious expression structured around the individual's experience of faith and belief, rather than around communal practice and belonging based on tradition, culture, or blood; one that can be changed easily instead of at great social and political cost; and one which thus sustains a view of proselytization and conversion as legally, ethically and religiously unproblematic. The point I am making here is not that the International Religious Freedom regime is some kind of ploy or conspiracy to Christianize the entire world, which would be a gross exaggeration, but rather that there are particular factors within American society, politics, and culture that lead this regime to have a Christian soft spot.

This Christian soft spot becomes even more tangible and visible in the Faith-Based Foreign Aid regime. Multiple forces were involved in bringing about the regime during President Bush's first term: religious lobbying, the president's biography and born-again experience, political calculations, and shifting philosophies—including among humanitarian and development scholars and practitioners—on the importance of religious actors in providing for the most vulnerable. All these elements converged on the view that religion should be considered a valuable resource in humanitarian and development efforts. These premises would lead to a more cooperative approach toward FBOs and a greater willingness to fund them, even the most pervasively religious ones, in order to deliver American aid abroad.

Since the regime's inception, its principal beneficiaries have been Christian agencies—especially Evangelical, but also Mainline Protestant and Catholic—which have secured the lion's share of US humanitarian and development assistance given to FBOs. As a result, the United States' international poverty reduction and emergency assistance has become ever more entangled and involved in the support and spread of Christianity worldwide. This is especially the case when funding has gone to pervasively religious Evangelical organizations, which often constitute part of the modern missionary enterprise that understands and practices development and humanitarian work abroad as a form of Christian witnessing or as a means of more actively seeking converts. Again, I want to sound a note of caution. I am not suggesting that encouraging Christianity through foreign aid is America's intended objective here. As I argued in chapter 4, this result is mostly a byproduct of a number of domestic, demographic, historical, institutional, and international factors which favor Christian agencies, compared to those of other traditions, as the institutions, cultures, and norms of the Faith-Based Foreign Aid regime facilitate a more structured and cooperative relationship between religion and American humanitarian and development policy.

---

[8] See also Castelli (2007a); Hurd (2014b); Sullivan (2005).

The second prevalent way in which the broader regime complex has intervened in global religious realities, thus potentially reshaping these, is by advancing a radically pluralist understanding of what religion is. The United States exhibits a highly diverse religious society. This is the result of multiple historical circumstances, including centuries of processes of voluntary and forced migration from all over the world, and a set of constitutional norms that powerfully disestablish religion from the state and free it within society in ways that are quite unique internationally. Therefore, along with its Christian soft spot and not necessarily in contradiction to it, the regime complex—above all through the International Religious Freedom regime, as well as in the context of the Religious Engagement and Faith-Based Foreign Aid regimes—has defended the rights, promoted the interests, and empowered through various forms of direct and indirect support an extremely wide variety of religious communities, groups, and actors.

These have not only included those groups from the main branches of major world religious traditions such as Islam, Judaism, or Buddhism,[9] but also religious groups—and here is where the distinctive American angle lies—from a disparate range of minority communities or smaller religious traditions which are generally either not legally recognized or viewed as illegitimate cults or sects across states and societies around the world. US international religious freedom policy and reports, for instance, have come to the defense of the rights of Jehovah's Witnesses in countries like Russia, of Scientologists in Germany, of Alevis and Ahmadis in multiple Muslim-majority countries, of Baha'is in Iran, and so on. Some of the most vocal critics of America's International Religious Freedom regime have even suggested that this policy may not go far enough in its recognition of religious practices. Its reports have been criticized, for example, for failing to mention the discrimination faced by women practicing certain forms of African traditional religions in places like the Central African Republic.[10]

Without wanting to get drawn into the debate about what constitutes legitimate or illegitimate religion, the point being made here is to suggest that what gets to be defined as such by the regimes is often historically and context specific, and that US foreign policymakers (and American-based scholars and analysts) will overwhelmingly tend to operate from a radically pluralist perspective which is likely to clash with narrower understandings of what constitutes religion elsewhere in the world.[11] This is likely to be the case especially with

---

[9] An entire regime is dedicated to Muslims and Islam. Jewish groups have been quite active in the religious freedom space, with the only non-Christian Ambassador-at-Large for International Religious Freedom by 2016 being a rabbi (i.e. Rabbi David Saperstein). International religious freedom reports, moreover, have extensively reported the violence and discrimination experienced, among others, by Rohingya Muslims in Myanmar, Tibetan Buddhists in China, or Jews in Europe and the Middle East.
[10] Hurd (2013c).
[11] This is not to say that everyone in the US subscribes to such a radically pluralist understanding of religion. Witness, for instance, suggestions by individuals tied to the Christian Right or anti-Jihad movement, that Islam should not be considered a religion, but rather a political ideology (Schulson 2017).

other states and societies that have adopted a more formal differentiation between official and traditional religions on the one hand, and unofficial or non-traditional religions on the other.

The third way in which the regime complex reflects, and thus potentially promotes globally, an American understanding of faith, is by seeking to support what US foreign policymakers identify as true, good, or useful religion. True, good, or useful religion is sought after, both explicitly and implicitly, in order to advance a wide range of international objectives—from solving environmental problems, promoting religious pluralism, or spreading democracy—as well as marginalizing what conversely is understood to be false, bad, or counterproductive religion.

What counts as true or false, good or bad, useful or counterproductive religion once more depends on a mix of American interests and values, whether domestic or international, religious or secular. In the best of cases true and good religion is peaceful, compassionate, ecumenical, tolerant, and liberal, in the classical sense of supporting human rights, democracy, and a market economy. There is greater uncertainty over whether true and good religion emphasizes conservative moral issues or progressive social justice ones, whether it should be political or apolitical, and whether it must be moderate or can also be fundamentalist (as long as it is not violent). In the unfortunate case that true or good religion cannot be clearly found or relied upon, the regimes turn to useful religion. This applies to religious actors or traditions that may have important value differences with American policymakers, but at least share some common security interests with the superpower.

The main target of the impulse to mobilize true, good, and useful religion, or at least reform religions along such lines, is Islam. The Muslim and Islamic Interventions regime is especially dedicated to this task, as are some initiatives of other regimes in the context of America's post-9/11 war on terror. A growing range of policies and programs have thus emerged designed to produce, empower, and legitimize "true" Muslims and "good" Islamic voices, actors, institutions, education, traditions, and theologies. These are often identified with the notion of moderate Muslims or Islam and by supporting these the intent is to oppose and replace religious interpretations and political narratives emanating from hostile organizations like Al Qaeda, the Islamic State of Iraq and Syria (ISIS), and the wider heterogeneous galaxy of extremist and violent Islamist actors. In the process, leading American policymakers—including presidents themselves—have intervened in religious and theological debates to adjudicate who can be considered a proper Muslim and who cannot, what is Islamic and what is not, what counts as moderate and what as extreme. Not only that, but both the neoconservatives in the Bush administration and President Obama himself, have gone as far as to suggest that an outright reformation—similar to the Protestant Reformation—is needed if Islam is to be comfortably accommodated within the value framework of twenty-first-century Western liberal modernity.[12]

While Islam lies at the center of many of the foreign policy regime complex's attempts to support and promote, mobilize and legitimize, certain religiosities over others, these efforts extend beyond any one particular religion. The International Religious Freedom regime, for instance, is intended to generate societies and states where individuals and communities can live and practice their religion freely not only in private but also publicly. At the same time, it seeks to produce a particular type of religious person and tradition, one that sustains and is compatible with pluralist, democratic, and capitalist societies. The Faith-Based Foreign Aid regime was a boon, especially during the Bush administration, for more conservative Christian Evangelical organizations wanting to promote their brand of theology and views of morality globally. With its launch under Secretary of State John Kerry, the Religious Engagement regime has appeared to favor, and thus empower, religious voices and actors that could contribute to America's national interest as defined by the progressive and Democratic Obama administration.

Ultimately, I contend, that if the champions and policymakers of the different religious foreign policy regimes had it completely their way, religiosity in foreign contexts would be transformed through the regime complex to resemble America's domestic faith-based and political landscape. This is characterized by a thriving plurality of denominations and religious traditions, but also by an overall Christian majority and Protestant-dominated culture; by faiths whose political theology generally supports democracy and free markets, while nonetheless exhibiting significant cleavages between conservative and progressive traditions; and by normative arrangements defining the public role of the sacred, structured around the two religion clauses – the Establishment and Free Exercise Clauses – of the US Constitution's First Amendment.

Religionizing World Politics

As the United States seeks to manage global religious realities driven by the conviction that "religion matters," as Secretary of State John Kerry put it,[13] the foreign policy regime complex simultaneously contributes to making the sacred matter even more. In other words, as the United States responds to the forces and actors that make up a postsecular world society—namely processes of religious resurgence and the emergence of postsecular consciousness—its foreign policy regime complex concurrently contributes to amplifying these very same dynamics through processes of religionization.

Religionization, I have shown, can take place through two mechanisms: subjective religious categorization and objective religious elevation. Religious categorization occurs when the regimes (re)produce a world where peoples, states, regions, events, and processes are chiefly defined along religious lines.

---

[12] See respectively Wolfowitz quoted in Ignatius (2003), and Obama quoted in Goldberg (2016).
[13] Kerry quoted in Casey (2015).

This projection of religious categories in and onto the world occurs especially in the context of the International Religious Freedom and the Muslim and Islamic Interventions regimes. Thus through the discourses, institutions, and practices of regimes such as these, the South Sudanese are labeled as Christians, insurgents in Iraq as Sunnis, Rohingyas in Burma as Muslims, political opponents to the Vietnamese regime as persecuted Buddhist Monks, the events of 9/11 explained as religiously inspired, terrorism identified as an Islamic or Muslim problem, violence in Syria described as sectarian, and curbing anti-Semitism presented as a religious freedom issue. When, for instance, the United States has as Special Representative to Muslim Communities in the State Department, it constructs through its institutions and practices a world wherein Muslim identity matters for political, economic, and security purposes. In parallel, the regime complex is premised on elevating, rather than marginalizing or excluding, the presence of religious voices and actors in the making and implementation of American foreign policy and the conduct of world politics more broadly—particularly those defined as true, good, or useful.

The implication of this argument is that we cannot completely disentangle, at the present moment, American foreign policy changes from global processes of religious resurgence. Put differently, our explanations of the growing political salience of religion globally may need to factor in not just—as many have suggested—a series of structural causes, such as the collapse of Communism, the spread of democracy and the participation of religious masses in politics, or various forms of crisis engendered by liberal modernity, capitalism, and globalization.[14] Instead, we should take more explicitly into consideration the agency and role played by the world's superpower in promoting changes associated with the growing political salience of religion globally. This role is particularly evident today with the emergence of the regime complex, but it may have even deeper historical origins in America's support of religiously inspired actors across Europe, the Middle East, Asia and other parts of the world during the Cold War and its fight against Communism.

Promoting and Diffusing Similar Religious Regimes in International Policy

A third, and final, international effect of America's foreign policy regime complex on religion is to promote the adoption or encourage the scaling up of similar religious regimes around the world—especially across Western states and multilateral institutions. This is occurring through two types of processes. The first is a fairly linear process of regime diffusion from the United States to other contexts. This may occur in direct or indirect ways. In the former case, much of the agency resides with American civil society actors and policymakers tied to the different regimes who purposely advocate and share

---

[14] These types of structural explanations for the resurgence of religion are offered for instance by Habermas (2006); Roy (2004); Thomas (2005); Toft, Philpott, and Shah (2011).

experiences across boundaries with the scope of promoting similar policies elsewhere. In the case of indirect processes of diffusion, agency resides mostly with non-American civil society actors and policymakers who carefully observe the superpower's experience and seek to reproduce or expand similar arrangements in their own contexts.

Linear processes of diffusion, whether direct or indirect, largely define the way in which elements of the international religious freedom and religious engagement agendas are traveling from the United States to other contexts. Indeed, ever since American foreign policymakers have started to give greater attention to religious freedom and engaging religious actors abroad, other countries like Canada, the United Kingdom, Germany, Italy, France, and EU institutions have launched similar offices and policies where none existed before, or sought to boost their own latent endeavors in these areas. A range of civil society institutions and initiatives have played a pivotal role in such processes of diffusion, acting in particular as connecting nodes and conveyer belts for the transmission of knowledge across the North American and transatlantic space. Featuring prominently among these are, for instance, the Berkley Center at Georgetown University, the Cambridge Institute on Religion and International Studies (CIRIS) at the University of Cambridge, the Bridging Voices initiative funded by the Henry Luce Foundation and the British Council, and the ReligioWest Project at the European University Institute, as well as regular events and workshops organized by the Italian think tank Istituto per gli Studi di Politica Internazionale (ISPI), in conjunction with the Italian Ministry of Foreign Affairs.

The second diffusion process involves more reciprocal mechanisms of knowledge exchange and mutual learning between the United States and non-American civil society actors and policymakers whereby Americans share with, but also draw from, the experiences of others. Compared to the International Religious Freedom and Religious Engagement regimes, where the United States is clearly in the driver's seat internationally, the Faith-Based Foreign Aid and the Muslim and Islamic Interventions regimes emerged in a different global context. These regimes came into being in the United States just as similar efforts were acquiring growing momentum in other countries and international institutions. In the case of both regimes, therefore, the United States has not necessarily been the primary vector of regime diffusion, but rather found itself participating in processes of knowledge circulation and mutual learning with and from other contexts. This said, given the sheer size and importance of the United States in the international arena, the superpower has often come to play a leading role in generating greater coordination and joint partnerships between different actors at the international level. This especially applies to counterterrorism interventions that target Muslims and Islam globally. Here the United States has been at the forefront of coordinating and funding a range of global and regional multilateral initiatives to counter Islamist extremism, such as *Hedayah* and the Global Counterterrorism Forum.

An important caveat is in order here. I have stressed throughout this sub-section the impact and effects that America's foreign policy regime complex has *potentially* had on global religious and secular realities. I emphasize the issue of potentiality rather than actuality because—as will be discussed further in the next section—far greater research is needed to unpack more fully the extent of America's influence and the causal pathways through which changes in US foreign policy are—if at all—bringing about changes across the globe.

Areas for Further Research: Looking Forward and Widening Horizons

Having outlined the contours of America's foreign policy regime complex on religion, in this section I put forward four broad areas for further research and reflection. The first area concerns the events taking place under the Trump administration and assessing whether the trends identified in this study and the theoretical framework developed here still hold in the context of ongoing developments. Second, there is a need for greater empirical probing into the extent to which religions—whether organizations, communities, or traditions—are changing globally in light of America's growing and institutionalized intervention in their midst, and if so, how. Third, further research is needed to compare the operationalization of religion in American foreign policy to similar processes taking place in other states and international institutions. Fourth, the analysis of this book can and should be put into dialogue with an ongoing debate about the challenge that the global resurgence of religion arguably poses to the state and to the contemporary Westphalian states-system more broadly.[15]

President Trump and the Regime Complex

How have the individual regimes and the overall regime complex fared under the Trump presidency? The book's analysis generally ends with the second Obama administration in 2016 and, at the time of writing, we are nearly halfway through President Trump's first term in office. Attention to ongoing developments—which I have discussed already in the concluding sections of each case study chapter and now bring together more coherently in this conclusion—is of value not only for updating as much as possible the book's historical narrative. It is also of value for assessing the strengths and weakness

---

[15] It must be noted that these areas are suggestions inspired by the theoretical premises underlying this book, as well as its empirical findings, and thus should not be read as exhausting all possible avenues for further thinking and research on the topic. Other areas, partially overlooked by this study, could include (a) explorations into the religious ideas and political theologies animating the enterprise of operationalizing religion in foreign and international policy; and (b) more targeted investigations into whether these policies are effective in promoting democracy, development, or peace as its advocates suggest, or not, as its critics maintain.

of its theoretical framework, and identify areas where this could be further re-fined in the future.

As of late 2018 we have witnessed under the Trump presidency processes of both regime continuity and change. Many of the foundational ideas, institutions, and practices constitutive of the American foreign policy regime complex have remained in place. More broadly, the current administration has not been shy about its public embrace of religion in general and of cer-tain religious agendas dear to the Religious Right in particular. This is hardly surprising considering that the administration includes many conservative Evangelicals as high up as Vice President Mike Pence, who describes him-self as "a Christian, a conservative, and a Republican, in that order."[16] When it comes to the changes taking place, these have tended to be of two kinds. On the one hand, the regimes appear to be evolving and adapting to the policy priorities of the new administration and its supporters in ways that could be expected by the book's theoretical model. On the other hand, there have been some important breaks with the past that cannot be entirely accounted for by the conceptual tools developed or employed by this study.[17]

Since Donald Trump took office, among the four regimes, the administra-tion has given particular attention to two of them, namely the International Religious Freedom and the Muslim and Islamic Interventions regimes. President Trump and Vice President Pence have spoken publicly on multiple occasions about religious freedom issues at home and abroad. Much of the regime's institutional infrastructure left behind by previous administrations has remained intact. Signaling the administration's high interest in this policy, a novel ambassador-at-large was appointed relatively quickly, in the figure of the political heavyweight Sam Brownback, a former Republican Senator and Governor and a key sponsor of the 1998 International Religious Freedom Act. Secretary of State Mike Pompeo has embraced full-heartedly the issue of inter-national religious freedom, especially when compared to President Trump's first Secretary of State Rex Tillerson. In July 2018, the first ever Ministerial to Advance Religious Freedom was held at the State Department, a major meeting that over three days brought together foreign ministers, international organizations officials, religious leaders, and civil society representatives from around the world to share experiences and coordinate efforts on this policy.

A few notable changes are taking place as well. First, in line with the waxing importance given to the regime, International Religious Freedom is replacing Religious Engagement as the core regime around which others are being more closely tied or aligned to. In other words, as we shall see better in a mo-ment, efforts appear under way to partially restructure the regime complex into a more nested type of regime under the International Religious Freedom

---

[16] Pence (2017).
[17] Much of the narrative here draws from what has already been discussed in the conclusions of chapters 3, 4, 5, and 6. For specific references to the facts mentioned here, the reader should consult these chapters.

umbrella. Second, while the International Religious Freedom regime has tended to have an implicit Christian soft spot over the past decades, attention to Christian concerns and communities has become even more overt and explicit under the Trump administration.

The fight against terrorism in general and ISIS in particular has been a major preoccupation of Donald Trump. In this context, policies targeting Muslims and interventions directed at Islam have also remained a constant with the present administration. Noteworthy, however, has been a shift away from the more cooperative and nuanced approaches adopted by President Obama, toward a much more conflictual and essentialist perspective. This has been particularly visible in President Trump's rhetoric, as well as that of many members of his administration, about the potential dangers posed by anyone identified as Muslim and in the emphasis placed on linking terrorism with Islam.

President Trump's travel ban, also known as the "Muslim ban", and the administration's repeated proposals to heighten the surveillance of Muslims, are a practical manifestation of this shift. Likewise, it has been no accident that various Muslim engagement positions still remain vacant at the time of writing (e.g., those of Special Envoy to the OIC and the Special Representative to Muslim Communities), and that the White House's customary *Iftar* dinner—at least since it was established during the Clinton presidency—was canceled in 2017 (the dinner was reinstated, in a reduced format, in 2018). The administration has also expressed an interest in rebranding Countering Violent Extremism (CVE) activities as "countering Islamic extremism" or "countering radical Islamic extremism." Whether such changes will take place is still unclear. President Trump's presence during the flashy inauguration of Saudi Arabia's Global Center for Combating Extremist Ideology (*Etidal* in Arabic), however, certainly shows the administration's commitment to engaging in the theological battle against Islamists. Moreover, the Trump presidency has so far prevalently focused on security and ideological responses to terrorism, while giving much less emphasis to other social, political, or economic factors.

The status and future prospects of the Faith-Based Foreign Aid and Religious Engagement regimes seem to be more uncertain instead. For the past year and a half, it remained unclear whether President Trump was going to reauthorize the White House and USAID's faith-based initiatives offices. The newly elected Republican president did appear to have some kind of informal and noninstitutionalized arrangement in place, an unofficial Evangelical advisory board that would advise the president and his administration on a wide range of issues that had little to do with supporting the vulnerable and poor, however. Furthermore, Donald Trump has exhibited a skeptical attitude toward foreign aid and plans to cut foreign assistance are under way.

Yet on May 3, 2018—on the National Day of Prayer—Trump issued an executive order launching his own Faith-Based and Opportunity Initiative. The Bush- and Obama-era faith-based offices in the White House and USAID have thus been reauthorized and given the initiative's new name. It is worth noting that along with the formal changes in name, two other more substantive shifts are taking place. First, rules demanding that FBOs clearly separate their operations from their faith commitments are being relaxed to accommodate the preferences of more pervasively religious organizations—often Evangelical in inspiration. Second, issues of religious freedom and persecution are being given greater consideration in the context of Trump's faith-based initiative. In this latter context, the status and well-being of Christians in the Middle East—especially of communities targeted by ISIS' violence in Iraq—has been a major concern of the administration and particularly of Vice President Pence. Estimates published by the *Washington Post*, for instance, suggest that total US aid to Christian and Yazidi communities in Iraq is likely to be in the order of $100 million for the 2018 fiscal year.[18]

Among all the regimes, Religious Engagement is undergoing the most dramatic changes as it is being radically downsized by the Trump administration. As of late 2018, no one has been appointed to replace Shaun Casey at the helm of the Office for Religion and Global Affairs, with the office rumored to be shut down or its operations moved under the Office for International Religious Freedom at State. While in its independent and institutionalized form the regime at the moment appears basically defunct, the notion of religious engagement has not completely vanished. Indeed, Donald Trump seems to have partially taken the matter in his own hands—most notably during his first foreign trip as US president, presented as a sort of "world religion tour,"[19] which included highly symbolic stops in Saudi Arabia, Israel, and the Vatican City.

Much of what is taking place at the moment—especially in the context of the International Religious Freedom, Faith-Based Foreign Aid, and Muslim and Islamic Intervention regimes—fits well with the analysis and theoretical framework developed in this study. The underlying axiom of this book is that in the context of a postsecular world society, pressures to operationalize or sustain existing regimes are expected to persist. Moreover, once institutionalized, a regime is likely to continue, also driven by particular processes of path dependency. Amid elements of continuity, though, the model expects that the arrival of a new administration constitutes a critical juncture which can lead to particular regime changes. Such changes, I have argued, are highly dependent on the influence that specific networks and coalitions of desecularizing actors may acquire within an administration at these moments. The Trump campaign and administration have relied quite heavily, among others, on the support of more conservative religious actors, mostly Evangelical but also Catholic and Jewish. The evolution we are seeing taking place in the case of the International Religious Freedom, Muslim and Islamic Interventions, and Faith-Based Foreign Aid regimes discussed here fits perfectly with these actors' normative preferences and interests, which are embedded in a range of

---

[18] Morello (2018).
[19] CFR (2018).

desecularizing discourses that I have laid out in the previous four chapters. The influence of the Religious Right on President Trump's foreign policy has been equally noticeable—for example, on the administration's controversial decision to move the American Embassy in Israel from Tel Aviv to Jerusalem.

More puzzling perhaps is the dramatic decline in the Religious Engagement regime. This development leads me to make two hypotheses on how the theoretical model could be further refined. First, given existing resistances—both normative and cultural, but also in terms of competing foreign policy interests—to the operationalization of religion in foreign policy, the why and how a particular regime is operationalized matters. Both the International Religious Freedom and the Faith-Based Foreign Aid regimes are the product of intense advocacy and lobbying from different and at times competing, but also well organized and broad-based, domestic constituencies. Likewise, both have been institutionalized through particular legal means, whether via a Congressional act in the former case or presidential executive orders in the latter. The Muslim and Islamic Interventions regime is a response—however problematic, according to many—to an obvious national security issue, which mobilizes intense domestic political and intellectual debate and activity. Religious engagement has generally been a more elite project, with scarce roots in domestic political or religious milieus, notable also in the fact that its operationalization has occurred comparatively later in time and thanks to a decision by a secretary of state, rather than Congress or the president. Moreover, although the regime may have some strategic value—especially according to the desecularizing experts championing it—it is not as intimately and explicitly tied to an immediate security threat as the Muslim and Islamic Interventions regime clearly is.

Second, the ideological composition and breadth of the desecularizing actors, and of the discourses supporting a particular regime, may matter too. The constellation of actors championing the International Religious Freedom, Faith-Based Foreign Aid, and Muslim and Islamic Interventions regimes is very diverse going from the right to the left—so to speak—of the political, scholarly, and religious spectrum. Hence, whether Democrats or Republicans are in power, these three regimes are likely to have a range of desecularizing actors who articulate discourses that can gain traction within any administration at any one given moment in time. The desecularizing actors supporting the Religious Engagement regime are somewhat diverse and are certainly not all theologically or politically progressive. Yet religious engagement desecularizing discourses—focusing either in the narrow sense on peacemaking or in the broader sense on international order—do appear to resonate overwhelmingly with the foreign policy ideas and preferences of Democratic administrations, who have tended to emphasize cooperation over conflict, the role of diplomacy over military action, and multilateralism over unilateralism.

Once we take these two conditions more explicitly into account, the current (as of late 2018) downsizing of the Religious Engagement regime may no longer appear that puzzling. Bearing all this in mind, then, we can expect the fortunes of this regime to wax again, but only under certain conditions: first, starting with the most probable, if a new Democratic administration gains hold of the White House and finds existing desecularizing discourses on religious engagement persuasive; second, if a discourse on religious engagement is developed and articulated by a novel epistemic community that is capable of resonating with the priorities of the Trump administration in particular and Republicans more generally; and third, if a broad-based domestic constituency develops which persuades Congress or the president to operationalize the Religious Engagement regime through legal measures, thus giving it more institutional weight than simply appearing as a pet project of a secretary of state.

Religious Changes and the "View from the Other Side"

Further in-depth research is needed to explore the impact of America's foreign policy regimes on religious realities both globally and in particular localities. Specifically, more probing is needed to examine the extent to which the operationalization of religion in foreign policy is reshaping sacred landscapes globally according to American values and interests. We have, in fact, very little systematic knowledge about what is currently occurring as the US foreign policy rubber hits the religious road around the world. This type of research—which should draw from a range of methods including case studies, ethnographic observations, surveys, and statistical analysis—could focus on three particularly pressing issues.

One aspect worthy of further investigation concerns the central claims made in this book, namely the effects that the regimes have had on certain religious traditions worldwide. These claims are the fruit of a particular theoretical framework, close analysis of American foreign policy discourses and practices, extensive interviews, and a review of the growing yet still limited cases and accounts available from the field. As such, more systematic attention can be given to exploring the extent to which, for instance, the regimes have actually favored certain religions (e.g., Christianity) over others, and certain religious minorities and sects more generally. More can also be done to assess the impact of the regime complex on the particular types of religiosities that come to be defined as good, true, or useful, especially within Islam but also across most other religious traditions.

Second, building on these premises, more attention needs to be paid to the potentially unintended (and presumably undesirable) religious and religio-political consequences brought about by the fact that the world's superpower is increasingly meddling in the affairs of faith-based actors and communities around the globe. For instance, some scholars close to the international religious freedom agenda may view a world where Christianity flourishes as a more democratic, free, and pro-American one,[20] and may thus welcome the

---

[20] For example, Shah and Hertzke (2016a, 2016b).

notion that the United States may be encouraging such developments. As the world's superpower becomes—or is simply perceived to become—ever more intertwined with the fortunes of Christianity globally, are Christian communities and institutions worldwide seen increasingly as extensions of American interests and influence? Are historical memories of entanglements between Christian missionaries and Western colonialism being revived, or are clash of civilizations narratives being sustained in the process? Most importantly, are such realities and perceptions generating backlashes and increasing the violence directed against Christians in foreign contexts?[21]

What about America's interventions within Islam? For instance, as US foreign policymakers seek to harness moderate Muslims and Islam for their agendas, to what extent do such policies undermine and delegitimize those same actors and political theologies viewed as true, good, or useful? This issue is particularly relevant in a context where, on the one hand, established Islamic institutions across the Muslim world are often discredited in light of longstanding political meddling in their affairs by Middle Eastern regimes themselves and, on the other, by the popular mistrust that exists toward America's intentions and role in the region. For this reason, US support for what gets to be viewed as moderate Muslims and Islam is often provided covertly. Secrecy, however, may generate further suspicion that any religious argument or actor appearing in line with American interests is not authentic, but the product of some kind of foreign influence.

Moreover, even if the United States were ever able to change the historical trajectory and theological direction of one of the world's greatest religions, such as Islam, the question remains whether the Christian Protestant experience invoked by presidents and their advisors provides a fruitful frame of reference. Can and should all religions follow the same Christian path? Does the Protestant Reformation offer an exemplary model to follow, given the religiously infused wars that it was closely entangled with in sixteenth- and seventeenth-century Europe? Not only that, but what safeguards have been put in place to avoid that those religions defined as useful today may turn out to be tomorrow's dangerous religion—just as yesterday's religious freedom fighters in Afghanistan, the *Mujahidin* and Osama Bin Laden, have become today's terrorists? While some critics of American's religious foreign policy regimes do raise similar questions, sustained scholarly research as well as governmental monitoring and evaluation exercises probing further into such thorny issues is sorely lacking.

Third, this study and others like it spend much time explaining and analyzing the institutional, cultural, and normative changes occurring in the bureaucracies responsible for making and implementing foreign policy. Important as this is, the changes that are occurring among religious actors and communities have generally received far less attention. Are religious actors and

---

[21] See in the case of India, for example, Cozad (2005); Subramanya (2015).

communities in the United States and around the world reorganizing themselves to welcome or resist a renewed era of religion–state entanglements and, if so, how? Are there any visible signs whereby such actors and communities are building greater capacity to effectively influence and steer American foreign policy according to their specific agendas, as the United States becomes more willing to partner with them?

Indeed, among both advocates and critics of these policies, some are starting to ask similar questions. William Vendley, of Religions for Peace and a supporter of greater state engagement with religion, notes how faith-based institutions and leaders "weren't built to be state-craft actors in the first instance."[22] He thus calls for greater attempts to chronicle "what is happening to the religious communities" all around the world as these are "learning," and "beginning to gear up and train themselves," to "become partners with states."[23] In a similar vein, but from a more critical perspective, Noah Salomon calls for greater attention to be paid to the "view from the other side."[24] In particular, his concern is with the ways that Sufi organizations are retooling themselves and the negative repercussion this process may have on their tradition as they assume the role of moderate and liberal Islam assigned to them by American policymakers in search for Islamic allies in a post-9/11 world. To sum up, then, future research should bring more to the fore the potentially transformative effects on, and the experience of, religious actors and communities as the United States seeks to include them in foreign policymaking and intervene in their midst.

The Operationalization of Religion in International and Comparative Perspective

This book seeks to contribute to the rapidly expanding literature that has emerged over the years exploring the causes, modalities, and consequences of the operationalization of religion in international policy. Yet more needs to be done still to understand the linkages as well as the differences between states. Three areas, I would argue, are of particular interest here.

One aspect that deserves further study is to better understand the drivers leading to the operationalization of religion taking place across different states and multilateral institutions around the world at this historical juncture. A possible starting point could be to draw on the theoretical framework developed and employed in this book to explain the particular American experience, and apply it to explain the emergence of similar regimes elsewhere. As similarities or differences appear from case to case, these could be used to confirm, critique, or further refine the theory and conceptual tools developed in this book.

---

[22] Vendley in Berkley Center (2014b, 36:14–37:23).
[23] Ibid.
[24] Salomon (2016).

A second area could build on this book's initial finding that multiple processes of regime diffusion from, to, and between the American case and other states and institutions are currently taking place. These dynamics of regime diffusion were mostly sketched out in this study rather than fully theorized or comprehensively demonstrated on an empirical basis. More work remains to be done, therefore, to identify the key mechanisms of diffusion at work across the different regimes and countries, the main agents and networks involved in such processes, what sustains them (including financially), how they relate to one another, and under what circumstances they succeed—or not—in their objectives to diffuse religious knowledge and policies across contexts.

Third, as religious foreign policies are emerging across different states and institutions, often Western-based, the time appears ripe to engage in greater comparative research. Elizabeth Shakman Hurd presents a wide-ranging view—and critique—of the operationalization of religion, and especially of religious freedom, in the foreign policies of the United States, the United Kingdom, and the EU.[25] What is generally missing still is a clear comparison which teases out differences, not just similarities, between cases. This type of research would do more than simply identify best practices that can be transplanted from one case to another, which is the main focus of a budding policy-driven transatlantic literature on the subject.[26] Rather, similar to the ongoing scholarly enterprise on comparative secularisms,[27] the type of research called for here would further the intellectual endeavor of understanding the context-specific nature of how religion is understood, operationalized, and managed in the foreign policies of countries with different histories, identities, state-institutional structures, religious demographics, religion–state settlements, and international interests.

Indeed, this type of work has already begun in certain quarters, although a more systematic approach would certainly be desirable. For instance, some have shown how European understandings of religious engagement or of international religious freedom—which Europeans mostly refer to as freedom of religion or belief (FoRB)—differ from how Americans approach these policies.[28] Others have explored how CVE policies vary substantially across different Western, Middle Eastern, and North African states, reflecting different national experiences and histories.[29] The field remains largely open for this kind of comparative research agenda on the operationalization of religion in international policy.

---

[25] Hurd (2015).
[26] Birdsall, Lindsay, and Tomalin (2015); Mandaville and Silvestri (2015); Thames (2014).
[27] For example Cady and Hurd (2010); Kuru (2009); Mayrl (2016).
[28] Annicchino (2013a); Wolff (2018).
[29] Awadallah, Lang, and Densmore (2017); Bettiza and Phillips (2012).

States, the Westphalian System, and the New Geopolitics of Religion

This book sits at the intersection of a complex debate around the (uncertain) future of the state and the Westphalian states-system in the context of a postsecular era of religious vitality and the destabilization of long taken-for-granted secular knowledge paradigms. Its arguments and findings partly confirm, partly refute, and above all complicate a general narrative in the discipline of IR that presents religion and its resurgence as a profound challenge to the modern state and the current international system.[30]

An important part of this narrative focuses on the threat posed by the growing political salience of religion to the centrality of the state as an institution, an actor, and as the ultimate source of political authority in contemporary international politics. One can easily understand why such a view has an important and widespread appeal. The nonstate character, transnational quality, and otherworldly outlook of most religious actors, networks, identities, and loyalties does lead to an understanding that as these become more important, the role of the territorially bounded, this-worldly state would decline. Such readings, I would suggest, are generally based on particular theoretical premises: on a modern outlook, present both in secular as well as faith-based milieus, that views religion and the state as mutually exclusive entities in competition with one another, locked into a zero-sum relationship.

This book's analysis, grounded in a postsecular and historical sociological theoretical premise, points instead toward another perspective. In this perspective, religions and their global resurgence are not simply a threat to the state, but can also become deeply intertwined through processes of desecularization with the exercise of state power internationally. I share thus Saeed's view that desecularization "does not entail an erosion of the secular disciplinary and symbolic powers of the nation-state, which may in fact be further strengthened through it."[31] What this study finds, in fact, is that with the growing salience of religious actors, communities, beliefs, symbols, and practices globally, governments become increasingly sensitive to the need to understand and govern the ebbs and flows of faith to their advantage. Indeed, this is the overall intention that underpins the United States' foreign policy regime complex on religion. By drawing from, mobilizing, and managing the sacred in its foreign policy, the United States is simultaneously seeking through religion to make itself more secure, extend its influence globally, and promote an international order that reflects its values and interests.

International religious freedom, for instance, is regularly framed as a policy beneficial to advancing either the wider US project of promoting democracy and human rights internationally or the narrower objective of defeating terrorism

---

[30] See, for example, Byrnes (2011); Huntington (1996); Mendelsohn (2012); Philpott (2002, 83–92); Rudolph and Piscatori (1997); Shani (2008); Thomas (2005).
[31] Saeed (2016, 24).

and resolving conflicts seen as a threat to its security. When it comes to faith-based initiatives, some note how FBOs and churches delivering aid in Africa do not simply supplant, but actually extend and complement contemporary forms of global secular humanitarian governance.[32] Similar conclusions can be drawn for America's Faith-Based Foreign Aid regime. Created as it is to tap into religious realities and partner with faith-based actors to improve distant lives, this regime also participates in governing people in the remotest corners of the world, or at least eliciting their goodwill toward the United States. The entire Muslim and Islamic Interventions regime is framed and executed in the context of fighting terrorism, projecting and cultivating American soft power, and reforming Muslim societies, states, and religiosities in line with US liberal values and security interests. Similar dynamics are at work in the religious engagement space. Former Secretary of State Kerry, for example, plainly acknowledged that the US engagement with religious actors and communities is chiefly designed "to make progress towards our foreign policy and our national security goals" and not "just for the sake of having interesting conversations."[33] The goals in question are explicitly spelt out in the US Strategy on Religious Leader and Faith Community Engagement as advancing liberal norms and institutions, improving the delivery of humanitarian and development assistance, fighting terrorism, and solving conflicts.[34] If all this sounds too ambitious, engaging religious actors is at the very least a valuable exercise to "gain intelligence", a former State Department official argues.[35]

In short, looking at it from the American foreign policy perspective, the global resurgence of religions does not seem to bring about the withering of the state. Instead, we may be witnessing the signs of a new or, better, renewed form of religious geopolitics which sees (certain) states and (certain) religions and religiosities as working in tandem for their mutual global benefit. Political and religious power have intersected in multiple and often mutually reinforcing ways from the dawn of times, from the Egypt of the Pharaohs, to Biblical Israel, Islamic Caliphates, Latin Christendom, and European colonialism. Yet it does seem, at least by looking at the religious turn in American foreign policy of the past two decades, that such interactions and overlaps are still occurring, albeit in new ways, today. Mara Willard, for instance, hints at such developments when arguing that:

> Religions are both agents and objects of imperial power . . . For those concerned about ways religion and national power interact, the establishment of an office of religious engagement at the State Department provides both continuity and change.[36]

---

[32] Agensky (2013); see also Lynch and Schwarz (2016).
[33] Kerry (2016).
[34] White House (2013).
[35] Nicole Bibbins Sedaca in Berkley Center (2013a, 14:52).
[36] Mara Willard in *The Immanent Frame* (2013).

The American case is not an isolated one, since the operationalization of religion is increasingly gaining momentum across Western states and institutions. Moreover, the international influence and power of countries like Saudi Arabia, Iran, Israel, or Russia today, for instance, appears to be increasingly entwined with the Islamic, Jewish, and Christian religious traditions, institutions, networks, and identities with which each country is closely related to.[37] Seen from this angle, the contours of a novel research agenda on the contemporary *geopolitics of religion* in international relations opens itself up for further exploration. This would include theoretical and empirical investigations into how particular states and religions interact in specific, mutually reinforcing, ways to increase their power and influence globally, including vis-à-vis their adversaries, whether states or religions.

Moreover, if the assessment of an international society witnessing states exercising their power globally through renewed forms of religious cooperation and entanglements holds true, then what is clearly being undermined are a number of key norms underpinning the modern Westphalian international system. Some suggest, for instance, that an erosion of Westphalian authority structures is occurring as transnational non-state actors like Al Qaeda have emerged, claiming to offer an alternative non-state-centric vision of world order and acting in the name of an Islamic *Umma* against the world's superpower and its allies.[38] I would add to this, however, that the Westphalian settlement may be undermined even further by the actions of the world's superpower, rather than by men in caves in Afghanistan. In particular, as America seeks to promote religious liberty and come to the rescue of persecuted communities abroad, as it funds FBOs to assist those in need across the globe, as it attempts to pacify Muslim societies and reform Islamic traditions, or as it engages religious actors around the world, it directly challenges two key premises of the Westphalian order upon which the modern international society of states rests.

First, such activities undermine at its very core the principle of state sovereignty and nonintervention. Famously and pithily captured by the *cuius regio, eius religio* formula (the ruler determines the religion of his realm), the principle of nonintervention was first and foremost intended to curtail foreign meddling in the domestic religious affairs of other sovereign states or political authorities. Second, American interference in the religious realm of others is generally designed to raise the profile of religion in world politics, rather than downplay or even ignore its significance. Such a move fundamentally upends an assumption that has animated much modern thinking about world politics. This is what Scott Thomas defines as the "Westphalian presumption":[39] namely, the notion that religion should be at best privatized or at least domesticated within the confines of states, but hardly allowed to participate in global

---

[37] See for instance Farquhar (2016); Garrard and Garrard (2008); Haynes (2001); Mearsheimer and Walt (2007); Nasr (2016).
[38] Mendelsohn (2012); Philpott (2002).
[39] Thomas (2005).

politics lest chaos and violence ensue. Put differently, this belief understands international order as resting on the religious genie being kept inside the state bottle. The religious turn in American foreign policy radically challenges such a presumption.

To conclude, a postsecular era may not necessarily bring about a less state-centric order, but is likely to put into question a Westphalian one which, historically, has emerged out of the European experience. Indeed, the norms and presumptions underpinning the modern Westphalian system appear undermined at their very core by the actions of the American foreign policy regime complex on religion, as well as by the multiple and complex global religious interventions that other Western and non-Western states are practicing in the context of the contemporary geopolitics of religion. In a way, we may well be back to the future. Regardless, we have only barely begun to understand and theorize what all of this means for world politics today, for how states and religions relate globally, what kind of power dynamics are at play, and what types of international norms and practices are emerging in an international system that it may be increasingly problematic to call Westphalian at the dawn of the twenty-first century.

APPENDIX 1 | Religious Foreign Policy Regimes' Norms,
Ideas, Institutions, and Practices

L EGEND: INDEPENDENT [I], National Security Council [NSC], State Department
[SD], United States Agency for International Development [USAID], White
House [WH]

INTERNATIONAL RELIGIOUS FREEDOM: NORMS, IDEAS, INSTITUTIONS, AND PRACTICES

	Norms (acts, rules, guidelines, etc.) and Ideas (strategies, reports, etc.)	Institutions (formal/permanent and "informal/temporary")	Practices (policies, initiatives, actions, etc.)
Clinton (1993–1996)		• "Advisory Committee on Religious Freedom Abroad" [SD]	
Clinton (1997–2000)	• State Department (1997), "United States Policies in Support of Religious Freedom: Focus on Christians" • Advisory Committee on Religious Freedom Abroad (1998), "Interim Report to the Secretary of State and to the President of the United States" • International Religious Freedom Act (1998)	• Office of International Religious Freedom (OIRF) [SD] • Ambassador-at-Large for International Religious Freedom (IRF Ambassador) [SD] • United States Commission on International Religious Freedom (USCIRF) [I] • Adviser for International Religious Freedom (IRF Adviser) [NSC]	• Monitoring and reporting • Diplomatic and policy actions • Capacity building in the foreign policy bureaucracy
Bush (2001–2004)		• OIRF [SD] • IRF Ambassador [SD] • USCIRF [I]	• Monitoring and reporting • Diplomatic and policy actions • Capacity building in the foreign policy bureaucracy
Bush (2005–2008)		• OIRF [SD] • IRF Ambassador [SD] • USCIRF [I]	• Monitoring and reporting • Diplomatic and policy actions • Capacity building in the foreign policy bureaucracy • Foreign assistance programming

Obama (2009–2012)	• IRF Office (2011), "Fact Sheet: Religious Freedom and National Security"	• OIRF [SD] • IRF Ambassador [SD] • USCIRF [I]	• Monitoring and reporting • Diplomatic and policy actions • Capacity building in the foreign policy bureaucracy • Foreign assistance programming • Capacity building abroad
Obama (2013–2016)	• Near East and South Central Asia Religious Freedom Act (2014)	• OIRF [SD] • IRF Ambassador [SD] • USCIRF [I] • Special Advisor for Religious Minorities in the Near East and South and Central Asia [SD]	• Monitoring and reporting • Diplomatic and policy actions • Capacity building in the foreign policy bureaucracy • Foreign assistance programming • Capacity building abroad • Focus on religious minorities in Muslim majority countries

FAITH-BASED FOREIGN AID: NORMS, IDEAS, INSTITUTIONS, AND PRACTICES

	Norms (acts, rules, guidelines, etc.) and Ideas (strategies, reports, etc.)	Institutions (formal/permanent and "informal/temporary")	Practices (policies, initiatives, actions, etc.)
Clinton (1993–1996)	• (Charitable Choice (1996))		
Clinton (1997–2000)			
Bush (2001–2004)	• Executive Order 13199: Establishment of White House Office of Faith-Based and Community Initiatives (2001) • Mexico City Policy (2001) • White House (2001), "Unlevel Playing Field: Barriers to Participation by Faith-Based and Community Organizations in Federal Social Service Programs" • Executive Order 13280: Responsibilities of the Department of Agriculture and the Agency for International Development with Respect to Faith-Based and Community Initiatives (2002)	• White House Office of Faith-Based and Community Initiatives (WHOFBCI) [WH] • Center for Faith-Based and Community Initiatives (CFBCI) [USAID] • Office of the US Global AIDS Coordinator [SD]	• Faith-Based Initiatives: Increases USAID engagement and funding of faith-based organizations (FBOs) • Mexico City Policy: Blocks funding for NGOs that perform or actively promote abortion as a method of family planning • President's Emergency Plan For AIDS Relief (PEPFAR): Funding made available also to FBOs for HIV/AIDS treatment, prevention and care programs (certain clauses privilege funding of FBOs over secular NGOs)

- United States Leadership Against HIV/AIDS, Tuberculosis, and Malaria Act (2003)
- Final Rule on Participation by Religious Organizations in USAID Programs (2004)

Bush (2005–2008)
- Tom Lantos and Henry J. Hyde United States Global Leadership Against HIV/AIDS, Tuberculosis, and Malaria Reauthorization Act (2008)

- WHOFBCI [WH]
- CFBCI [USAID]
- Office of the US Global AIDS Coordinator [SD]

- Faith-Based Initiatives: Increases USAID engagement and funding of FBOs
- Mexico City Policy: Blocks funding for NGOs that perform or actively promote abortion as a method of family planning
- PEPFAR: Funding made available also to FBOs for HIV/AIDS treatment, prevention and care programs (certain clauses privilege funding of FBOs over secular NGOs)

	Norms (acts, rules, guidelines, etc.) and Ideas (strategies, reports, etc.)	Institutions (formal/permanent and "informal/temporary")	Practices (policies, initiatives, actions, etc.)
Obama (2009–2012)	• Mexico City Policy—Revoked (2009) • White House (2010), "A New Era of Partnerships: Report of Recommendations to the President" • Executive Order 13559: Fundamental Principles and Policymaking Criteria for Partnerships With Faith-Based and Other Neighborhood Organizations (2010)	• White House Office of Faith-Based and Neighborhood and Partnerships (WHOFBNP) [WH] • "President's Advisory Council on Faith-Based and Neighborhood Partnerships" [WH] • CFBCI [USAID] • Office of the US Global AIDS Coordinator and Health Diplomacy [SD]	• Faith-Based Initiatives 2.0: Further expansion and mainstreaming of engagement and funding of FBOs across USAID programs • PEPFAR: Funding made available also to FBOs for HIV/AIDS treatment, prevention and care programs (clauses that privilege funding of FBOs over secular NGOs are removed)
Obama (2013–2016)	• PEPFAR Stewardship and Oversight Act (2013)	• WHOFBNP [WH] • "President's Advisory Council on Faith-Based and Neighborhood Partnerships" [WH] • CFBCI [USAID] • Office of the US Global AIDS Coordinator and Health Diplomacy [SD]	• Faith-Based Initiatives 2.0: Further expansion and mainstreaming of engagement and funding of FBOs across USAID programs • PEPFAR: Funding made available also to FBOs for HIV/AIDS treatment, prevention and care programs (clauses that privilege funding of FBOs over secular NGOs are removed)

MUSLIM AND ISLAMIC INTERVENTIONS: NORMS, IDEAS, INSTITUTIONS, AND PRACTICES

	Norms (acts, rules, guidelines, etc.) and Ideas (strategies, reports, etc.)	Institutions (formal/permanent and "informal/temporary")	Practices (policies, initiatives, actions, other)
Clinton (1993–1996)		• "Policy planning activities, workshops, and study groups" [SD]	• Symbolic gestures and practices (Speeches, Mosque visits, *Iftar* dinners, other)
Clinton (1997–2000)		• "Policy planning activities, workshops, and study groups" [SD]	• Symbolic gestures and practices (Speeches, Mosque visits, *Iftar* dinners, other)
Bush (2001–2004)	•White House (2002), "National Security Strategy"	• "Evolving 'Strategic Communications / Muslim World' Policy Coordination Committees (PCC)" [NSC] • Under Secretary of State for Public Diplomacy and Public Affairs [SD]	• Symbolic gestures and practices (Speeches, Mosque visits, *Iftar* dinners, other) • Freedom Agenda in the Broader Middle East: Military interventions (Iraq and Afghanistan), diplomatic engagements, and programs (MEPI) • War of Ideas: Improve America's image in the Muslim world

	Norms (acts, rules, guidelines, etc.) and Ideas (strategies, reports, etc.)	Institutions (formal/permanent and "informal/temporary")	Practices (policies, initiatives, actions, other)
Bush (2005–2008)	• White House (2006), "National Security Strategy" • PCC (2007), "US National Strategy for Public Diplomacy and Strategic Communication"	• "Evolving 'Strategic Communications / Muslim World' PCCs" [NSC] • Under Secretary of State for Public Diplomacy and Public Affairs [SD] • Special Envoy to the Organization of Islamic Conference/Cooperation (OIC) [SD]	• Symbolic gestures and practices (Speeches, Mosque visits, *Iftar* dinners, other) • Freedom Agenda in the Broader Middle East: Military interventions (Iraq and Afghanistan), diplomatic engagements (Palestinian elections) and programs (MEPI, BMENA) • War of Ideas: Improve America's image in the Muslim world; support moderate Muslims; *madrassa* reform programs
Obama (2009–2012)	• President Obama (2009), "A New Beginning" (address in Cairo to Muslim communities around the world) • White House (2010), "A New Era of Partnerships: Report of Recommendations to the President" • White House (2011), "Empowering Local Partners to Prevent Violent Extremism in the United States"	• "President's Advisory Council on Faith-Based and Neighborhood Partnerships" [WH] • Global Engagement Directory [NSC] • Special Envoy to the OIC [SD] • Special Representative to Muslim Communities [SD]	• Gobal Muslim Engagement: Symbolic gestures and practices (Speeches, Mosque visits, *Iftar* dinners, other); addressing Muslim policy grievances (Israeli-Palestinian Conflict, Guantanamo); programs (economic, education, civil society, science, culture)

			• Countering Violent Extremism (CVE): rhetorically delinking Islam from terrorism; generate, support, and promote counter/alternative religious and political narratives to those of violent (Muslim) extremists; community engagement; international cooperation and global capacity building (*Hedayah*)
		• Evolving Countering Violent Extremism (CVE) institutions, [NSC, SD, USAID]	
Obama (2013–2016)	• State Department & USAID (2016), "Joint Strategy on Countering Violent Extremism"	• Global Engagement Directory [NSC] • Special Envoy to the OIC [SD] • Special Representative to Muslim Communities [SD] • Evolving CVE institutions, [NSC, SD, USAID]	• Gobal Muslim Engagement: Symbolic gestures and practices (Speeches, Mosque visits, *Iftar* dinners, other); addressing Muslim policy grievances (Israeli-Palestinian Conflict, Guantanamo, Iraq); programs (economic, education, civil society, science, culture) • CVE: rhetorically delinking Islam from terrorism; generate, support, and promote counter/alternative religious and political narratives to those of violent (Muslim) extremists; community engagement; international coordination and global capacity building (*Hedayah*, White House CVE Summit, Global Counterterrorism Forum, Global Fund for Community Engagement and Resilience)

RELIGIOUS ENGAGEMENT: NORMS, IDEAS, INSTITUTIONS, AND PRACTICES

	Norms (acts, rules, guidelines, etc.) and Ideas (strategies, reports, etc.)	Institutions (formal/permanent and "informal/temporary")	Practices (policies, initiatives, actions, other)
Clinton (1993–1996)			
Clinton (1997–2000)	Advisory Committee on Religious Freedom Abroad (1998), "Interim Report to the Secretary of State and to the President of the United States"	• "Advisory Committee on Religious Freedom Abroad" [SD]	
Bush (2001–2004)			
Bush (2005–2008)			
Obama (2009–2012)	• White House (2010), "A New Era of Partnerships: Report of Recommendations to the President" • Interagency Working Group on Religion & Global Affairs (2010/2012), "Religious Engagement Reports" • Religion and Foreign Policy Working Group (2012), "Ensuring the Opportunity for Mutual Council and Collaboration: A White Paper of the Religion and Foreign Policy Working Group of the Secretary of State's Strategic Dialogue with Civil Society"	• "President's Advisory Council on Faith-Based and Neighborhood Partnerships" [WH] • "Religion & Global Affairs Forum" [SD] • "Interagency Working Group on Religion & Global Affairs" [WH, SD, USAID] • "Religion and Foreign Policy Working Group" [SD]	

| Obama (2013–2016) | • White House (2013), "US Strategy on Religious Leader and Faith Community Engagement"
• State Department guidelines on the matter of compliance with the Establishment Clause (2013/2015) | • "Religion and Foreign Policy Working Group" [SD]
• Office of Religion and Global Affairs (RGA) [SD]
• Special Representative for Religion in Global Affairs [SD]
• Special Envoy to the OIC [SD]
• Special Representative to Muslim Communities [SD]
• Special Envoy to Monitor and Combat Anti-Semitism [SD] | • Office of Religion and Global Affairs (RGA) tasked with: Advising the Secretary on policy matters as they relate to religion; supporting posts and bureaus in assessing religious dynamics and engaging religious actors; serving as a first point of entry for those seeking to engage the State Department on matters of religion and global affairs
• Issues of particular interest include: conflict resolution, counterterrorism, discrimination and social justice (e.g., Islamophobia, anti-Semitism, gender, refugees), climate change, and anti-corruption |

APPENDIX 2 | List of Interviewees

Surname, Name	Title and Affiliation (Year of Interview)
Abrams, Elliott	Senior Fellow, Council on Foreign Relations (2010, 2011)
Ahmed, Akbar	Ibn Khaldun Chair of Islamic Studies, American University (2011)
Beutel, Alejandro J.	Researcher, National Consortium for the Study of Terrorism and Responses to Terrorism, University of Maryland (2015)
Birdsall, Judd	Managing Director, Cambridge Institute on Religion and International Studies (2015)
Braniff, William	Executive Director, National Consortium for the Study of Terrorism and Responses to Terrorism, University of Maryland (2015)
Brinkmoeller, Mark	Senior Director, US Community Partnerships, One Campaign (2010, 2011)
Cesari, Jocelyne	Senior Fellow, Berkley Center for Religion, Peace, and World Affairs, Georgetown University (2015)
Chapman, Beth	Director of Outreach and Advancement, Trinity Forum (2011)
Cromartie, Michael	Vice President, Ethics and Public Policy Center (2011)
Cusimano Love, Maryann	Associate Professor, Catholic University of America (2011)
Farr, Thomas	Senior Fellow, Berkley Center for Religion, Peace, and World Affairs, Georgetown University (2010, 2011)

Surname, Name	Title and Affiliation (Year of Interview)
Faskianos, Irina	Vice President National Program & Outreach, Council on Foreign Relations (2011)
Former NSC Official	Consultant and Strategic Advisor, former National Security Council Staff (2010)
Fornea, Stan	Chaplain, US Navy Commander, White House Military Office (2011)
Gallespie, Anne	Clergy Director, Christ Church, Alexandria, Virginia (2011)
Glain, Stephen	Freelance Journalist (2010)
Grand, Stephen	Director, Project on US Relations with the Islamic World, Brookings Institution (2011)
Grieboski, Joseph	Founder, Institute on Religion and Public Policy (2011)
Grim, Brian	Senior Researcher, Pew Research Center Forum on Religion & Public Life (2011)
Hart, Tom	Senior Director of US Government Relations, One Campaign (2011)
Henne, Peter	Research Associate, Pew Research Center Religion & Public Life (2015)
Hertzke, Allen	Professor, University of Oklahoma (2011)
Hoover, Dennis	Vice President for Research and Publications, Institute for Global Engagement (2011)
Inboden, William	Assistant Professor, University of Texas at Austin (2011)
Johnston, Douglas	President, International Center for Religion and Diplomacy (2011)
Katulis, Brian	Senior Fellow, Center for American Progress (2015)
Lateef, Asma	Director, Bread for the World Institute, Bread for the World (2011)
Lugo, Luis	Director, Pew Research Center Forum on Religion and Public Life (2010)
Lundquist, Kristen	Program Officer for Religion, Security and Gender, Institute for Global Engagement (2011)
Maginnis, Robert	Senior Fellow, Family Research Council (2011)
Marshall, Katherine	Senior Fellow, Berkley Center for Religion, Peace, and World Affairs, Georgetown University (2011)
Marshall, Paul	Senior Fellow, Center for Religious Freedom, Hudson Institute (2010, 2011)
Metallo, Thomas	Associate Professor, Liberty University (2010)

Surname, Name	Title and Affiliation (Year of Interview)
Meyer, David	Associate Professor, Regent University (2010)
Moroccan Diplomat	Embassy of the Kingdom of Morocco to the United States of America (2011)
Natsios, Andrew	Professor, Georgetown University (2011)
OIRF Official 1	Office of International Religious Freedom, United States Department of State (2011)
OIRF Official 2	Office of International Religious Freedom, United States Department of State (2015)
Otis, Pauletta	Professor, Marine Corps University (2011)
Policy Planning Official	Policy Planning, United States Department of State (2011)
Prodromou, Elizabeth	Assistant Professor, Boston University and USCIRF Commissioner (2011)
RGA Official	Office of Religion and Global Affairs, United States Department of State (2015)
Rodgers, Mark	Principal, Clapham Group and former Chief of Staff to Senator Rick Santorum (2011)
Rogers, Melissa	Director, Center for Religion and Public Affairs, Wake Forest University Divinity School (2011)
Roller, George	Executive Director, Center for Christian Statesmanship (2011)
Seiple, Chris	President, Institute for Global Engagement (2011)
State Department Official	Foreign Affairs Analyst, United States Department of State (2015)
Szmania, Susan	Senior Researcher, National Consortium for the Study of Terrorism and Responses to Terrorism, University of Maryland (2015)
USAID CFBCI Official 1	Center for Faith-Based and Community Initiatives, USAID (2010, 2011)
USAID CFBCI Official 2	Center for Faith-Based and Community Initiatives, USAID (2015)
USAID Official	Senior Conflict Advisor, USAID (2015)
USCIRF Official 1	United States Commission on International Religious Freedom (2010, 2011)
USCIRF Official 2	United States Commission on International Religious Freedom (2011)
USIP Official	Senior Program Officer, United States Institute of Peace (2015)
Vaïsse, Justin	Senior Fellow, Brookings Institution (2011)

Surname, Name	Title and Affiliation (Year of Interview)
Weaver, Heather	Staff Attorney, American Civil Liberties Union (2011)
Wehner, Peter	Senior Fellow, Ethics and Public Policy Center (2011)
WHOFBI Official	Office of Faith-Based and Neighborhood Partnerships, The White House (2010)

BIBLIOGRAPHY

Abrams, Elliott. 2010. Personal Communication. Washington, DC, June 21, 2010.

Abrams, Elliott. 2011. Personal Communication. Washington, DC, June 27, 2011.

Acharya, Amitav. 2013. "The R2P and Norm Diffusion: Towards a Framework of Norm Circulation." *Global Responsibility to Protect* 5 (4): 466–479.

Adamson, Fiona. 2005. "Global Liberalism Versus Political Islam: Competing Ideological Frameworks in International Politics." *International Studies Review* 7 (4): 547–569.

Adcock, Cassie S. 2014. "Debating Conversion, Silencing Caste: the Limited Scope of Religious Freedom." *Journal of Law and Religion* 29 (3): 363–377.

Adler, Emanuel, and Peter M. Haas. 1992. "Conclusion: Epistemic Communities, World Order, and the Creation of a Reflective Research Program." *International Organization* 46 (1): 367–390.

Agensky, Jonathan C. 2013. "Dr Livingstone, I Presume? Evangelicals, Africa and Faith-Based Humanitarianism." *Global Society* 27 (4): 454–474.

Agensky, Jonathan C. 2017. "Recognizing Religion: Politics, History, and the 'Long 19th Century'." *European Journal of International Relations* 23 (4), 729–755.

Agha, Aleem, and Nick Schifrin. 2012. "Koran Burning at U.S. Base Sparks Afghan Protests." *ABC News*, http://abcnews.go.com/International/quran-burning-us-base-draws-afghan-protests/story?id=15756570 (accessed June 15, 2013).

Ahmed, Akbar S. 2003. *Islam Under Siege: Living Dangerously in a Post-honor World.* Cambridge: Polity Press.

Ahmed, Akbar S. 2007. *Journey into Islam: the Crisis of Globalization.* Washington, DC: Brookings Institution Press.

Ahmed, Akbar S. 2010. *Journey into America: the Challenge of Islam.* Washington, DC: Brookings Institution Press.

Aikman, David. 2004. *A Man of Faith: The Spiritual Journey of George W. Bush* Nashville, TN: W. Publishing Group.

Al Jazeera. 2012. "US Envoy to OIC Discusses Anti-Islam Video." *Al Jazeera*, https://www.youtube.com/watch?v=sWqqiWln5lo (accessed July 15, 2013).

Albright, Madeleine K. 2006. *The Mighty and the Almighty: Reflections on America, God, and World Affairs.* Large print ed. New York: Harper.

Albright, Madeleine K. 2015. "The Future of Religion and Diplomacy: A Conversation with Madeleine Albright and Officials from the State Department's Office of Religion and Global Affairs." Washington, DC: Newseum Institute, https://www.youtube.com/watch?v=HLnacnOmAfY (accessed April 23, 2016).

Alden, Chris, and Amnon Aran. 2012. *Foreign Policy Analysis: New Approaches.* London: Routledge.

Alexander, Ari. 2011. "Administrator Shah Speaks to Faith-Based Leaders at White House Feed the Future Event." *Impact Blog, USAID,* https://blog.usaid.gov/2011/01/administrator-shah-speaks-to-faith-based-leaders-at-white-house-feed-the-future-event/ (accessed July 17, 2012).

Alexander, Ruth. 2013. "Are There Really 100,000 New Christian Martyrs Every Year?" *BBC,* http://www.bbc.co.uk/news/magazine-24864587 (accessed August 2, 2018).

American Civil Liberties Union (ACLU). 2009. "White House Announces Troubling Faith-Based Order, ACLU Says Administration Is Heading Into Uncharted Waters, (American Civil Liberties Union)," http://www.aclu.org/religion-belief/white-house-announces-troubling-faith-based-order-aclu-says-administration-heading-u (accessed September 5, 2011).

American Civil Liberties Union (ACLU). 2011. "ACLU Comments on a USAID Proposed Rule—Part 205: Participation by Religious Organizations in USAID Programs, (American Civil Liberties Union)," http://www.aclu.org/religion-belief/aclu-comments-usaid-proposed-rule-part-205-participation-religious-organizations-usa (accessed November 10, 2011).

American Civil Liberties Union (ACLU) et al. 2014. "Coalition Letter to Obama Administration on Countering Violent Extremism (CVE) Program," https://www.aclu.org/files/assets/141218_cve_coalition_letter_2.pdf (accessed June 10, 2015).

American Enterprise Institute (AEI). 2015. "Edge of Extinction: The Eradication of Religious and Ethnic Minorities in Iraq." *American Enterprise Institute,* https://www.youtube.com/watch?v=8QK_pD1REJw (accessed June 30, 2016).

Amr, Hady. 2009. "The Opportunity of the Obama Era: Can Civil Society Help Bridge Divides between the United States and a Diverse Muslim World?." *Analysis Paper 1.* Doha: Brookings Doha Center, http://www.brookings.edu/research/papers/2009/10/11-civil-society-amr (accessed May 22, 2012).

Amstutz, Mark R. 2014. *Evangelicals and American Foreign Policy.* New York: Oxford University Press.

Anderson, Benedict. 2006. *Imagined Communities: Reflections on the Origin and Spread of Nationalism.* New Edition ed. London: Verso.

Annicchino, Pasquale, ed. 2013a. *Freedom of Religion or Belief in Foreign Policy. Which One?* Florence: European University Institute; ReligioWest.

Annicchino, Pasquale. 2013b. "Recent Developments Concerning the Promotion of Freedom of Religion or Belief in Italian Foreign Policy." *Review of Faith & International Affairs* 11 (3): 61–68.

Appleby, R. Scott. 2000. *The Ambivalence of the Sacred: Religion, Violence, and Reconciliation.* Lanham, MD: Rowman & Littlefield.

Appleby, R. Scott, and Richard Cizik. 2010. "Engaging Religious Communities Abroad: A New Imperative for U.S. Foreign Policy." *Report of the Task Force on*

Religion and the Making of U.S. Foreign Policy. Chicago: Chicago Council on Global Affairs, http://www.thechicagocouncil.org/UserFiles/File/Task Force Reports/ 2010 Religion Task Force_Full Report.pdf (accessed April 4, 2011).

Asad, Talal. 1993. *Genealogies of Religion: Discipline and Reasons of Power in Christianity and Islam.* Baltimore: Johns Hopkins University Press.

Asad, Talal. 2003a. *Formations of the Secular: Christianity, Islam, Modernity.* Palo Alto, CA: Stanford University Press.

Asad, Talal. 2003b. "Secularism, Nation-State, Religion." In *Formations of the Secular: Christianity, Islam, Modernity,* edited by Talal Asad, 181–201. Palo Alto, CA: Stanford University Press.

Asad, Talal. 2011. "Thinking About Religion, Belief, and Politics." In *The Cambridge Companion to Religious Studies,* edited by Robert A. Orsi, 36–57. Cambridge: Cambridge University Press.

Awadallah, Alia, Hardin Lang, and Kristy Densmore. 2017. "Losing the War of Ideas: Countering Violent Extremism in the Age of Trump." Washington, DC: Center for American Progress, https://www.americanprogress.org/issues/ security/reports/2017/08/17/437457/losing-war-ideas/ (accessed July 30, 2018).

Aydin, Cemil. 2017. *The Idea of the Muslim World: A Global Intellectual History.* Cambridge, MA: Harvard University Press.

Bacevich, Andrew, and Elizabeth Prodromou. 2004. "God Is Not Neutral: Religion and US Foreign Policy after 9/11." *Orbis* 48 (1): 43–54.

Banta, Benjamin. 2013. "Analysing Discourse as a Causal Mechanism." *European Journal of International Relations* 19 (2): 379–402.

Baran, Zeyno (ed.). 2004. "Understanding Sufism and its Potential Role in US Policy." Washington, DC: Nixon Center Conference Report, http://www.hudson. org/content/researchattachments/attachment/451/understanding_suffism.pdf (accessed June 20, 2014).

Barbato, Mariano, and Friedrich Kratochwil. 2009. "Towards a Post-secular Political Order?" *European Political Science Review* 1 (3): 317–340.

Barber, Benjamin. 1992. "Jihad vs. McWorld." *Atlantic Monthly* 269 (3): 53–65.

Barkawi, Tarak, and George Lawson. 2017. "The International Origins of Social and Political Theory." In *International Origins of Social and Political Theory,* edited by Tarak Barkawi and George Lawson, 1–7. Bingley, UK: Emerald Publishing Limited.

Barnett, Michael. 2011. *Empire of Humanity: A History of Humanitarianism.* Ithaca, NY: Cornell University Press.

Barnett, Michael. 2015. "Religion and the Liberal International Order." In *Faith, Freedom, and Foreign Policy: Challenges for the Transatlantic Community,* edited by Michael Barnett, Clifford Bob, Nora Fisher Onar, Anne Jenichen, Michael Leigh, and Lucian N. Leustean, 8–29, http://www.bosch-stiftung.de/content/language1/ downloads/Transatlantic_Academy_2015_Report.pdf (accessed June 1, 2015). Washington, DC: Transatlantic Academy.

Barnett, Michael N., and Martha Finnemore. 1999. "The Politics, Power, and Pathologies of International Organizations." *International Organization* 53 (4): 699–732.

Barnett, Michael, and Janice Gross Stein, eds. 2012. *Sacred Aid: Faith and Humanitarianism.* Oxford: Oxford University Press.

Baumgartner, Frank R., and Beth L. Leech. 1998. *Basic Interests: The Importance of Groups in Politics and in Political Science.* Princeton, NJ: Princeton University Press.

BBC. 2006. "Bush's Language Angers US Muslims." *BBC*, http://news.bbc.co.uk/1/hi/4785065.stm (accessed April 14, 2011).

Beach, Derek, and Rasmus Brun Pedersen. 2013. *Process-tracing Methods: Foundations and Guidelines.* Ann Arbor: University of Michigan Press.

Beaman, Lori G. 2003. "The Myth of Pluralism, Diversity, and Vigor: The Constitutional Privilege of Protestantism in the United States and Canada." *Journal for the Scientific Study of Religion* 42 (3): 311–325.

Beckford, James A. 2012. "SSSR Presidential Address—Public Religions and the Post-secular: Critical Reflections." *Journal for the Scientific Study of Religion* 51 (1): 1–19.

Beeson, Amy. 2010. "Who Gets to Give Aid? American Faith-Based Organizations and the Politics of Belief." *Harvard Political Review*, http://harvardpolitics.com/covers/religion-in-america/who-gets-to-give-aid/ (accessed April 30, 2015).

Belfer Center. 2016. "Conversations in Diplomacy: Shaun Casey." Belfer Center, Harvard University, https://soundcloud.com/belfercenter/conversations-in-diplomacy-shaun-casey-march-23-2016 (accessed June 18, 2016).

Bellin, Eva. 2008. "Faith in Politics New Trends in the Study of Religion and Politics." *World Politics* 60 (2): 315–347.

Belshaw, Deryke Gerald Rooten, Robert Calderisi, and Chris Sugden, eds. 2001. *Faith in Development: Partnership Between the World Bank and the Churches of Africa.* Washington, DC: World Bank and Regnum Books International.

Benard, Cheryl. 2003. "Civil Democratic Islam: Partners, Resources, and Strategies." Santa Monica, CA: RAND Corporation, http://www.rand.org/pubs/monograph_reports/2005/MR1716.pdf (accessed February 7, 2009).

Benedetti, Carlo. 2006. "Islamic and Christian Inspired Relief NGOs: Between Tactical Collaboration and Strategic Diffidence?" *Journal of International Development* 18 (6): 849–859.

Bennett, Andrew. 2013. "The Mother of All Isms: Causal Mechanisms and Structured Pluralism in International Relations Theory." *European Journal of International Relations* 19 (3): 459–481.

Berger, Peter L. 1969. *The Sacred Canopy: Elements of a Sociological Theory of Religion.* New York: Anchor Books.

Berger, Peter L. 1999a. "The Desecularization of the World: A Global Overview." In *The Desecularization of the World: Resurgent Religion and World Politics*, edited by Peter L. Berger, 1–18. Grand Rapids, MI: Ethics and Public Policy Center; Eermans Publishing.

Berger, Peter L., ed. 1999b. *The Desecularization of the World: Resurgent Religion and World Politics.* Grand Rapids, MI: Ethics and Public Policy Center; Eermans Publishing.

Berger, Peter L. 2014. "An Ancient Habit: Proselytization." *The American Interest*, http://www.the-american-interest.com/2014/12/24/proselytization/ (accessed January 19, 2015).

Berger, Peter L., Grace Davie, and Effie Fokas. 2008. *Religious America, Secular Europe?: A Theme and Variation.* Aldershot: Ashgate.

Berkley Center. 2008. "International Religious Freedom Policy—Panel 3: The Critique from the Muslim World." Washington, DC: Georgetown University Berkley Center for Religion, Peace, and World Affairs, https://www.youtube.com/watch?v=AJIWa-I1z8Y (accessed June 4, 2015).

Berkley Center. 2009. "Faith Complex: Jacqueline Salmon on White House Faith-Based Initiatives (PART ONE)." https://www.youtube.com/watch?v=B1Jl5_rmx30 (accessed July 5, 2015).

Berkley Center. 2010a. "Keynote Debate: Proselytism and Religious Freedom in the 21st Century." Washington, DC: Georgetown University Berkley Center for Religion, Peace, and World Affairs, https://www.youtube.com/watch?v=c4XmX0ypnnw (accessed June 4, 2015).

Berkley Center. 2010b. "Report of the Georgetown Symposium on Proselytism & Religious Freedom in the 21st Century." Washington, DC: Georgetown University Berkley Center for Religion, Peace, and World Affairs, http://repository.berkleycenter.georgetown.edu/100303ProselytismReport.pdf (accessed June 4, 2015).

Berkley Center. 2013a. "Evaluating the State Department's Office of Faith-Based Community Initiatives." Washington, DC: Georgetown University Berkley Center for Religion, Peace, and World Affairs, https://www.youtube.com/watch?v=TO7wavjBoI4 (accessed May 19, 2016).

Berkley Center. 2013b. "Proselytism and Religious Freedom in the 21st Century: The Political Implications of Proselytism." Washington, DC: Georgetown University Berkley Center for Religion, Peace, and World Affairs, https://www.youtube.com/watch?v=1wRD_7pevj4 (accessed June 4, 2015).

Berkley Center. 2014a. "Is International Religious Freedom Policy Becoming Respectable?" Washington, DC: Georgetown University Berkley Center for Religion, Peace, and World Affairs, https://www.youtube.com/watch?v=Z4-dnmwajsQ.

Berkley Center. 2014b. "Religion, The Missing Dimension of Statecraft: A Twentieth Anniversary Reflection." Washington, DC: Georgetown University Berkley Center for Religion, Peace, and World Affairs, https://www.youtube.com/watch?v=5PThhuYXog8 (accessed May 19, 2016).

Berkley Center. 2015. "The Gathering Storm: Religious Persecution and Legislative Responses." Washington, DC: Georgetown University: Berkley Center for Religion, Peace, and World Affairs, https://www.youtube.com/watch?v=9b4UK2Sdy24.

Berkley Center. 2016a. "Radicals, Religion, and Peace: Global Security in an Age of Terror: Panel 2." Washington, DC: Georgetown University Berkley Center for Religion, Peace, and World Affairs, https://www.youtube.com/watch?v=nNYFeZDHdAw (accessed December 10, 2016).

Berkley Center. 2016b. "Religious Studies Scholars and Government Engagement with Religion." Washington, DC: Georgetown University Berkley Center for Religion, Peace, and World Affairs, https://www.youtube.com/watch?v=cu_JYTlN_hQ (accessed December 10, 2016).

Berkley Center. 2017. "Best Practices in International Religious Freedom Policy." Washington, DC: Georgetown University Berkley Center for Religion, Peace, and

World Affairs, https://www.youtube.com/watch?v=Xq-T8o-k1uQ (accessed July 20, 2018).

Berkowitz, Bill. 2013. "Obama's Faith-Based Diplomacy." *buzzflash.com*, http://truth-out.org/buzzflash/commentary/obama-s-faith-based-diplomacy (accessed July 2, 2015).

Bettiza, Gregorio. 2015. "Constructing Civilisations: Embedding and Reproducing the 'Muslim world' in American Foreign Policy Practices and Institutions Since 9/11." *Review of International Studies* 41 (3): 575–600.

Bettiza, Gregorio, and Filippo Dionigi. 2015. "How Do Religious Norms Diffuse? Institutional Translation and International Change in a Postsecular World Society." *European Journal of International Relations* 21 (3): 621–646.

Bettiza, Gregorio, and Christopher Phillips. 2012. "Islam Is in the Eye of the Beholder: Explaining the Variance in American and European Discourses and Practices towards 'Islam' and 'Muslims'." Unpublished paper.

Bilmes, Linda J., and Joseph E. Stiglitz. 2008. *The Three Trillion Dollar War: The True Cost of the Iraq Conflict.* New York: Norton.

Bin Laden, Osama. 1996. "Bin Laden's Fatwa." https://en.wikisource.org/wiki/Osama_bin_Laden%27s_Declaration_of_War (accessed June 26, 2015).

Birdsall, Judd. 2012. "Obama and the Drama Over International Religious Freedom Policy: An Insider's Perspective." *Review of Faith & International Affairs* 10 (3): 33–41.

Birdsall, Judd. 2013. "The State Department's Great Leap Faithward." *Huffington Post*, http://www.huffingtonpost.com/judd-birdsall/state-department-faith-based-office_b_3744290.html (accessed April 22, 2016).

Birdsall, Judd. 2014a. "Sue Breeze on British Foreign Policy and Religion." *Review of Faith & International Affairs* 12 (3): 75–77.

Birdsall, Judd. 2014b. "Why It Is the Best and Worst Time to Be IRF Ambassador." *Cornerstone*, http://berkleycenter.georgetown.edu/responses/why-it-is-the-best-and-worst-time-to-be-irf-ambassador-1c589442-18f9-4502-8624-91eabc2c272f (accessed April 22, 2016).

Birdsall, Judd. 2015. Skype Communication. April 8, 2015.

Birdsall, Judd, Jane Lindsay, and Emma Tomalin. 2015. "Toward Religion-Attentive Foreign Policy: A Report on an Anglo-American Dialogue." Centre for Religion and Public Life at the University of Leeds, Religious Freedom Project at Georgetown University, and Institute for Global Engagement, https://globalengage.org/faith-international-affairs/reports/toward-religion-attentive-foreign-policy-a-report-on-an-anglo-american-dial (accessed May 23, 2017).

Bjelopera, Jerome P. 2014. "Countering Violent Extremism in the United States." Washington, DC: Congressional Research Service, https://www.fas.org/sgp/crs/homesec/R42553.pdf (accessed April 10, 2015).

Bjornson, Leah. 2013. "Canada's New Office of Religious Freedom Raises Concerns." *The Peak*, http://www.the-peak.ca/2013/03/canadas-new-office-of-religious-freedom-raises-concerns/ (accessed July 29, 2016).

Blackman, Alexandra Domike. 2018. "Religion and Foreign Aid." *Politics and Religion* 11 (3): 522–552.

Bob, Clifford. 2005. *The Marketing of Rebellion: Insurgents, Media, and International Activism.* Cambridge: Cambridge University Press.

Bob, Clifford. 2015. "Religious Activists and Foreign Policy in the West." In *Faith, Freedom, and Foreign Policy: Challenges for the Transatlantic Community,* edited by Michael Barnett, Clifford Bob, Nora Fisher Onar, Anne Jenichen, Michael Leigh, and Lucian N. Leustean, 94–111, http://www.bosch-stiftung.de/content/language1/downloads/Transatlantic_Academy_2015_Report.pdf (accessed June 1, 2015). Washington, DC: Transatlantic Academy.

Boorstein, Michelle. 2012. "Federal Lawsuit Charges Religious Freedom Commission with Discriminating against Muslims." *Washington Post,* http://www.washingtonpost.com/blogs/under-god/post/federal-lawsuit-charges-religious-freedom-commission-with-discriminating-against-muslims/2012/06/08/gJQAs62NOV_blog.html (accessed August 19, 2012).

Bornstein, Erica. 2002. "Developing Faith: Theologies of Economic Development in Zimbabwe." *Journal of Religion in Africa* 32 (1): 4–31.

Borschel-Dan, Amanda. 2014. "Christian Zionists Funding Israel Immigration Still Scares Jews." *The Times of Israel,* http://www.timesofisrael.com/christian-zionists-funding-israel-immigration-still-scares-jews (accessed July 18, 2015).

Boston Globe. 2006. "USAID Contracts with Faith-Based Organizations." *Boston Globe,* October 30, 2011.

Brinkmoeller, Mark. 2010. Personal Communication. Washington, DC, June 8, 2010.

Brinkmoeller, Mark. 2011. Personal Communication. Washington, DC, July 12, 2011.

Broome, André, and Joel Quirk. 2015. "Governing the World at a Distance: The Practice of Global Benchmarking." *Review of International Studies* 41 (5): 819–841.

Brownstein, Ronald. 1999. "Charity Begins at Church, Gov. Bush Says." *Los Angeles Times,* http://articles.latimes.com/1999/jul/23/news/mn-58823 (accessed November 2, 2011).

Bruce, Steve. 2011. *Secularization: In Defence of an Unfashionable Theory.* Oxford: Oxford University Press.

Bull, Hedley. 2002. *The Anarchical Society: A Study of Order in World Politics.* Third ed. Basingstoke: Palgrave Macmillan.

Burkhalter, Holly. 2004. "The Politics of AIDS: Engaging Conservative Activists." *Foreign Affairs* 83 (1): 8–14.

Burnett, Stanton. 1994. "Implications for the Foreign Policy Community." In *Religion, the Missing Dimension of Statecraft,* edited by Douglas M. Johnston and Cynthia Sampson. New York: Oxford University Press.

Buruma, Ian. 2004. "Lost In Translation: The Two Minds of Bernard Lewis." *The New Yorker,* http://www.newyorker.com/magazine/2004/06/14/lost-in-translation-3 (accessed June 21, 2016).

Busby, Joshua William. 2007. "Bono Made Jesse Helms Cry: Jubilee 2000, Debt Relief, and Moral Action in International Politics." *International Studies Quarterly* 51 (2): 247–275.

Bush, George W. 2001a. "'Islam Is Peace' Says President: Remarks by the President at Islamic Center of Washington, DC." Islamic Center of Washington, DC, https://georgewbush-whitehouse.archives.gov/news/releases/2001/09/20010917-11.html (accessed January 10, 2012).

Bush, George W. 2001b. "Remarks on Signing Executive Orders With Respect to Faith-Based and Community Initiatives." Washington, DC, http://www.presidency.ucsb.edu/ws/?pid=45707 (accessed January 10, 2012).

Bush, George W. 2002. "George Bush's Speech to the UN General Assembly." *The Guardian*, http://www.guardian.co.uk/world/2002/sep/12/iraq.usa3 (accessed June 13, 2012).

Bush, George W. 2008. "Special Islamic Envoy." *C-Span*, http://www.c-span.org/video/?204208-1/special-islamic-envoy&start=5 (accessed January 10, 2012).

Bush, George W. 2010. *Decision Points*. New York: Crown Publishers.

Buzan, Barry. 2004. *From International to World Society?: English School Theory and the Social Structure of Globalisation*. Cambridge: Cambridge University Press.

Buzan, Barry. 2018. "Revisiting World Society." *International Politics* 55 (1): 125–140.

Buzan, Barry, and George Lawson. 2013. "The Global Transformation: The Nineteenth Century and the Making of Modern International Relations." *International Studies Quarterly* 57 (3): 620–634.

Byrnes, Timothy A. 2011. *Reverse Mission: Transnational Religious Communities and the Making of US Foreign Policy*. Washington, DC: Georgetown University Press.

Cady, Linell, and Elizabeth Shakman Hurd, eds. 2010. *Comparative Secularisms in a Global Age*. New York: Palgrave Macmillan.

Calhoun, Craig J., Mark Juergensmeyer, and Jonathan VanAntwerpen, eds. 2011. *Rethinking Secularism*. Oxford: Oxford University Press.

Calhoun, Craig, Eduardo Mendieta, and Jonathan VanAntwerpen, eds. 2013. *Habermas and Religion*. Cambridge: Polity Press.

Cambridge Institute on Religion & International Studies (CIRIS). 2015. "Interview: Shaun Casey, U.S. Special Rep for Religion and Global Affairs." Cambridge Institute on Religion & International Studies, http://ciris.org.uk/2015/05/07/interview-with-the-u-s-special-representative-for-religion-and-global-affairs-shaun-casey/ (accessed December 5, 2016).

Camilleri, Joseph A. 2012. "Postsecularist Discourse in an 'Age of Transition'." *Review of International Studies* 38 (5): 1019–1039.

Canellos, Peter S., and Kevin Baron. 2006. "A US Boost to Graham's Quest for Converts." *Boston Globe*, http://archive.boston.com/news/nation/articles/2006/10/08/a_us_boost_to_grahams_quest_for_converts/ (accessed April 13, 2011).

Capoccia, Giovanni, and R. Daniel Kelemen. 2007. "The Study of Critical Junctures: Theory, Narrative, and Counterfactuals in Historical Institutionalism." *World Politics* 59 (3): 341–369.

Carbonnier, Gilles. 2013. "Religion and Development: Reconsidering Secularism as the Norm." *International Development Policy* 4 (1): 1–5.

Carlsnaes, Walter. 1992. "The Agency-Structure Problem in Foreign Policy Analysis." *International Studies Quarterly* 36 (3): 245–270.

Carlsnaes, Walter, and Stefano Guzzini. 2011. "Introduction." In *Foreign Policy Analysis: Volume I*, edited by Walter Carlsnaes and Stefano Guzzini, xix–xxxv. Thousand Oaks, CA: Sage Publications.

Carothers, Thomas. 2007. "U.S. Democracy Promotion During and After Bush." Washington, DC: Carnegie Endowment for International Peace, https://

carnegieendowment.org/files/democracy_promotion_after_bush_final.pdf (accessed May 12, 2014).

Casanova, José. 1994. *Public Religions in the Modern World*. Chicago, IL: University of Chicago Press.

Casanova, José. 2010. "Transcript of Dr. Casanova's remarks delivered at the Symposium on Proselytism and Religious Freedom in the 21st Century." Georgetown Symposium on Proselytism & Religious Freedom in the 21st Century, Georgetown University, http://repository.berkleycenter.georgetown.edu/100303ProselytismReport.pdf (accessed July 12, 2015).

Casanova, José. 2011. "The Secular, Secularizations, Secularisms." In *Rethinking Secularism*, edited by Craig J. Calhoun, Mark Juergensmeyer, and Jonathan VanAntwerpen, 54–74. Oxford: Oxford University Press.

Casey, Shaun. 2015. "The Future of Religion and Diplomacy." *DipNote Blog*, https://www.humanrights.gov/dyn/2015/03/the-future-of-religion-and-diplomacy/ (accessed April 26, 2016).

Casey, Shaun. 2016. "Why We #EngageAmerica and the World on Religion and Foreign Policy." *White House Blog*, https://www.whitehouse.gov/blog/2016/04/26/why-we-engageamerica-and-world-religion-and-foreign-policy (accessed April 26, 2016).

Cassidy, Elizabeth K. 2013. "The United States' Approach to Promoting International Religious Freedom: the 1998 International Religious Freedom Act." In *Freedom of Religion or Belief in Foreign Policy. Which One?*, edited by Pasquale Annicchino, 52–58, http://cadmus.eui.eu/bitstream/handle/1814/30059/Religiowest_Annicchino_web.pdf?sequence=2 (accessed May 2014). Florence: European University Institute; ReligioWest.

Castelli, Elizabeth A. 2005. "Praying for the Persecuted Church: US Christian Activism in the Global Arena." *Journal of Human Rights* 4 (3): 321–351.

Castelli, Elizabeth A. 2007a. "Persecution Complexes: Identity Politics and the 'War on Christians.'" *Differences* 18 (3): 152–180.

Castelli, Elizabeth A. 2007b. "Theologizing Human Rights: Christian Activism and the Limits of Religious Freedom." In *Non-Governmental Politics*, edited by Michel Feher, Gaëlle Krikorian, and Yates McKee, 673–687. New York: Zone Books.

Castelli, Elizabeth A. 2016. "Paradoxes of international religious freedom." *The Immanent Frame*, http://blogs.ssrc.org/tif/2016/05/05/paradoxes-of-international-religious-freedom/ (accessed April 6, 2017).

Cavanaugh, William T. 2009. *The Myth of Religious Violence: Secular Ideology and the Roots of Modern Conflict*. Oxford: Oxford University Press.

Center for American Progress (CAP). 2009. "JFK, Barack Obama & Religion in Presidential Politics." Washington, DC: Center for American Progress, https://www.youtube.com/watch?v=5YKSO7J9Qdg (accessed May 3, 2015).

Center for Faith Based and Community Initiatives (CFBCI) Official 1. 2010. Personal Communication. Washington, DC, June 23, 2010.

Center for Faith Based and Community Initiatives (CFBCI) Official 1. 2011. Personal Communication. Washington, DC, July 6, 2011.

Centre for Research and Evidence on Security Threats (CREST). 2016. "The Counter Jihad Movement, *CREST Primer*." The Centre for Research and Evidence on Security Threats, https://crestresearch.ac.uk/resources/counter-jihad-movement/ (accessed June 6, 2018).

Center for the Study of Islam and Democracy (CSID). 2010. "Plenary Session Roundtable: Perspectives on Muslim Engagement featuring Farah Pandith." *U.S. Relations with the Muslim World: One Year After Cairo*, (Washington, DC: Center for the Study of Islam and Democracy), http://www.usip.org/events/us-relations-the-muslim-world-one-year-after-cairo (accessed June 10, 2011).

Cesari, Jocelyne. 2015. Skype Communication. May 18, 2015.

Cesari, Jocelyne. 2017. "To Curb Political Violence in Its Name, Islam Needs to Be Independent of Political Power, Not Reformed Even Further." *Middle East Monitor*, https://www.middleeastmonitor.com/20170401-to-curb-political-violence-in-its-name-islam-needs-to-be-independent-of-political-power-not-reformed-even-further/ (accessed April 10, 2017).

Checkel, Jeffrey T. 2005. "International Institutions and Socialization in Europe: Introduction and Framework." *International Organization* 59 (4): 801–826.

Checkel, Jeffrey T. 2006. "Tracing Causal Mechanisms." *International Studies Review* 8 (2): 362–370.

Cheney, Dick. 2006. "Vice President's Remarks at the World Affairs Council of Philadelphia Luncheon Honoring Professor Bernard Lewis." Philadelphia: Park Hyatt Philadelphia at the Bellevue, http://georgewbush-whitehouse.archives.gov/news/releases/2006/05/20060501-3.html (accessed August 10, 2012).

Chowdhury Fink, Naureen, and Rafia Bhulai. 2016. "Advancing CVE Research: The Roles of Global and Regional Coordinating Bodies." *CT-MORSE: Countering-Terrorism Monitoring, Resporting and Support Mechanisms* (European Commission), http://ct-morse.eu/wp-content/uploads/2016/07/Report-CVE-Mapping-Research.pdf (accessed January 29, 2017).

Claassen, Ryan L. 2015. *Godless Democrats and Pious Republicans?: Party Activists, Party Capture, and the "God Gap."* New York: Cambridge University Press.

Clarke, Gerard. 2007. "Agents of Transformation? Donors, Faith-Based Organisations and International Development." *Third World Quarterly* 28 (1): 77–96.

Clarke, Gerard, and Michael Jennings, eds. 2008a. *Development, Civil society and Faith-based Organisations: Bridging the Sacred and the Secular*. Basingstoke: Palgrave Macmillan.

Clarke, Gerard, and Michael Jennings. 2008b. "Introduction." In *Development, Civil Society and Faith-Based Organisations: Bridging the Sacred and the Secular*, edited by Gerard Clarke and Michael Jennings, 1–16. Basingstoke: Palgrave Macmillan.

Clarkson, Frederick. 2014. "An Uncharitable Choice: The Faith-Based Takeover of Federal Programs." Political Research Associates, http://www.politicalresearch.org/2014/10/10/an-uncharitable-choice-the-faith-based-takeover-of-federal-programs/-sthash.Kq5DCkXP.I7Il9DAw.dpbs (accessed July 1, 2016).

Clinton, William J. 1994. "Remarks to the Jordanian Parliament in Amman, Jordan." http://www.presidency.ucsb.edu/ws/index.php?pid=49373-ixzz1jMTDy8vx (accessed December 20, 2011).

Clyne, Melissa. 2015. "Frank Wolf: Obama Won't Help Mideast Christians, Congress Should." *Newsmax*, http://www.newsmax.com/Newsmax-Tv/Frank-Wolf-ISIS-Christians-persecution/2015/04/21/id/639819/-ixzz3dPQ3RnVw (accessed May 8, 2015).

Collins, Chris. 2013. "If We Want an AIDS-Free Generation, Why Are We Cutting PEPFAR?" *Huffington Post*, http://www.huffingtonpost.com/chris-collins/pepfar-cuts-hiv-aids_b_3101250.html (accessed May 29, 2015).

Connolly, William E. 1999. *Why I Am Not a Secularist*. Minneapolis: University of Minnesota Press.

Cooper, Melinda. 2015. "The Theology of Emergency: Welfare Reform, US Foreign Aid and the Faith-Based Initiative." *Theory, Culture & Society* 32 (2): 53–77.

Cottle, Michelle. 2003. "Bible Brigade." *New Republic*, https://newrepublic.com/article/66874/bible-brigade (accessed March 2, 2011).

Council of the European Union. 2013. "EU Guidelines on the Promotion and Protection of Freedom of Religion or Belief." Luxembourg: Foreign Affairs Council Meeting, https://eeas.europa.eu/sites/eeas/files/137585.pdf (accessed April 4, 2015).

Council on Foreign Relations (CFR). 2018a. "President Trump's World Religion Tour." Religion and Foreign Policy Conference Call (Council on Foreign Relations), https://www.cfr.org/conference-calls/president-trumps-world-religion-tour (accessed August 3, 2018).

Council on Foreign Relations (CFR). 2018b. "Religious Literacy in Global Affairs: Event with Diane L. Moore, Farah Pandith and Chris Seiple." CFR Religion and Foreign Policy Workshop, New York: Council on Foreign Relations, https://www.cfr.org/event/religious-literacy-global-affairs?utm_medium=email&utm_source=religion&utm_content=053018&sp_mid=56710697&sp_rid=Zy5iZXRoa XphQGV4ZXRlci5hYy51awS2 (accessed June 17, 2018).

Cox, Brian, and Daniel Philpott. 2003. "Faith-Based Diplomacy: An Ancient Idea Newly Emergent." *Faith & International Affairs* 1 (2): 31–40.

Cozad, Laurie. 2005. "The United States' Imposition of Religious Freedom: The International Religious Freedom Act and India." *India Review* 4 (1): 59–83.

Croft, Stuart. 2007. "Thy Will Be Done: The New Foreign Policy of Americas Christian Right." *International Politics* 44 (6): 692–710.

Cromartie, Michael, ed. 2005. *Religion, Culture, and International Conflict: A Conversation*. Oxford: Rowman & Littlefield.

Cromartie, Michael. 2011. Personal Communication. Washington, DC, June 15, 2011.

Curtis, Simon, and Marjo Koivisto. 2010. "Towards a Second 'Second Debate'? Rethinking the Relationship between Science and History in International Theory." *International Relations* 24 (4): 433–455.

Dabiq. 1436. "The Extinction of the Grayzone." *Dabiq* (7): 54–66.

Dalacoura, Katerina. 2011. *Islamist Terrorism and Democracy in the Middle East*. New York: Cambridge University Press.

Dallmayr, Fred R., and Abbas Manoochehri. 2007. *Civilizational Dialogue and Political Thought: Tehran Papers, Global Encounters*. Lanham, MD: Lexington Books.

Danan, Liora, and Alice Hunt. 2007. "Mixed Blessings: US Government Engagement with Religion in Conflict-Prone Settings." *A Report of the Post-Conflict Reconstruction Project*. Washington, DC: Center for International and Strategic Studies (CSIS), http://csis.org/publication/mixed-blessings (accessed February 17, 2010).

Dassa Kaye, Dalia, Frederic Wehrey, Audra K. Grant, and Dale Stahl. 2008. "More Freedom, Less Terror? Liberalization and Political Violence in the Arab World." Santa Monica, CA: RAND Corporation, http://www.rand.org/content/dam/rand/pubs/monographs/2008/RAND_MG772.pdf (accessed April 22, 2010).

Davis, Derek, ed. 2010. *The Oxford Handbook of Church and State in the United States.* Oxford: Oxford University Press.

De Cordier, Bruno. 2009. "The 'Humanitarian Frontline', Development and Relief, and Religion: What Context, Which Threats and Which Opportunities?" *Third World Quarterly* 30 (4): 663–684.

Deneulin, Séverine, and Masooda Bano. 2009. *Religion in Development: Rewriting the Secular Script.* London: Zed.

Deneulin, Séverine, and Carole Rakodi. 2011. "Revisiting Religion: Development Studies Thirty Years On." *World Development* 39 (1): 45–54.

Desch, Michael C. 2013. "The Coming Reformation of Religion in International Affairs? The Demise of the Secularization Thesis and the Rise of New Thinking About Religion." In *Religion and International Relations: A Primer for Research*, edited by Michael C. Desch and Daniel Philpott, 14–55, http://rmellon.nd.edu/assets/101872/religion_and_international_relations_report.pdf (accessed May 20, 2014).

Desert News. 2018. "Q&A: Former State Department Official Talks Faith and Politics." *Desert News*, https://www.deseretnews.com/article/900009383/qanda-former-state-department-official-talks-faith-and-politics.html (accessed July 31, 2018).

DiIulio, John J. 2007. *Godly Republic: A Centrist Civic Blueprint for America's Faith-based Future.* Berkeley: University of California Press.

Dilger, Hansjörg. 2009. "Doing Better? Religion, the Virtue-Ethics of Development, and the Fragmentation of Health Politics in Tanzania." *Africa Today* 56 (1): 89–110.

Dionne, E. J. 2006. "Obama's Eloquent Faith." *Washington Post*, http://www.washingtonpost.com/wp-dyn/content/article/2006/06/29/AR2006062901778.html.

Dionne, Kim Yi. 2014. "Will an Organization Receiving U.S. Government Funds Get Away with Discriminatory Hiring Practices?" *Monkey Cage*, https://www.washingtonpost.com/news/monkey-cage/wp/2014/03/28/will-an-organization-receiving-u-s-government-funds-get-away-with-discriminatory-hiring-practices/ (accessed July 19, 2015).

Djerejian, Edward P. 1992. "The U.S. and the Middle East in a Changing World." Address by Secretary Djerejian at Meridian House International, Washington, DC, http://www.disam.dsca.mil/pubs/Vol 14_4/Djerejian.pdf (accessed April 30, 2011).

Dressler, Markus. 2014. "Beyond Religio-Secularism: Toward a Political Critique." *The Immanent Frame*, http://blogs.ssrc.org/tif/2014/02/25/beyond-religio-secularism-toward-a-political-critique/ (accessed March 5, 2014).

Dressler, Markus, and Arvind-pal Singh Mandair. 2011. *Secularism and Religion-making.* New York: Oxford University Press.

Drezner, Daniel W. 2011. "Does Obama Have a Grand Strategy?" *Foreign Affairs* 90 (4): 57–68.

DuBois, Joshua. 2010. "Vatican Interfaith Conference: Keynote Remarks." Holy See's Conference on Interfaith Action, Rome, http://www.whitehouse.gov/blog/2010/10/14/vatican-interfaith-conference-keynote-remarks (accessed August 20, 2012).

DuBois, Joshua. 2013. *The President's Devotional: The Daily Readings That Inspired President Obama.* New York: HarperOne.

Dueck, Colin. 2010. *Hard Line: The Republican Party and US Foreign Policy Since World War II.* Princeton, NJ: Princeton University Press.

Dueck, Colin. 2011. "The Accommodator: Obama's Foreign Policy." *Policy Review* 169 (Oct./Nov.): 13–28.

Eisenstadt, Shmuel N. 2000. "Multiple Modernities." *Daedalus* 129 (1): 1–29.

Emon, Anver. 2015. "Is ISIS Islamic? Why It Matters for the Study of Islam." *The Immanent Frame,* http://blogs.ssrc.org/tif/2015/03/27/is-isis-islamic-why-it-matters-for-the-study-of-islam/ (accessed April 18, 2016).

Epstein, Helen. 2005. "God and the Fight against AIDS." *New York Review of Books* 52 (7): 47–51.

Esposito, John L. 1999. *The Islamic Threat: Myth or Reality?* New York: Oxford University Press.

Esposito, John L. 2002. *Unholy War: Terror in the Name of Islam.* New York: Oxford University Press.

Esposito, John L. 2007. "It's the Policy, Stupid: Political Islam and US Foreign Policy." *Prince Alwaleed bin Talal Center for Muslim-Christian Understanding,* https://acmcu.georgetown.edu/the-policy-stupid (accessed July 1, 2011).

Esposito, John L., and Dalia Mogahed. 2007. *Who Speaks for Islam?: What a Billion Muslims Really Think.* New York: Gallup Press.

Esposito, John L., and John O. Voll. 1996. *Islam and Democracy.* New York: Oxford University Press.

Esposito, John L., and John O. Voll. 2000. "Islam and the West: Muslim Voices of Dialogue." *Millennium: Journal of International Studies* 29 (3): 613–639.

Evertz, Scott H. 2010. "How Ideology Trumped Science: Why PEPFAR Has Failed to Meet Its Potential." Washington, DC: Center for American Progress, https://cdn.americanprogress.org/wp-content/uploads/issues/2010/01/pdf/pepfar.pdf (accessed June 25, 2015).

Falwell, Jerry. 2002. "Falwell On Islam, Mohammed." *CBS News,* http://www.cbsnews.com/video/watch/?id=2808715n (accessed January 10, 2010).

Farquhar, Michael. 2016. *Circuits of Faith: Migration, Education, and the Wahhabi Mission.* Palo Alto, CA: Stanford University Press.

Farr, Thomas F. 2008a. "Diplomacy in an Age of Faith: Religious Freedom and National Security." *Foreign Affairs* 87 (2): 110–124.

Farr, Thomas F. 2008b. *World of Faith and Freedom: why International Religious Liberty Is Vital to American National Security.* New York: Oxford University Press.

Farr, Thomas F. 2010a. Personal Communication. Washington, DC, June 15, 2010.

Farr, Thomas F. 2010b. "Undefender of the Faith." *Foreign Policy,* http://www.foreignpolicy.com/articles/2010/04/05/undefender_of_the_faith (accessed December 1, 2012).

Farr, Thomas F. 2016. "The Saperstein Effect: It Depends on Kerry." *Religious Freedom Institute*, https://www.religiousfreedominstitute.org/cornerstone/2016/7/5/the-saperstein-effect-it-depends-on-kerry (accessed September 7, 2016).

Farr, Thomas F. 2017. "Religious Freedom and the Common Good: The Importance of Religious Actors and Ideas in Public Life." *Cardus*, https://s3.amazonaws.com/berkley-center/170223FarrReligiousFreedomCommonGoodCardusReport.pdf (accessed April 8, 2017).

Farr, Thomas F., and Dennis R. Hoover. 2009. "The Future of U.S. International Religious Freedom Policy: Recommendations for the Obama Administration." Washington, DC: Georgetown University: Berkley Center for Religion, Peace, and World Affairs, https://globalengage.org/content/IRFpolicyreport_final_lowres.pdf (accessed March 21, 2011).

Faskianos, Irina. 2011. Phone Communication. Washington, DC/New York, June 27, 2011.

Feddes, Morgan. 2011. "Just Before Shut Down, Congress Reauthorizes the U.S. Commission on International Religious Freedom." *Christianity Today*, http://blog.christianitytoday.com/ctpolitics/2011/12/just_before_shu.html (accessed August 20, 2012).

Federal Register. 2011. "Proposed Rules." *Federal Register* 76 (58): 16712–16714.

Fernando, Mayanthi. 2005. "The Republic's 'Second Religion': Recognizing Islam in France." *Middle East Report* 35 (2): http://www.merip.org/mer/mer235/republics-second-religion (accessed July 9, 2012).

Ferrara, Pasquale. 2013a. *Global Religions and International Relations: A Diplomatic Perspective*. New York: Palgrave Macmillan.

Ferrara, Pasquale. 2013b. "Reporting on Religious Freedom: The 'Governmental' Approach and the Issue of Legitimacy." In *Freedom of Religion or Belief in Foreign Policy. Which One?*, edited by Pasquale Annicchino, 59–65, http://cadmus.eui.eu/bitstream/handle/1814/30059/Religiowest_Annicchino_web.pdf?sequence=2 (accessed May 2014). Florence: European University Institute; ReligioWest.

Finke, Roger, and Rodney Stark. 1992. *The Churching of America, 1776–1990: Winners and Losers in Our Religious Economy*. New Brunswick, NJ: Rutgers University Press.

Finke, Roger, and Rodney Stark. 1998. "Religious Choice and Competition." *American Sociological Review* 63 (5): 761–766.

Finke, Roger, and Rodney Stark. 2005. *The Churching of America, 1776–2005: Winners and Losers in Our Religious Economy*. New Brunswick, NJ: Rutgers University Press.

Finnemore, Martha, and Kathryn Sikkink. 1998. "International Norm Dynamics and Political Change." *International Organization* 52 (4): 887–917.

Fioretos, Orfeo. 2011. "Historical Institutionalism in International Relations." *International Organization* 65 (2): 367–399.

Foreign & Commonwealth Office (FCO). 2015. "Freedom of Religion or Belief Toolkit: How the FCO Can Help Promote and Protect This Human Right." London: Foreign & Commonwealth Office, https://www.gov.uk/government/uploads/system/uploads/attachment_data/file/561516/Freedom_of_Religion_or_Belief_Toolkit_-_2016.pdf (accessed June 30, 2016).

Former NSC Official. 2010. Personal Communication. Washington, DC, June 16, 2010.

Forst, Brian, and Akbar S. Ahmed. 2005. *After Terror: Promoting Dialogue Among Civilizations.* Cambridge: Polity Press.

Fox, Jonathan. 2006. "World Separation of Religion and State Into the 21st Century." *Comparative Political Studies* 39 (5): 537–569.

Fox News. 2015. "Fear Christian Minorities Face 'Extinction' in Middle East." *Fox News,* https://www.youtube.com/watch?v=nowo7pIgBls (accessed July 14, 2016).

Freedom from Religious Persecution Act of 1997. H. R. 1685, *105th Congress* (1997–1998).

Froese, Paul, and F. Carson Mencken. 2009. "A US Holy War? The Effects of Religion on Iraq War Policy Attitudes." *Social Science Quarterly* 90 (1): 103–116.

Frum, David, and Richard Norman Perle. 2003. *An End to Evil: How to Win the War on Terror.* 1st ed. New York: Random House.

Frykholm, Amy. 2013. "Under Hillary Clinton, the State Department Pursued Greater Religious Engagement." *Religion & Politics,* http://religionandpolitics.org/2013/05/08/since-hillary-clintons-tenure-the-state-department-pursues-greater-religious-engagement/ (accessed July 29, 2016).

Fukuyama, Francis. 1992. *The End of History and the Last Man.* New York: The Free Press.

Fukuyama, Francis. 2004. "The Neoconservative Moment." *National Interest* 76 (2): 57–68.

Furman, Dick. 2010. "Haiti Revisited: A Surgeon's Diary." *Samaritan's Purse,* http://www.samaritanspurse.org/index.php/articles/haiti_revisited_a_surgeons_diary_day_6/ (accessed November 11, 2011).

Garrard, John, and Carol Garrard. 2008. *Russian Orthodoxy Resurgent: Faith and Power in the New Russia.* Princeton, NJ: Princeton University Press.

George, Alexander L., and Andrew Bennett. 2005. *Case Studies and Theory Development in the Social Sciences.* Cambridge, MA: The MIT Press.

George, Robert P. 2014. "U.S. Efforts to Hold Accountable Countries of Particular Concern." Testimony Before the Subcommittee on Africa, Global Health, Global Human Rights, and International Organizations of the House Committee on Foreign Affairs on Protecting Religious Freedom, Washington, DC, http://www.uscirf.gov/sites/default/files/May 22 testimony final draft Tuesdayrev2.pdf (accessed July 6, 2015).

Gerges, Fawaz A. 1999. *America and Political Islam: Clash of Cultures or Clash of Interests?* Cambridge: Cambridge University Press.

Gerson, Michael. 2014. "Michael Gerson: Looking Back on a Decade of PEPFAR." *Patheos,* http://www.patheos.com/blogs/philosophicalfragments/2014/07/16/michael-gerson-looking-back-on-a-decade-of-pepfar/ (accessed August 1, 2015).

Gertz, Bill. 2014. "Surrender in the War of Ideas." *Washington Free Beacon,* http://freebeacon.com/national-security/surrender-in-the-war-of-ideas/ (accessed June 5, 2016).

Ghandour, Abdel-Rahman. 2003. "Humanitarianism, Islam and the West: Contest or Co-operation." *Humanitarian Exchange* (25): 14–17.

Gjelten, Tom. 2018. "Trump's National Security And State Department Picks Alarm American Muslims." *NPR,* https://www.npr.org/2018/04/06/599856473/

trump-and-muslims-a-warming-abroad-a-cooling-at-home?t=1532451260168 (accessed July 25, 2018).

Glassman, James K. 2008a. "Public Diplomacy 2.0: A New Approach to Global Engagement." Washington, DC: New America Foundation, http://2001-2009. state.gov/r/us/2008/112605.htm (accessed May 26, 2016).

Glassman, James K. 2008b. "Opening Statement of James K. Glassman." Senate Foreign Relations Committee, Washington, DC, https://www.aei.org/publication/opening-statement-of-james-k-glassman/ (accessed May 26, 2016).

Goldberg, Jeffrey. 2010. "The Most Influential Muslim at the White House?," http://www.theatlantic.com/international/archive/2010/04/the-most-influential-muslim-at-the-white-house/38587 (accessed August 27, 2011).

Goldberg, Jeffrey. 2016. "The Obama Doctrine." *The Atlantic*, http://www.theatlantic.com/magazine/archive/2016/04/the-obama-doctrine/471525/ (accessed May 14, 2016).

Gonzalez, David. 2001. "U.S. Aids Conversion-Minded Quake Relief in El Salvador." *New York Times*, http://www.nytimes.com/2001/03/05/world/05SALV.html?pagewanted=1 (accessed April 11, 2015).

Gopin, Marc. 1997. "Religion, Violence, and Conflict Resolution." *Peace & Change* 22 (1): 1–31.

Gopin, Marc. 2000. *Between Eden and Armageddon: The Future of World Religions, Violence, and Peacemaking*. Oxford: Oxford University Press.

Gopin, Marc. 2002. *Holy War, Holy Peace: How Religion Can Bring Peace to the Middle East*. Oxford: Oxford University Press.

Gorski, Philip S. 2003. "Historicizing the Secularization Debate: An Agenda for Research." In *Handbook for the Sociology of Religion*, edited by Michelle Dillon, 110–122. Cambridge: Cambridge University Press.

Gorski, Philip S. 2013. "What is Critical Realism? And Why Should You Care?" *Contemporary Sociology: A Journal of Reviews* 42 (5): 658–670.

Gorski, Philip S., David Kyuman Kim, John Torpey, and Jonathan VanAntwerpen. 2012a. "The Post-Secular in Question." In *The Post-Secular in Question: Religion in Contemporary Society*, edited by Philip Gorski, David Kyuman Kim, John Torpey, and Jonathan VanAntwerpen, 1–22. New York: New York University Press.

Gorski, Philip S., David Kyuman Kim, John Torpey, and Jonathan VanAntwerpen, eds. 2012b. *The Post-Secular in Question: Religion in Contemporary Society*. New York: New York University Press.

Graham, David A. 2017. "A Short History of U.S. Presidents Explaining Islam to Muslims." *The Atlantic*, https://www.theatlantic.com/international/archive/2017/05/american-presidents-explain-islam-to-muslim/527415/ (accessed June 20, 2018).

Green, Edward C. 2003. "Faith-Based Organizations: Contributions to HIV Prevention." Washington, DC: USAID, https://www.researchgate.net/publication/254441593_Faith-Based_Organizations_Contributions_to_HIV_Prevention (accessed January 24, 2010).

Green, Edward C. 2011. *Broken Promises: How the AIDS Establishment Has Betrayed the Developing World*. New York: Routledge.

Green, Emma. 2017. "'Protecting Religious Freedom Is a Foreign-Policy Priority of the Trump Administration': How—and When—Will the White House Carry Out Its Verbal Commitment to Protect Persecuted Minorities Overseas?" *The Atlantic*, https://www.theatlantic.com/international/archive/2017/05/religious-freedom-trump-administration/526320/ (accessed July 22, 2018).

Green, Mark. 2018. "Help Is on the Way for Middle Eastern Christians." *Wall Street Journal*, https://www.wsj.com/articles/help-is-on-the-way-for-middle-eastern-christians-1528931329 (accessed July 26, 2018).

Grieboski, Joseph. 2011a. "The Case for Pulling the Plug on the US Commission on International Religious Freedom." *Huffington Post*, http://www.huffingtonpost.com/joseph-k-grieboski/us-commission-international-religious-freedom_b_1010590.html (accessed February 25, 2012).

Grieboski, Joseph. 2011b. Personal Communication. Alexandria, VA, June 3, 2011.

Grim, Brian J., and Roger Finke. 2010. *The Price of Freedom Denied: Religious Persecution and Conflict in the Twenty-first Century*. Cambridge: Cambridge University Press.

Gunn, T. Jeremy. 2004. "The United States and the Promotion of Freedom of Religion and Belief." In *Facilitating Freedom of Religious Belief: A Deskbook*, edited by Tore Lindholm, W. Cole Durham Jr., Elizabeth A. Sewell, and Bahia G. Tahzib-Lie, 617–642. The Hague: Martinus Nijhoff.

Gunn, T. Jeremy. 2013. "The Politics of Religious Freedom: Competing Claims in the United States (and Other Places)." In *Freedom of Religion or Belief in Foreign Policy. Which One?*, edited by Pasquale Annicchino, 32–37, http://cadmus.eui.eu/bitstream/handle/1814/30059/Religiowest_Annicchino_web.pdf?sequence=2 (accessed May 2014). Florence: European University Institute; ReligioWest.

Guth, James L. 2009. "Religion and American Public Opinion: Foreign Policy Issues." In *The Oxford Handbook of Religion and American Politics*, edited by James L. Guth, Lyman A. Kellstedt, and Corwin E. Smidt, 243–265. New York: Oxford University Press.

Guth, James L. 2011. "Religious Factors and American Public Support for Israel: 1992–2008." Annual meeting of the American Political Science Association, Seattle, WA, September 1–4, 2011.

Guth, James L., Corwin E. Smidt, and Lyman A. Kellstedt, eds. 2009. *The Oxford Handbook of Religion and American Politics*. New York: Oxford University Press.

Gutkowski, Stacey. 2013. *Secular War: Myths of Religion, Politics and Violence*. London: I. B. Tauris.

Gutkowski, Stacey. 2016. "We Are the Very Model of a Moderate Muslim State: The Amman Messages and Jordan's Foreign Policy." *International Relations* 30 (2): 206–226.

Guzzini, Stefano. 2012. "The Framework of Analysis: Geopolitics Meets Foreign Policy Identity Crises." In *The Return of Geopolitics in Europe?: Social Mechanisms and Foreign Policy Identity Crises*, edited by Stefano Guzzini, 45–74. Cambridge: Cambridge University Press.

Haas, Peter M. 1992. "Introduction: Epistemic Communities and International Policy Coordination." *International Organization* 46 (1): 1–35.

Haass, Richard N. 2003. "Toward Greater Democracy in the Muslim World." *Washington Quarterly* 26 (3): 137–148.

Habermas, Jürgen. 2006. "Religion in the Public Sphere." *European Journal of Philosophy* 14 (1): 1–25.

Habermas, Jürgen. 2008a. *Between Naturalism and Religion: Philosophical Essays.* Cambridge: Polity Press.

Habermas, Jürgen. 2008b. "Notes on Post-Secular Society." *New Perspectives Quarterly* 25 (4): 17–29.

Habermas et al., Jürgen, ed. 2010. *An Awareness of What Is Missing: Faith and Reason in a Post-secular Age* Cambridge: Polity Press.

Habermas, Jürgen, and Eduardo Mendieta. 2010. "A Postsecular World Society?: On the Philosophical Significance of Postsecular Consciousness and the Multicultural World Society—An Interview with Jürgen Habermas." *The Immanent Frame,* http://blogs.ssrc.org/tif/wp-content/uploads/2010/02/A-Postsecular-World-Society-TIF.pdf (accessed October 11, 2011).

Habermas, Jürgen, and Joseph Ratzinger. 2006. *Dialectics of Secularization: On Reason and Religion.* San Francisco: Ignatius Press.

Hackett, Rosalind I. J., ed. 2014. *Proselytization Revisited: Rights Talk, Free Markets and Culture Wars.* Abingdon: Routledge.

Hackett, Rosalind I. J., Mark Silk, and Dennis Hoover. 1999. "Religious Persecution as a U.S. Policy Issue." Proceedings of a Consultation held at the Center for the Study of Religion and Public Life, Trinity College, Hartford, CT, http://www.trincoll.edu/depts/csrpl/Religious Persecution/relperse.pdf (accessed June 10, 2015).

Hajer, Maarten A. 1993. "Discourse Coalition and the Institutionalization of Practice: The Case of Acid Rain in Britain." In *The Argumentative Turn in Policy Analysis and Planning,* edited by Frank Fischer and John Forester, 43–76. Durham, NC: Duke University Press.

Hall, Charles F. 1997. "The Christian Left: Who Are They and How Are They Different from the Christian Right?" *Review of Religious Research* 39 (1): 27–45.

Hall, Peter A. 1993. "Policy Paradigms, Social Learning, and the State: the Case of Economic Policymaking in Britain." *Comparative Politics* 25 (3): 275–296.

Halliday, Fred. 2003. *Islam and the Myth of Confrontation: Religion and Politics in the Middle East.* London: I. B. Tauris.

Hallward, Maia Carter 2008. "Situating the 'Secular': Negotiating the Boundary Between Religion and Politics." *International Political Sociology* 2 (1): 1–16.

Halper, Stefan A., and Jonathan Clarke. 2004. *America Alone: the Neo-Conservatives and the Global Order.* Cambridge: Cambridge University Press.

Hamid, Shadi. 2016. "How Iraq Warped Obama's Worldview." *The Atlantic,* http://www.theatlantic.com/international/archive/2016/03/obama-doctrine-iraq-islam/473148 (accessed May 14, 2016).

Hanson, Hilary. 2015. "Befuddled Pat Robertson Declares Islam Is Not A Religion, Again." *Huffington Post,* http://www.huffingtonpost.com/entry/pat-robertson-islam-not-religion_us_56671841e4b08e945ff111a9 (accessed September 21, 2016).

Hart, Tom. 2011. Personal Communication. Washington, DC, July 8, 2011.

Hartman, Andrew. 2015. *A War for the Soul of America: A History of the Culture Wars.* Chicago: University of Chicago Press.

Hasdorff, Terri. 2006. "Faith-Based Organizations and U.S. Programming in Africa: Testimony by Terri Hasdorff Director of the Center for Faith-Based and Community Initiatives United States Agency for International Development." Subcommittee on Africa, Global Human Rights and International Operations International Relations Committee U.S. House of Representatives, Washington, DC: http://pdf.usaid.gov/pdf_docs/pdacio34.pdf (accessed May 14, 2010).

Hasenclever, Andreas, Peter Mayer, and Volker Rittberger. 2000. "Integrating Theories of International Regimes." *Review of International Studies* 26 (1): 3–33.

Hatzopoulos, Pavlos, and Fabio Petito, eds. 2003. *Religion in International Relations: the Return from Exile*. 1st ed. Basingstoke: Palgrave Macmillan.

Haynes, Jeffrey. 2001. "Transnational Religious Actors and International Politics." *Third World Quarterly* 22 (2): 143–158.

Haynes, Jeffrey. 2006. "Religion and International Relations in the 21st Century: Conflict or Co-operation?" *Third World Quarterly* 27 (3): 535–541.

Haynes, Jeffrey. 2014. *Faith-Based Organizations at the United Nations*. New York: Palgrave Macmillan.

Haynes, Jeffrey. 2017. "Donald Trump, 'Judeo-Christian Values,' and the 'Clash of Civilizations'." *Review of Faith & International Affairs* 15 (3): 66–75.

Hearn, Julie. 2002. "The 'Invisible' NGO: US Evangelical Missions in Kenya." *Journal of Religion in Africa* 32 (1): 32–60.

Hehir, J. Bryan, ed. 2004. *Liberty and Power: A Dialogue on Religion and U.S. Foreign Policy in an Unjust World*. Washington, DC: Brookings Institution Press.

Henne, Peter S. 2018. "Trump's Administration Does Little for International Religious Freedom." *The Globe Post*, https://theglobepost.com/2018/07/24/trump-international-religious-freedom/ (accessed July 24, 2018).

Herberg, Will. 1955. *Protestant-Catholic-Jew: An Essay in American Religious Sociology*. Chicago: University of Chicago Press.

Hertzke, Allen D. 2001a. "The Faith Factor in Foreign Policy: Religious Constituencies and Congressional Initiative on Human Rights." *Extensions*, http://www.ou.edu/special/albertctr/extensions/spring2001/Hertzke.html (accessed November 6, 2010).

Hertzke, Allen D. 2001b. "The Political Sociology of the Crusade against Religious Persecution." In *The Influence of Faith: Religious Groups and U.S. Foreign Policy*, edited by Elliott Abrams, 69–94. Lanham, MD: Rowman & Littlefield Publishers.

Hertzke, Allen D. 2004. *Freeing God's Children: the Unlikely Alliance for Global Human Rights*. Lanham, MD: Rowman & Littlefield.

Hertzke, Allen D., ed. 2013. *The Future of Religious Freedom: Global Challenges*. New York: Oxford University Press.

Hertzke, Allen D., and Daniel Philpott. 2000. "Defending the Faiths." *National Interest* 61 (Fall): 74–81.

Hill, Christopher. 2003. *The Changing Politics of Foreign Policy*. New York: Palgrave Macmillan.

Hirsh, Michael. 2016. "Team Trump's Message: The Clash of Civilizations Is Back." *Politico*, http://www.politico.com/magazine/story/2016/11/donald-trump-team-islam-clash-of-civilizations-214474 (accessed February 2, 2017).

Hobson, John M., and Stephen Hobden, eds. 2002. *Historical Sociology of International Relations*. Cambridge: Cambridge University Press.

Hobson, John, George Lawson, and Justin Rosenberg. 2010. "Historical Sociology." In *The International Studies Encyclopaedia*, edited by Robert A. Denemark. Malden, MA: Wiley-Blackwell.

Hoover, Dennis R. 2011. Phone Communication. Washington, DC, July 15, 2011.

Hoover, Dennis R., ed. 2014. *Religion and American Exceptionalism*. New York: Routledge.

Hoover, Dennis R., and Douglas Johnston, eds. 2012. *Religion and Foreign Affairs: Essential Readings*. Waco, TX: Baylor University Press.

Horowitz, Michael. 1995. "New Intolerance Between Crescent and Cross." *Wall Street Journal*, July 5, 1995.

Hout, Michael, and Claude S. Fischer. 2014. "Explaining Why More Americans Have No Religious Preference: Political Backlash and Generational Succession, 1987–2012." *Sociological Science* 1: 423–447.

Hudson, John. 2016. "Growth of Islamic State Forces State Department Overhaul." *Foreign Policy*, http://foreignpolicy.com/2016/02/01/growth-of-islamic-state-forces-state-department-overhaul (accessed August 28, 2016).

Huliaras, Asteris. 2008. "The Evangelical Roots of US Africa Policy." *Survival* 50 (6): 161–182.

Huntington, Samuel P. 1993a. "The Clash of Civilizations?" *Foreign Affairs* 72 (3): 22–49.

Huntington, Samuel P. 1993b. "If Not Civilizations, What? Paradigms of the Post-cold War World." *Foreign Affairs* 72 (5): 186–194.

Huntington, Samuel P. 1996. *The Clash of Civilizations and the Remaking of World Order*. New York: Simon & Schuster.

Hurd, Elizabeth Shakman. 2008. *The Politics of Secularism in International Relations*. Princeton, NJ: Princeton University Press.

Hurd, Elizabeth Shakman. 2012a. "Believing in Religious Freedom." *The Immanent Frame*, http://blogs.ssrc.org/tif/2012/03/01/believing-in-religious-freedom/ (accessed February 15, 2013).

Hurd, Elizabeth Shakman. 2012b. "International Politics After Secularism." *Review of International Studies* 38 (5): 943–961.

Hurd, Elizabeth Shakman. 2012c. "The Tragedy of Religious Freedom in Syria." *Chicago Tribune*, http://articles.chicagotribune.com/2012-03-29/news/ct-perspec-0329-syria-20120329_1_religious-freedom-alawites-and-christians-syrian-revolt (accessed August 20, 2012).

Hurd, Elizabeth Shakman. 2013a. "Losing Faith in Faith-based Outreach." *Al Jazeera*, http://america.aljazeera.com/articles/2013/9/24/faith-based-communityinitiativesstatedepartment.html (accessed December 20, 2013).

Hurd, Elizabeth Shakman. 2013b. "Religious Difference and Religious Freedom." *PluRel*, http://www.tf.uio.no/english/research/projects/goba/project-hub/blog/plurel/rett-og-religion/religious-difference-and-religious-freedom.html (accessed December 20, 2013).

Hurd, Elizabeth Shakman. 2013c. "What's Wrong with Promoting Religious Freedom?" *Foreign Policy*, http://www.foreignpolicy.com/2013/06/12/whats-wrong-with-promoting-religious-freedom (accessed December 20, 2013).

Hurd, Elizabeth Shakman. 2014a. "International 'Religious Freedom' Agenda Will Only Embolden ISIS." *Religion Dispatches*, http://religiondispatches.org/international-religious-freedom-agenda-will-only-embolden-isis/ (accessed May 16, 2015).

Hurd, Elizabeth Shakman. 2014b. "Religious Freedom, American-Style." *Quaderni di Diritto e Política Ecclesiastica* 22 (1): 231–242.

Hurd, Elizabeth Shakman. 2014c. "Response to Daniel Philpott: The Politics of Religious Freedom." *Religion Dispatches*, http://religiondispatches.org/response-to-daniel-philpott-the-politics-of-religious-freedom/ (accessed May 16, 2015).

Hurd, Elizabeth Shakman. 2015. *Beyond Religious Freedom: The New Global Politics of Religion*. Princeton, NJ: Princeton University Press.

Hurd, Elizabeth Shakman. 2016. "*Beyond Religious Freedom*—An introduction." *The Immanent Frame*, http://blogs.ssrc.org/tif/2016/03/17/beyond-religious-freedom-an-introduction/ (accessed April 9, 2017).

Hurd, Elizabeth Shakman, and Winnifred Fallers Sullivan. 2014. "Symposium: Rethinking Religious Freedom." *Journal of Law and Religion* 29 (3): 358–509.

Husain, Ed. 2013. "A Global Venture to Counter Violent Extremism." Policy Innovation Memorandum no. 37. New York: Council on Foreign Relations, https://www.cfr.org/report/global-venture-counter-violent-extremism (accessed August 3, 2016).

Hussain, Rashad. 2010. "Remarks at the UN Third Global Forum of the Alliance of Civilizations." Rio de Janeiro: UN Third Global Forum of the Alliance of Civilizations, http://www.state.gov/p/io/142790.htm.

Hussain, Rashad. 2012. "Remarks: Protecting the Rights of Christians and Religious Minorities in the Muslim World." The Second National Baptist-Muslim Dialogue, Newton, MA, http://www.state.gov/p/io/rm/2012/201433.htm (accessed April 19, 2015).

Hussain, Rashad, and Al-Husein N. Madhany. 2008. "Reformulating the Battle of Ideas: Understanding the Role of Islam in Counterterrorism Policy." Washington, DC: Brookings Institution, http://www.brookings.edu/~/media/research/files/papers/2008/8/counterterrorism hussain/o8_counterterrorism_hussain.pdf (accessed March 21, 2011).

Ignatius, David. 2003. "The Read on Wolfowitz." *Washington Post*, https://www.washingtonpost.com/archive/opinions/2003/01/17/the-read-on-wolfowitz/9e5b63af-403d-4414-8b11-ee61c41c17c5 (accessed May 30, 2011).

Ikenberry, G. John. 2001. *After Victory: Institutions, Strategic Restraint, and the Rebuilding of Order After Major Wars*. Princeton, NJ: Princeton University Press.

Ikenberry, G. John. 2011. *Liberal Leviathan: The Origins, Crisis, and Transformation of the American World Order*. Princeton, NJ: Princeton University Press.

Inboden, William. 2010. *Religion and American Foreign Policy, 1945–1960: the Soul of Containment*. Cambridge: Cambridge University Press.

Inboden, William. 2011. "Phone Communication." Washington, DC, June 29, 2011.

Inboden, William. 2012. "Religious Freedom and National Security: Why the U.S. Should Make the Connection." Policy Review 175. Stanford University: Hoover

Institution, http://www.hoover.org/publications/policy-review/article/129086 (accessed March 5, 2013).

International Religious Freedom Act of 1998 (IRFA). H. R. 2431, *105th Congress* (1997–1998). https://www.congress.gov/105/plaws/publ292/PLAW-105publ292.pdf.

International Religious Freedom Roundtable. n.d. "Purpose Statement." http://www.aicongress.org/wp-content/uploads/2012/05/IRF-Roundtable-Web-Update.pdf (accessed April 30, 2015).

Jackson, Patrick Thaddeus. 2011. *The Conduct of Inquiry in International Relations: Philosophy of Science and its Implications for the Study of World Politics.* New York: Routledge.

Jenkins, Philip. 2011. *The Next Christendom: The Coming of Global Christianity.* Oxford: Oxford University Press.

Johnson, Stephen, Helle C. Dale, and Patrick Cronin. 2005. "Strengthening U.S. Public Diplomacy Requires Organization, Coordination, and Strategy." Washington, DC: The Heritage Foundation, http://dh7863-34.intermedia.net/learn/articles/publicdiplomacy_heritageaug05.pdf (accessed September 24, 2013).

Johnston, Douglas M., ed. 2003. *Faith-Based Diplomacy: Trumping Realpolitik.* Oxford: Oxford University Press.

Johnston, Douglas M. 2011a. Personal Communication. Washington, DC, June 10, 2011.

Johnston, Douglas M. 2011b. *Religion, Terror, and Error: US Foreign Policy and the Challenge of Spiritual Engagement.* Santa Barbara, CA: Praeger Publishers.

Johnston, Douglas M., and Cynthia Sampson, eds. 1994. *Religion, the Missing Dimension of Statecraft.* New York: Oxford University Press.

Jones, Nelson. 2014. "Are Christians Really the World's Most Persecuted Religious Group?" *New Statesman*, http://www.newstatesman.com/lifestyle/2014/04/are-christians-really-world-s-most-persecuted-religious-group (accessed May 29, 2015).

Joseph, Jonathan, and Colin Wight, eds. 2010. *Scientific Realism and International Relations.* London: Palgrave Macmillan.

Juergensmeyer, Mark. 2008. *Global Rebellion: Religious Challenges to the Secular State, from Christian Militias to al Qaeda.* Berkeley: University of California Press.

Kaaya, Sadab Kitatta. 2014. "Anti-Gay Group Fires All Staff." *The Observer*, http://www.observer.ug/index.php?option=com_content&view=article&id=33371&catid=78&Itemid=116 (accessed July 21, 2016).

Kaiser Family Foundation. 2017. "Fact Sheet: The U.S. President's Emergency Plan for AIDS Relief (PEPFAR)." Kaiser Family Foundation, https://www.kff.org/global-health-policy/fact-sheet/the-u-s-presidents-emergency-plan-for/ (accessed July 25, 2018).

Kaoma, Kapya. 2014. *American Culture Warriors in Africa: A Guide to the Exporters of Homophobia and Sexism.* Somerville, MA: Political Research Associates.

Kaplan, David E. 2005a. "The Enemy of My Enemy . . ." *US News*, https://web.archive.org/web/20050425084622/http://www.usnews.com/usnews/news/articles/050425/25roots.b2.htm (accessed February 1, 2012).

Kaplan, David E. 2005b. "Hearts, Minds, and Dollars: In an Unseen Front in the War on Terrorism, America is Spending Millions . . . To Change the Very Face of Islam." *US News*, http://www.usnews.com/usnews/news/articles/050425/25roots_print.htm (accessed February 1, 2012).

Kaplan, David E. 2006. "Of Jihad Networks and the War of Ideas." *US News*, http://www.usnews.com/usnews/news/articles/060622/22natsec.htm (accessed February 1, 2012).

Kaplan, Esther. 2004. "The Bush AIDS Machine." *The Nation*, http://www.thenation.com/article/bush-aids-machine/ (accessed August 4, 2016).

Karpov, Vyacheslav. 2010. "Desecularization: A Conceptual Framework." *Journal of Church and State* 52 (2): 232–270.

Katulis, Brian, Rudy deLeon, and John Craig. 2015. "The Plight of Christians in the Middle East: Supporting Religious Freedom, Pluralism, and Tolerance During a Time of Turmoil." Washington, DC: Center for American Progress, https://cdn.americanprogress.org/wp-content/uploads/2015/03/ChristiansMiddleEast-report.pdf (accessed June 6, 2015).

Keohane, Robert O., and David G. Victor. 2011. "The Regime Complex for Climate Change." *Perspectives on Politics* 9 (1): 7–23.

Kepel, Gilles. 1994. *The Revenge of God: The Resurgence of Islam, Christianity and Judaism in the Modern World*. Cambridge: Polity Press.

Kerry, John. 2015. "Toward a Better Understanding of Religion and Global Affairs." *DipNote*, https://blogs.state.gov/stories/2015/09/05/toward-better-understanding-religion-and-global-affairs (accessed April 15, 2016).

Kerry, John. 2016. "Remarks at Rice University's Baker Institute for Public Policy." Rice University, Houston, TX, https://2009-2017.state.gov/secretary/remarks/2016/04/256618.htm (accessed March 20, 2017).

Kerry, John, Shaun Casey, and Melissa Rogers. 2013. "Remarks at the Launch of the Office of Faith-Based Community Initiatives." US Department of State, Washington, DC, https://2009-2017.state.gov/secretary/remarks/2013/08/212781.htm (accessed March 20, 2017).

King, David. 2012. "The New Internationalists: World Vision and the Revival of American Evangelical Humanitarianism, 1950–2010." *Religions* 3 (4): 922–949.

Kirby, Dianne. 2003. "Harry Truman's Religious Legacy: The Holy Alliance, Containment and the Cold War." In *Religion and the Cold War*, edited by Dianne Kirby, 77–102. New York: Palgrave Macmillan.

Klotz, Audie, and Cecelia Lynch. 2006. "Translating Terminologies." *International Studies Review* 8 (2): 356–362.

Kniss, Fred, and David Todd Campbell. 1997. "The Effect of Religious Orientation on International Relief and Development Organizations." *Journal for the Scientific Study of Religion* 36 (1): 93–103.

Kopsa, Andy. 2013. "Obama Still Funding Failed 'Faith-Based' Programmes." *Al Jazeera*, http://www.aljazeera.com/indepth/opinion/2013/03/2013326111715591221.html (accessed August 4, 2016).

Kopsa, Andy. 2014. "Obama's Evangelical Gravy Train." *The Nation*, http://www.thenation.com/article/obamas-evangelical-gravy-train/ (accessed August 4, 2016).

Kranish, Michael. 2006. "Religious Right Wields Clout: Secular Groups Losing Funding Amid Pressure." *Boston Globe*, http://www.boston.com/news/nation/articles/2006/10/09/religious_right_wields_clout/ (accessed October 27, 2011).

Krasner, Stephen D. 1983. *International Regimes*. Ithaca, NY: Cornell University Press.

Kratochwil, Friedrich, and John Gerard Ruggie. 1986. "International Organization: A State of the Art on an Art of the State." *International Organization* 40 (4): 753–775.

Kristol, William, and Robert Kagan. 1996. "Toward a Neo-Reaganite Foreign Policy." *Foreign Affairs* 75 (4): 18–32.

Kuo, David. 2006. *Tempting Faith: An Inside Story of Political Seduction.* New York: The Free Press.

Kuo, David, and John J. DiIulio. 2008. "The Faith to Outlast Politics." *New York Times,* http://www.nytimes.com/2008/01/29/opinion/29kuo.html?pagewanted=print (accessed October 25, 2011).

Kurki, Milja. 2006. "Causes of a Divided Discipline: Rethinking the Concept of Cause in International Relations Theory." *Review of International Studies* 32 (2): 189–216.

Kurki, Milja. 2007. "Critical Realism and Causal Analysis in International Relations." *Millennium: Journal of International Studies* 35 (2): 361–378.

Kuru, Ahmet T. 2009. *Secularism and State Policies Toward Religion: the United States, France, and Turkey.* Cambridge: Cambridge University Press.

Laborde, Cécile. 2014. "Three Approaches to the Study of Religion." *The Immanent Frame,* http://blogs.ssrc.org/tif/2014/02/05/three-approaches-to-the-study-of-religion/ (accessed April 28, 2015).

Land, Richard. 1997. "Freedom from Religious Persecution Act of 1997, Part II—Private Witnesses." Hearing Before the Committee on International Relations, House of Representatives, Washington, DC, http://commdocs.house.gov/committees/intlrel/hfa45691.000/hfa45691_of.htm (accessed April 28, 2011).

Lawson, George. 2007. "Historical Sociology in International Relations: Open Society, Research Programme and Vocation." *International Politics* 44 (4): 343–368.

Lewis, Bernard. 1990. "The Roots of Muslim Rage." *The Atlantic Monthly* 266 (3): 47–60.

Lewis, Bernard. 1997. "The West and the Middle East." *Foreign Affairs* 76 (1): 114–130.

Lewis, Bernard. 2001. "The Revolt of Islam: When Did the Conflict with the West Begin, and How Could It End?" *The New Yorker,* http://www.newyorker.com/magazine/2001/11/19/the-revolt-of-islam (accessed May 25, 2011).

Lewis, Bernard. 2002a. "The Day After." American Enterprise Institute conference on Post-Saddam Iraq, Washington, DC.

Lewis, Bernard. 2002b. "Time for Toppling." *Wall Street Journal,* http://www.wsj.com/articles/SB1033089910971012713 (accessed May 20, 2011).

Lewis, Bernard. 2002c. "A War of Resolve." *Wall Street Journal,* http://www.wsj.com/articles/SB1019783516427073880 (accessed May 20, 2011).

Lewis, Bernard. 2002d. *What Went Wrong?: The Clash Between Islam and Modernity in the Middle East.* London: Weidenfeld & Nicolson.

Lieven, Anatol. 2005. *America Right or Wrong: an Anatomy of American Nationalism.* London: Harper Perennial.

Linklater, Andrew. 2009. "Historical Sociology." In *Theories of International Relations,* edited by Scott Burchill, Andrew Linklater, Richard Devetak, Jack Donnelly, Matthew Paterson, Christian Reus-Smit, and Jacqui True, 136–158. New York: Palgrave Macmillan.

Lipset, Seymour Martin. 1996. *American Exceptionalism: a Double-Edged Sword.* New York: Norton.

Lipsky, Alyson B. 2011. "Evaluating the Strength of Faith: Potential Comparative Advantages of Faith-Based Organizations Providing Health Services in Sub-Saharan Africa." *Public Administration and Development* 31 (1): 25–36.

Lisovskaya, Elena, and Vyacheslav Karpov. 2010. "Orthodoxy, Islam, and the Desecularization of Russia's State Schools." *Politics and Religion* 3 (2): 276–302.

Lupovici, Amir. 2009. "Constructivist Methods: a Plea and Manifesto for Pluralism." *Review of International Studies* 35 (1): 195–218.

Luttwak, Edward. 1994. "The Missing Dimension." In *Religion, the Missing Dimension of Statecraft*, edited by Douglas M. Johnston, and Cynthia Sampson, 8–19. New York: Oxford University Press.

Lynch, Cecelia, and Tanya B. Schwarz. 2016. "Humanitarianism's Proselytism Problem." *International Studies Quarterly* 60 (4): 636–646.

Lynch, Marc. 2010. "Rhetoric and Reality: Countering Terrorism in the Age of Obama." Washington, DC: Center for a New American Security, http://www.cnas.org/files/documents/publications/CNAS_Rhetoric and Reality_Lynch.pdf (accessed July 19, 2011).

Lynch, Timothy J. 2008. "Kristol Balls: Neoconservative Visions of Islam and the Middle East." *International Politics* 45 (2): 182–211.

Mabee, Brian. 2007. "Levels and Agents, States and People: Micro-Historical Sociological Analysis and International Relations." *International Politics* 44 (4): 431–449.

Mabee, Brian. 2011. "Historical Institutionalism and Foreign Policy Analysis: The Origins of the National Security Council Revisited." *Foreign Policy Analysis* 7 (1): 27–44.

Mahmood, Saba. 2012. "Religious Freedom, the Minority Question, and Geopolitics in the Middle East." *Comparative Studies in Society and History* 54 (2): 418–446.

Mahoney, James. 2000. "Path Dependence in Historical Sociology." *Theory and Society* 29 (4): 507–548.

Mahoney, James, Erin Kimball, and Kendra L. Koivu. 2009. "The Logic of Historical Explanation in the Social Sciences." *Comparative Political Studies* 42 (1): 114–146.

Mamdani, Mahmood. 2002. "Good Muslim, Bad Muslim: A Political Perspective on Culture and Terrorism." *American Anthropologist* 104 (3): 766–775.

Mandaville, Peter. 2001. *Transnational Muslim Politics: Reimagining the Umma, Transnationalism*. London: Routledge.

Mandaville, Peter. 2005. *Global Political Islam*. London: Routledge.

Mandaville, Peter. 2010a. "Transformative Partnerships in U.S.-Muslim World Relations: Empowering Networks for Community Development and Social Change." The Brookings Project on U.S. Relations with the Islamic World: 2010 U.S.-Islamic World Forum Papers. Washington, DC: Brookings Institution, http://www.brookings.edu/~/media/research/files/papers/2010/6/us-muslim-relations-mandaville/06_us_muslim_relations_mandaville.pdf (accessed February 30, 2011).

Mandaville, Peter. 2010b. "Whither U.S. Engagement with Muslims?" *Foreign Policy*, http://mideast.foreignpolicy.com/posts/2010/06/04/whither_us_engagement_with_muslims (accessed February 30, 2011).

Mandaville, Peter. 2017. "The Future of Religion and U.S. Foreign Policy under Trump." Washington, DC: The Brookings Institution, https://www.brookings.edu/research/the-future-of-religion-and-u-s-foreign-policy-under-trump/ (accessed July 30, 2018).

Mandaville, Peter, and Melissa Nozell. 2017. "Engaging Religion and Religious Actors in Countering Violent Extremism." Special Report 413. Washington, DC: United States Institute of Peace, https://www.usip.org/sites/default/files/SR413-Engaging-Religion-and-Religious-Actors-in-Countering-Violent-Extremism.pdf (accessed July 28, 2018).

Mandaville, Peter, and Sarah Silvestri. 2015. "Integrating Religious Engagement into Diplomacy: Challenges & Opportunities." *Issues in Governance Studies* 67. Washington, DC: Brookings Institution, http://www.brookings.edu/~/media/research/files/papers/2015/01/29-religious-engagement-diplomacy-mandaville-silvestri/issuesingovstudiesmandavillesilvestriefinal.pdf (accessed June 24, 2016).

Mansfield, Stephen. 2003. *The Faith of George W. Bush*. New York: Penguin.

Markoe, Lauren. 2015. "Religious Leaders Call on President Obama to Appoint Special Envoy for Persecuted Christians." *Huffington Post*, http://www.huffingtonpost.com/2015/04/24/obama-middle-east-christians_n_7130650.html (accessed June 3, 2015).

Marsden, Lee. 2008. *For God's Sake: the Christian Right and US Foreign Policy*. London: Zed Books.

Marsden, Lee. 2011. "Religion, Identity and American Power in the Age of Obama." *International Politics* 48 (2): 326–343.

Marsden, Lee. 2012. "Bush, Obama and a Faith-Based US Foreign Policy." *International Affairs* 88 (5): 953–974.

Marshall, Katherine, and Lucy Keough. 2004. "Mind, Heart, and Soul in the Fight Against Poverty." Washington, DC: World Bank Publications, http://siteresources.worldbank.org/EXTDEVDIALOGUE/Resources/Mind_heart_soul.pdf (accessed November 24, 2010).

Marshall, Katherine, and Marisa Bronwyn Van Saanen. 2007. *Development and Faith: Where Mind, Heart, and Soul Work Together*. Washington, DC: World Bank Publications.

Marshall, Paul A. 2011. Personal Communication. Washington, DC, June 16, 2011.

Marshall, Paul A., and Lela Gilbert. 1997. *Their Blood Cries Out: The Growing Worldwide Persecution of Christians*. Dallas, TX: Word Publishing.

Marshall, Paul A., Lela Gilbert, and Roberta Green. 2009. *Blind Spot: When Journalists Don't Get Religion*. New York: Oxford University Press.

Marshall, Paul A., Lela Gilbert, and Nina Shea. 2013. *Persecuted: The Global Assault on Christians*. Nashville, TN: Thomas Nelson.

Martin, David. 1978. *A General Theory of Secularization*. Oxford: Blackwell.

Marty, Martin E., and R. Scott Appleby, eds. 1991–1995. *The Fundamentalism Project*, vols. 1–5. Chicago: University of Chicago Press.

Mavelli, Luca, and Fabio Petito. 2012. "The Postsecular in International Relations: an Overview." *Review of International Studies* 38 (5): 931–942.

Mavelli, Luca, and Fabio Petito, eds. 2014. *Towards a Postsecular International Politics: New Forms of Community, Identity, and Power*. Basingstoke: Palgrave Macmillan.

May, Peter J., and Ashley E. Jochim. 2013. "Policy Regime Perspectives: Policies, Politics, and Governing." *Policy Studies Journal* 41 (3): 426–452.

Mayrl, Damon. 2016. *Secular Conversions: Political Institutions and Religious Education in the United States and Australia, 1800–2000*. Cambridge: Cambridge University Press.

McAlister, Melani. 2008. "The Politics of Persecution." *Middle East Research and Information Project* 249 (39): 18–27.

McAlister, Melani. 2012. "The Persecuted Body: Evangelical Internationalism, Islam, and the Politics of Fear." In *Facing Fear: The History of an Emotion in Global Perspective*, edited by Michael Laffan and Max Weiss, 133–161. Princeton, NJ: Princeton University Press.

McAlister, Melani. 2013. "State Department Finds Religion, But Whose?" *Religion Dispatches*, http://religiondispatches.org/state-department-finds-religion-but-whose/ (accessed September 9, 2016).

McAlister, Melani. 2018. *The Kingdom of God Has No Borders: A Global History of American Evangelicals*. New York: Oxford University Press.

McCants, William. 2015. "Islamic Scripture Is Not the Problem. And Funding Muslim Reformers Is Not the Solution." *Markaz*, http://www.brookings.edu/blogs/markaz/posts/2015/06/16-islamic-scripture-not-problem-mccants (accessed June 10, 2016).

McDougall, Walter A. 1997. *Promised Land, Crusader State: the American Encounter with the World Since 1776*. Boston: Houghton Mifflin.

McInerney, Stephen. 2011. "The Federal Budget and Appropriations for Fiscal Year 2011: Democracy, Governance, and Human Rights in the Middle East." Washington, DC: The Project on Middle East Democracy, http://pomed.org/wordpress/wp-content/uploads/2010/04/fy11-budget-analysis-final.pdf (accessed January 16, 2012).

McKenzie, Robert L. 2016. "Countering Violent Extremism in America: Policy Recommendations for the Next President." Brookings Big Ideas for America. Washington, DC: Brookings Institution, https://www.brookings.edu/research/countering-violent-extremism-in-america-policy-recommendations-for-the-next-president/ (accessed December 13, 2016).

McMaster, H. R. 2017. "HR McMaster Briefing on Trip Statement." White House, Washington, DC, https://www.c-span.org/video/?c4670112/hr-mcmaster-briefing-trip (accessed June 7, 2017).

McNeil, Donald G. Jr. 2015. "U.S. Push for Abstinence in Africa Is Seen as Failure Against H.I.V." *New York Times*, http://www.nytimes.com/2015/02/27/health/american-hiv-battle-in-africa-said-to-falter.html?_r=1 (accessed July 9, 2015).

Mead, Walter Russell. 2006. "God's Country." *Foreign Affairs* 85 (5): 24–43.

Mearsheimer, John J. 1990. "Why We Will Soon Miss the Cold War." *The Atlantic Monthly* 266 (2): 35–50.

Mearsheimer, John J., and Stephen M. Walt. 2007. *The Israel Lobby and US Foreign Policy*. New York: FSG.

Menchik, Jeremy. 2017. "The Constructivist Approach to Religion and World Politics." *Comparative Politics* 49 (4): 561–581.

Mendelsohn, Barak. 2012. "God vs. Westphalia: Radical Islamist Movements and the Battle for Organizing the World." *Review of International Studies* 38 (3): 589–613.

Military Religious Freedom Foundation (MRFF). 2008. "Shocking Video of Evangelical Christian Missionaries Embedded with American Combat Troops in Afghanistan." Military Religious Freedom Foundation, http://www.militaryreligiousfreedom.org/weekly-watch/12-12-08/travel_the_road.html (accessed March 11, 2010).

Miller, Greg, and Scott Higham. 2015. "In a Propaganda War, U.S. Tried to Play by the Enemy's Rules." *Washington Post*, https://www.washingtonpost.com/world/national-security/in-a-propaganda-war-us-tried-to-play-by-the-enemys-rules/2015/05/08/6eb6b732-e52f-11e4-81ea-0649268f729e_story.html?utm_term=.76cd60e91969 (accessed August 29, 2016).

Milligan, Susan. 2006. "Together, but Worlds Apart: Christian Aid Groups Raise Suspicion in Strongholds of Islam." *Boston Globe*, http://www.boston.com/news/world/asia/articles/2006/10/10/together_but_worlds_apart/ (accessed October 30, 2011).

Milliken, Jennifer. 1999. "The Study of Discourse in International Relations: a Critique of Research and Methods." *European Journal of International Relations* 5 (2): 225–254.

Ministero degli Affari Esteri. 2012. "Roma: Anche in Italia un Osservatorio sulla Libertà Religiosa." http://www.esteri.it/mae/it/sala_stampa/archivionotizie/approfondimenti/2012/06/20120622_roma.html (accessed September 16, 2012).

Mirahmadi, Hedieh, Mehreen Farooq, and Waleed Ziad. 2012. "Pakistan's Civil Society: Alternative Channels to Countering Violent Extremism." Washington, DC: World Organization for Resource Development and Education (WORDE), http://www.worde.org/wp-content/uploads/2012/10/WORDE-Report-Pakistan-Civil-Society-Alternative-Channels-to-CVE.pdf (accessed June 11, 2016).

Mirahmadi, Hedieh, Waleed Ziad, Mehreen Farooq, and Robert D. Lamb. 2015. "Empowering Pakistan's Civil Society to Counter Global Violent Extremism." Forum Papers. Washington, DC: The Brookings Project on U.S. Relations with the Islamic World: U.S.-Islamic World, http://www.worde.org/wp-content/uploads/2015/01/Brookings-WORDE-Empowering-Pakistans-Civil-Society-for-Counter-Global-Violent-Extremism.pdf (accessed June 11, 2016).

Moghul, Haroon. 2013. "Islam's Scholars for Dollars." *Public Discourse*, http://www.thepublicdiscourse.com/2013/09/10861/ (accessed July 5, 2016).

Moll, Rob. 2008. "The Father of Faith-Based Diplomacy." *Christianity Today*, http://www.christianitytoday.com/ct/2008/september/29.54.html (accessed April 24, 2010).

Morello, Carol. 2018. "Under Pressure from Pence, U.S. Aid Is Directed to Christian, Yazidi Communities in Iraq." *Washington Post*, https://www.washingtonpost.com/world/national-security/under-pressure-from-pence-us-aid-directed-to-christian-yazidi-communities-in-iraq/2018/06/15/815d8e60-6f4c-11e8-afd5-778aca903bbe_story.html?noredirect=on&utm_term=.cd571bacf265 (accessed July 26, 2018).

Moroccan Diplomat. 2011. Personal Communication. Washington, DC, July 14, 2011.

Muedini, Fait. 2015. *Sponsoring Sufism: How Governments Promote "Mystical Islam" in their Domestic and Foreign Policies*. Basingstoke: Palgrave Macmillan.

Mugabi, Stephen. 2003. "Building God's Kingdom through Microenterprise Development: A Christian vision for transformational development." *Transformation* 20 (3): 133–138.

Muravchik, Joshua, and Charlie Szrom. 2008. "In Search of Moderate Muslims." Washington, DC: American Enterprise Institute, https://www.aei.org/publication/in-search-of-moderate-muslims/ (accessed April 3, 2011).

Nan, Susan Allen, Zachariah Cherian Mampilly, and Andrea Bartoli, eds. 2011. *Peacemaking: From Practice to Theory*. Santa Barbara, CA: Praeger.

Narayan, Deepa, Raj Patel, Kai Schafft, Anne Rademacher, and Sarah Koch-Schulte. 2000. "Voices of the Poor: Can Anyone Hear Us? Voices From 47 Countries." Washington, DC: World Bank, http://siteresources.worldbank.org/INTPOVERTY/Resources/335642-1124115102975/1555199-1124115187705/vol1.pdf (accessed August 30, 2015).

Nasr, Vali. 2016. "The War for Islam." *Foreign Policy*, http://foreignpolicy.com/2016/01/22/the-war-for-islam-sunni-shiite-iraq-syria/ (accessed December 19, 2016).

Nasser-Eddine, Minerva, Bridget Garnham, Katerina Agostino, and Gilbert Caluya. 2011. "Countering Violent Extremism (CVE) Literature Review." Counter Terrorism and Security Technology Centre: Australian Government Department of Defence: Defence Science and Technology Organisation, http://dspace.dsto.defence.gov.au/dspace/bitstream/1947/10150/1/DSTO-TR-2522 PR.pdf (accessed September 7, 2016).

National Association of Evangelicals (NAE). 1996. "Statement of Conscience Concerning Worldwide Religious Persecution." National Association of Evangelicals, Washington, DC: http://nae.net/worldwide-religious-persecution/ (accessed October 25, 2010).

National Association of Evangelicals (NAE). 2004. "For the Health of the Nation: An Evangelical Call to Civic Responsibility." Washington, DC: National Association of Evangelicals, http://www.nae.net/images/content/For_The_Health_Of_The_Nation.pdf (accessed November 21, 2010).

National Association of Evangelicals (NAE). 2015. "Letter to President on Religious Minorities Post." Washington, DC: National Association of Evangelicals.

National Council of Churches (NCC). 1998. "NCC Public Policy Office Offers Qualified Support For Nickles-Lieberman Bill on Religious Persecution." National Council of Churches, Washington, DC, http://www.ncccusa.org/news/news90.html (accessed October 27, 2010).

Natsios, Andrew S. 2011. Personal Communication. Washington, DC, June 3, 2011.

Nau, Henry R. 2010. "Obama's Foreign Policy." *Policy Review*, http://www.hoover.org/research/obamas-foreign-policy (accessed March 1, 2016).

Neuhaus, Richard John. 1984. *The Naked Public Square: Religion and Democracy in America*. Grand Rapids, MI: William B. Eerdmans.

Norris, Pippa, and Ronald Inglehart. 2004. *Sacred and Secular: Religion and Politics Worldwide*. Cambridge: Cambridge University Press.

Nozell, Melissa, and Susan Hayward. 2014. "Religious Leaders Countering Extremist Violence: How Policy Changes Can Help." *The Olive Branch*. United States Institute of Peace, http://www.usip.org/olivebranch/religious-leaders-countering-extremist-violence-how-policy-changes-can-help (accessed September 20, 2016).

Obama, Barack. 2006. "Transcript: Obama's 2006 Sojourners/Call to Renewal Address on Faith and Politics." Sojourners/Call to Renewal Conference, Washington, DC, https://sojo.net/articles/transcript-obamas-2006-sojournerscall-renewal-address-faith-and-politics-sthash.8s1KIgfq.dpuf (accessed February 17, 2010).

Obama, Barack. 2008. "Obama Delivers Speech on Faith in America." Zanesville, OH, http://www.nytimes.com/2008/07/01/us/politics/01obama-text.html?_r=1&pagewanted=all (accessed April 19, 2010).

Obama, Barack. 2009a. "President Barack Obama's Inaugural Address." Washington, DC, http://www.whitehouse.gov/blog/inaugural-address (accessed June 10, 2012).

Obama, Barack. 2009b. "President Obama Addresses Muslim World in Cairo." *Washington Post*, http://www.washingtonpost.com/wp-dyn/content/article/2009/06/04/AR2009060401117.html.

Obama, Barack. 2011. "Remarks by the President on the Middle East and North Africa." US Department of State, Washington, DC, http://www.whitehouse.gov/the-press-office/2011/05/19/remarks-president-middle-east-and-north-africa (accessed June 12, 2012).

Obama, Barack. 2014a. "Remarks by the President at National Prayer Breakfast." Washington Hilton, Washington, DC, https://www.whitehouse.gov/the-press-office/2014/02/06/remarks-president-national-prayer-breakfast (accessed June 1, 2016).

Obama, Barack. 2014b. "Statement by the President on ISIL." The White House, Washington, DC, https://www.whitehouse.gov/the-press-office/2014/09/10/statement-president-isil-1 (accessed July 29, 2016).

Obama, Barack. 2015. "Remarks by the President in Closing of the Summit on Countering Violent Extremism." Summit on Countering Violent Extremism, The White House, Washington, DC, https://www.whitehouse.gov/the-press-office/2015/02/18/remarks-president-closing-summit-countering-violent-extremism (accessed July 2, 2016).

Office of Inspector General (OIG). 2009. "Audit of USAID's Faith-based and Community Initiatives." Office of Inspector General: Audit Report NO. 9-000-09-009-P. Washington, DC: Office of Inspector General, US Agency for International Development, http://www.usaid.gov/oig/public/fy09rpts/9-000-09-009-p.pdf (accessed October 25, 2015).

Office of Inspector General (OIG). 2011. "Review of the Centers for Disease Control and Prevention's Oversight of the President's Emergency Plan for Aids Relief Funds for Fiscal Years 2007 through 2009." Washington, DC: Office of Inspector General, http://oig.hhs.gov/oas/reports/region4/41004006.pdf (accessed October 25, 2015).

Office of the Press Secretary. 2015. "Statement by the Press Secretary on the Murder of Egyptian Citizens." The White House, Washington, DC, https://

obamawhitehouse.archives.gov/the-press-office/2015/02/15/statement-press-secretary-murder-egyptian-citizens (accessed July 30, 2016).

Office of International Religious Freedom (OIRF). 2000. "2000 Report on International Religious Freedom." Washington, DC: US Department of State, https://www.state.gov/j/drl/rls/irf/2010/index.htm (accessed June 4, 2015).

Office of International Religious Freedom (OIRF). 2002. "2002 Report on International Religious Freedom." Washington, DC: US Department of State, http://www.state.gov/j/drl/rls/irf/2002/index.htm (accessed June 4, 2015).

Office of International Religious Freedom (OIRF). 2009. "2009 Report on International Religious Freedom." Washington, DC: US Department of State, http://www.state.gov/j/drl/rls/irf/2009/index.htm (accessed June 4, 2015).

Office of International Religious Freedom (OIRF). 2010. "2010 Report on International Religious Freedom." Washington, DC: US Department of State, http://www.state.gov/g/drl/rls/irf/2010/index.htm (accessed June 4, 2015).

Office of International Religious Freedom (OIRF). 2011a. "Fact Sheet: Office of International Religious Freedom Bureau of Democracy, Human Rights and Labor." Washington, DC: US Department of State, http://iipdigital.usembassy.gov/st/english/texttrans/2011/08/20110817164823suo.9397634.html-axzz4BeugsFfo (accessed August 22, 2011).

Office of International Religious Freedom (OIRF). 2011b. "Fact Sheet: Religious Freedom and National Security." Washington, DC: US Department of State, http://www.state.gov/j/drl/rls/fs/2011/170635.htm (accessed August 22, 2011).

Office of International Religious Freedom (OIRF). 2013. "Fact Sheet: U.S. Policy and Programs in Support of International Religious Freedom." Washington, DC: US Department of State, http://www.state.gov/r/pa/prs/ps/2013/05/209666.htm (accessed August 24, 2015).

Office of International Religious Freedom (OIRF) Official 1. 2011. Personal Communication. Washington, DC, June 13, 2011.

Office of International Religious Freedom (OIRF) Official 2. 2015. Personal Communication. Washington, DC, April 23, 2015.

Office of Religion and Global Affairs' (RGA) Official. 2015. Personal Communication. Washington, DC, April 23, 2015.

Olasky, Marvin. 1992. The Tragedy of American Compassion. Washington, DC: Regnery Publishing.

Olasky, Marvin. 2000. Compassionate Conservatism: What It Is, What It Does, and How It Can Transform America. New York: The Free Press.

Olivier, Jill, Clarence Tsimpo, Regina Gemignani, Mari Shojo, Harold Coulombe, Frank Dimmock, Minh Cong Nguyen, Harrison Hines, Edward J. Mills, and Joseph L. Dieleman. 2015. "Understanding the Roles of Faith-based Health-care Providers in Africa: Review of the Evidence With a Focus on Magnitude, Reach, Cost, and Satisfaction." The Lancet 386 (10005): 1765–1775.

Olson, Laura R. 2007. "Whither the Religious Left? Religiopolitical Progressivism in Twenty-First Century America." In From Pews to Polling Places: Faith and Politics in the American Religious Mosaic, edited by J. Matthew Wilson, 53–80. Washington, DC: Georgetown University Press.

Pally, Marcia. 2013. "The New Evangelicals: Evangelicals who Have Left the Right." *The Immanent Frame*, http://blogs.ssrc.org/tif/2013/01/15/evangelicals-who-have-left-the-right/ (accessed April 18, 2015).

Patel, Faiza, and Meghan Koushik. 2017. "Countering Violent Extremism." New York: Brennan Center for Justice at New York University School of Law, http://www.brennancenter.org/sites/default/files/publications/Brennan Center CVE Report_0.pdf (accessed April 27, 2017).

Patel, Faiza, and Andrew Lindsay. 2018. "Countering Violent Extremism Programs in the Trump Era." New York: Brennan Center for Justice: New York University School of Law, https://www.brennancenter.org/blog/countering-violent-extremism-programs-trump-era (accessed July 30, 2018).

Patomäki, Heikki, and Colin Wight. 2000. "After Postpositivism? The Promises of Critical Realism." *International Studies Quarterly* 44 (2): 213–237.

Patterson, Eric. 2011. *Politics in a Religious World: Building a Religiously Informed US Foreign Policy*. New York: Continuum.

Pease, Emily. 2009. "US Efforts to Reform Education in the Middle East." Education Reform in the Middle East, http://theyonseijournal.com/wp-content/uploads/2012/08/p23_1.pdf (accessed August 25, 2016).

Pelkmans, Mathijs. 2009. "The 'Transparency' of Christian Proselytizing in Kyrgyzstan." *Anthropological Quarterly* 82 (2): 423–445.

Pence, Mike. 2017. "Remarks by Vice President Pence at the World Summit in Defense of Persecuted Christians." World Summit in Defense of Persecuted Christians, Washington, DC, https://www.whitehouse.gov/briefings-statements/remarks-vice-president-pence-world-summit-defense-persecuted-christians/ (accessed July 24, 2018).

Pershing, Ben. 2013. "Frank Wolf to Retire After 17 Terms in Congress; N.Va. Seat Will Be a Prime Battleground in 2014." *Washington Post*, https://www.washingtonpost.com/local/virginia-politics/frank-wolf-to-retire-after-17-terms-in-congress-northern-va-seat-to-be-a-battleground-in-2014/2013/12/17/712bb608-6749-11e3-a0b9-249bbb34602c_story.html (accessed June 14, 2015).

Petito, Fabio, Daniel Philpott, Silvio Ferrari, and Judd Birdsall. 2016. "FoRB—Recognising our differences can be our strength: Enhancing transatlantic cooperation on promoting Freedom of Religion or Belief." *Policy Briefing*, University of Sussex, https://www.sussex.ac.uk/webteam/gateway/file.php?name=3534-gs-policy-briefing-summer-web.pdf&site=11 (accessed December 10, 2016).

Petito, Fabio, and Scott M. Thomas. 2015. "Encounter, Dialogue, and Knowledge: Italy as a Special Case of Religious Engagement in Foreign Policy." *Review of Faith & International Affairs* 13 (2): 40–51.

Pew Research Center. 2006. "The Great Divide: How Westerners and Muslims View Each Other." *Global Attitudes & Trends*. Washington, DC: Pew Research Center, http://www.pewglobal.org/2006/06/22/the-great-divide-how-westerners-and-muslims-view-each-other (accessed May 7, 2012).

Pew Research Center. 2008. "Is the 'God Gap' Closing?" Washington, DC: Pew Research Center: Religion and Public Life, http://www.pewforum.org/2008/02/21/is-the-god-gap-closing/ (accessed April 29, 2018).

Pew Research Center. 2009a. "Global Restrictions on Religion." Washington, DC: Pew Forum on Religion & Public Life, http://www.pewforum.org/uploadedFiles/Topics/Issues/Government/restrictions-fullreport.pdf (accessed February 12, 2010).

Pew Research Center. 2009b. "President Obama's Advisory Council on Faith-Based and Neighborhood Partnerships." Washington, DC: Pew Forum on Religion & Public Life, http://www.pewforum.org/2009/08/18/president-obamas-advisory-council-on-faith-based-and-neighborhood-partnerships/ (accessed March 3, 2010).

Pew Research Center. 2009c. "Shifting Boundaries: The Establishment Clause and Government Funding of Religious Schools and Other Faith-Based Organizations." Washington, DC: Pew Forum on Religion & Public Life, http://www.pewforum.org/2009/05/14/shifting-boundaries-the-establishment-clause-and-government-funding-of-religious-schools-and-other-faith-based-organizations/ (accessed April 6, 2010).

Pew Research Center. 2011. "Rising Restrictions on Religion: One-third of the World's Population Experiences an Increase." Washington, DC: Pew Forum on Religion & Public Life, http://www.pewforum.org/uploadedFiles/Topics/Issues/Government/RisingRestrictions-web.pdf (accessed January 10, 2012).

Pew Research Center. 2012. "Lobbying for the Faithful: Religious Advocacy Groups in Washington, D.C." Washington, DC: Pew Forum on Religion & Public Life, http://www.pewforum.org/uploadedFiles/Topics/Issues/Government/ReligiousAdvocacy_web.pdf (accessed May 11, 2012).

Pew Research Center. 2014a. "For 2016 Hopefuls, Washington Experience Could Do More Harm than Good: Military Service Top Positive, Atheism Top Negative for Potential Candidates." Washington, DC: Pew Research Center, http://www.people-press.org/2014/05/19/for-2016-hopefuls-washington-experience-could-do-more-harm-than-good/ (accessed June 3, 2018).

Pew Research Center. 2014b. "Religious Hostilities Reach Six-Year High." Washington, DC: Pew Forum on Religion & Public Life, http://www.pewforum.org/files/2014/01/RestrictionsV-full-report.pdf (accessed June 4, 2015).

Pew Research Center. 2015. "America's Changing Religious Landscape." Washington, DC: Pew Forum on Religion & Public Life, http://www.pewforum.org/2015/05/12/americas-changing-religious-landscape/ (accessed June 4, 2015).

Pew Research Center. 2016. "Israel's Religiously Divided Society." Washington, DC: Pew Research Center, file:///Users/gregorio/Downloads/Israel-Survey-Full-Report.pdf.

Phillips, Kevin. 2006. *American Theocracy: The Peril and Politics of Radical Religion, Oil, and Borrowed Money in the 21st Century*. New York: Viking.

Philpott, Daniel, Thomas F. Farr, and Timothy Samuel Shah. 2017. "Response to Persecution: Findings of the *Under Caesar's Sword Project* on Global Christian Communities." University of Notre Dame and the Religious Freedom Project at the Berkley Center for Religion, Peace, and World Affairs, http://ucs.nd.edu/assets/233538/ucs_report_2017_web.pdf (accessed July 3, 2018).

Philpott, Daniel. 2000. "The Religious Roots of Modern International Relations." *World Politics* 52 (2): 206–245.

Philpott, Daniel. 2002. "The Challenge of September 11 to Secularism in International Relations." *World Politics* 55 (1): 66–95.

Philpott, Daniel. 2007. "Explaining the Political Ambivalence of Religion." *American Political Science Review* 101 (3): 505–525.

Philpott, Daniel. 2009. "Has the Study of Global Politics Found Religion?" *Annual Review of Political Science* (12): 183–202.

Philpott, Daniel. 2012. *Just and Unjust Peace: an Ethic of Political Reconciliation.* New York: Oxford University Press.

Philpott, Daniel. 2014. "Religious Freedom Advocates Resemble ISIS? Really?" *Arc of the Universe,* http://arcoftheuniverse.info/taking-issue-with-religious-freedoms-latest-critics (accessed May 16, 2015).

Philpott, Daniel, and Timothy Samuel Shah. 2016. "In Defense of Religious Freedom: New Critics of a Beleaguered Human Right." *Journal of Law and Religion* 31 (3): 380–395.

Piccio, Lorenzo 2013. "Top USAID Grant Implementers: A Primer." *Devex,* https://www.devex.com/news/top-usaid-grant-implementers-a-primer-81197 (accessed July 31, 2015).

Pierson, Paul. 2004. *Politics in Time: History, Institutions, and Social Analysis.* Princeton, NJ: Princeton University Press.

Pipes, Daniel. 2002. *Militant Islam Reaches America.* New York: Norton.

Pipes, Daniel. 2011. "The U.S. Government Builds Mosques and Madrassahs." *Lion's Den: Daniel Pipes Blog,* http://www.danielpipes.org/blog/2004/02/the-us-government-builds-mosques-and (accessed December 20, 2011).

Podhoretz, Norman. 2007. *World War IV: The Long Struggle Against Islamofascism.* New York: Doubleday.

Policy Coordinating Committee. 2007. "U.S. National Strategy for Public Diplomacy and Strategic Communication." Washington, DC: Strategic Communication and Public Diplomacy Policy Coordinating Committee, http://www.au.af.mil/au/awc/awcgate/state/natstrat_strat_comm.pdf (accessed August 25, 2012).

Policy Planning Official. 2011. Personal Communication. Washington, DC, June 24, 2011.

Porges, Marisa L. 2010. "The Saudi Deradicalization Experiment." Expert Brief. Council on Foreign Relations, http://www.cfr.org/radicalization-and-extremism/saudi-deradicalization-experiment/p21292 (accessed September 18, 2011).

Posner, Sarah. 2009. "Obama's Faithful Flock." *The Nation,* http://www.thenation.com/article/obamas-faithful-flock/ (accessed January 10, 2010).

Pouliot, Vincent. 2007. "'Sobjectivism': Toward a Constructivist Methodology." *International Studies Quarterly* 51 (2): 359–384.

President's Emergency Plan for AIDS Relief (PEPFAR). 2012. "A Firm Foundation: The PEPFAR Consultation on the Role of Faith-based Organizations in Sustaining Community and Country Leadership in the Response to HIV/AIDS." Washington, DC: United States Department of State, http://www.pepfar.gov/documents/organization/195614.pdf (accessed March 30, 2015).

Preston, Andrew. 2012. *Sword of the Spirit, Shield of Faith: Religion in American War and Diplomacy.* New York: Knopf.

Prince, Ruth, Philippe Denis, and Rijk van Dijk. 2009. "Introduction to Special Issue: Engaging Christianities: Negotiating HIV/AIDS, Health, and Social Relations in East and Southern Africa." *Africa Today* 56 (1): v–xviii.

Prodromou, Elizabeth H. 2011. Personal Communication. Washington, DC, June 7, 2011.

Project on Middle East Democracy (POMED). 2010. "Obama's Cairo Speech, One Year Later." The Project on Middle East Democracy, http://pomed.org/blog-post/democracy-promotion/obamas-cairo-speech-one-year-later-2/ (accessed August 2, 2010).

Public Broadcasting Service (PBS). 2009. "Religion and Obama's First 100 Days." *Religion & Ethics Newsweekly*, http://www.pbs.org/wnet/religionandethics/2009/05/01/may-1-2009-religion-and-obamas-first-100-days/2866/ (accessed September 4, 2011).

Public Broadcasting Service (PBS). 2012. "USAID Administrator Rajiv Shah." *Religion & Ethics Newsweekly*, http://www.pbs.org/wnet/religionandethics/2012/02/17/february-17-2012-usaid-administrator-rajiv-shah/10313/ (accessed July 16, 2015).

Putnam, Robert D., and David E. Campbell. 2010. *American Grace: How Religion Divides and Unites Us.* New York: Simon & Schuster.

Rabasa, Angel, Cheryl Benard, Peter Chalk, C. Christine Fair, Theodore W. Karasik, Rollie Lal, Ian O. Lesser, and David E. Thale. 2004. "The Muslim World After 9/11." Santa Monica, CA: RAND Corporation, http://www.rand.org/content/dam/rand/pubs/monographs/2004/RAND_MG246.pdf (accessed May 10, 2010).

Rabasa, Angel, Cheryl Benard, Lowell H. Schwartz, and Peter Sickle. 2007. "Building Moderate Muslim Networks." Santa Monica, CA: RAND Corporation, http://www.rand.org/pubs/monographs/2007/RAND_MG574.pdf (accessed May 10, 2010).

Ramamurthy, Pradeep. 2010. "Introducing Rashad Hussain." *The White House Blog*, https://www.whitehouse.gov/blog/2010/03/05/introducing-rashad-hussain (accessed September 8, 2010).

Raustiala, Kal, and David G. Victor. 2004. "The Regime Complex for Plant Genetic Resources." *International Organization* 58 (2): 277–309.

Religion and Foreign Policy Working Group. 2012. "Ensuring the Opportunity for Mutual Councel and Collaboration." A White Paper of the Religion and Foreign Policy Working Group of the Secretary of State's Strategic Dialogue with Civil Society. Washington, DC: US Department of State, https://globalengage.org/content/1300_Religion__Foreign_Policy_Working_Group_Submitted_WP_16Oct2012.pdf (accessed April 30, 2015).

Religion, State and Society. 2011. "Special Issue: The Changing Nature of Military Chaplaincy." *Religion, State and Society* 39 (1): 1–124.

Reus-Smit, Christian. 2002. "Imagining Society: Constructivism and the English School." *British Journal of Politics & International Relations* 4 (3): 487–509.

Reus-Smit, Christian. 2008. "Reading History Through Constructivist Eyes." *Millennium: Journal of International Studies* 37 (2): 395–414.

Reuters. 2010. "Obama Names U.S. Envoy to Muslim World Body." *Reuters*, http://www.reuters.com/article/us-obama-muslims-envoy-idUSTRE61C1SE20100213 (accessed January 28, 2011).

Review of Faith & International Affairs. 2009. "Special Issue: The Past and Future of the Military Chaplaincy." *Review of Faith & International Affairs* 7 (4): 1–82.

Review of Faith & International Affairs. 2014. "Special Issue: The Internationalization of International Religious Freedom Policy." *Review of Faith & International Affairs* 12 (3): 1–77.

Ricks, Thomas E. 2006. *Fiasco: The American Military Adventure in Iraq.* New York: Penguin.

Ricksmay, Thomas E. 2014. "Starship Troopers vs. Pork-Eating Crusaders: How Military and Civilian Cultures Prevent Strategic Corporals." *Foreign Policy,* http://foreignpolicy.com/2014/05/21/starship-troopers-vs-pork-eating-crusaders-how-military-and-civilian-cultures-prevent-strategic-corporals/ (accessed October 8, 2016).

Riesebrodt, Martin. 2012. *The Promise of Salvation: A Theory of Religion.* Chicago: University of Chicago Press.

Review of International Studies. 2012. "Special Issue: The Postsecular in International Relations." *Review of International Studies* 38 (5): 931–1115.

Robinson, Eugene. 2012. "George W. Bush's Greatest Legacy—His Battle against AIDS." *Washington Post,* https://www.washingtonpost.com/opinions/eugene-robinson-george-w-bushs-greatest-legacy--his-battle-against-aids/2012/07/26/gJQAumGKCX_story.html?utm_term=.159d97c9f6e9 (accessed March 2, 2014).

Rock, Stephen R. 2011. *Faith and Foreign Policy: the Views and Influence of U.S. Christians and Christian Organizations.* New York: Continuum International.

Rodgers, Mark. 2011. Personal Communication. Washington, DC, June 8, 2011.

Rogers, Melissa. 2010. "Continuity and Change: Faith-Based Partnerships Under Obama and Bush." *Brookings Institution,* http://www.brookings.edu/opinions/2010/1213_faith_based_rogers.aspx (accessed April 18, 2011).

Rogers, Melissa. 2011. Personal Communication. Washington, DC, June 28, 2011.

Rogers, Melissa. 2018. "President Trump Just Unveiled a New White House 'Faith' Office. It Actually Weakens Religious Freedom." *Washington Post,* https://www.washingtonpost.com/news/acts-of-faith/wp/2018/05/14/president-trump-just-unveiled-a-new-white-house-faith-office-it-actually-weakens-religious-freedom/?noredirect=on&utm_term=.44604be84c7a (accessed July 25, 2018).

Rogers, Melissa, and E. J. Dionne. 2008. "Serving People in Need, Safeguarding Religious Freedom: Recommendations for the New Administration on Partnerships with Faith-based Organizations." Washington, DC: Brookings Institution, http://www.brookings.edu/papers/2008/12_religion_dionne.aspx (accessed June 17, 2013).

Roosevelt, Franklin Delano. 1941. "The Four Freedoms." Washington, DC, http://www.americanrhetoric.com/speeches/fdrthefourfreedoms.htm (accessed May 2, 2015).

Ropp, Steve C., Thomas Risse-Kappen, and Kathryn Sikkink. 1999. *The Power of Human Rights: International Norms and Domestic Change.* Cambridge: Cambridge University Press.

Rosenau, William. 2006. "Waging the 'War of Ideas,'" Santa Monica, CA: RAND Corporation, http://www.rand.org/pubs/reprints/RP1218.html (accessed December 17, 2015).

Rosensaft, Menachem 2010. "Morocco Is a Friend and Must Be Treated as Such." *Huffington Post*, http://www.huffingtonpost.com/menachem-rosensaft/morocco-is-a-friend-and-m_b_630387.html (accessed May 31, 2015).

Roy, Olivier. 2004. *Globalized Islam: The Search for a New Ummah*. New York: Columbia University Press.

Roy, Olivier, and Justin Vaisse. 2008. "How to Win Islam Over." *New York Times*, http://www.nytimes.com/2008/12/21/opinion/21roy.html (accessed October 2, 2010).

Rudolph, Susanne Hoeber, and James P. Piscatori, eds. 1997. *Transnational Religion and Fading States*. Boulder, CO: Westview Press.

Saeed, Sadia. 2016. *Politics of Desecularization: Law and the Minority Question in Pakistan*. New York: Cambridge University Press.

Sager, Rebecca. 2010. *Faith, Politics, and Power: the Politics of Faith-based Initiatives*. New York: Oxford University Press.

Saiya, Nilay. 2015. "The Religious Freedom Peace." *International Journal of Human Rights* 19 (3): 369–382.

Salomon, Noah. 2016. "The New Global Politics of Religion: A View from the Other Side." *The Immanent Frame*, http://blogs.ssrc.org/tif/2016/04/26/the-new-global-politics-of-religion-a-view-from-the-other-side/ (accessed April 4, 2017).

Sandal, Nukhet A. 2011. "Religious Actors as Epistemic Communities in Conflict Transformation: the Cases of South Africa and Northern Ireland." *Review of International Studies* 37 (3): 929–949.

Santelli, John S., Ilene S. Speizer, and Zoe R. Edelstein. 2013. "Abstinence Promotion Under PEPFAR: The Shifting Focus of HIV Prevention for Youth." *Global Public Health* 8 (1): 1–12.

Sapersteine, David N. 2015. "Announcement of Knox Thames' Appointment." Unclassified email.

Sauer, Abe. 2011. "Our Government-Funded Mission to Make Haiti Christian: Your Tax Dollars, Billy Graham's Son, Monsanto and Sarah Palin." *The Awl*, http://www.theawl.com/2011/01/our-government-funded-mission-to-make-haiti-christian-your-tax-dollars-billy-grahams-son-monsanto-and-sarah-palin (accessed January 30, 2014).

Schmid, Alex P. 2013. "Radicalisation, De-Radicalisation, Counter-Radicalisation: A Conceptual Discussion and Literature Review." ICCT Research Paper. The Hague: International Centre for Counter-Terrorism, http://www.icct.nl/download/file/ICCT-Schmid-Radicalisation-De-Radicalisation-Counter-Radicalisation-March-2013.pdf (accessed May 17, 2016).

Schulson, Michael. 2017. "Why Do So Many Americans Believe that Islam Is a Political Ideology, Not a Religion?" *Washington Post*, https://www.washingtonpost.com/news/acts-of-faith/wp/2017/02/03/why-do-so-many-americans-believe-that-islam-is-a-political-ideology-not-a-religion/?utm_term=.c3a550820817 (accessed August 3, 2018).

Secretary of State for the Home Department. 2010. "Pursue, Prevent, Protect, Prepare: The United Kingdom's Strategy for Countering International Terrorism." London: Secretary of State for the Home Department, https://www.

gov.uk/government/uploads/system/uploads/attachment_data/file/228907/
7833.pdf (accessed July 29, 2016).

Seiple, Chris. 2007. "Memo to the State: Religion and Security." *Review of Faith &*
International Affairs 5 (1): 39–42.

Seiple, Chris. 2011. Phone Communication. Washington, DC, July 7, 2011.

Seiple, Chris, and Dennis R. Hoover. 2013. "Religious Freedom and Global Security."
In *The Future of Religious Freedom: Global Challenges*, edited by Allen D. Hertzke,
315–330. Oxford: Oxford University Press.

Seiple, Chris, Dennis R. Hoover, and Pauletta Otis, eds. 2013. *The Routledge Handbook*
of Religion and Security. Abingdon: Routledge.

Seiple, Robert A., and Dennis Hoover, eds. 2004. *Religion and Security: the New Nexus*
in International Relations. Lanham, MD: Rowman & Littlefield.

Sen, Amartya. 1999. *Assessing Human Development: Human Development Report 1999.*
New York: United Nations Development Program.

Shah, Timothy Samuel, and Allen D. Hertzke, eds. 2016a. *Christianity and Freedom.*
Vol. 1. Historical Perspectives. Cambridge: Cambridge University Press.

Shah, Timothy Samuel, and Allen D. Hertzke, eds. 2016b. *Christianity and Freedom.*
Vol. 2. Contemporary Perspectives. Cambridge: Cambridge University Press.

Shah, Timothy Samuel, and Monica Duffi Toft. 2006. "Why God Is Winning." *Foreign*
Policy (155): 39–43.

Shah, Timoty Samuel, Alfred Stepan, and Monica Duffy Toft, eds. 2012. *Rethinking*
Religion and World Affairs. New York: Oxford University Press.

Shani, Giorgio. 2008. "Toward a Post Western IR: The Umma, Khalsa Panth,
and Critical International Relations Theory." *International Studies Review* 10
(4): 722–734.

Sharp, Jeremy M. 2010. "U.S. Foreign Assistance to the Middle East: Historical
Background, Recent Trends, and the FY2011 Request." *CRS Report for Congress.*
Washington, DC: Congressional Research Service, http://www.fas.org/sgp/crs/
mideast/RL32260.pdf (accessed March 5, 2011).

Shea, Nina. 1997. *In the Lion's Den: A Shocking Account of Persecution and Martyrdom*
of Christians Today and how We Should Respond. Nashville, TN: Broadman &
Holman Publishers.

Sheikh, Mona Kanwal. 2012. "How Does Religion Matter? Pathways to Religion in
International Relations." *Review of International Studies* 38 (2): 365–392.

Sheline, Annelle. 2017. "Middle East Regimes Are Using 'Moderate' Islam to Stay in
Power." *POMEPS Studies: Adaptation Strategies of Islamist Movements* 27 (April
2017): 47–48.

Sil, Rudra, and Peter J. Katzenstein. 2010. "Analytic Eclecticism in the Study of World
Politics: Reconfiguring Problems and Mechanisms across Research Traditions."
Perspectives on Politics 8 (2): 411–431.

Simmons, Beth A., Frank Dobbin, and Geoffrey Garrett. 2006. "Introduction: The
International Diffusion of Liberalism." *International Organization* 60 (4): 781–810.

Singh, Jang, Emily Carasco, Goran Svensson, Greg Wood, and Michael Callaghan.
2005. "A Comparative Study of the Contents of Corporate Codes of Ethics in
Australia, Canada and Sweden." *Journal of World Business* 40 (1): 91–109.

Smith, Christian. 2003. *The Secular Revolution: Power, Interests, and Conflict in the Secularization of American Public Life*. Berkeley: University of California Press.

Smith, Christian. 2008. "Future Directions in the Sociology of Religion." *Social Forces* 86 (4): 1561–1589.

Smith, Gary Scott. 2006. *Faith and the Presidency: from George Washington to George W. Bush*. New York: Oxford University Press.

Smock, David. 2004. "Ijtihad: Reinterpreting Islamic Principles for the Twenty-first Century." *Religion and Peacemaking Program: Special Report*. Washington, DC: United States Institute of Peace, http://www.usip.org/sites/default/files/sr125.pdf (accessed April 8, 2011).

Smock, David. 2006. "Religious Contributions to Peacemaking: When Religion Brings Peace." *Not War, Peaceworks No. 55*. Washington, DC: United States Institute of Peace, http://origin.usip.org/pubs/peaceworks/pw55.pdf (accessed April 8, 2011).

Smock, David, and Qamar-ul Huda. 2009. "Islamic Peacemaking Since 9/11." *Religion and Peacemaking Program: Special Report*. Washington, DC: United States Institute of Peace, http://www.usip.org/sites/default/files/islamicpeacemaking.pdf (accessed April 8, 2011).

Spirnak, Madelyn E. 2009. "Remarks by the Acting Deputy Assistant Secretary, Bureau of Near Eastern Affairs at the Center for the Study of Islam and Democracy's Annual Banquet." Center for the Study of Islam and Democracy, Washington, DC, http://www.state.gov/p/nea/rls/rm/2009/123119.htm.

State Department Official. 2015. Personal Communication. Washington, DC, April 21, 2015.

Steinfels, Peter. 2006. "In Politics, the 'God Gap' Overshadows Other Differences." *New York Times*, http://www.nytimes.com/2006/12/09/us/politics/09beliefs.html (accessed September 27, 2010).

Steinitz, Lucy Y. 2006. "Meeting the Challenge with God on our Side." *International Review of Mission* 95 (376–377): 92–103.

Su, Anna. 2016. *Exporting Freedom, Religious Liberty and American Power*. Cambridge, MA: Harvard University Press.

Subramanya, Rupa. 2015. "Uncle Sam May Be Indirectly Funding Religious Conversion in India." *First Post*, http://www.firstpost.com/india/uncle-sam-may-be-indirectly-funding-religious-conversion-in-india-2176175.html (accessed June 9, 2015).

Sullivan, Winnifred Fallers. 2005. *The Impossibility of Religious Freedom*. Princeton, NJ: Princeton University Press.

Sullivan, Winnifred Fallers. 2009. "Waking Up to Still Being a Faith-Based Nation." *The Immanent Frame*, http://blogs.ssrc.org/tif/2009/01/22/waking-up-to-still-being-a-faith-based-nation/ (accessed April 22, 2011).

Tannenwald, Nina. 2005. "Ideas and Explanation: Advancing the Theoretical Agenda." *Journal of Cold War Studies* 7 (2): 13–42.

Taylor, Charles. 2007. *A Secular Age*. Cambridge, MA: Harvard University Press.

Thames, Knox. 2012. "Making Freedom of Religion or Belief a True EU Priority." EUI Working Paper; RSCAS 2012/41. Florence: ReligioWest, European

University Institute, http://cadmus.eui.eu/handle/1814/23357 (accessed February 1, 2013).

Thames, Knox. 2014. "Forging a Trans-Atlantic Partnership on Religious Freedom." *Review of Faith & International Affairs* 12 (3): 1–8.

Thaut, Laura C. 2009. "The Role of Faith in Christian Faith-Based Humanitarian Agencies: Constructing the Taxonomy." *Voluntas: International Journal of Voluntary and Nonprofit Organizations* 20 (4): 319–350.

The Economist. 2010. "The Limits of Freedom and Faith." *The Economist,* http://www.economist.com/node/15833005 (accessed August 20, 2012).

The Economist. 2016. "The EU and Religious Freedom: Europe Names a Slovak to Tell the World about Liberty of Thought." *The Economist,* http://www.economist.com/blogs/erasmus/2016/05/eu-and-religious-freedom (accessed December 11, 2016).

The Economist. 2017. "Freedom's Many Meanings: America's Point-Man on Religious Liberty is Contentious." *The Economist,* https://www.economist.com/erasmus/2017/07/30/americas-point-man-on-religious-liberty-is-contentious (accessed September 29, 2018).

The Immanent Frame. 2010/2011. "Religious Freedom." *The Immanent Frame,* http://blogs.ssrc.org/tif/category/exchanges/religion-american-politics/religious-freedom/ (accessed December 19, 2014).

The Immanent Frame. 2012/2013. "The Politics of Religious Freedom." *The Immanent Frame,* http://blogs.ssrc.org/tif/the-politics-of-religious-freedom/page/2/ (accessed December 19, 2014).

The Immanent Frame. 2013. "Off the Cuff: Engaging Religion at the Department of State." *The Immanent Frame,* http://blogs.ssrc.org/tif/2013/07/30/engaging-religion-at-the-department-of-state/ (accessed December 19, 2014).

The Immanent Frame. 2014. "Beyond Critique." *The Immanent Frame,* http://blogs.ssrc.org/tif/beyond-critique/ (accessed December 19, 2014).

Thomas, Jolyon B. 2014. "Japan's Preoccupation with Religious Freedom." PhD diss., Princeton University.

Thomas, Jolyon B. 2016. "Religious Freedom, Past and Future." *The Immanent Frame,* http://blogs.ssrc.org/tif/2016/03/31/religious-freedom-past-and-future/ (accessed April 9, 2017).

Thomas, Scott. 2004. "Building Communities of Character: Foreign Aid Policy and Faith-Based Organizations." *SAIS Review of International Affairs* 24 (2): 133–148.

Thomas, Scott. 2005. *The Global Resurgence of Religion and the Transformation of International Relations: the Struggle for the Soul of the Twenty-first Century.* Basingstoke: Palgrave Macmillan.

Thomas, Scott. 2010. "A Globalized God." *Foreign Affairs* 89 (6): 93–101.

Time. 2005. "The 25 Most Influential Evangelicals in America." *Time,* http://content.time.com/time/specials/packages/0,28757,1993235,00.html (accessed April 20, 2011).

Tocqueville, Alexis de. 2000. *Democracy in America.* The Complete and Unabridged Volumes I and II ed. New York: Bantam.

Toft, Monica Duffy, Daniel Philpott, and Timothy Samuel Shah. 2011. *God's Century: Resurgent Religion and Global Politics.* New York: Norton.

Tomalin, Emma. 2013. *Religions and Development* Abingdon: Routledge.

Trump, Donald J. 2016. "Donald Trump on Muslims." *C-SPAN*, https://www.you-tube.com/watch?v=-szoKY-3PbQ (accessed April 28, 2017).

Trump, Donald J. 2017. "Trump Vows to Abolish Radical Islamic Terrorism." *CNN*, https://www.youtube.com/watch?v=UINLiN7LBoc (accessed April 28, 2017).

Trump, Donald J. 2018. "Remarks by President Trump at the National Day of Prayer." The White House, Washington, DC, https://www.whitehouse.gov/briefings-statements/remarks-president-trump-national-day-prayer/ (accessed July 25, 2018).

United States Agency for International Development (USAID). 2008. *The Center for Faith-Based and Community Initiatives: Strategic Partnerships Guidebook.* Washington, DC: United States Agency for International Development.

United States Agency for International Development (USAID). 2009a. *Issue Brief: The Role of Religious Leaders and Communities in Development Efforts in Asia and The Middle East.* Washington, DC: United States Agency for International Development, http://pdf.usaid.gov/pdf_docs/Pdacp350.pdf (accessed August 2, 2015).

United States Agency for International Development (USAID). 2009b. *Religion, Conflict & Peacebuilding: An Introductory Programming Guide.* Washington, DC: United States Agency for International Development, http://pdf.usaid.gov/pdf_docs/Pnadr501.pdf (accessed January 20, 2011).

United States Agency for International Development (USAID). 2011. *The CFBCI Newsletter*, April 22, 2011. Washington, DC: United States Agency for International Development.

United States Agency for International Development (USAID). 2012. *The CFBCI Newsletter*, April 19, 2012. Washington, DC: United States Agency for International Development.

United States Agency for International Development (USAID). 2013. *The CFBCI Newsletter*, February 28, 2013. Washington, DC: United States Agency for International Development.

United States Agency for International Development (USAID) Official. 2015. Skype Communication. July 7, 2015.

United States Commission on International Religious Freedom (USCIRF). 2011. *Annual Report 2011*. Washington, DC: United States Commission on International Religious Freedom, http://www.uscirf.gov/images/book with cover for web.pdf (accessed June 21, 2012).

United States Commission on International Religious Freedom (USCIRF). 2013. *Annual Report 2013*. Washington, DC: United States Commission on International Religious Freedom, http://www.uscirf.gov/sites/default/files/resources/2013 USCIRF Annual Report (2).pdf (accessed May 23, 2015).

United States Commission on International Religious Freedom (USCIRF). 2015. *Annual Report 2015*. Washington, DC: United States Commission on International Religious Freedom, http://www.uscirf.gov/sites/default/files/USCIRF Annual Report 2015%282%29.pdf (accessed May 28, 2017).

United States Commission on International Religious Freedom (USCIRF). 2017. *2017 Annual Report*. Washington, DC: United States Commission on

International Religious Freedom, http://www.uscirf.gov/sites/default/files/2017. USCIRFAnnualReport.pdf (accessed May 28, 2017).

United States Commission on International Religious Freedom (USCIRF) Official 1. 2010. Personal Communication. Washington, DC, June 22, 2010.

United States Commission on International Religious Freedom (USCIRF) Official 1. 2011. Personal Communication. Washington, DC, June 16, 2011.

United States Government (USG). 1998. "A National Security Strategy for a New Century." Washington, DC: United States Government, http://www. globalsecurity.org/military/library/policy/national/nss-9810.htm (accessed August 30, 2011).

United States Government (USG). 1999. "A National Security Strategy for a New Century." Washington, DC: United States Government, http://www. globalsecurity.org/military/library/policy/national/index.html (accessed August 30, 2011).

United States Government (USG). 2002. "The National Security Strategy of the United States of America." Washington, DC: United States Government, http:// www.globalsecurity.org/military/library/policy/national/index.html (accessed August 30, 2011).

United States Government (USG). 2006. "The National Security Strategy of the United States of America." Washington, DC: United States Government, http://www.globalsecurity.org/military/library/policy/national/nss-060316.htm (accessed August 30, 2011).

United States Government (USG). 2010. "The National Security Strategy." Washington, DC: United States Government, http://www.whitehouse.gov/sites/default/files/ rss_viewer/national_security_strategy.pdf (accessed August 30, 2011).

United States Government (USG). 2016. "Department of State & USAID Joint Strategy on Countering Violent Extremism." Washington, DC: Department of State and United States Agency for International Development, http://www.state. gov/documents/organization/257913.pdf (accessed December 5, 2016).

United States Government (USG). 2017. "The National Security Strategy of the United States of America." Washington, DC: United States Government, https:// www.whitehouse.gov/wp-content/uploads/2017/12/NSS-Final-12-18-2017-0905. pdf (accessed July 24, 2018).

United States Government (USG). 2018. "National Strategy for Counterterrorism of the United States of America." Washington, DC: The White House, https:// www.whitehouse.gov/wp-content/uploads/2018/10/NSCT.pdf (accessed January 15, 2019).

United States Institute of Peace (USIP) Official. 2015. Personal Communication. Washington, DC, April 23, 2015.

US Department of State. 1997. "United States Policies in Support of Religious Freedom: Focus on Christians." Washington, DC: US Department of State: Bureau of Democracy, Human Rights, and Labor Affairs, http://www.state.gov/www/ global/human_rights/980123_acrfa_interim.html-presidential (accessed June 11, 2010).

US Department of State. 1998. "Advisory Committee on Religious Freedom Abroad: Interim Report to the Secretary of State and to the President of the United States." Washington, DC: US Department of State: Bureau of Democracy, Human Rights, and Labor, http://www.state.gov/www/global/human_rights/980123_acrfa_interim.html-presidential (accessed October 23, 2010).

US Department of State. 2010. "Voices: Inaugural Newsletter." Washington, DC: United States Department of State: Office of the Special Representative to Muslim Communities, http://www.state.gov/documents/organization/155334.pdf (accessed April 2, 2011).

US Department of State. 2016a. "Fact Sheet: Religion and Global Affairs." Washington, DC: US Department of State: Bureau of Public Affairs, http://www.state.gov/r/pa/pl/238144.htm (accessed December 13, 2016).

US Department of State. 2016b. "Meeting of the Transatlantic Policy Network on Religion and Diplomacy (TPNRD)." *Media Note.* Office of the Spokesperson, US Department of State, https://www.state.gov/r/pa/prs/ps/2016/06/258658.htm (accessed December 13, 2016).

US Department of State. 2017. "Religion and Global Affairs: One-Pager." Washington, DC: US Department of State: Religion and Global Affairs, https://www.state.gov/s/rga/265814.htm (accessed May 22, 2017).

US Government Accountability Office (GAO). 2005. "U.S. Public Diplomacy: Interagency Coordination Efforts Hampered by the Lack of a National Communication Strategy." Washington, DC: United States Government Accountability Office, http://www.gao.gov/new.items/d05323.pdf (accessed July 26, 2011).

US Government Accountability Office (GAO). 2013. "International Religious Freedom Act: State Department and Commission Are Implementing Responsibilities but Need to Improve Interaction." Washington, DC: United States Government Accountability Office, https://www.gao.gov/assets/660/653335.pdf (accessed June 22, 2015).

US Government Accountability Office (GAO). 2017. "Countering Violent Extremism: Actions Needed to Define Strategy and Assess Progress of Federal Efforts." Washington, DC: United States Government Accountability Office, http://www.gao.gov/assets/690/683984.pdf (accessed April 28, 2017).

US–Muslim Engagement Project. 2009. "Changing Course: A New Direction for U.S. Relations with the Muslim World." Report of the Leadership Group on US–Muslim Engagement. Washington, DC, http://www.usmuslimengagement.org/index.php?option=com_content&task=view&id=21&Itemid=50 (accessed June 13, 2011).

Vaisse, Justin. 2011. Personal Communication. Washington, DC, June 10, 2011.

Van der Veer, Peter. 2001. *Imperial Encounters: Religion and Modernity in India and Britain.* Princeton, NJ: Princeton University Press.

Wald, Kenneth D., and Allison Calhoun-Brown. 2018. *Religion and Politics in the United States.* 8th ed. Lanham, MD: Rowman & Littlefield Publishers.

Waldman, Peter 2004. "A Historian's Take on Islam Steers U.S. in Terrorism Fight." *Wall Street Journal,* http://www.wsj.com/articles/SB107576070484918411 (accessed May 30, 2016).

Wallin, Jesse. 2011. "The Role of Faith-Based Organizations in Haiti's Reconstruction." *Harvard Humanitarian & Development NGOs Blog,* http://hausercenter.org/

iha/2011/02/15/the-role-of-faith-based-organizations-in-haitis-reconstruction/ (accessed November 1, 2011).

Waltz, Kenneth N. 1959. *Man, the State and War: a Theoretical Analysis.* New York: Columbia University Press.

Wang, Regina. 2012. "Billy Graham No Longer Thinks Mormonism Is a Cult." *Time,* http://newsfeed.time.com/2012/10/19/billy-graham-no-longer-thinks-mormonism-is-a-cult/ (accessed May 4, 2013).

Warren, Rick. 2015. "Pastor Rick Warren: 'The church invented the hospital.'" *C-SPAN,* https://www.youtube.com/watch?v=1xaZDo-EuYU (accessed September 18, 2015).

Warsi, Sayeeda. 2013. "An International Response to a Global Crisis: A Conversation with Baroness Warsi on Religious Freedom." Georgetown University, Washington, DC, http://berkleycenter.georgetown.edu/events/an-international-response-to-a-global-crisis-a-conversation-with-baroness-warsi-on-religious-freedom (accessed June 16, 2015).

Weaver, Heather L. 2011. Phone Communication. Washington, DC, July 14, 2011.

Wendt, Alexander. 1987. "The Agent-Structure Problem in International Relations Theory." *International Organization* 41 (3): 335–370.

Wendt, Alexander. 1999. *Social Theory of International Politics.* Cambridge: Cambridge University Press.

White House. 2001. "Unlevel Playing Field: Barriers to Participation by Faith-Based and Community Organizations in Federal Social Service Programs." Washington, DC: White House Office of Faith-Based and Community Initiatives, http://georgewbush-whitehouse.archives.gov/news/releases/2001/08/unlevelfield.html (accessed August 5, 2014).

White House. 2008. "The Quiet Revolution—The President's Faith-Based and Community Initiative: A Seven-Year Progress Report." Washington, DC: The White House, http://georgewbush-whitehouse.archives.gov/government/fbci/The-Quiet-Revolution.pdf (accessed October 26, 2010).

White House. 2009. "The Bush Record: President Bush's Global Health Initiatives Are Saving Lives Around the World." *The Bush Record.* Washington, DC: The White House, https://georgewbush-whitehouse.archives.gov/infocus/bushrecord/factsheets/globalhealth.html (accessed July 25, 2018).

White House. 2010. "A New Era of Partnerships: Report of Recommendations to the President." President's Advisory Council on Faith-Based and Neighborhood Partnerships. Washington, DC: The White House, https://obamawhitehouse.archives.gov/sites/default/files/docs/ofbnp-council-final-report.pdf (accessed September 15, 2010).

White House. 2011. "Empowering Local Partners to Prevent Violent Extremism in the United States." Washington, DC: The White House, https://www.whitehouse.gov/sites/default/files/empowering_local_partners.pdf (accessed October 30, 2011).

White House. 2013. "U.S. Strategy on Religious Leader and Faith Community Engagement." Washington, DC: The White House, http://www.state.gov/s/rga/strategy/ (accessed July 20, 2016).

White House. 2015. "Fact Sheet: The White House Summit on Countering Violent Extremism." Washington, DC: The White House, https://www.whitehouse.gov/the-press-office/2015/02/18/fact-sheet-white-house-summit-countering-violent-extremism (accessed May 3, 2016).

White House. 2016. "Fact Sheet: Promoting and Protecting Religious Freedom Around the Globe." Washington, DC: The White House, https://www.whitehouse.gov/the-press-office/2016/08/10/fact-sheet-promoting-and-protecting-religious-freedom-around-globe (accessed July 19, 2016).

White House. 2018. "Executive Order on the Establishment of a White House Faith and Opportunity Initiative." Washington, DC: The White House, https://www.whitehouse.gov/presidential-actions/executive-order-establishment-white-house-faith-opportunity-initiative/ (accessed July 25, 2018).

White House. n.d. "Charitable Choice: The Facts." The White House, http://georgewbush-whitehouse.archives.gov/government/fbci/guidance/charitable.html (accessed September 2, 2010).

White House Office of Faith-Based Initiatives (WHOFBI) Official. 2010. Personal Communication. Washington, DC, June 24, 2010.

Widmaier, Wesley W., Mark Blyth, and Leonard Seabrooke. 2007. "Exogenous Shocks or Endogenous Constructions? The Meanings of Wars and Crises." *International Studies Quarterly* 51 (4): 747–759.

Wight, Colin. 1999. "They Shoot Dead Horses Don't They? Locating Agency in the Agent-structure Problematique." *European Journal of International Relations* 5 (1): 109–142.

Wight, Colin. 2004. "Theorizing the Mechanisms of Conceptual and Semiotic Space." *Philosophy of the Social Sciences* 34 (2): 283–299.

WikiLeaks. n.d. "Engaging Indonesian Youth—NSC Ramamurthy Discusses Cairo Vision." *WikiLeaks*, https://wikileaks.org/plusd/cables/10JAKARTA159_a.html (accessed June 11, 2016).

Wiktorowicz, Quintan. 2004. *Islamic Activism: a Social Movement Theory Approach, Indiana series in Middle East studies*. Bloomington: Indiana University Press.

Wiktorowicz, Quintan. 2014. "The Foreign Policy Essay: It is Time to Fund Domestic Counter-Radicalization." *Lawfare*, https://www.lawfareblog.com/foreign-policy-essay-it-time-fund-domestic-counter-radicalization (accessed May 29, 2016).

Wilcox, Clyde, and Carin Larson. 2006. *Onward Christian Soldiers?: The Religious Right in American Politics*. Boulder, CO: Westview Press.

Willard, Mara. 2014. "Shaun Casey Talks About Leading the State Department's Faith-Based Office." *Religion & Politics*, http://religionandpolitics.org/2014/03/04/shaun-casey-talks-about-leading-the-state-departments-faith-based-office/ (accessed October 12, 2016).

Wilson, Erin K. 2012. *After Secularism: Rethinking Religion in Global Politics*. Basingstoke: Palgrave Macmillan.

Wison, Carter A. 2000. "Policy Regimes and Policy Change." *Journal of Public Policy* 20 (3): 247–274.

Witte, John Jr. 2001. "A Primer on the Rights and Wrongs of Proselytism." *Cumberland Law Review* 31 (3): 619–629.

Wolff, Sarah. 2018. "EU Religious Engagement in the Southern Mediterranean: Much Ado About Nothing?" *Mediterranean Politics* 23 (1): 161–181.

Wood, Graeme. 2015. "What ISIS Really Wants?" *The Atlantic*, http://www.theatlantic.com/magazine/archive/2015/03/what-isis-really-wants/384980/ (accessed August 1, 2016).

World Vision. 2015. "World Vision U.S.: 2015 Annual Review." World Vision, https://www.worldvision.org/wp-content/uploads/2015-annual-report-brochure-F3.pdf (accessed December 3, 2016).

Wuthnow, Robert. 2009. *Boundless Faith: the Global Outreach of American Churches.* Berkeley: University of California Press.

Zaharna, R.S. 2009. "Obama, U.S. Public Diplomacy and the Islamic World." *World Politics Review*, http://www.american.edu/soc/faculty/upload/Zaharna-public-diplomacy-islamic-world.pdf (accessed March 23, 2012).

Zogby, James J. 2018. "Taking the US International Religious Freedom Commission from Bad to Worse." *The New Arab*, https://www.alaraby.co.uk/english/comment/2018/5/28/us-international-religious-freedom-commission-from-bad-to-worse (accessed May 30, 2018).

Zubaida, Sami. 2016. "Islamic Reformation?" *Open Democracy*, https://www.opendemocracy.net/arab-awakening/sami-zubaida/islamic-reformation (accessed December 5, 2016).

Pence, Mike, 96, 135–36, 199, 205, 222, 223–24
Pentecostalism, 124
PEPFAR. *See* President's Emergency Plan for AIDS Relief
Perle, Richard, 149, 150
Persecution Project Foundation, 58
Personal Responsibility and Work Opportunity Reconciliation Act, 102–3
persuasion, 40, 70
Petito, Fabio, 29
Pew Forum on Religion, 73, 75
Pew Research Center on Religion and Public Life, 36, 182–83, 202
phenomenological secularism, 43n77
Philippines, 186
Philpott, Daniel, 21, 49–50, 63, 179n23, 179, 180, 214
Pius XII, Pope, 174–75
Planned Parenthood, 114
Poland, 28, 174–75
policy paradigms, 37–39
political salience of religion, 5n8, 5–6, 29–30, 31–32, 33, 210–11, 219, 230. *See also* resurgence of religion
defined, 27n20
Muslim and Islamic Interventions regime and, 141, 142, 169
trends in, 26–28
political secularism, 45
Pompeo, Mike, 95–96, 172, 205, 222
Population Services International (PSI), 114
positive essentialization of religion, 45–46, 86, 163, 171, 211–12
post-Cold War era, 1–2, 3–4, 5, 7, 10, 13, 14, 207–8, 213
Faith-Based Foreign Aid regime in, 108–9
International Religious Freedom regime in, 58, 59, 64–65, 66
Muslim and Islamic Interventions regime in, 138–39, 140–41
postsecularism in, 23, 25, 26, 28, 33, 41, 53–54
regimes as novel developments of, 210

Religious Engagement regime in, 175–76, 178
postsecular consciousness, 5–6, 26–27, 31–32, 33–34, 218
critical postsecular perspective, 29
defined, 5–6
Faith-Based Foreign Aid regime and, 106, 108–9
forms taken by, 28–30
International Religious Freedom regime and, 59, 62, 63, 64
Muslim and Islamic Interventions regime and, 140–41
normative postsecular perspective, 29
Religious Engagement regime and, 176, 183
sociological postsecular perspective, 28–29
postsecularism
defined, 26
Faith-Based Foreign Aid regime and, 100–1, 132–33
International Religious Freedom regime and, 57, 66
Muslim and Islamic Interventions regime and, 141, 172
Religious Engagement regime and, 189
Westphalian system and, 230, 233
postsecular world society, 5–6, 19, 210–11, 218, 224–25
defined, 31
emergence of, 26–33
foreign policy theorizing in, 21–54
International Religious Freedom regime and, 59, 64
Religious Engagement regime and, 200–1, 202
poststructural discourse theory (PDT), 17–18, 40n68
Pouliot, Vincent, 16
Powell, Colin, 150, 169n153
Presidential Advisory Council, 116–17, 121
President's Emergency Plan for AIDS Relief (PEPFAR), 2–3, 100, 110, 112–14, 115, 120–21, 122, 123–24, 126, 128, 130–31, 134–35, 136, 212

President's Emergency Plan for AIDS
    Relief (PEPFAR) (*cont.*)
  budget of, 99–100, 112–13
  conscience clause of, 113–14, 119
  diluting theology of, 119–20
  distinctly theological style of, 113–14
Prince, Ruth, 130–31
Prince Alwaleed Bin Talal Center for
    Muslim-Christian Understanding,
    35–36, 145
process tracing, 18n48, 18
Prodromou, Elizabeth, 78n91, 91, 102
Project on US Relations with the
    Islamic World, 36, 145
proselytism and conversion, 84–86, 90,
    98–99, 125–26
prostitution, 113–14, 119, 130–31
Protestantism, 13, 49, 214–15, 227. *See
    also* Evangelicalism; Mainline
    Protestantism
  Faith-Based Foreign Aid regime and,
    98, 127–28
  International Religious Freedom
    regime and, 61, 65–66, 77–78, 81,
    83–84, 85, 87–88
  Muslim and Islamic Interventions
    regime and, 166–67
  Religious Engagement regime
    and, 174–75
Protestant particularism, 83, 86, 95
Protestant Reformation, 166–67,
    217–18, 227
Public Diplomacy 2.0, 154
Pursue, Prevent, Protect, Prepare (UK
    strategy), 168n148

Al Qaeda, 3, 41, 91–92, 137–38, 141, 144,
    146, 148, 149, 151–52, 153, 160, 166,
    173, 217–18, 232

radical pluralism, 83–84, 86, 87, 216–17
Radio Free Europe, 152–53
Radio Sawa, 152–53
Ramadan, 152–53
Ramamurthy, Pradeep, 158–60, 162n116
RAND Corporation, 36, 143–44, 151
Rauf, Feisal Abdul, 145, 146n43, 182n39

Reagan, Ronald, 56, 174–75
Reformulating the Battle of Ideas
    (report), 157
regime complexes, 22–23. *See also*
    foreign policy regime complex
reifying the role of religion, 162–63,
    194, 211
religion (defining), 15–16
Religion, Conflict, and Peacebuilding
    program (University of Notre
    Dame), 35–36
Religion, Conflict, and Peace Initiative
    (Harvard University), 36
*Religion: The Missing Dimension of
    Statecraft* (edited volume), 178
Religion and Diplomacy
    Conference, 190
*Religion and Foreign Policy Conference
    Call* series, 182–83
Religion and Foreign Policy Initiative,
    36, 73, 182–83
Religion and Foreign Policy Working
    Group, 186–87, 189, 197–98
Religion and Global Affairs Forum,
    185, 186–87
Religion and Peacemaking Program, 36,
    147, 179
religionization through categorization,
    10n19, 50–51, 218–19
  defined, 9–10
  Faith-Based Foreign Aid regime
    and, 130
  International Religious Freedom
    regime and, 91–92
  Muslim and Islamic Interventions
    regime and, 167–68
  Religious Engagement regime and,
    199–200
religionization through elevation, 50,
    51, 218–19
  defined, 9–10
  Faith-Based Foreign Aid regime
    and, 130–31
  International Religious Freedom
    regime and, 91
  Muslim and Islamic Interventions
    regime and, 167, 168